R

Pakistan
a country study

Federal Research Division
Library of Congress
Edited by
Peter R. Blood
Research Completed
April 1994

ıith tendril and geometric
.lace of Mirrors), Lahore

Sixth Edition, First Printing, 1995.

Library of Congress Cataloging-in-Publication Data

Pakistan: a country study / Federal Research Division, Library of Congress ; edited by Peter R. Blood. — 6th ed.
p. cm. — (Area handbook series, ISSN 1057–5294) (DA Pam ; 550–48)
"Supersedes the 1984 edition of Pakistan: a country study, edited by Richard F. Nyrop"—T.p. verso.
"Research completed April 1994."
Includes bibliographical references (pp. 333–361) and index.
ISBN 0–8444–0834–4
1. Pakistan. I. Blood, Peter R., 1952– . II. Library of Congress. Federal Research Division. III. Series. IV. Series: DA Pam ; 550–48.
DS376.9.P376 1995 94–17247
954.91—dc20 CIP

Reprinted without alteration on acid-free paper.

Bernan
Lanham, Maryland
December 1995

Foreword

This volume is one in a continuing series of books prepared by the Federal Research Division of the Library of Congress under the Country Studies/Area Handbook Program sponsored by the Department of the Army. The last two pages of this book list the other published studies.

Most books in the series deal with a particular foreign country, describing and analyzing its political, economic, social, and national security systems and institutions, and examining the interrelationships of those systems and the ways they are shaped by cultural factors. Each study is written by a multidisciplinary team of social scientists. The authors seek to provide a basic understanding of the observed society, striving for a dynamic rather than a static portrayal. Particular attention is devoted to the people who make up the society, their origins, dominant beliefs and values, their common interests and the issues on which they are divided, the nature and extent of their involvement with national institutions, and their attitudes toward each other and toward their social system and political order.

The books represent the analysis of the authors and should not be construed as an expression of an official United States government position, policy, or decision. The authors have sought to adhere to accepted standards of scholarly objectivity. Corrections, additions, and suggestions for changes from readers will be welcomed for use in future editions.

Louis R. Mortimer
Chief
Federal Research Division
Library of Congress
Washington, DC 20540–5220

Acknowledgments

The authors wish to acknowledge the contributions of the writers of the 1984 edition of *Pakistan: A Country Study*, edited by Richard F. Nyrop. Portions of their work were incorporated into this volume.

The authors are also grateful to individuals in various United States government agencies and diplomatic and private institutions who shared their time, research materials, and expertise about Pakistan. Special thanks are owed to the Embassy of Pakistan in Washington; to Anne T. Sweetser for her helpful comments on Pakistani society and culture; and to Mustapha Kamal Pasha at the American University and Barbara Leitch LePoer at the Congressional Research Service, Library of Congress, for their insightful comments on various parts of the manuscript. Thanks are also given to Ralph K. Benesch, who oversees the Country Studies/Area Handbook Program for the Department of the Army.

The authors also wish to thank members of the Federal Research Division staff who contributed directly to the preparation of the manuscript. These people include Sandra W. Meditz, who reviewed all drafts and served as liaison with the sponsoring agency; Robert L. Worden and Andrea M. Savada, who reviewed each chapter and made numerous suggestions and points of clarification; Ilona Peterson, who provided current information about AIDS in Pakistan; David P. Cabitto, who provided graphics support; Marilyn L. Majeska, who managed editing and edited portions of the manuscript; Alberta J. King, who provided bibliographic assistance; Andrea T. Merrill, who managed production; and Barbara Edgerton and Izella Watson, who did the word processing.

Also involved in preparing the text were Sheila Ross, who edited the chapters; Catherine Schwartzstein, who performed the final prepublication editorial review; Joan C. Cook, who compiled the index; and Janie L. Gilchrist, David P. Cabitto, and Stephen C. Cranton, who prepared the camera-ready copy.

Harriett R. Blood prepared the topography and drainage map; other maps and charts were prepared by Maryland Mapping and Graphics. Meg Blood designed the illustrations for the cover and the title page of each chapter.

Finally, the authors acknowledge the generosity of the individuals and the public and private agencies who allowed their photographs to be used in this study.

Contents

List of Figures

Preface

This edition supersedes the 1984 edition of *Pakistan: A Country Study*, edited by Richard F. Nyrop. Like its predecessor, the present book is an attempt to treat in a compact and objective manner the dominant historical, social, economic, political, and national security aspects of contemporary Pakistan. Sources of information included scholarly books, journals, and monographs; official reports and documents of governments and international organizations; foreign and domestic newspapers and periodicals; and interviews with individuals with special competence in South Asian affairs. Relatively up-to-date economic data were available from several sources, but the sources were not always in agreement. Most demographic data should be viewed as well-informed estimates.

Chapter bibliographies appear at the end of the book; brief comments on some of the more valuable sources for further reading appear at the conclusion of each chapter. Measurements are given in the metric system; a conversion table is provided to assist readers unfamiliar with the metric system (see table 1, Appendix). For the convenience of the reader, a brief chronology of the major eras and events of South Asian and Pakistani history is included (see table A).

The transliteration of various words and phrases posed a problem. For many words of Arabic origin—such as Muslim, Quran, and *zakat*—the authors followed a modified version of the system adopted by the United States Board on Geographic Names. In numerous instances, however, the authors adhered to the spelling used by the government and people of Pakistan. There is thus some variance in spellings: for example, the Prophet Muhammad, but Mohammad Ali Jinnah. The reader should also note that the term *Khan*, which appears with numerous names (for example, Ayub Khan, Ghaffar Khan, and Yahya Khan), is an honorific and is almost never a surname.

The body of the text reflects information available as of April 1994. Certain other portions of the text, however, have been updated. The Introduction discusses significant events that have occurred since the completion of research, and the Chronology and Country Profile include updated information as available.

Table A. Chronology of Important Events

Period	Description
ANCIENT EMPIRES	
ca. 2500–1600 B.C.	Indus Valley culture.
ca. 1500–500 B.C.	Migrations of Indo-Aryan-speaking tribes; the Vedic Age.
ca. 563–483 B.C.	Life of Siddhartha Gautama—the Buddha; founding of Buddhism.
ca. 321–180 B.C.	Mauryan Empire; reign of Ashoka (ca. 274–236 B.C.); spread of Buddhism.
ca. 180 B.C.–A.D. 150	Saka dynasties in Indus Valley.
ca. A.D. 78–ca. 200	Kushan Empire; Gandharan art flourishes.
ca. A.D. 319–ca. 600	Gupta Empire; classical age in northern India.
COMING OF ISLAM	
711	Muhammad bin Qasim, an Arab general, conquers Sindh and incorporates it into Umayyad Caliphate.
1001–1030	Mahmud of Ghazni raids Indian subcontinent from Afghanistan.
1192	Muhammad of Ghor defeats Rajputs.
1206–1526	Delhi Sultanate.
1398	Timur destroys Delhi.
MUGHAL PERIOD	
1526	Babur defeats last Lodhi sultan in first Battle of Panipat, thus laying foundation of Mughal Empire.
1556	Akbar victorious in second Battle of Panipat.
1556–1605	Reign of Akbar.
1605–27	Reign of Jahangir; in 1612 East India Company opens first trading post (factory).
1628–58	Reign of Shah Jahan, builder of Taj Mahal.
1658–1707	Reign of Aurangzeb, last great Mughal ruler.
1707–1858	Lesser emperors; decline of Mughal Empire.
BRITISH PERIOD	
1757	Battle of Plassey and British victory over Mughal forces in Bengal; conventional date for beginning of British rule in India.
1799–1839	Sikh kingdom established in Punjab under Maharaja Ranjit Singh.
1830s	Introduction of British education and other reform measures.
1838–42	First Anglo-Afghan War.
1843	British annex Sindh, Hyderabad, and Khairpur.
1845–50	Sikh Wars; British annex Punjab; Kashmir sold to Dogra Dynasty, to be ruled under British paramountcy.
1857–58	Uprising, variously known as Indian Mutiny, Sepoy Rebellion, and by Indian nationalists as First War of Independence.
1858	East India Company dissolved; rule of India under British crown (the British Raj) begins; marks formal end of Mughal Empire.
1878–80	Second Anglo-Afghan War.
1885	Indian National Congress formed.
1893	Durand Line established as boundary between Afghanistan and British India.
1905	Partition of Bengal.
1906	All-India Muslim League founded.

Table A. Chronology of Important Events

Period		Description
1909		Morley-Minto Reforms establish separate electorates for Muslims.
1911		Partition of Bengal annulled.
1916		Congress-Muslim League Pact (often referred to as Lucknow Pact) signed.
1919		Montague-Chelmsford Reforms; Third Anglo-Afghan War.
1935		Government of India Act of 1935.
1940		Muslim League adopts "Pakistan Resolution" demanding separate nation for Muslims of India. "Two Nations Theory" articulated by Muslim League leader Mohammad Ali Jinnah and others.
1946	August	Muslim League observes "Direct Action Day." Widespread communal rioting spreads to many parts of India.
1947	June	Legislation introduced in British Parliament calling for independence and partition of India; communal rioting and mass movements of population begin, resulting in next months in 250,000 deaths and up to 24 million refugees.
INDEPENDENT PAKISTAN		
1947	August	Partition of British India; India achieves independence and incorporates West Bengal and Assam; Pakistan is created and incorporates East Bengal (East Wing, or East Pakistan) and territory in the northwest (West Wing, or West Pakistan); Jinnah becomes governor general of Pakistan; Liaquat Ali Khan becomes prime minister.
	October	Start of first Indo-Pakistani War over sovereignty of Kashmir.
1948	September	Jinnah dies; Khwaja Nazimuddin becomes governor general.
1949	January	United Nations-arranged cease-fire between Pakistan and India takes effect, ending first Indo-Pakistani War.
1951	October	Liaquat assassinated; Nazimuddin becomes prime minister; Ghulam Mohammad becomes governor general.
1955	August	Ghulam Mohammad resigns; succeeded by Iskander Mirza.
	October	"One Unit Plan" establishes the four provinces of West Pakistan as one administrative unit.
1956	March	Constitution adopted; Mirza becomes president.
1958	October	Mirza abrogates constitution and declares martial law; Mirza sent into exile; General Mohammad Ayub Khan, chief martial law administrator (CMLA), assumes presidency.
1965	August	Start of second Indo-Pakistani War over Kashmir.
1969	March	Martial law declared; Ayub Khan resigns; CMLA General Agha Mohammad Yahya Khan assumes presidency.
1970	July	One Unit Plan abolished; four provinces reestablished in West Pakistan.
	December	First general elections; Awami League under Sheikh Mujibur Rahman (Mujib) secures absolute majority in new National Assembly; West Pakistan-dominated government declines to convene assembly.
1971	March	East Pakistan attempts to secede, beginning civil war; Mujib imprisoned in West Pakistan; the "independent, sovereign republic of Bangladesh" first proclaimed from captured radio station in Chittagong.
	April	Formal declaration of independence of Bangladesh issued; government-in-exile formed in Calcutta.

Table A. Chronology of Important Events

Period		Description
	December	India invades East Pakistan; India first nation to recognize Bangladesh; Pakistani military surrenders to Indian armed forces, marking Bangladeshi independence; Yahya Khan resigns; Zulfiqar Ali Bhutto becomes CMLA and president of Pakistan.
1972	July	Bhutto and India's prime minister, Indira Gandhi, conclude Simla Agreement, adjusting 1949 cease-fire line between Pakistan and India and creating new Line of Control.
1973	August	New constitution goes into effect; Bhutto becomes prime minister.
1976	January	Diplomatic relations established between Pakistan and Bangladesh.
1977	March	General elections; massive victory by Bhutto's party evokes widespread rioting and protest.
	July	General Mohammad Zia ul-Haq, chief of the army staff, appoints himself CMLA and proclaims martial law.
1978	September	Zia ul-Haq becomes nation's sixth president, replacing Fazal Elahi Chaudhry.
1979	February	Islamic penal code introduced.
	April	Zulfiqar Ali Bhutto hanged.
	November	Mob storms and burns down United States Embassy in Islamabad, killing two Americans and two Pakistani employees; United States cultural centers in Rawalpindi and Lahore also torched; attacks in response to Iranian-inspired rumors that United States citizens responsible for November 20 attack on Grand Mosque in Mecca.
	December	Large-scale movements of Soviet troops and military equipment into Afghanistan.
1980	January	United States president Jimmy Carter pledges military assistance to help Pakistan defend itself against Soviet threat; Carter offers US$400 million, rejected by Zia as "peanuts."
1983	August	President Zia ul-Haq announces that martial law will be lifted in 1985 but warns that army will retain key role in future governments.
1985	January	Non-Islamic banking abolished.
	February	General elections held for National Assembly.
	March	Mohammad Khan Junejo invited by Zia to form civilian cabinet.
	July	Economy declared to be in conformity with Islam.
1986	August	Movement for the Restoration of Democracy launches campaign against government, demanding new general elections; Benazir Bhutto arrested in Karachi.
	December	New federal cabinet sworn into office by President Zia with Junejo continuing as prime minister.
1988	May	Prime Minister Junejo expands federal government to include five new ministers and three new ministers of state; President Zia dismisses Junejo government, dissolves national and provincial assemblies, and orders new elections to be held within ninety days.
	August	Zia, the United States ambassador to Pakistan, and top army officials killed in mysterious airplane crash near Bahawalpur in Punjab; Ghulam Ishaq Khan, chairman of Senate, sworn in as acting president; General Mirza Aslam Beg becomes chief of the army staff.

Table A. Chronology of Important Events

Period		Description
	October	Joint United States-Pakistani investigatory committee concludes that Zia's death was caused by "criminal act of sabotage."
	November	Elections held for National Assembly; Pakistan People's Party (PPP) wins ninety-three out of 207 seats contested.
	December	Benazir Bhutto sworn in as first female prime minister of a Muslim nation; PPP and MQM parties sign "Karachi Declaration," an accord to restore peace in Sindh; Pakistan and India sign accords at South Asian Association for Regional Cooperation (SAARC) summit in Islamabad, including agreement not to attack each other's nuclear facilities.
1989	February	Soviet Union completes withdrawal of troops from Afghanistan.
	June	Combined Opposition Parties, consisting of most opposition groups, formed in National Assembly, with Ghulam Mustafa Jatoi as leader.
	September	Pakistan's largest ever military exercise, Zarb-e-Momin (Sword of the Faithful), commences.
	October	Pakistan rejoins Commonwealth of Nations (withdrew in 1972 to protest recognition of Bangladesh by member states).
1990	May–June	Ethnic troubles mount in Sindh; rift develops between PPP and coalition partners.
	August	President Ghulam Ishaq Khan dismisses Prime Minister Benazir Bhutto, her cabinet, and National Assembly; orders new elections for October 24, 1990; Ghulam Mustafa Jatoi becomes caretaker prime minister.
	October	United States president George Bush unable to deliver annual certification that Pakistan does not possess nuclear weapons as condition of continued assistance and arms and technology transfers, leading to cutoff of most aid. National elections held; Benazir Bhutto's PPP loses to coalition of rightist parties.
	November	Mian Nawaz Sharif elected prime minister.
1991	February	Prime Minister Nawaz Sharif liberalizes economy, lifts controls on foreign currency entering country, and announces policies to encourage new investment; numerous pro-Iraq demonstrations and widespread public opposition to Nawaz Sharif's support of Desert Storm, but pro-United Nations stance reiterated.
	May	Shariat Bill adopted by National Assembly.
	July	Opposition members call upon president to dismiss government because of deteriorating law and order situation, particularly in Sindh.
1992	December	Babri Mosque in Ayodya, India, destroyed by Hindu fundamentalists seeking to build Hindu temple on contested site; communal violence mounts over incident; Pakistan asks Indian government to protect Muslims in India.
1993	January	General Asif Nawaz Janjua, chief of the army staff, dies of a heart attack and is replaced with Lieutenant General Abdul Waheed; Aimal Kansi, a Pakistani, shoots two Central Intelligence Agency employees to death and wounds three others in Washington, before fleeing the country.
	April	President Ishaq Khan dismisses government of Prime Minister Nawaz Sharif, citing corruption.
	June	Twenty-two Pakistani troops are killed while undertaking peacekeeping duties in Somalia.

Table A. Chronology of Important Events

Period		Description
	July	President Ishaq Khan and Prime Minister Nawaz Sharif resign under pressure from military; World Bank officer Moeen Qureshi named caretaker prime minister pending elections in October. Wassim Sajjad becomes acting president; India rejects Pakistan's proposal to sign regional nuclear test ban treaty.
	October	Benazir Bhutto's PPP wins slim margin in national elections and builds coalition government; Benazir appointed prime minister.
	November	PPP stalwart, Farooq Leghari, defeats acting president, Wassim Sajjad, and becomes president.
1994	January	Benazir opens first all-female police station in Rawalpindi.
	August	Pakistan places its troops on high alert along the Line of Control after India deploys two more army divisions in Kashmir; former Prime Minister Nawaz Sharif makes public statement claiming that Pakistan possesses nuclear weapons.
1995	March	Terrorist attack on streets of Karachi kills two American employees of United States consulate and draws international attention to mounting law and order problems in Pakistan.
	July	United States press carries allegations by United States intelligence officials that Pakistan has surreptitiously received fully operable medium-range M–11 ballistic missiles from China.

Country Profile

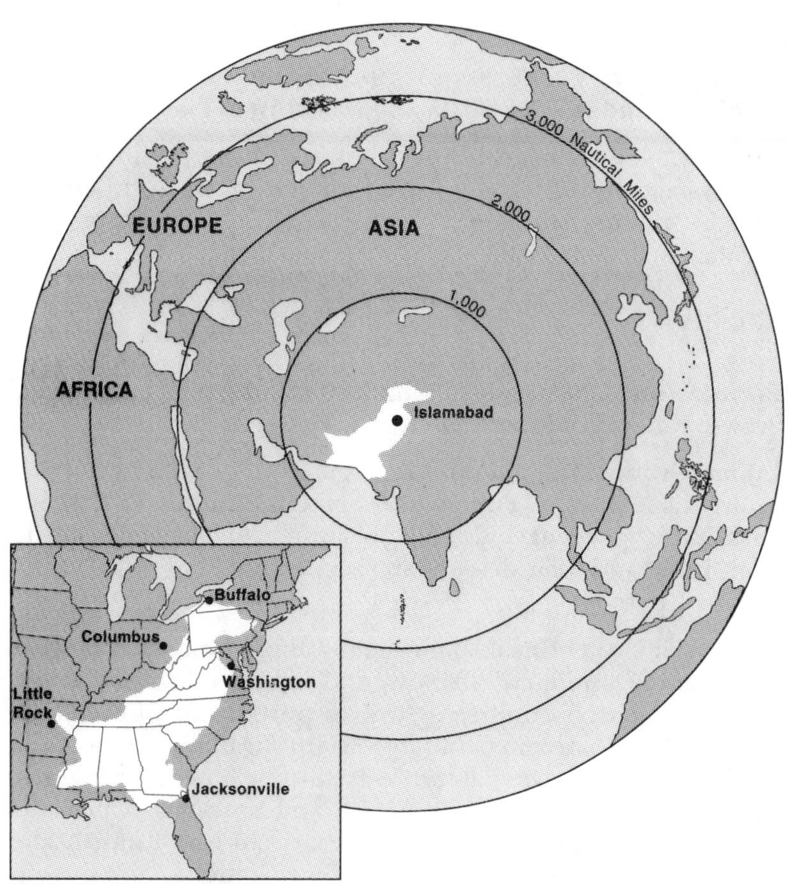

Country

Formal Name: Islamic Republic of Pakistan.

Short Form: Pakistan.

Term for Citizens: Pakistani(s).

Capital: Islamabad (Islamabad Capital Territory).

Date of Independence: August 14, 1947, from Britain.

NOTE—The Country Profile contains updated information as available.

Geography

Size: Total land area estimated to be 796,095 square kilometers.

Topography: Three major geographic areas: northern highlands, Indus River plain, and Balochistan Plateau.

Climate: Generally arid; hot summers, cool or cold winters; wide variations of temperature in given locale and between coastal area on Arabian Sea and glacial regions of northern highlands; little rainfall.

Society

Population: 1994 (July) estimated at 129 million; annual growth rate officially estimated at 3.1 percent.

Ethnic Groups: In general, percentages of population similar to linguistic groups: Punjabis 66 percent, Sindhis 13 percent, Pakhtuns 9 percent, Baloch 3 percent, *muhajirs* (immigrants from India and their descendants) 8 percent, and other ethnic groups 1 percent.

Language: Urdu official language, but English in general use in government, military, business, and higher education. Urdu spoken as native tongue by only 8 percent of population, Punjabi by 48 percent, Punjabi variant Siraiki by 10 percent, Sindhi by 12 percent, Pakhtu or Pashto by 8 percent, Balochi by 3 percent, Hindko by 2 percent, and Brahui by 1 percent. Native speakers of other languages, including English and Burushaski, account for 8 percent of population.

Religion: About 97 percent of Pakistanis are Muslim, 77 percent of whom are Sunni and 20 percent Shia; remaining 3 percent of population divided equally among Christian, Hindu, and other religions.

Education and Literacy: In 1992 overall literacy rate estimated at more than 36 percent for adult population. Literacy rates substantially lower for women. In 1990 only forty-five educated women for every 100 educated men. Education organized into five levels: primary (grades one through five); middle (grades six through eight); high (grades nine and ten); intermediate (grades eleven and twelve); and university undergraduate and graduate programs. Preparatory classes (*kachi,* or nursery) formally incorporated into system in 1988.

Health and Welfare: Substandard housing, inadequate sanitation and water supply, and widespread malnutrition contribute to spread of disease and to high infant, childhood, and maternal mortality. In the mid-1990s, leading causes of death gastroenteritis, respiratory infections, congenital abnormalities, tuberculosis, malaria, and typhoid fever.

Economy

Salient Features: Low-income country with promising growth, but transition to middle-income nation held back by chronic problems, including rapidly rising population, sizable government deficits, heavy dependence on foreign aid, large military expenditures, and recurrent governmental instability.

Gross Domestic Product (GDP): In FY 1993, equivalent of US$50.8 billion, or about US$408 per capita; GDP growth rate averaged 5.3 percent a year between 1950 and 1993.

Agriculture: Declined over the past four decades from 53 percent of GDP in 1950 to 25 percent of GDP in FY 1993, but still employs 48 percent of labor force. Pakistan notable for having world's largest continuous irrigation canal system.

Industry: Leading growth component of economy, industry (including mining, manufacturing, and utilities) accounted for 21.7 percent of GDP in FY 1993, up from 8 percent in FY 1950, and employed 13 percent of labor force.

Services: Services (including construction, trade, transportation and communications, and other services) accounted for 53.3 percent of GDP in FY 1993 and employed 39 percent of labor force. About 7 percent of civilian work force employed in construction, 13 percent in trade, 5 percent in transportation, and 14 percent in other services.

Energy: Firewood, bagasse, and dung major energy sources. Small crude oil production; over 90 percent of petroleum requirements imported. Natural gas, oil, and hydroelectric power major domestic commercial energy sources. Substantial deposits of poor-quality coal. Energy supplies constrain industrialization.

Foreign Trade: United States and Japan largest trading partners. In FY 1993 United States accounted for 13.7 percent of Pakistan's exports and 11.2 percent of its imports. Japan accounted for 6.6 percent of exports and 14.2 percent of imports. Germany, Britain, and Saudi Arabia important trading partners. Hong Kong important export market. China significant supplier of imports. Trade with India negligible. Cotton and rice major exports; petrochemicals, chemicals, machinery, and transportation equipment major imports.

Balance of Payments and External Debt: Negative balance of trade in early and mid-1990s. In FY 1992, exports US$6.9 billion and imports US$9.3 billion, resulting in trade deficit of approximately US$2.4 billion. Trade deficit expected to increase to US$2.5 billion in 1993. World Bank estimated US$24.1 billion external debt in 1992.

Foreign Aid: Dependent on foreign aid for development efforts and balancing debt payments. United States largest donor of aid since independence, but all United States military aid and all new civilian commitments ended October 1990.

Currency and Exchange Rate: Rupee (Rs) divided into 100 paisa. US$1 = Rs30.30 in February 1994.

Fiscal Year: July 1 to June 30.

Transportation and Telecommunications

Roads: Road system approximately 180,000 kilometers in 1992; asphalt roads about 51 percent of total. Work on four-lane 339-kilometer highway between Lahore and Islamabad began January 1993. Number of motor vehicles estimated at nearly 2 million in 1992, including 932,000 motorcycles, 454,000 automobiles, 220,000 tractors, 157,000 trucks and vans, and 37,000 buses.

Railroads: 8,775 kilometers total; 7,718 kilometers broad gauge, 445 kilometers meter gauge, and 610 kilometers less than meter gauge; 1,037 kilometers broad-gauge double track; 286 kilometers electrified; most government owned.

Civil Aviation: International airports at Karachi, Islamabad, Lahore, Peshawar, and Quetta. Pakistan International Airlines national carrier.

Ports: Major ports at Karachi, Port Muhammad bin Qasim, Gwadar, and Pasni.

Telecommunications: Telegraph and telephone systems

government owned; more than 1.6 million telephone connections in March 1993. Radio and telephone dominated by government corporations; Pakistan Broadcasting Corporation had monopoly on radio broadcasting, with home service of 270 hours daily in twenty languages and world service of ten hours daily in two languages in 1995; nineteen AM and eight FM broadcasting stations. Government-controlled Pakistan Television Corporation (PTV) transmits daily; privately owned People's Television Network transmits on eight channels; twenty-nine television broadcast stations; more than 2 million television sets in use in 1995.

Government and Politics

Government: Has shifted among various forms of parliamentary, military, and presidential governments in pursuit of political stability. The 1973 constitution, as amended in 1985, provides for parliamentary system with president as head of state and popularly elected prime minister as head of government. Bicameral legislature, Majlis-i-Shoora (Council of Advisers), consists of Senate (upper house) and National Assembly (lower house).

Politics: Return of democracy and open political debate after death of General Mohammad Zia ul-Haq in 1988; politics characterized by varied and volatile mix of ethnic and regional alliances. Provincialism and ethnic rivalries continue to impede progress toward national integration. Major political parties include Pakistan People's Party, Pakistan Muslim League (Nawaz Sharif faction), Muhajir Qaumi Mahaz, Awami National Party, Jamaat-i-Islami, Jamiat-ul-Ulama-i-Islam, and Solidarity Movement (Tehrik-i-Istiqlal).

Judicial System: Supreme Court, provincial high courts, and other lesser courts exercise civil and criminal jurisdiction. Federal Shariat Court decides if a civil law is repugnant to injunctions of Islam.

Administrative Divisions: Four provinces—Balochistan, North-West Frontier Province, Punjab, and Sindh; one territory—Federally Administered Tribal Areas; one capital territory—Islamabad Capital Territory; and Pakistani-administered portion of disputed Jammu and Kashmir region—Azad (Free) Kashmir and the Northern Areas.

Foreign Relations: Member of United Nations, Commonwealth of Nations, Economic Cooperation Organization, South Asian Association for Regional Cooperation, and numerous other international organizations. Relations with United States historically close but turbulent. Acrimonious relations with India and fallout from Soviet occupation of Afghanistan (1979-89) have been defining factors in recent foreign policy.

National Security

Armed forces: Active army strength in 1994 was 520,000, with 300,000 reserve personnel; navy, 22,000, with 5,000 reserve personnel; air force, 45,000, with 8,000 reserve personnel; paramilitary forces—including National Guard, Frontier Corps, Pakistan Rangers, Mehran Force, Coast Guard, and Maritime Security Agency—exceeded 300,000.

Major Military Units: Army organized in nine corps. Under corps headquarters, twenty-one divisions. Navy organized in four commands, COMPAK—the fleet; COMLOG—logistics; COMFORNAV—naval installations in the north of Pakistan; and COMKAR—naval headquarters at Karachi. Air force organized in eighteen squadrons to defend three air defense districts—north, central, and south.

Military Equipment: Army equipment includes tanks, mostly of Chinese manufacture but some United States-made armored personnel carriers, artillery pieces, motorized rocket launchers, mortars, air defense guns, TOW antitank guided weapons, surface-to-surface missiles, ship-to-surface missiles, and surface-to-air missiles. Navy equipment includes submarines with United States Harpoon missiles, destroyers, guided missile frigates, frigates, surface-to-air missiles, torpedo craft, minehunters, combat aircraft, and armed helicopters. Air force equipment includes F–16 fighters (mainstay of force), Chinese J–6s and J–5s, French Mirages, and C–130 Hercules transport aircraft.

Defense Budget: US$3.5 billion in FY 1994, representing 26 percent of government spending and about 9 percent of gross national product.

Foreign Military Relations: Principal military tie with United States, but relationship periodically strained. China, a steady source of military equipment, has joined Pakistan in cooperative ventures in weapons production. Security relationships also with Saudi Arabia, Persian Gulf states, Iran, and Turkey.

International Security Forces: Pakistani troops contributed to various international security initiatives, including United States-led alliance in Persian Gulf War and United Nations peacekeeping efforts in Somalia and Bosnia. Pakistan has sent peacekeeping observers to Croatia, Iraq-Kuwait border zones, Liberia, Mozambique, and Western Sahara.

Internal Security and Police: Internal security occasionally threatened by regional interests, particularly by sectarian violence in Sindh in early 1990s. Police often perceived as abusers of civil rights. Widespread violent crime and narcotics-related incidents constitute potential threats to domestic security.

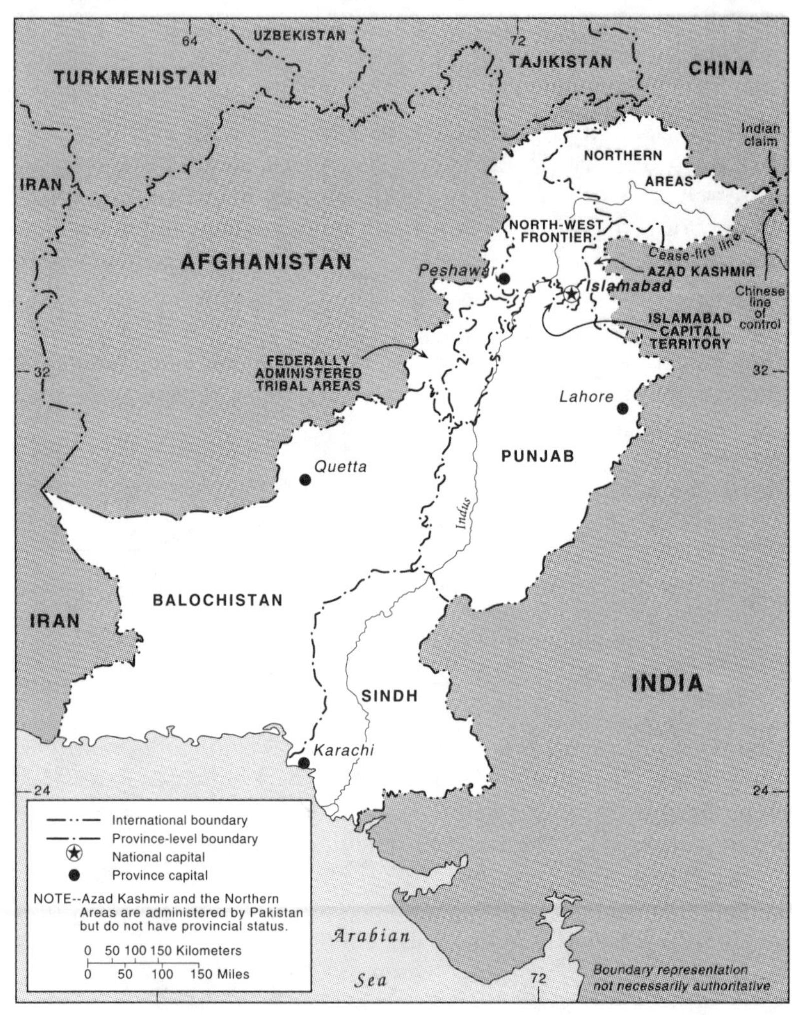

Figure 1. Administrative Divisions of Pakistan, 1994

Introduction

PAKISTAN BECAME AN INDEPENDENT STATE in 1947, the realization of a yearning by India's Muslims, who feared domination by the Hindu majority in a postcolonial India. As the British made their final plans to surrender the "Jewel in the Crown" of their empire, the earlier, elite "Two Nations Theory," premised on the notion of a separate homeland for the subcontinent's Muslim minority, had broadened its popular appeal and evolved into a collective vision championed by Muslims of all backgrounds. After independence, a debate commenced among contending groups over further refinement of that vision. Agreement on what system of government the new nation should adopt—a critical aspect of the debate—was never fully reached. Indeed, few nations have in so short a period undergone as many successive political and constitutional experiments as has Pakistan. This irresolution contributed, in the decades following independence, to a recurrent pattern of crisis: repeated coups and extended periods in which martial law replaced civilian government, violent deaths of several national leaders, periodic strife among ethnic groups, and, most traumatically, a civil war that divided the country in two.

The struggle over the character and soul of Pakistan continues. Although democracy returned to Pakistan in 1988 after a long lapse, it is on trial daily, its continuation by no means certain. Definition of the vision of what Pakistan represents is still being contested from many opposing quarters.

Pakistan's status in the world has changed dramatically in the nearly one-half century of its existence as an independent state. In the twilight years of the Cold War, it achieved international stature as a "frontline" state during the Soviet occupation of neighboring Afghanistan. With the Soviet departure from Afghanistan in the late 1980s and the end of the Cold War, Pakistan's role in the world arena has become less visible, and its voice has diminished to the level of many other developing states competing in the new world order. Yet, during the years it spent in support of the Afghan struggle against Soviet domination, Pakistan impressed upon the world community a new appreciation of its standing among Islamic nations and of its ideological commitment to causes it champions.

In terms of its military and economic development, Pakistan is a "threshold" state. The world's first Islamic "de facto" nuclear-weapons state, it has long been at loggerheads with its larger and more powerful neighbor, India, which, like Pakistan, denies having built nuclear weapons but not its ability to do so at the "turn of a screw." A nation well positioned to serve as an economic model for other developing countries in the post-Cold War era—especially the Islamic states of the former Soviet Union—Pakistan has shown steady and impressive long-term economic growth and is successfully making the transition from an overwhelmingly agricultural to an industrial economy. Yet, despite its considerable achievements in technology and commerce, Pakistan confronts many of the same problems it faced at its birth. The nation has one of the world's highest population growth rates, making it difficult for the government to address the problems of poverty and attendant ills that affect so many in its society. Indeed, social development has lagged behind economic gains. Quality of life indicators—literacy rates, especially among women, human rights, and universal access to heath care—have shown Pakistan to be a country with serious deficiencies.

Throughout history, Pakistan has been strongly affected by its geostrategic placement as a South Asian frontier located at the juncture of South Asia, West Asia, and Central Asia. Scholars have called Pakistan the "fulcrum of Asia" because since antiquity invaders have traversed this frontier carrying with them the seeds of great civilizations. The armies of Islam came to South Asia through the same mountain passes in the northwest of Pakistan that the Indo-Aryans, Alexander the Great, the Kushans, and others had earlier entered.

Present-day Pakistan has been shaped by its rich history, pre-Islamic as well as Islamic, but colored in particular by the exigencies of its troubled and bloody birth as a nation in 1947. The partitioning of British India into India and Pakistan was preceded and accompanied by communal riots of unprecedented violence and scope that forced millions of Hindu, Muslim, and Sikh refugees to flee across the new international borders.

The partition plan that led to the separate states of India and Pakistan was drawn up in an atmosphere of urgency as a swell of religious and ethnic unrest shook India. Under guidelines established with the help of Britain's last viceroy in India, Lord Louis Mountbatten, the perplexing task of establishing the new

boundaries of Pakistan was accomplished. Most Indian Muslims lived either on the dusty plains of Punjab or in the humid delta of Bengal. Contiguous Muslim-majority districts in Punjab and Bengal were awarded to Pakistan under the plan's guidelines. The additional task of deciding the status of the more than 500 semiautonomous princely states of India still remained. All but three of these quickly acceded to either Pakistan or India. But the two largest princely states, Jammu and Kashmir (usually just called Kashmir) and Hyderabad, and one small state, Junagadh, posed special problems. Hyderabad and Junagadh were located within territory awarded to India but were both Hindu majority states ruled by a Muslim leader. These states hesitated but were quickly incorporated by force into India.

The status of the third state, Kashmir, which had borders with both India and Pakistan, proved especially problematic. Unlike Hyderabad and Junagadh, Kashmir had a Muslim majority and was ruled by a Hindu. Kashmir's maharaja was reluctant to accede to either Pakistan or India, but when threatened by a Muslim uprising (with outside support from Pakistani tribesmen) against his unpopular rule, he hurriedly signed the documents of accession, in October 1947, required by India before it would provide aid. Pakistan then launched an active military and diplomatic campaign to undo the accession, which it maintained was secured by fraud. Kashmir was subsequently divided by the occupying armies of both nations, the Indians holding two-thirds of the state, including the Muslim-dominated Vale of Kashmir and the Hindu-majority region of Jammu to the south, while the Pakistanis controlled the western third, which they called Azad (Free) Kashmir. India and Pakistan fought two major wars to maintain or seize control over this state: in 1947–48 and in 1965. Kashmir's contested and indeterminate status continues dangerously to complicate relations between South Asia's two most powerful states.

The bifurcated Pakistan that existed from August 1947 to December 1971 was composed of two parts, or wings, known as East Pakistan and West Pakistan, separated by 1,600 kilometers of Indian territory. Observers pointed out, however, that the people of the two wings were estranged from each other in language and cultural traditions: that the Bengali "monsoon Islam" of the East Wing was alien to the "desert Islam" of the West Wing. The East Wing, notable for its Bengali ethnic homogeneity and its collective Bangla cultural and linguistic heritage, contained over half of the population of Pakistan and sharply contrasted with the ethnic and linguistic diversity of the West Wing. The West Wing consisted of four major ethnic groups—Punjabis, Pakhtuns, Sindhis, and Baloch. The *muhajirs* (see Glossary) constituted a fifth important group. The political leaders of Pakistan, however—particularly those of West Pakistan—asserted that the Islamic faith and a shared fear of "Hindu India" provided an indestructible bond joining the two societies into one nation. This assertion proved flawed. A culture of distrust grew between the two wings, fueled by imbalances of representation in the government and military. Furthermore, Bengali politicians argued that the economic "underdevelopment" of East Pakistan was a result of the "internal colonialism" of the rapacious capitalist class of West Pakistan. In the final analysis, real and perceived inequities would fray this "indestructible" bond holding the country together. Less than a quarter century after the country's founding, Pakistan would fission, the eastern wing becoming the independent nation of Bangladesh.

It was neither Pakistan's precarious security nor its cultural and ethnic diversity, but rather characteristics deeply rooted in the nation's polity that most impeded its early democratic development. The essentials for such a process—disciplined political parties and a participatory mass electorate—were missing in Pakistan's first years as an independent state. The All-India Muslim League, the party that led the struggle for Pakistan, failed to mature into a stable democratic party with a national following capable of holding together the nation's diverse ethnic and cultural groups. Instead, it disintegrated into rival factions soon after independence. Lack of a consensus over prospective Islamic provisions for the nation's governance, Bengali resentment over the West Pakistanis' initial imposition of Urdu as the national language, and the reluctance of West Pakistani politicians to share power with politicians of the East Wing—all were factors that delayed the acceptance of Pakistan's first constitution until nine years after independence. The nation was also dealt a severe psychological blow when in September 1948, only thirteen months after independence, Mohammad Ali Jinnah—known reverentially as the Quaid-i-Azam (Great Leader)—died. Jinnah's role in the creation of Pakistan had been so dominant that it has been observed that he had neither peers nor associates, only lieutenants and aides. Jinnah's primary lieutenant, Liaquat Ali Khan, the nation's first prime minister, was assassinated in October 1951.

Jinnah's and Liaquat's leadership, so critical to the nation in its infancy, was replaced in the early and mid-1950s by the generally lackluster, often inept performances of the nation's politicians. Those few politicians who were effective were all too willing to play upon the emotions of an electorate as yet unaccustomed to open democratic debate. The ethnic and provincial causes championed by these politicians too often took precedence over national concerns. The government was weak and unable to quell the violence and ethnic unrest that distracted it from building strong parliamentary institutions.

Believing that Pakistan's first attempt at establishing a parliamentary system of government failed, in the late 1950s the military ousted the "inefficient and rascally" politicians. During this period, however, the belief that democracy was the "natural state" of Pakistan and an important political goal was not entirely abandoned. Mohammad Ayub Khan, Pakistan's first "soldier-statesman," regarded himself as more of a reformer than an autocrat and, as chief martial law administrator, early on acknowledged the need to relinquish some military control. In his unique governmental system called the "Basic Democracies," Ayub Khan became the "civilian" head of a military regime. Ayub Khan's "democracy from above" allowed for controlled participation of the electorate and was supposed to capture the peculiar "genius" of Pakistan. To his critics, however, Ayub Khan's political system was better characterized as a form of "representational dictatorship." In 1969 an ailing Ayub Khan was forced to resign following nationwide rioting against his regime's perceived corruption, spent economic policies, and responsibility for Pakistan's defeat in the 1965 Indo-Pakistani War over Kashmir. Ayub Khan was briefly succeeded by his army commander in chief, General Agha Mohammad Yahya Khan, who would best be remembered for presiding over the two most traumatic and psychologically devastating events in the country's history: the humiliating defeat of Pakistan's armed forces by India and the secession of East Pakistan.

The East Wing of Pakistan had not benefited greatly from Ayub Khan's "Decade of Progress," with its gains in agricultural production and trade. Bengali politicians wanted to improve what they considered to be the second-class political and economic status of their province vis-à-vis West Pakistan, just as they had earlier agitated for greater cultural and linguistic recognition. The country's first nationwide direct elections were held in December 1970. The East Pakistan-based Awami League, campaigning on a platform calling for almost total provincial autonomy, won virtually all the seats allotted to the East Wing and was thereby assured a majority in the national legislature.

The results of Pakistan's first nationwide experiment in democracy were not honored. Fearing Bengali dominance in the nation's political affairs, West Pakistani politicians, led by Pakistan People's Party (PPP) leader Zulfiqar Ali Bhutto and supported by senior army officers, most of whom were Punjabis, pressured Yahya Khan to postpone the convening of the National Assembly. When the Bengalis of East Pakistan revolted openly at this turn of events, the Pakistani military banned the Awami League, arrested its leader, Sheikh Mujibur Rahman, and began a massive military crackdown. In the savage civil war that followed, tens of thousands of Bengalis were killed, and an estimated 10 million people took refuge in India. In early December 1971, India entered the war and within weeks decisively defeated the Pakistani military. From the aftermath of the war and the dismemberment of Pakistan came the birth of a new nation: Bangladesh.

To most Pakistanis, the news of Pakistan's defeat came as a numbing shock—their military was both disgraced and condemned for its brutal crackdown in East Pakistan. Literally overnight, the country had lost its status as the largest Muslim nation in the world. Gone, too, were any illusions of military parity with India.

Pakistan soon recovered under the charismatic leadership of Zulfiqar Ali Bhutto, who launched a forceful campaign to restore the people's self-confidence and to repair Pakistan's tarnished image abroad. Initially, Bhutto was sworn in as president and chief martial law administrator, the two positions he took over from Yahya Khan. Although he soon revoked formal martial law, he governed autocratically until he was overthrown in 1977.

A man of contradictions, and a product of a privileged feudal background, the Western-educated Bhutto nonetheless expounded populist themes of shared wealth, national unity, and the need to restore political democracy under the slogan "Islam our Faith, Democracy our Polity, Socialism our Economy." Bhutto nationalized a large number of the most important manufacturing, insurance, and domestically owned banking industries—actions that substantially slowed economic growth.

By the mid-1970s, Bhutto's autocratic tendencies were interfering with his ability to govern. His determination to crush any and all potential opposition had become obsessive. Bhutto purged his party of real or imagined opponents, created a praetorian security force answerable only to himself, brought the prestigious civil service under his personal control, and sacked military officers who possessed what he described as "Bonapartist tendencies." Fatefully, Bhutto then named General Mohammad Zia ul-Haq—a relatively junior and obscure general—to hold the top army post. Most observers had predicted that Bhutto's PPP would retain control of the National Assembly in the elections of March 1977, but the margin of the PPP's victory was so overwhelming that charges of fraud were immediately made, and riots erupted throughout the country. General Zia was well positioned to act against Bhutto. He abruptly informed the nation that he had taken over as the chief martial law administrator but assured the people that the military desired only to supervise fair elections, which he said would be held in ninety days. This was the first of many promises Zia did not keep. As the elections approached, Zia announced that criminal charges were being brought against Bhutto and postponed the elections until after Bhutto had been tried in court. Bhutto was found guilty of complicity in the murder of a political opponent, and later hanged. The memory of Bhutto and the circumstances surrounding his fall became a rallying cry for his daughter, Benazir, who, during the 1980s, sought revenge as she began her political ascent in steadfast opposition to Zia and martial law.

Zia ul-Haq's eleven years of rule left a profound—and controversial—legacy on Pakistani society. Zia's military junta differed in important aspects from the earlier military regime of Ayub Khan. Like Zia, Ayub Khan had been contemptuous of politicians; his style of governing was autocratic in the tradition of the British Raj and its Mughal predecessors. Nevertheless, Ayub Khan welcomed Western influences in his quest for economic development, and he introduced various reform measures, such as the Muslim Family Laws Ordinance, which provided protection for women within their families. Moreover, early in his rule, Ayub Khan isolated the army from the governmental decision-making process and instead relied heavily on senior civil servants and a few conservative politicians.

Zia's rule, by contrast, was notable for the high visibility of a small number of army officers and for his fervent advocacy of a more stringent version of Islamic orthodoxy. Zia made clear his desire to supplant the prevailing legal system with Islamic law, the sharia (see Glossary), and championed a role for Islam that was more state directed and less a matter of personal choice. He proclaimed that all laws had to conform with Islamic tenets and values and charged the military with protecting the nation's ideology as well as its territorial integrity. His establishment of the Federal Shariat Court to examine laws in light of the injunctions of Islam further involved the state in religious affairs.

The crucial and perplexing question of the role Islam should play in Pakistan existed before the creation of the nation and remains unresolved today. Jinnah supplied a historical reference to the dilemma, stating in his inaugural address, "You will find that in course of time Hindus would cease to be Hindus and Muslims would cease to be Muslims, not in the religious sense, because that is the personal faith of each individual, but in the political sense as citizens of the State." Although each of Pakistan's indigenous constitutions has defined Pakistan as an Islamic state, determining what this means in practice has usually been left open to individual preference. Zia elevated the tempo of the debate over the role of Islam in Pakistani society by directly involving the state with religion.

The Soviet invasion of Afghanistan in December 1979 and its nine-year occupation of that country not only had a direct impact on Pakistani society in general but also held vital importance for Zia's leadership, influencing his domestic and international image as well as the survival of his regime. From the beginning of his rule, Zia was regarded by much of the world community as a usurper of power and as something of an international pariah. He furthered his isolation by deciding, early in his regime, to pursue the development of nuclear weapons, a program begun earlier by Bhutto. Building on the long and close relationship between the United States and Pakistan dating from the early years of the Cold War, United States president Jimmy Carter and his administration worked energetically but unsuccessfully to discourage Pakistan's nuclear program and finally suspended all economic and military aid on April 6, 1979. The execution of Bhutto two days earlier had added to

United States displeasure with the Zia regime and Pakistan. Relations with the United States soured further when a Pakistani mob burned down the United States Embassy in November 1979.

The Soviet invasion of Afghanistan abruptly ended Pakistan's estrangement from the United States. Within days, Pakistan once again became Washington's indispensable frontline ally against Soviet expansionism. Massive military and economic assistance flowed into Pakistan despite Zia's continued pursuit of nuclear weapons technology. Pakistan's nuclear program made major advances in the 1980s. Moreover, the change in geostrategic circumstances following the occupation of neighboring Afghanistan allowed Zia to postpone the promised elections repeatedly while he consolidated his position. Foreign assistance provided a stimulus to the economy and became an important means by which Zia neutralized his opponents. The war, depicted by Zia and the Afghan resistance as a holy war of believers versus nonbelievers, facilitated Zia's efforts to transform Pakistan into a state governed by Islamic law.

The war in Afghanistan had many profound and disturbing residual effects on Pakistani society. Pakistan absorbed more than 3.2 million Afghan refugees into its North-West Frontier Province and Balochistan. The influx of so many displaced people threatened to overwhelm the local economies as refugees competed with Pakistanis for resources. With the refugees came an arsenal of weapons. Domestic violence increased dramatically during the war years, and observers spoke dismally of a "Kalashnikov culture" asserting itself in Pakistani society.

By the time of Zia's death in an airplane explosion in August 1988, an agreement had been signed signaling the end of Soviet military intervention in Afghanistan, and the Soviet pullout had already begun. Domestic politics in Pakistan were surprisingly tranquil as Pakistan prepared for a transition of power and elections to the National Assembly, which Zia had earlier dissolved. An era seemed to have ended and a new, more promising one to have begun. The prospect for genuine democracy in Pakistan appeared to have dramatically improved, and Pakistan appeared to have reached a watershed in its political development.

After her party won a plurality of seats in the parliamentary elections of November 1988, Benazir Bhutto formed a fragile coalition government and assumed the position of prime minister. She became the first freely elected leader in Pakistan since her father was deposed and the first woman to hold such a high position in a Muslim country. Confronted by severe disadvantages from the start, Benazir soon discovered that the art of governance was considerably more difficult than orchestrating opposition politics. An experienced politician but an inexperienced head of government, she was outmaneuvered by her political opposition, intimidated by the military, and diverted from her reform program. Benazir was also frustrated by her inability to control the spreading social disorder, the widespread banditry, and the mounting ethnic violence between Sindhis and *muhajirs* in her home province of Sindh. A prolonged struggle between Bhutto and the provincial government of Mian Nawaz Sharif in Punjab culminated in bureaucrat-turned-president Ghulam Ishaq Khan's siding with Nawaz Sharif against Benazir. Empowered by the Eighth Amendment provisions of the constitution—a direct legacy of the Zia ul-Haq regime, which strengthened the powers of the president at the expense of the prime minister—Ishaq Khan dismissed Benazir in August 1990 for alleged corruption and her inability to maintain law and order. He also dismissed her cabinet and dissolved the National Assembly as well as the Sindh and North-West Frontier Province provincial assemblies and ordered new elections for October.

The elections brought Nawaz Sharif's Islamic Democratic Alliance (Islami Jamhoori Ittehad—IJI) coalition to power, and for a brief period there appeared to be a workable relationship between the new prime minister and the president. Yet this alliance soon unraveled over policy differences, specifically over the question of who had the power to appoint the top army commander. In charges similar to those Ishaq Khan had before brought against Benazir, Nawaz Sharif was accused in early 1993 of "corruption and mismanagement." Nawaz Sharif, like Benazir before him, was dismissed and parliament dissolved—without a vote of confidence ever having been taken in the legislature. This time, however, the Supreme Court overturned the president's action, declaring it unconstitutional. The court restored both the prime minister and parliament. The Supreme Court's ruling, which served as a stunning rebuke to Ishaq Khan, succeeded in defusing his presidentially engineered crisis and, more important, allowed Ishaq Khan's opponents to boldly challenge the legitimacy of the civil-military bureaucracy that had so often interrupted the process of democratic nation building.

The crisis in government continued as Ishaq Khan, still resolved to undermine the prime minister, brazenly manipulated provincial politics, dissolving the provincial assemblies in Punjab and the North-West Frontier Province. Fears of military intervention and the reimposition of martial law loomed as the ongoing feud between the president and prime minister threatened to bring effective government to a standstill. Although the army ultimately intervened in mid-1993 to break the stalemate and convinced both men to step down, fears of a military takeover were unfounded. The army proved sensitive to the spirit of the times and exercised admirable restraint as it assumed a new and benign role as arbiter rather than manipulator of the nation's politics.

A caretaker government led by World Bank official Moeen Qureshi was installed in July 1993, with the mandate to preside over new elections for the national and provincial assemblies. The caretaker government surprised everyone with its vigor and impressed Pakistanis and international observers alike. During his three-month tenure, Qureshi earned the accolade "Mr. Clean" by initiating an impressive number of reform measures. Qureshi published lists of unpaid debts and prevented debtor-politicians from running for office. He also devalued the currency and cut farm subsidies and public-service expenditures. Because the Qureshi caretaker government was temporary and not much constrained by the realpolitik of Pakistani society, observers doubted that any succeeding government would be able to match its record and boldness of action.

In October 1993, Qureshi fulfilled his primary mandate of holding new elections for the national and provincial assemblies. The contest was now between two staunch adversaries—Nawaz Sharif and Benazir Bhutto—and their respective parties. Although Benazir's PPP received less of the popular vote than Nawaz Sharif's Pakistan Muslim League (PML-N), it won a narrow plurality of seats in the National Assembly, enabling Benazir to form a government. Presidential elections were held in November, and Farooq Leghari, a member of Benazir's party, won, thereby strengthening her position.

In a political culture that traditionally placed great emphasis on the personal characteristics of its leaders and considerably less on the development of its democratic institutions, the personality of these leaders has always been of paramount, and many would argue exaggerated, importance. The case of Benazir Bhutto, Pakistan's prime minister in mid-1995, is no exception. Benazir's return to the pinnacle of Pakistani politics in October 1993 was portrayed with great theater as a redemptive second coming for the country's self-proclaimed "Daughter of Destiny." Benazir pledged this time to fulfill some of the promises she had failed to keep during her first tenure as prime minister. These included calming the potentially explosive ethnic problems in the country, strengthening a treasury overburdened with debt, reconstructing a financial system weakened by corruption, managing a burgeoning population with inadequate access to social services and one making heavy demands on the country's fragile ecology, enforcing women's rights in a decidedly male-dominated society, and forging a consensus on the role of Islam in contemporary Pakistani society. Above all, Benazir promised to steer Pakistan further along the road to democracy—a difficult and sensitive task in a country whose power structure has traditionally been authoritarian and whose politics have been socially divisive and confrontational.

As before, Benazir faces a continual challenge from Nawaz Sharif, who appears to be pursuing the same destabilizing political strategies that succeeded in paralyzing her first government. For a short while, following Benazir's return to power, her public rhetoric and that of her opponent seemed less confrontational than before and tended to stress themes of political stability, cooperation, and accommodation. This period of détente was short-lived, however, as a familiar pattern in Pakistani politics soon reasserted itself, with vigorous opposition attempts to bring down Benazir's government. Unrestrained and sometimes chimerical criticism fueled opposition-orchestrated general strikes, which continued unabated throughout 1994 and into 1995. In response, Benazir branded her opposition as traitorous and "antistate." By the end of the first half of 1995, relations had become so vitriolic between Benazir and Nawaz Sharif that in June, Nawaz Sharif accused Benazir of being "part of the problem" of the escalating violence in Karachi, and Benazir, for her part, leveled an accusation of treason against the former prime minister and chief rival, only months after her government had arrested Nawaz Sharif's father for alleged financial crimes.

Promising to be true to her reform agenda, Benazir unveiled a government budget in June 1994 that called for lowering import duties, making the rupee convertible on the current account, broadening the tax base, and holding down defense spending. These measures will be strengthened by Pakistan's receipt of most of the US$2.5 billion in aid requested at a meeting of international donors in 1994. In order to receive US$1.4 billion in preferential International Monetary Fund (IMF—see Glossary) credits, Pakistan agreed to a three-year structural adjustment program of fiscal austerity and deficit cutting. Under guidelines set by the IMF, Pakistan hopes to raise its gross domestic product (GDP—see Glossary) growth to an average of 6.5 percent per year while eventually lowering inflation to 5 percent. Whether this goal can be reached depends largely on raising Pakistan's export earnings, which suffered in the past few years primarily as a result of a drought, a major flood, and a plant virus "leaf curl" that has devastated cotton production.

Most observers believe that Pakistan's greatest economic advantage is its people: the country possesses a reservoir of entrepreneurial and technical skills necessary for rapid economic growth and development. The textile industry is especially critical to Pakistan's development. This dynamic sector in the economy—a major producer of cotton cloth and yarn—should benefit from the phaseout of textile import quotas under the General Agreement on Tariffs and Trade (GATT). By late 1994, Pakistan's official foreign-exchange reserves had risen from below US$300 million the previous year to more than US$3 billion. The government's continuing strategy of privatizing state-owned enterprises appears to be invigorating the economy and attracting substantial foreign investment in the country's stock exchanges. An optimistic Benazir stated that "Pakistan is poised for an economic takeoff" and noted that in the "new world of today, trade had replaced aid."

Although Pakistan's recent economic gains are encouraging, the country faces a number of long-term impediments to growth. The most serious of these are rapid population growth, governmental neglect of social development, continued high inflation and unemployment, a bloated and inefficient bureaucracy, widespread tax evasion and corruption, a weak infrastructure, and defense expenditures that consume more than 25 percent (some estimates are as high as 40 percent) of government spending.

Benazir will also need to address Pakistan's most pressing social problems if her reform program is to have a lasting effect. Many of these problems are caused by the skewed distribution of resources in Pakistan. Although the middle class is growing, wealth has remained largely in the control of the nation's elite. Agitation caused by the unfulfilled promise of rising expectations is fueled by sophisticated media, which extend a glimpse of a better life to every village and *basti* (barrio).

Pakistan must also work to protect its international image. In mid-1995 human rights violations continued to be widely reported, including arbitrary arrest and detention, torture of prisoners, and incidents of extrajudicial killings by overzealous police, most often in connection with government efforts to restore law and order to troubled Sindh. The government, faced with unprecedented levels of societal violence, has been forced to take strong action. Prime Minister Benazir Bhutto pledged to use "ruthlessness" where necessary to confront and to root out ethnic and religious militants. Pakistan is also challenged by pervasive narcotics syndicates, which wield great influence in Karachi, as well as in Peshawar in the North-West Frontier Province. Pakistan has become one of the world's leading producers of heroin, supplying a reported 20 to 40 percent of the heroin consumed in the United States and 70 percent of that consumed in Europe. Pakistan also has an expanding domestic market for illicit drugs—a scourge that is having a devastating effect on Pakistani society. The Pakistan government estimates that there are 2.5 million drug addicts in the country—1.7 million of them addicted to heroin.

A particularly worrisome problem is Pakistan's unwanted role as a base for Islamic militants. These militants come from a wide range of Arab countries, including Algeria, Tunisia, Egypt, Iraq, Jordan, Saudi Arabia, and Sudan, as well as nations in Central Asia and the Far East, and are mostly based in the North-West Frontier Province. Many of these militants participated in the war in Afghanistan but now serve other, often extremist, causes. An attack that killed two American employees of the United States consulate in Karachi in March 1995 has drawn international attention to the growing terrorist activity in Pakistan.

Pakistan's most pressing foreign relations problem is still Kashmir. India routinely accuses Pakistan of supporting a Kashmiri "intifadah"—a Muslim uprising in Indian-controlled areas of Kashmir. The rebellion, which is centered in the Vale of Kashmir, a scenic intermontane valley with a Muslim majority, has claimed 20,000 lives since 1990. Pakistan claims only to have lent moral and political support to Muslim and Sikh separatist sentiments in Kashmir and the Indian state of Punjab, respectively, while it accuses India of creating dissension in Pakistan's province of Sindh. The Kashmir issue has now broadened in scope and has taken on a new and ominous dimension. In February 1993, then Central Intelligence Agency director James Woolsey testified before Congress that the arms race between India and Pakistan represented the "most probable prospect" for the future use of nuclear weapons. These sentiments were echoed the following year by United Nations secretary general Boutros-Ghali, who cautioned that an escalation of hostilities between Pakistan and India could lead to an accident, with "disastrous repercussions." Tensions on the military Line of Control between Pakistani-controlled Azad Kashmir and Indian-held Kashmir remained high in mid-1995.

In August 1994, former Prime Minister Nawaz Sharif made an announcement calculated to showcase his hard-line stance on Kashmir, embarrass Benazir's government, and further complicate its relations with the United States over the two countries' most sensitive bilateral issue—Pakistan's clandestine nuclear weapons program. He stated, "If India dares to attack Azad Kashmir, it will have to face the Pakistani atom bomb. I declare that Pakistan is in possession of an atom bomb."

Nawaz Sharif's statement fortified the position of United States supporters of the Pressler Amendment of the Foreign Assistance Act, which has suspended United States aid and most military arms sales to Pakistan since October 1990. Under the amendment, the president must make the required annual certification to Congress that Pakistan does not possess a nuclear weapon. The last certification had been given—guardedly—by President George Bush in November 1989.

The timing of Nawaz Sharif's statement also threatened to undermine President William J. Clinton's earlier South Asian nonproliferation initiative: a proposal to Congress to authorize the release to Pakistan of twenty-eight F–16 fighter airplanes (purchased before the aid cutoff) in return for a verifiable cap on Pakistan's production of fissile nuclear material. In mid-1995, following a visit to the United States by Benazir Bhutto, the Clinton administration and Congress appeared to be moving toward agreement to significantly relax the Pressler Amendment and other "country specific" sanctions that Pakistanis believe unfairly penalize their country for its nuclear program while overlooking India's program. Relaxation of the sanctions could yet be derailed as new accusations by United

States intelligence officials surfaced in the United States press in early July 1995 alleging that Pakistan had surreptitiously received fully operable medium-range M–11 ballistic missiles from China. The Clinton administration, however, maintains that there is no conclusive proof that the missiles have been delivered, and until there is, there will be no change regarding sanctions.

Events in Pakistan point to a nation undergoing profound and accelerated change but one very much indebted to its past. Change in Pakistan is perhaps most turbulent in the metropolis of Karachi—Pakistan's economic hub and a city whose well-being may offer a glimpse of the future prospects of the nation. In mid-1995 Karachi continued to be plagued by a volatile combination of sectarian, ethnic, political, and economic unrest. The city of more than 12 million seems, in the words of one Pakistan watcher, to have fallen almost into a Hobbesian state of "all against all," as religious, political, and criminal gangs—many well armed—wage a battle for control. In a city that is growing by more than 400,000 people a year and has an unemployment rate as high as 14 percent, recruits for feuding religious and political factions are easily found. The violence left as many as 1,000 dead in 1994 and showed little sign of abating in 1995. The army, ordered to provide a measure of security for the city, pulled out in December 1994 after a two- and one-half-year presence, tiring of its police role and mindful that Karachi's streets were becoming too dangerous for its troops.

There are many explanations for the lawlessness and disorder in Karachi. Economists cite rampant economic growth. Sociologists cite problems arising from Sunni (see Glossary) and Shia (see Glossary) divisions in Islam and from linguistic and ethnic competition, primarily between Urdu-speaking *muhajirs* and native Sindhis. The government complains of unruly political parties that are sometimes too willing to include criminal and drug-trafficking elements in their ranks, and it even raises the specter of the "hidden hand" of Indian agents provocateurs intent on destabilizing Pakistan.

In the final analysis, Karachi may present the greatest risk as well as the greatest potential for the nation's future. Some observers are predicting that the success or failure of Benazir's leadership will ultimately rest on whether she succeeds in managing the crisis in Karachi. On the one hand, if the city continues to be mired in anarchy and violence, its reputation as a cosmopolitan symbol of the new Pakistan will be tarnished. If security does not improve, foreign investors are likely to stay away, delaying Pakistan's much-anticipated economic takeoff. On the other hand, if the situation in Pakistan's largest "urban laboratory" improves, the lessons learned can be applied elsewhere in the nation.

Benazir's father, former Prime Minister Zulfiqar Ali Bhutto, wrote in 1977, "Politics is not the conversion of a flowering society into a wasteland. Politics is the soul of life. It is my eternal romance with the people. Only the people can break this eternal bond." These words highlighted his philosophy of bringing politics to the street and deriving strength from the masses. This philosophy served his daughter well during her years as an opposition figure but considerably less so during her first term as prime minister. Whether or not Benazir can keep the allegiance of the people while presiding over the maturation of Pakistan's democratic institutions will largely depend on her understanding of her nation's complex political legacy.

July 10, 1995 Peter R. Blood

Chapter 1. Historical Setting

Artist's rendition of tile mosaic of horsemen and soldiers from the Pictured Wall, Lahore Fort, Punjab. Artwork represents seventeenth-century tessellated tile work of the Mughal period.

WHEN BRITISH ARCHAEOLOGIST Sir Mortimer Wheeler was commissioned in 1947 by the government of Pakistan to give a historical account of the new country, he entitled his work *Five Thousand Years of Pakistan.* Indeed, Pakistan has a history that can be dated back to the Indus Valley civilization (ca. 2500–1600 B.C.), the principal sites of which lay in present-day Sindh and Punjab provinces. Pakistan was later the entryway for the migrating pastoral tribes known as Indo-Aryans, or simply Aryans, who brought with them and developed the rudiments of the broad and evolutionary religio-philosophical system later recognized as Hinduism. They also brought an early version of Sanskrit, the base of Urdu, Punjabi, and Sindhi, languages that are spoken in much of Pakistan today.

Hindu rulers were eventually displaced by Muslim invaders, who, in the tenth, eleventh, and twelfth centuries, entered northwestern India through the same passes in the mountains used earlier by the Aryans. The culmination of Muslim rule in the Mughal Empire (1526–1858, with effective rule between 1560 and 1707) encompassed much of the area that is today Pakistan. Sikhism, another religious movement that arose partially on the soil of present-day Pakistan, was briefly dominant in the Punjab and in the northwest in the early nineteenth century. These regimes subsequently fell to the expanding power of the British, whose empire lasted from the eighteenth century to the mid-twentieth century, until they too left the scene, yielding power to the successor states of India and Pakistan.

The departure of the British was a goal of the Muslim movement championed by the All-India Muslim League (created in 1906 to counter the Hindu-dominated Indian National Congress), which strove for both political independence and cultural separation from the Hindu-majority regions of British India. These objectives were reached in 1947, when British India received its independence as two new sovereign states. The Muslim-majority areas in northwestern and eastern India were separated and became Pakistan, divided into the West Wing and East Wing, respectively. The placement of two widely separated regions within a single state did not last, and in 1971 the East Wing broke away and achieved independence as Bangladesh.

The pride that Pakistan displayed after independence in its long and multicultural history has disappeared in many of its officially sponsored textbooks and other material used for teaching history (although the Indus Valley sites remain high on the list of the directors of tourism). As noted anthropologist Akbar S. Ahmed has written in *History Today*, "In Pakistan the Hindu past simply does not exist. History only begins in the seventh century after the advent of Islam and the Muslim invasion of Sindh."

Early Civilizations

From the earliest times, the Indus Valley region has been both a transmitter of cultures and a receptacle of different ethnic, linguistic, and religious groups. Indus Valley civilization appeared around 2500 B.C. along the Indus River valley in Punjab and Sindh. This civilization, which had a writing system, urban centers, and a diversified social and economic system, was discovered in the 1920s at its two most important sites: Mohenjo-daro, in Sindh near Sukkur, and Harappa, in Punjab south of Lahore (see fig. 2). A number of other lesser sites stretching from the Himalayan foothills in Indian Punjab to Gujarat east of the Indus River and to Balochistan to the west have also been discovered and studied. How closely these places were connected to Mohenjo-daro and Harappa is not clearly known, but evidence indicates that there was some link and that the people inhabiting these places were probably related.

An abundance of artifacts have been found at Harappa—in fact, the archaeological yield there has been so rich that the name of that city has often been equated with the Indus Valley civilization (Harappan culture) it represents. Yet the site was damaged in the latter part of the nineteenth century when engineers constructing the Lahore-Multan railroad used brick from the ancient city for ballast. Fortunately, the site at Mohenjo-daro has been less disturbed in modern times and shows a well-planned and well-constructed city of brick.

Indus Valley civilization was essentially a city culture sustained by surplus agricultural produce and extensive commerce, which included trade with Sumer in southern Mesopotamia in what is today Iraq. Copper and bronze were in use, but not iron. Mohenjo-daro and Harappa were cities built on similar plans of well-laid-out streets, elaborate drainage systems, public baths, differentiated residential areas, flat-roofed brick houses, and fortified administrative and religious centers enclosing meeting halls and granaries. Weights and measures were standardized. Distinctive engraved stamp seals were used, perhaps to identify property. Cotton was spun, woven, and dyed for clothing. Wheat, rice, and other food crops were cultivated, and a variety of animals were domesticated. Wheel-made pottery—some of it adorned with animal and geometric motifs—has been found in profusion at all the major Indus Valley sites. A centralized administration has been inferred from the cultural uniformity revealed, but it remains uncertain whether authority lay with a priestly or a commercial oligarchy.

By far the most exquisite but most obscure artifacts unearthed to date are the small, square steatite seals engraved with human or animal motifs. Large numbers of the seals have been found at Mohenjo-daro, many bearing pictographic inscriptions generally thought to be a kind of script. Despite the efforts of philologists from all parts of the world, however, and despite the use of computers, the script remains undeciphered, and it is unknown if it is proto-Dravidian or proto-Sanskrit. Nevertheless, extensive research on the Indus Valley sites, which has led to speculations on both the archaeological and the linguistic contributions of the pre-Aryan population to Hinduism's subsequent development, has offered new insights into the cultural heritage of the Dravidian population still dominant in southern India. Artifacts with motifs relating to asceticism and fertility rites suggest that these concepts entered Hinduism from the earlier civilization. Although historians agree that the civilization ceased abruptly, at least in Mohenjo-daro and Harappa, there is disagreement on the possible causes for its end. Conquering hordes of Aryan invaders from central and western Asia have long been thought by historians to have been the "destroyers" of Indus Valley civilization, but this view is increasingly open to scientific scrutiny and reinterpretation. Other, perhaps more plausible explanations include recurrent floods caused by tectonic earth movement, soil salinity, and desertification.

Until the entry of the Europeans by sea in the late fifteenth century, and with the exception of the Arab conquests of Muhammad bin Qasim in the early eighth century, the route taken by peoples who migrated to India has been through the mountain passes, most notably the Khyber Pass, in northwestern Pakistan. Although unrecorded migrations may have taken place earlier, it is certain that migrations increased in the sec-

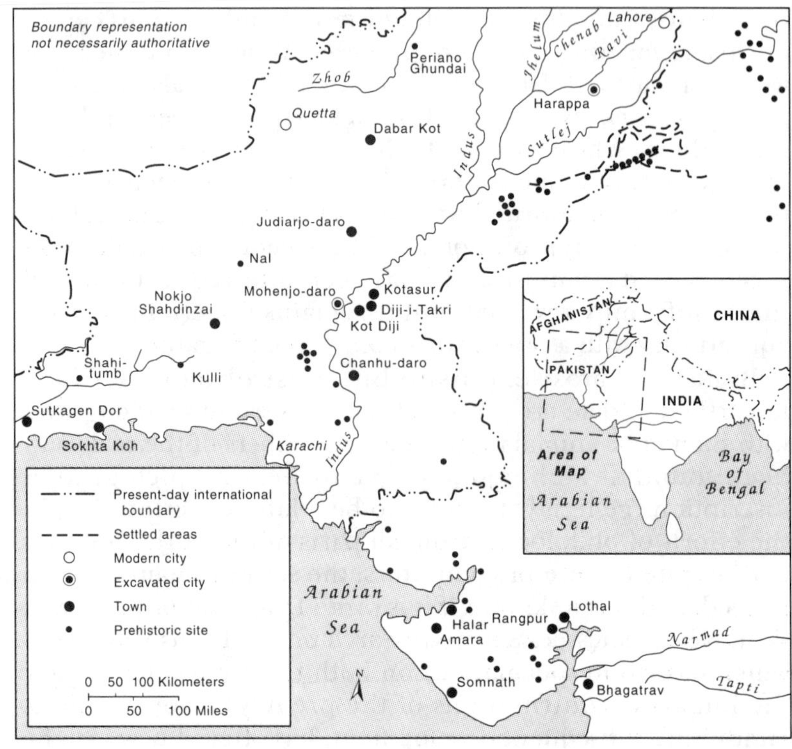

Source: Based on information from Robert Eric Mortimer Wheeler, *Early India and Pakistan: To Ashoka*, New York, 1968, 95; and Joseph E. Schwartzberg, ed., *A Historical Atlas of South Asia*, New York, 1992, 9.

Figure 2. Indus Valley Culture Sites, ca. 2500–1600 B.C.

ond millennium B.C. The records of these people—who spoke an Indo-European language—are literary, not archaeological, and were preserved in the Vedas, collections of orally transmitted hymns. In the greatest of these, the "Rig Veda," the Aryan speakers appear as a tribally organized, pastoral, and pantheistic people. The later Vedas and other Sanskritic sources, such as the Puranas (literally, "old writings"—an encyclopedic collection of Hindu legends, myths, and genealogy), indicate an eastward movement from the Indus Valley into the Ganges Valley (called Ganga in Asia) and southward at least as far as the Vindhya Range, in central India. A social and political system evolved in which the Aryans dominated, but various indigenous peoples and ideas were accommodated and absorbed. The caste system that remained characteristic of Hinduism also evolved. One theory is that the three highest castes—Brahmins, Kshatriyas, and Vaishyas—were composed of Aryans, while a lower caste—the Sudras—came from the indigenous peoples.

By the sixth century B.C., knowledge of Indian history becomes more focused because of the available Buddhist and Jain sources of a later period. Northern India was populated by a number of small princely states that rose and fell in the sixth century B.C. In this milieu, a phenomenon arose that affected the history of the region for several centuries—Buddhism. Siddhartha Gautama, the Buddha, or "Enlightened One" (ca. 563–483 B.C.), was born in the Ganges Valley. His teachings were spread in all directions by monks, missionaries, and merchants. The Buddha's teachings proved enormously popular when considered against the more obscure and highly complicated rituals and philosophy of Vedic Hinduism. The original doctrines of the Buddha also constituted a protest against the inequities of the caste system, thereby attracting large numbers of followers.

At about the same time, the semi-independent kingdom of Gandhara, roughly located in northern Pakistan and centered in the region of Peshawar, stood between the expanding kingdoms of the Ganges Valley to the east and the Achaemenid Empire of Persia to the west. Gandhara probably came under the influence of Persia during the reign of Cyrus the Great (559–530 B.C.). The Persian Empire fell to Alexander the Great in 330 B.C., and he continued his march eastward through Afghanistan and into India. Alexander defeated Porus, the Gandharan ruler of Taxila, in 326 B.C. and marched on to the Ravi River before turning back. The return march through Sindh and Balochistan ended with Alexander's death at Babylon in 323 B.C.

Greek rule did not survive in northwestern India, although a school of art known as Indo-Greek developed and influenced art as far as Central Asia. The region of Gandhara was conquered by Chandragupta (r. ca. 321–ca. 297 B.C.), the founder of the Mauryan Empire, the first universal state of northern India, with its capital at present-day Patna in Bihar. His grandson, Ashoka (r. ca. 274–ca. 236 B.C.), became a Buddhist. Taxila became a leading center of Buddhist learning. Successors to Alexander at times controlled the northwestern region of present-day Pakistan and even the Punjab after Mauryan power waned in the region.

The northern regions of Pakistan came under the rule of the Sakas, who originated in Central Asia in the second century B.C. They were soon driven eastward by Pahlavas (Parthians related to the Scythians), who in turn were displaced by the Kushans (also known as the Yueh-Chih in Chinese chronicles).

The Kushans had earlier moved into territory in the northern part of present-day Afghanistan and had taken control of Bactria. Kanishka, the greatest of the Kushan rulers (r. ca. A.D. 120–60), extended his empire from Patna in the east to Bukhara in the west and from the Pamirs in the north to central India, with the capital at Peshawar (then Purushapura) (see fig. 3). Kushan territories were eventually overrun by the Huns in the north and taken over by the Guptas in the east and the Sassanians of Persia in the west.

The age of the imperial Guptas in northern India (fourth to seventh centuries A.D.) is regarded as the classical age of Hindu civilization. Sanskrit literature was of a high standard; extensive knowledge in astronomy, mathematics, and medicine was gained; and artistic expression flowered. Society became more settled and more hierarchical, and rigid social codes emerged that separated castes and occupations. The Guptas maintained loose control over the upper Indus Valley.

Northern India suffered a sharp decline after the seventh century. As a result, Islam came to a disunited India through the same passes that Aryans, Alexander, Kushans, and others had entered.

Islam in India

The initial entry of Islam into India came in the first century after the death of the Prophet Muhammad (see Basic Tenets of Islam, ch. 2). The Umayyad caliph in Damascus sent an expedition to Balochistan and Sindh in 711 led by Muhammad bin Qasim (for whom Karachi's second port is named). The expedition went as far north as Multan but was not able to retain that region and was not successful in expanding Islamic rule to other parts of India. Coastal trade and the presence of a Muslim colony in Sindh, however, permitted significant cultural exchanges and the introduction into the subcontinent of saintly teachers (Sufi—see Glossary). Muslim influence grew with conversions.

Almost three centuries later, the Turks and the Afghans spearheaded the Islamic conquest in India through the traditional invasion routes of the northwest. Mahmud of Ghazni

Dhyani Buddha, second-century Buddha statue from the historic site of Taxila Courtesy Prints and Photographs Division, Library of Congress

(979–1030) led a series of raids against Rajput kingdoms and rich Hindu temples and established a base in the Punjab for future incursions. Mahmud's tactics originated the legend of idol-smashing Muslims bent on plunder and forced conversions, a reputation that persists in India to the present day.

During the last quarter of the twelfth century, Muhammad of Ghor invaded the Indo-Gangetic Plain, conquering in succession Ghazni, Multan, Sindh, Lahore, and Delhi. His successors established the first dynasty of the Delhi Sultanate, the Mamluk Dynasty (*mamluk* means "slave") in 1211 (however, the Delhi Sultanate is traditionally held to have been founded in 1206). The territory under control of the Muslim rulers in Delhi expanded rapidly. By mid-century, Bengal and much of central India were under the Delhi Sultanate. Several Turko-Afghan dynasties ruled from Delhi: the Mamluk (1211–90), the Khalji (1290–1320), the Tughlaq (1320–1413), the Sayyid (1414–51), and the Lodhi (1451–1526). As Muslims extended their rule into southern India, only the Hindu kingdom of Vijayanagar remained immune, until it too fell in 1565. There were also kingdoms independent of Delhi in the Deccan, Gujarat, Malwa (central India), and Bengal. Nevertheless, almost all of the area in present-day Pakistan remained generally under the rule of Delhi.

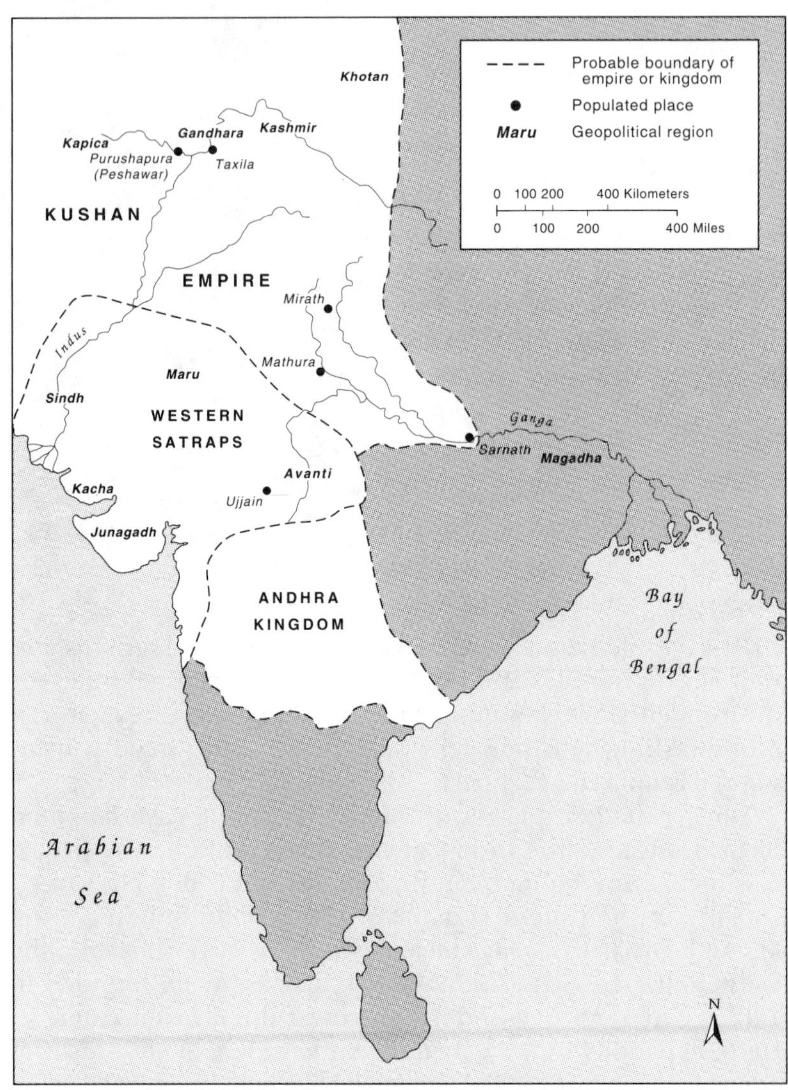

Source: Based on information from William C. Brice, ed., *An Historical Atlas of Islam*, Leiden, 1981, 47–53; and C. Collin Davies, *An Historical Atlas of the Indian Peninsula*, London, 1959, 15.

Figure 3. Kushan Empire, ca. A.D. 150

The sultans of Delhi enjoyed cordial, if superficial, relations with Muslim rulers in the Near East but owed them no allegiance. The sultans based their laws on the Quran and the sharia (see Glossary) and permitted non-Muslim subjects to practice their religion only if they paid *jizya* (see Glossary), or head tax. The sultans ruled from urban centers—while military camps and trading posts provided the nuclei for towns that sprang up in the countryside. Perhaps the greatest contribution of the sultanate was its temporary success in insulating the subcontinent from the potential devastation of the Mongol invasion from Central Asia in the thirteenth century. The sultanate ushered in a period of Indian cultural renaissance resulting from the stimulation of Islam by Hinduism. The resulting "Indo-Muslim" fusion left lasting monuments in architecture, music, literature, and religion. The sultanate suffered from the sacking of Delhi in 1398 by Timur (Tamerlane) but revived briefly under the Lodhis before it was conquered by the Mughals.

The Mughal Period

India in the sixteenth century presented a fragmented picture of rulers, both Muslim and Hindu, who lacked concern for their subjects and who failed to create a common body of laws or institutions. Outside developments also played a role in shaping events. The circumnavigation of Africa by the Portuguese explorer Vasco da Gama in 1498 allowed Europeans to challenge Arab control of the trading routes between Europe and Asia. In Central Asia and Afghanistan, shifts in power pushed Babur of Ferghana (in present-day Uzbekistan) southward, first to Kabul and then to India. The dynasty he founded endured for more than three centuries.

Claiming descent from both Chinggis Khan (Genghis Khan) and Timur, Babur combined strength and courage with a love of beauty, and military ability with cultivation. Babur concentrated on gaining control of northwestern India. He did so in 1526 by defeating the last Lodhi sultan on the field of Panipat, a town just northwest of Delhi. Babur then turned to the tasks of persuading his Central Asian followers to stay on in India and of overcoming other contenders for power, mainly the Rajputs and the Afghans. He succeeded in both tasks but died shortly thereafter in 1530. The Mughal Empire was one of the largest centralized states in premodern history and was the precursor to the British Indian Empire (see fig. 4).

The perennial question of who was the greatest of the six "Great Mughals" receives varying answers in present-day Pakistan and India. Some favor Babur the pioneer and others his great-grandson, Shah Jahan (r. 1628–58), builder of the Taj

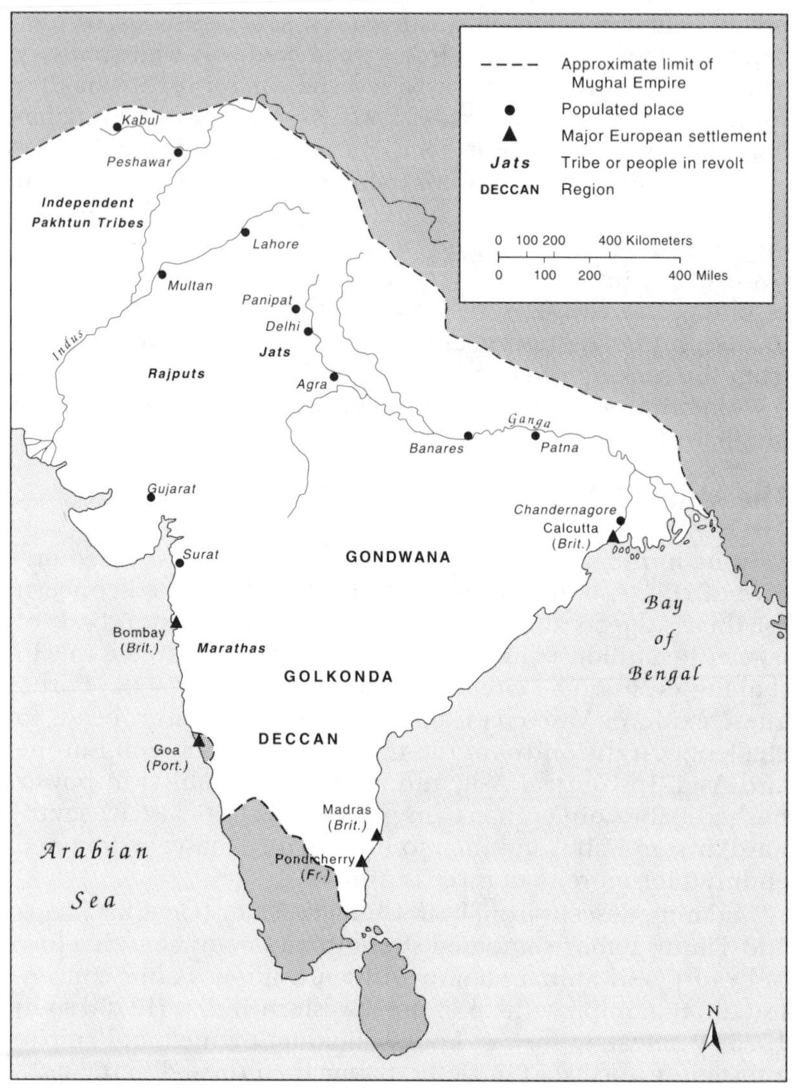

Source: Based on information from Joseph E. Schwartzberg, ed., *A Historical Atlas of South Asia*, New York, 1992, 46.

Figure 4. Mughal Empire, Late Seventeenth Century

Mahal and other magnificent buildings. The other two towering figures of the era by general consensus were Akbar (r. 1556–1605) and Aurangzeb (r. 1658–1707). Both rulers expanded the empire greatly and were able administrators. Akbar was known for his religious tolerance and administrative genius, while Aurangzeb was a pious Muslim and fierce protector of orthodox Islam in an alien and heterodox environment.

Akbar succeeded his father, Humayun (r. 1530–40 and 1555–56), whose rule was interrupted by the Afghan Sur Dynasty, which rebelled against him. It was only just before his death that Humayun was able to regain the empire and leave it to his son. In restoring and expanding Mughal rule, Akbar based his authority on the ability and loyalty of his followers, irrespective of their religion. In 1564 the *jizya* on non-Muslims was abolished, and bans on temple building and Hindu pilgrimages were lifted.

Akbar's methods of administration reinforced his power against two possible sources of challenge—the Afghan-Turkish aristocracy and the traditional interpreters of Islamic law, the ulama (see Glossary). He created a ranked imperial service based on ability rather than birth, whose members were obliged to serve wherever required. They were remunerated with cash rather than land and were kept away from their inherited estates, thus centralizing the imperial power base and ensuring its supremacy. The military and political functions of the imperial service were separate from those of revenue collection, which was supervised by the imperial treasury. This system of administration, known as the *mansabdari*, was based on loyal service and cash payments and was the backbone of the Mughal Empire; its effectiveness depended on personal loyalty to the emperor and his ability and willingness to choose, remunerate, and supervise.

Akbar declared himself the final arbiter in all disputes of law derived from the Quran and the sharia. He backed his religious authority primarily with his authority in the state. In 1580 he also initiated a syncretic court religion called the Din-i-Ilahi (Divine Faith). In theory, the new faith was compatible with any other, provided that the devotee was loyal to the emperor. In practice, however, its ritual and content profoundly offended orthodox Muslims. The ulama found their influence undermined. The concept of Islam as a superior religion with a historic mission in the world appeared to be compromised. The syncretism of the court and its tolerance of both Hindus and unorthodox Shia (see Glossary) sects among Muslims triggered a reaction among Sunni (see Glossary) Muslims. In the fratricidal war of succession that closed the reign of Akbar's grandson Shah Jahan in 1658, the aristocracy supported the austere military commander Aurangzeb against his learned and eclectic brother Dara Shikoh, whom Aurangzeb defeated in battle and later had decapitated in 1662.

Aurangzeb's reign ushered in the decline of the Mughal Empire. Aurangzeb, who in the latter half of his long rule assumed the title "Alamgir," or "world-seizer," was known for aggressively expanding the empire's frontiers and for his militant enforcement of orthodox Sunni Islam. During his reign, the Mughal Empire reached its greatest geographical extent, yet his policies also led to its dissolution. Although he was an outstanding general and a rigorous administrator, his reign was characterized by a decline in fiscal and military standards as security and luxury increased. Land rather than cash became the usual means of remunerating high-ranking officials, and divisive tendencies in his large empire further undermined central authority.

In 1679 Aurangzeb reimposed the hated *jizya* on Hindus. Coming after a series of other taxes and also discriminatory measures favoring Sunni Muslims, this action by the "prayer-monger," as he was called, incited rebellion among Hindus and others in many parts of the empire—Jat, Sikh, and Rajput forces in the north and Maratha forces in the Deccan. The emperor managed to crush the rebellions in the north, but at a high cost to agricultural productivity and to the legitimacy of Mughal rule. Aurangzeb was compelled to move his headquarters to Daulatabad in the Deccan to mount a costly campaign against Maratha guerrilla fighters, which lasted twenty-six years until he died in 1707 at the age of ninety. Aurangzeb, oppressed by a sense of failure, isolation, and impending doom, lamented that in life he "came alone" and would "go as a stranger."

In the century and one-half that followed, effective control by Aurangzeb's successors weakened. Succession to imperial and even provincial power, which had often become hereditary, was subject to intrigue and force. The *mansabdari* system gave way to the *zamindari* system, in which high-ranking officials took on the appearance of hereditary landed aristocracy with powers of collecting rents. As Delhi's control waned, other contenders for power emerged and clashed, thus preparing the way for the eventual British takeover.

Vasco da Gama led the first documented European expedition to India, sailing into Calicut on the southwest coast in 1498. In 1510 the Portuguese captured Goa, which became the seat of their activity. Under Admiral Alfonso de Albuquerque,

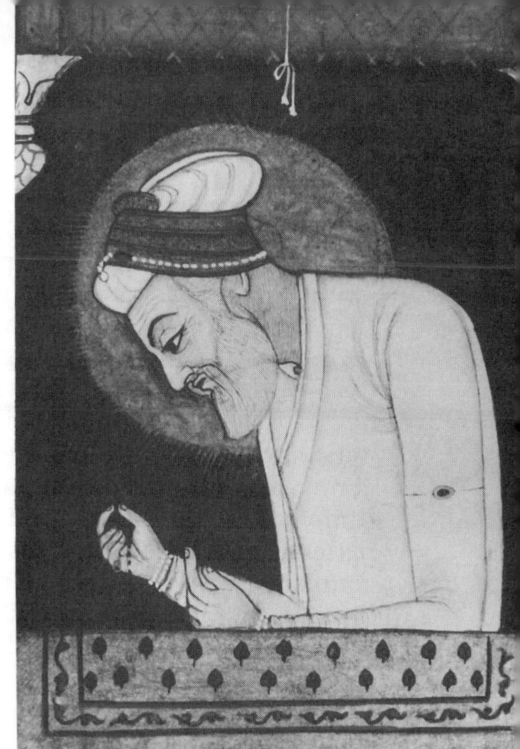

Mughal painting of Aurangzeb, the last of the Great Mughals Courtesy Prints and Photographs Division, Library of Congress

Portugal successfully challenged Arab power in the Indian Ocean and dominated the sea routes for a century. Jesuits came to "convert, to converse, and to record" observations of India. The Protestant countries of the Netherlands and England, upset by the Portuguese monopoly, formed private trading companies at the turn of the seventeenth century to challenge the Portuguese.

Mughal officials permitted the new carriers of India's considerable export trade to establish trading posts (factories) in India. The Dutch East India Company concentrated mainly on the spice trade from present-day Indonesia. Britain's East India Company carried on trade with India. The French East India Company also set up factories.

During the wars of the eighteenth century, the factories served not only as collection and transshipment points for trade but also increasingly as fortified centers of refuge for both foreigners and Indians. British factories gradually began to apply British law to disputes arising within their jurisdiction. The posts also began to grow in area and population. Armed company servants were effective protectors of trade. As rival contenders for power called for armed assistance and as individual European adventurers found permanent homes in India, British and French companies found themselves more and more involved in local politics in the south and in Bengal. Plots and counterplots climaxed when British East India Company forces, led by Robert Clive, decisively defeated the larger but divided forces of Nawab Siraj-ud-Dawlah at Plassey (Pilasi) in Bengal in 1757.

Company Rule

It was not until the middle of the nineteenth century that almost all of the territory that constitutes Pakistan and India came under the rule of the British East India Company. The patterns of territorial acquisition and rule as applied by the company in Sindh and Punjab and the manner of governance became the basis for direct British rule in the British Indian Empire and indirect rule in the princely states under the paramountcy of the crown.

Although the British had earlier ruled in the factory areas, the beginning of British rule is often dated from the Battle of Plassey. Clive's victory was consolidated in 1764 at the Battle of Buxar (in Bihar), where the emperor, Shah Alam II, was defeated. As a result, Shah Alam was coerced to appoint the company to be the *diwan* (collector of revenue) for the areas of Bengal, Bihar, and Orissa (this pretense of Mughal control was abandoned in 1827). The company thus became the supreme, but not the titular, power in much of the Ganges Valley, and company agents continued to trade on terms highly favorable to them.

The area controlled by the company expanded during the first three decades of the nineteenth century by two methods. The first was the use of subsidiary agreements (*sanad*) between the British and the local rulers, under which control of foreign affairs, defense, and communications was transferred from the ruler to the company and the rulers were allowed to rule as they wished (up to a limit) on other matters. This development created what came to be called the Native States, or Princely India, that is, the world of the maharaja and his Muslim counterpart, the *nawab.* The second method was outright military conquest or direct annexation of territories; it was these areas that were properly called British India. Most of northern India was annexed by the British.

At the start of the nineteenth century, most of present-day Pakistan was under independent rulers. Sindh was ruled by the Muslim Talpur *mirs* (chiefs) in three small states that were annexed by the British in 1843. In the Punjab, the decline of the Mughal Empire allowed the rise of the Sikhs, first as a military force and later as a political administration in Lahore. The kingdom of Lahore was at its most powerful and expansive during the rule of Maharaja Ranjit Singh, when Sikh control was extended beyond Peshawar, and Kashmir was added to his dominions in 1819. After Ranjit Singh died in 1839, political conditions in the Punjab deteriorated, and the British fought two wars with the Sikhs. The second of these wars, in 1849, saw the annexation of the Punjab, including the present-day North-West Frontier Province, to the company's territories. Kashmir was transferred by sale in the Treaty of Amritsar in 1850 to the Dogra Dynasty, which ruled the area under British paramountcy until 1947.

As the British increased their territory in India, so did Russia expand in Central Asia. The East India Company signed treaties with a number of Afghan rulers and with Ranjit Singh. Russia backed Persian ambitions in western Afghanistan. In 1838 the company's actions brought about the First Anglo-Afghan War (1838–42). Assisted by Sikh allies, the company took Kandahar and Kabul and made its own candidate amir. The amir proved unpopular with the Afghans, however, and the British garrison's position became untenable. The retreat of the British from Kabul in January 1842 was one of the worst disasters in British military history, as a column of more than 16,000 (about one-third soldiers, the rest camp followers) was annihilated by Afghan tribesmen as they struggled through the snowbound passes on their way back to India. The British later sent a punitive expedition to Kabul, which it burned in retribution, but made no attempt to reoccupy Afghanistan.

In the Punjab, annexed in 1849, a group of extraordinarily able British officers, serving first the company and then the British crown, governed the area. They avoided the administrative mistakes made earlier in Bengal. A number of reforms were introduced, although local customs were generally respected. Irrigation projects later in the century helped the Punjab become the granary of northern India (see Irrigation, ch. 3). The respect gained by the new administration could be gauged by the fact that within ten years Punjabi troops were fighting for the British elsewhere in India to subdue the uprising of 1857–58 (see the British Raj, this ch.). The Punjab was to become the major recruiting area for the British Indian Army, recruiting both Sikhs and Muslims.

The British Raj

The uprising of 1857–58 became the great divide in nineteenth-century South Asian history. Understated by British historians as the Indian Mutiny or Sepoy Rebellion and referred to with some exaggeration by later Indian nationalists as the First War of Independence, the uprising nevertheless heralded the formal end of the Mughal Empire and marked the end of company rule in India as well. In general, the uprising was a reaction to British expansionism and the outcome of the policies of modernization and annexation of Governor General Lord Dalhousie (1848–56), especially in Oudh (Avadh, now part of the Indian state of Uttar Pradesh) in 1856. The immediate spark for mutiny by the sepoys (Indian soldiers employed by the East India Company) was the introduction of the new Enfield rifle, which had cartridges, allegedly greased with cow or pig fat, the tips of which had to be bitten off before loading. Both Muslim and Hindu soldiers were outraged at this offense to their religious scruples and refused to comply. British officers responded by summarily dismissing regiment after regiment from the Bengal Army for refusing to load their weapons. The mutiny was ignited at the cantonment at Meerut, north of Delhi, when all three of the sepoy regiments rose in revolt against the British, killing some British officers before heading for Delhi to restore Bahadur Shah II to imperial glory. Although the area of fighting was limited to northern and central India and participation was limited to sepoys of the Bengal army and some princely states, the uprisings lasted a year and were a severe blow to British confidence. In putting down the rebellion, British troops were aided substantially by their recently recruited troops from the Punjab.

The uprising of 1857–58 heralded the formal end of the Mughal Empire and marked as well the end of company rule in India. The British Parliament passed the Government of India Act of 1858, which transferred authority to the British crown, represented in India by the governor general, who thereafter also had the title of viceroy. Queen Victoria was proclaimed empress of India in 1877.

The Victorian model of administration in British India became the standard reference point for law, order, and probity in Pakistan. At the apex of the administration stood the governor general, almost always a British peer. The governor general held supreme legislative and executive powers and was responsible directly to the secretary of state for India, a member of the British cabinet. British India was divided into provinces (*suba*) for administrative purposes, each headed, depending on size and importance, by a governor or lieutenant governor. Provinces were divided into divisions, and these in turn were divided into districts (*zilla*), the basic administrative units, encompassing substantial territory and population. In many cases, the provinces and districts followed the lines of those created by the Mughals.

The district officer was the linchpin of the system. The officer was revenue collector as well as dispenser of justice and was called district collector, district magistrate, and, in some areas, deputy commissioner (the DC) with equal validity. District officers were usually drawn from the prestigious meritocracy, the Indian Civil Service. Recruitment to the Indian Civil Service was competitive, based on examination of young men with a British classical education. Exclusively British at its beginning, the Indian Civil Service was forced to open its doors slightly to successful Indian candidates. After 1871 district boards and municipal committees were established to assist the district officers in their administrative functions. Thus elective politics, in however limited a form, was introduced to the subcontinent. The governor general was also known as the viceroy and crown representative when dealing with Indian princes. Relations between the British crown and Indian princes were set out in an elusive doctrine of "paramountcy." The princes promised loyalty and surrendered all rights to conduct foreign or defense policy; the crown promised noninterference in internal affairs (except in cases of gross maladministration or injustice) and protection from external and internal enemies.

The British Raj was socially and politically conservative, but it brought profound economic change to the subcontinent. For strategic, administrative, and commercial reasons, the British improved transportation and communications and kept them in good repair. Coal mines were opened in Bihar and Bengal, and irrigation canals were laid out in the Yamuna (also seen as Jumna), Ganges, and Indus valleys; the Indus Valley became the largest irrigated area in the world. The expansion of irrigation in the Punjab led to the development of canal colonies, settled mainly by Sikhs and Muslims, and the designation of the Punjab as the granary of India. Law and order guaranteed a high rate of return on British, and later Indian, investment in these enterprises.

Racial criteria were also used in a dramatic overhaul of the British Indian Army. The number of British soldiers was increased relative to the Indians, and Indians were excluded from artillery and technical services. A theory of "martial races" was used to accelerate recruitment from among "loyal" Sikhs, Punjabi Muslims, Dogras, Gurkas, and Pakhtuns (Pathans—see Glossary) and to discourage enlistment of "disloyal" Bengalis and high-caste Hindus.

The Forward Policy

British policy toward the tribal peoples on the northwest frontier vacillated between caution and adventurism during the latter half of the nineteenth century. Some viceroys opposed extending direct administration or defense beyond the Indus River. Others favored a more assertive posture, or "forward policy." The latter's view prevailed, partly because Russian advances in Central Asia gave their arguments credence. In 1874 Sir Robert Sandeman was sent to improve British relations with the Baloch tribes and the khan of Kalat. In 1876 Sandeman concluded a treaty with the khan that brought his territories—including Kharan, Makran, and Las Bela—under British suzerainty. The Second Anglo-Afghan War was fought in 1878–80, sparked by the Afghan amir's refusal to accept a British diplomatic mission to Kabal. When British forces subsequently occupied much of Afghanistan, a treaty (Treaty of Gandamak) was concluded in May 1879, which forced Afghanistan to accept Britain's control of its foreign affairs and to cede to the British various frontier areas, including the districts of Pishin, Sibi, Harnai, and Thal Chotiali. During succeeding years, other tribal areas were forcibly occupied by the British. In 1883 the British leased the Bolan Pass, southeast of Quetta, from the khan of Kalat on a permanent basis, and in 1887 some areas of Balochistan were declared British territory.

A similar forward policy was pursued farther north. A British political agent was stationed in Gilgit in 1876 to report on Russian activities as well as on developments in the nearby states of Hunza and Nagar. In 1889 the Gilgit Agency was made permanent. A British expedition was sent against Hunza and Nagar, which submitted to British control. A new *mir* from the ruling family of Hunza was appointed by the British. British garrisons were established in Hunza and Chitral in 1892. A formal protectorate was declared over Chitral and Gilgit in 1893.

Also in 1893, Sir Mortimer Durand negotiated an agreement with Amir Abdur Rahman Khan of Afghanistan to fix an only partially surveyed line (the Durand Line) running from Chitral to Balochistan to designate the areas of influence for the Afghans and the British. Each party pledged not to interfere in the other's lands. This agreement brought under British domination territory and peoples that had not yet been conquered and would become the source of much difficulty between Pakistan and Afghanistan in the future (see Boundaries, ch. 2; Foreign Policy, ch. 4).

The establishment of British hegemony in the northwest frontier regions did not lead to direct administration similar to that in other parts of India. Local customary law continued, as did the traditional lines of authority and social customs upheld by the *maliks* (tribal chiefs). To a large extent, the frontier was little more than a vast buffer zone with Afghanistan between the British and Russian empires in Asia and a training ground for the British Indian Army.

The Seeds of Muslim Nationalism

The uprising of 1857–58 was the last fitful assertion of an all but moribund Mughal Empire. Mutinous sepoys had marched from Meerut, the site of the first outbreak, to Delhi proclaiming their intention to restore the poet-emperor Bahadur Shah II to power. British forces with Punjabi sepoys recaptured Delhi and banished the emperor to Burma, where he died in penury in 1862. British distrust of Muslim aristocracy resulted from the rebellious sepoys' attempt to restore the power of the emperor. Muslim leaders were alleged to have had a major role in planning and leading the revolt, although the revolt itself was a series of badly planned and uncoordinated uprisings and the principal leaders, Nana Sahib and Tantia Topi, were Hindus. In the eyes of British rulers, Muslim leaders had been discredited.

As a consequence, the landed Muslim upper classes in the north Indian heartland retreated into cultural and political isolation, while fellow Muslims in the Punjab were rewarded for assisting the British. The former failed to reemerge economically and produced no large group comparable to the upwardly mobile British-educated Hindu middle class. They did not revise the doctrines of Islam to meet the challenges posed by alien rule, Christian missionaries, and revivalist Hindu sects, such as the Arya Samaj, attempting reconversion to Hinduism. The former Muslim rulers of India were in danger of becoming a permanent noncompetitive class in the British Raj at the very time the forces of Indian nationalism were gathering strength.

One response to British rule came to be known as the Deoband Movement, which was led by the ulama, who were expanding traditional Islamic education. The ulama also sought to reform the teaching of Islamic law and to promote its application in contemporary Muslim society. They promoted publications in Urdu, established fund-raising drives, and undertook other modern organizational work on an all-India basis. While most Deobandis eventually were to support the Indian National Congress and a united India, a group that favored the creation of Pakistan later emerged as the core of the Jamiat-ul-Ulama-i-Islam party (see Political Dynamics, ch. 4).

Another response was led by Syed Ahmad Khan (1817–98, known as Sir Syed) and was called the Aligarh Movement after the Muhammadan Anglo-Oriental College (now Aligarh Muslim University), which he founded in 1875 at Aligarh in north-central India (see Education, ch. 2). Sir Syed considered access to British education as the best means of social mobility for the sons of the Muslim gentry under colonial rule.

Meanwhile, the beginnings of the Indian nationalist movement were to be discerned in the increasing tendency to form all-India associations representing various interests. English-speaking Indians, predominantly middle-class but from different parts of the country, were discovering the efficacy of associations and public meetings in propagating their views to a wider audience and in winning the attention of the British government. In 1885 the Indian National Congress (also referred to as Congress) was founded to formulate proposals and demands to present to the British.

A national, all-India forum, Congress was an umbrella organization. Many of its members envisioned a long British period of tutelage and advocated strictly constitutionalist and gradualist reforms, but after World War I, Congress argued for a speedy end to alien rule. The idea of the territorial integrity of India and opposition to any sectarian division of India, however, always remained sacrosanct to Congress.

Although Sir Syed often voiced demands similar to those made by the founders of Congress—local self-government, Indian representation on the viceroy's and the governors' councils, and equal duties for Indian members of the Indian Civil Service and the judicial service—he remained aloof when

Congress was founded and advised his followers not to join it, because he thought the organization would be dominated by Hindus and would inevitably become antigovernment. It has been argued that Sir Syed's fear of Hindu domination sowed the seeds for the "Two Nations Theory" later espoused by the All-India Muslim League (also referred to as the Muslim League), founded in 1906, and led to its demand for a separate state for the Muslims of India—reinforcing his view that the British were the only guarantors of the rights of the Muslims. Sir Syed argued that education and not politics was the key to Muslim advancement. Graduates of Aligarh generally made their careers initially in administration, not politics, and thus were not greatly affected by the introduction of representative institutions at the provincial level by the India Councils Act of 1892.

Events in Bengal proved that agitation was as useful as politics. Lord Curzon (George Nathaniel Curzon), the viceroy, partitioned the large province of Bengal (which then included Bihar and Orissa) in 1905. Although the province was unwieldy, Curzon's plan divided the Bengali speakers by creating the new province of Eastern Bengal and Assam and reducing the original province to western Bengal, Bihar, and Orissa. The eastern province had a Muslim majority.

A massive antipartition campaign was launched against the British by Hindus in Bengal, using constitutional methods as well as terrorism spearheaded by revolutionaries. The partition of Bengal was annulled in 1911. The province of Eastern Bengal and Assam was dissolved, Bengal proper was reunited, Assam was separated, and a new province of Bihar and Orissa was created. Although the reunited Bengal province had a small Muslim majority, ambitious Muslims in the province were disgruntled and looked to the Muslim League for better prospects.

The All-India Muslim League had been founded in Dhaka to promote loyalty to the British and "to protect and advance the political rights of the Muslims of India and respectfully represent their needs and aspirations to the Government." It was also stated that there was no intention to affect the rights of other religious groups. Earlier that same year, a group of Muslims—the Simla Delegation—led by Aga Khan III, met the viceroy and put forward the concept of "separate electorates." If the proposal were accepted, Muslim members of elected bodies would be chosen from electorates composed of Muslims only, and the number of seats in the elected bodies allotted to Muslims would be at least proportional to the Muslim share of the population, but preferably "weighted" to give Muslims a share in seats somewhat higher than their proportion of the population. The principles of communal representation, separate electorates, and weightage were included in the Government of India Act of 1909 and were expanded to include such other groups as Sikhs and Christians in later constitutional enactments.

Beginnings of Self-Government

The Government of India Act of 1909—also known as the Morley-Minto Reforms (John Morley was the secretary of state for India, and Gilbert Elliot, fourth earl of Minto, was viceroy)—gave Indians limited roles in the central and provincial legislatures, known as legislative councils. Indians had previously been appointed to legislative councils, but after the reforms some were elected to them. At the center, the majority of council members continued to be government-appointed officials, and the viceroy was in no way responsible to the legislature. At the provincial level, the elected members, together with unofficial appointees, outnumbered the appointed officials, but responsibility of the governor to the legislature was not contemplated. Morley made it clear in introducing the legislation to the British Parliament that parliamentary self-government was not the goal of the British government.

The granting of separate electorates and communal representation was welcomed by Muslims but opposed by Congress. The Muslim League was pleased by the apparent British intention to support and safeguard Muslim interests in the subcontinent. Separate electorates remained a part of the Muslim League platform even after the independence of Pakistan. Congress opposition was understandable. As the majority community in most provinces, Hindus stood to lose from weighted minority representation. Congress also presented itself as a national secular party and could not support identification of voters with a particular community.

The Morley-Minto Reforms were a milestone. Step by step, the elective principle was introduced for membership in Indian legislative councils. The "electorate" was limited, however, to a small group of upper-class Indians. These elected members increasingly became an "opposition" to the "official government." Communal electorates were later extended to other communities and made a political factor of the Indian tendency toward group identification through religion. The practice created certain vital questions for all concerned. The intentions of the British were questioned. How humanitarian was their concern for the minorities? Were separate electorates a manifestation of "divide and rule?"

For Muslims it was important both to gain a place in all-India politics and to retain their Muslim identity, objectives that required varying responses according to circumstances, as the example of Mohammad Ali Jinnah illustrates. Jinnah, who was born in 1876, studied law in England and began his career as an enthusiastic liberal in Congress on returning to India. In 1913 he joined the Muslim League, which had been shocked by the 1911 annulment of the partition of Bengal into cooperating with Congress to make demands on the British. Jinnah continued his membership in Congress until 1919. During this dual membership period, he was described by a leading Congress spokesperson as the "ambassador of Hindu-Muslim unity."

India's important contributions to the efforts of the British Empire in World War I stimulated further demands by Indians and further response from the British. Congress and the Muslim League met in joint session in December 1916. Under the leadership of Jinnah and Pandit Motilal Nehru (father of Jawalharlal Nehru), unity was preached, and a proposal for constitutional reform was made that included the concept of separate electorates. The resulting Congress-Muslim League Pact (often referred to as the Lucknow Pact) was a sincere effort to compromise. Congress accepted the separate electorates demanded by the Muslim League, and the Muslim League joined with Congress in demanding self-government. The pact was expected to lead to permanent and constitutional united action.

In August 1917, the British government formally announced a policy of "increasing association of Indians in every branch of the administration and the gradual development of self-governing institutions with a view to the progressive realization of responsible government in India as an integral part of the British Empire." Constitutional reforms were embodied in the Government of India Act of 1919—also known as the Montagu-Chelmsford Reforms (Edwin Samuel Montagu was Britain's secretary of state for India; the Marquess of Chelmsford was viceroy). These reforms represented the maximum concessions the British were prepared to make at that time. The franchise was extended, and increased authority was given to central and provincial legislative councils, but the viceroy remained responsible only to London.

The changes at the provincial level were significant, as the provincial legislative councils contained a considerable majority of elected members. In a system called "dyarchy," the nation-building departments of government—agriculture, education, public works, and the like—were placed under ministers who were individually responsible to the legislature. The departments that made up the "steel frame" of British rule—finance, revenue, and home affairs—were retained by executive councillors, who were often, but not always, British and who were responsible to the governor.

The 1919 reforms did not satisfy political demands in India. The British repressed opposition, and restrictions on the press and on movement were reenacted. An apparently unwitting example of violation of rules against the gathering of people led to the massacre at Jalianwala Bagh in Amritsar in April 1919. This tragedy galvanized such political leaders as Jawaharlal Nehru (1889–1964) and Mohandas Karamchand Gandhi (1869–1948) and the masses who followed them to press for further action.

The Allies' post-World War I peace settlement with Turkey provided an additional stimulus to the grievances of the Muslims, who feared that one goal of the Allies was to end the caliphate of the Ottoman sultan. After the end of the Mughal Empire, the Ottoman caliph had become the symbol of Islamic authority and unity to Indian Sunni Muslims. A pan-Islamic movement, known as the Khilafat Movement, spread in India. It was a mass repudiation of Muslim loyalty to British rule and thus legitimated Muslim participation in the Indian nationalist movement. The leaders of the Khilafat Movement used Islamic symbols to unite the diverse but assertive Muslim community on an all-India basis and bargain with both Congress leaders and the British for recognition of minority rights and political concessions.

Muslim leaders from the Deoband and Aligarh movements joined Gandhi in mobilizing the masses for the 1920 and 1921 demonstrations of civil disobedience and noncooperation in response to the massacre at Amritsar. At the same time, Gandhi endorsed the Khilafat Movement, thereby placing many Hindus behind what had been solely a Muslim demand.

Despite impressive achievements, however, the Khilafat Movement failed. Turkey rejected the caliphate and became a secular state. Furthermore, the religious, mass-based aspects of the movement alienated such Western-oriented constitutional politicians as Jinnah, who resigned from Congress. Other Muslims also were uncomfortable with Gandhi's leadership. British historian Sir Percival Spear wrote that "a mass appeal in his [Gandhi's] hands could not be other than a Hindu one. He could transcend caste but not community. The [Hindu] devices he used went sour in the mouths of Muslims." In the final analysis, the movement failed to lay a lasting foundation of Indian unity and served only to aggravate Hindu-Muslim differences among masses that were being politicized. Indeed, as India moved closer to the self-government implied in the Montagu-Chelmsford Reforms, rivalry over what might be called the spoils of independence sharpened the differences between the communities.

The political picture in India was not at all clear when the mandated decennial review of the Government of India Act of 1919 became due in 1929. Prospects of further constitutional reforms spurred greater agitation and a frenzy of demands from different groups. The commission in charge of the review was headed by Sir John Simon, who recommended further constitutional change, but it was not until 1935 that a new Government of India Act was passed. Three consecutive roundtable conferences were held in London in 1930, 1931, and 1932, at which a wide variety of interests from India were represented. The major disagreement concerned the continuation of separate electorates, which Gandhi and Congress strongly opposed. As a result, the decision was forced on the British government. Prime Minister Ramsay MacDonald issued his "communal award," which continued the system of separate electorates at both the central and the provincial level.

The principal result of the act was "provincial autonomy." The dyarchical system was discontinued, and all subjects were placed under ministers who were individually and collectively responsible to the former legislative councils, which were renamed legislative assemblies. (In a few provinces, including Bengal, a bicameral system was established; the upper house continued to be called a legislative council.) Almost all assembly members were elected, with the exception of some special and otherwise unrepresented groups. After the elections, provincial chief ministers and cabinets took office, although the governors had limited "emergency powers." Sindh was separated from Bombay and became a province. The 1919 reforms had earlier been introduced in the North-West Frontier Province. Balochistan, however, retained special status; it had no legislature and was governed by an "agent general to the governor general." At the center, the act essentially provided for the establishment of dyarchy, but it also provided for a federal system that included the princes. The princes refused to join a system that might force them to accept decisions made by elected politicians. Thus, the full provisions of the 1935 act did not come into force at the center.

The Two Nations Theory

Events in the late 1920s and 1930s led Muslims to begin to think that their destiny might be in a separate state, a concept that developed into the demand for partition. Motilal Nehru convened an "all-party" conference in 1929 to suggest changes that would lead to independence when the British took up the report of the Simon Commission. The majority of the delegates demanded the end of the system of separate electorates. Jinnah, in turn, put forward fifteen points that would satisfy Muslim interests—in particular, the retention of separate electorates or the creation of "safeguards" to prevent a Hindu-controlled legislature. Jinnah's proposals were rejected, and from then on cooperation between Hindus and Muslims in the independence movement was rare.

In his presidential address to the Muslim League session at Allahabad in 1930, the leading modern Muslim philosopher in South Asia, Sir Muhammad Iqbal (1876–1938), described India as Asia in miniature, in which a unitary form of government was inconceivable and religious community rather than territory was the basis for identification. To him, communalism in its highest sense was the key to the formation of a harmonious whole in India. Therefore, he demanded the establishment of a confederated India to include a Muslim state consisting of Punjab, North-West Frontier Province, Sindh, and Balochistan. In subsequent speeches and writings, Iqbal reiterated the claims of Muslims to be considered a nation "based on unity of language, race, history, religion, and identity of economic interests."

Iqbal gave no name to his projected state. That was done by a group of students at Cambridge in Britain who issued a pamphlet in 1933 entitled *Now or Never.* They opposed the idea of federation, denied that India was a single country, and demanded partition into regions, the northwest receiving national status as a "Pakistan." They explained the term as follows: "Pakistan . . . is . . . composed of letters taken from the names of our homelands: that is, Punjab, Afghania [North-West Frontier Province], Kashmir, Iran, Sindh, Tukharistan, Afghanistan, and Balochistan. It means the land of the Paks, the spiritually pure and clean."

In 1934 Jinnah returned to the leadership of the Muslim League after a period of residence in London, but found it divided and without a sense of mission. He set about restoring a sense of purpose to Muslims, and he emphasized the Two Nations Theory.

The 1937–40 period was critical in the growth of the Two Nations Theory. Under the 1935 Government of India Act, elections to the provincial legislative assemblies were held in 1937. Congress gained majorities in seven of the eleven provinces. Congress took a strictly legalistic stand on the formation of provincial ministries and refused to form coalition governments with the Muslim League, even in the United Provinces (Uttar Pradesh in contemporary India), which had a substantial Muslim minority, and vigorously denied the Muslim League's claim to be the only true representative of Indian Muslims. This claim, however, was not substantiated because the Muslim League had done poorly in the elections, especially in the Muslim-majority provinces such as Punjab and the North-West Frontier Province. The conduct of Congress governments in the Muslim-minority provinces permanently alienated the Muslim League.

By the late 1930s, Jinnah was convinced of the need for a unifying issue among Muslims, and Pakistan was the obvious answer. At its annual session in Lahore on March 23, 1940, the Muslim League resolved that the areas of Muslim majority in northwestern and eastern India should be grouped together to constitute independent states—autonomous and sovereign—and that any independence plan without this provision was unacceptable to Muslims. Federation was rejected. The Lahore Resolution was often referred to as the "Pakistan Resolution"; however, the word *Pakistan* did not appear in it.

An interesting aspect of the Pakistan movement was that it received its greatest support from areas in which Muslims were a minority. In those areas, the main issue was finding an alternative to replacing British rule with Congress, that is, Hindu, rule.

Toward Partition

Congress predictably opposed all proposals for partition and advocated a united India with a strong center and a fully responsible parliamentary government. To many, notably to Jawaharlal Nehru, the idea of a sovereign state based on a common religion seemed a historical anachronism and a denial of democracy. From 1940 on, reconciliation between Congress and the Muslim League became increasingly difficult, if not impossible.

During World War II, the Muslim League and Congress adopted different attitudes toward British rule. British priorities were driven by the expediencies of defense, and war was declared abruptly without any prior consultation with Indian politicians. Congress ministers in the provinces resigned in protest. As a consequence, Congress, with most of its leaders in jail for opposition to the Raj, lost its political leverage over the British. The Muslim League, however, followed a course of cooperation, gaining time to consolidate. The British appreciated the loyalty and valor of the British Indian Army, many of whose members were Punjabi Muslims. The Muslim League's success could be gauged from its sweep of 90 percent of the Muslim seats in the 1946 election, compared with only 4.5 percent in the 1937 elections. The 1946 election was, in effect, a plebiscite among Muslims on Pakistan. In London it became clear that there were three parties in any discussion on the future of India: the British, Congress, and the Muslim League.

Spurred by the Japanese advance in Asia and forceful persuasion from Washington, British prime minister Winston Churchill's coalition war government in 1942 had dispatched Sir Stafford Cripps to India with a proposal for settlement. The plan provided for dominion status after the war for an Indian union of British Indian provinces and princely states wishing to accede to it, a separate dominion for those who did not, and firm defense links between Britain and an Indian union. Cripps himself was sympathetic to Indian nationalism. However, his mission failed, and Gandhi described it as "a post-dated check on a crashing bank."

In August 1942, Gandhi launched the "Quit India Movement" against the British. Jinnah condemned the movement. The government retaliated by arresting about 60,000 individuals and outlawing Congress. Communal riots increased. Talks between Jinnah and Gandhi in 1944 proved as futile as negotiations between Gandhi and the viceroy.

In July 1945, the Labour Party came to power in Britain with a large majority. Its choices in India were limited by the decline of British power and the necessity of retaining Indian links in imperial defense. General unrest in India spread, and, when a naval mutiny in Bombay broke out in 1945, British officials came to the conclusion that independence was the only alternative to forcible retention of control over an unwilling dependency. The viceroy, Lord Wavell, met with Indian leaders in Simla in 1945 to decide what form of interim government would be acceptable. No agreement was reached.

New elections to the provincial and central legislatures were ordered, and a three-man team came to India from Britain to discuss plans for self-government. The Cabinet Mission Plan, proposed by Cripps, represented Britain's last, desperate attempt to transfer the power it retained over India to a single union. The mission put forward a three-tier federal form of government in which the central government would be limited to power over defense, foreign relations, currency, and communications; significant other powers would be delegated to the provinces. The plan also prescribed the zones that would be created: northeastern Bengal and Assam would be joined to form a zone with a slight Muslim majority; in the northwest, Punjab, Sindh, North-West Frontier Province, and Balochistan would be joined for a clear Muslim majority; and the remainder of the country would be the third zone, with a clear Hindu majority. The approximation of the boundaries of a new Pakistan was clear from the delineation of the zones. The mission also suggested the right of veto on legislation by communities that saw their interests adversely affected. Finally, the mission proposed that an interim government be established immediately and that new elections be held.

Congress and the Muslim League emerged from the 1946 elections as the two dominant parties, although the Muslim League again was unable to capture a majority of the Muslim seats in the North-West Frontier Province. At first, both parties seemed to accept the Cabinet Mission Plan, despite many reservations, but the subsequent behavior of the leaders soon led to bitterness and mistrust. Nehru effectively quashed any prospect of the plan's success when he announced that Congress would not be "fettered" by agreements with the British, thereby making it clear that Congress would use its majority in the newly created Constituent Assembly to write a constitution that conformed to its ideas. The formation of an interim government was also controversial. Jinnah demanded equality between the Muslim League and Congress, a proposal rejected by the viceroy. The Muslim League boycotted the interim government, and each party disputed the right of the other to appoint Muslim ministers, a prerogative Jinnah claimed belonged solely to the Muslim League.

When the viceroy proceeded to form an interim government without the Muslim League, Jinnah called for demonstrations, or "Direct Action," on August 16, 1946. Communal rioting broke out on an unprecedented scale, especially in Bengal and Bihar. The massacre of Muslims in Calcutta brought Gandhi to the scene, where he worked with the Muslim League provincial chief minister, Hussain Shahid Suhrawardy. Gandhi's and Suhrawardy's efforts calmed fears in Bengal, but rioting quickly spread elsewhere and continued well into 1947. Jinnah permitted the Muslim League to enter the interim government in an effort to stem further communal violence. Disagreements among the ministers paralyzed the government, already haunted by the specter of civil war.

In February 1947, Lord Mountbatten was appointed viceroy with specific instructions to arrange for a transfer of power by June 1948. Mountbatten assessed the situation and became convinced that Congress was willing to accept partition as the price for independence, that Jinnah would accept a smaller Pakistan than the one he demanded (that is, all of Punjab and Bengal), and that Sikhs would learn to accept a division of Punjab. Mountbatten was convinced by the rising temperature of communal emotions that the June 1948 date for partition was too distant and persuaded most Indian leaders that immediate acceptance of his plan was imperative.

On June 3, 1947, British prime minister Clement Attlee introduced a bill in the House of Commons calling for the independence and partition of India. On July 14, the House of Commons passed the India Independence Act, by which two independent dominions were created on the subcontinent; the princely states were left to accede to either. The partition plan stated that contiguous Muslim-majority districts in Punjab and Bengal would go to Pakistan, provided that the legislatures of the two provinces agreed that the provinces should be partitioned—they did. Sindh's legislature and Balochistan's *jirga* (council of tribal leaders) agreed to join Pakistan. A plebiscite was held in the Sylhet District of Assam, and, as a result, part of the district was transferred to Pakistan. A plebiscite was also held in the North-West Frontier Province. Despite a boycott by Congress, the province was deemed to have chosen Pakistan. The princely states, however, presented a more difficult problem. All but three of the more than 500 states quickly acceded to Pakistan or India under guidelines established with the aid of Mountbatten. The states made their decisions after giving consideration to the geographic location of their respective areas and to their religious majority. Two states hesitated but were quickly absorbed into India: Hyderabad, the most populated of the princely states, whose Muslim ruler desired independence; and Junagadh, a small state with a Muslim prince that tried to accede to Pakistan despite its majority Hindu population. The accession of the third state, Jammu and Kashmir, also could not be resolved peacefully, and its indeterminate status has poisoned relations between India and Pakistan ever since (see Survival in a Harsh Environment, ch. 5).

Throughout the summer of 1947, as communal violence mounted, preparations for partition proceeded in Delhi. Assets were divided, boundary commissions were set up to demarcate frontiers, and British troops were evacuated. The military was restructured into two forces. Law and order broke down in different parts of the country. Civil servants were given the choice of joining either country; British officers could retire with compensation if not invited to stay on. Jinnah and Nehru tried unsuccessfully to quell the passions of communal fury that neither fully understood. On August 14, 1947, Pakistan and India achieved independence. Jinnah became the first governor general of the Dominion of Pakistan.

Independent Pakistan

Problems at Independence

In August 1947, Pakistan was faced with a number of problems, some immediate but others long term. The most important of these concerns was the role played by Islam. Was Pakistan to be a secular state serving as a homeland for Muslims of the subcontinent, or was it to be an Islamic state governed by the sharia, in which non-Muslims would be second-class citizens? The second question concerned the distribution of power between the center and the provincial governments, a question that eventually led to the dissolution of the country with the painful loss of the East Wing (East Bengal, later East Pakistan, now Bangladesh) in 1971, an issue that remained unresolved in the early 1990s.

The territory of Pakistan was divided into two parts at independence, separated by about 1,600 kilometers of Indian territory. The 1940 Lahore Resolution had called for independent "states" in the northwest and the northeast. This objective was changed, by a 1946 meeting of Muslim League legislators, to a call for a single state (the acronym *Pakistan* had no letter for Bengal). Pakistan lacked the machinery, personnel, and equipment for a new government. Even its capital, Karachi, was a second choice—Lahore was rejected because it was too close to the Indian border. Pakistan's economy seemed unviable after severing ties with India, the major market for its commodities. And, much of Punjab's electricity was imported from Indian power stations.

Above all other concerns were the violence and the refugee problem: Muslims were fleeing India; Hindus and Sikhs were fleeing Pakistan. Jinnah's plea to regard religion as a personal matter, not a state matter, was ignored. No one was prepared for the communal rioting and the mass movements of population that followed the June 3, 1947, London announcement of imminent independence and partition. The most conservative estimates of the casualties were 250,000 dead and 12 million to 24 million refugees. The actual boundaries of the two new states were not even known until August 17, when they were announced by a commission headed by a British judge. The boundaries—unacceptable to both India and Pakistan—have remained.

West Pakistan lost its Hindus and Sikhs. These communities had managed much of the commercial activity of West Pakistan. The Sikhs were especially prominent in agricultural colonies. They were replaced largely by Muslims from India, mostly Urdu speakers from the United Provinces. Although some people, especially Muslims from eastern Punjab (in India), settled in western Punjab (in Pakistan), many headed for Karachi and other cities in Sindh, where they took the jobs vacated by departing Hindus. In 1951 close to half of the population of Pakistan's major cities were immigrants (*muhajirs*—refugees from India and their descendants).

The aspirations for Pakistan that had been so important to Muslims in Muslim-minority provinces and the goals for the new state these urban refugees supported were not always compatible with those of the traditional rural people already inhabiting Pakistan, whose support for the concept of Pakistan came much later. Pakistani society was polarized from its inception.

The land and people west of the Indus River continued to pose problems. The most immediate problem was the continued presence of a Congress government in the North-West Frontier Province, a government effective at the grassroots level and popular despite the loss in the plebiscite. Led by Khan Abdul Ghaffar Khan and his Khudai-i-Khitmagar (Servants of God, a Congress faction), this group was often referred to as the Red Shirts after its members' attire. Ghaffar Khan asked his followers not to participate in the July 1947 plebiscite.

Pakistan also had to establish its legitimacy against a possible challenge from Afghanistan. Irredentist claims from Kabul were based on the ethnic unity of tribes straddling the border; the emotional appeal of "Pakhtunistan," homeland of the Pakhtuns, was undeniable. However, Pakistan upheld the treaties Britain had signed with Afghanistan and refused to discuss the validity of the Durand Line as the international border (see The Forward Policy, this ch.). Relations with Afghanistan were hostile, resulting in the rupture of diplomatic and commercial relations and leading Afghanistan to cast the only vote against Pakistan's admission to the United Nations (UN) in 1947.

The India Independence Act left the princes theoretically free to accede to either dominion. The frontier princely states of Dir, Chitral, Amb, and Hunza acceded quickly to Pakistan while retaining substantial autonomy in internal administration and customary law. The khan of Kalat in Balochistan declared independence on August 15, 1947, but offered to negotiate a special relationship with Pakistan. Other Baloch *sardar* (tribal chiefs) also expressed their preference for a separate identity. Pakistan took military action against them and the khan and brought about their accession in 1948. The state of Bahawalpur, with a Muslim ruler and a Muslim population, acceded to Pakistan, as did Khairpur.

The maharaja of Jammu and Kashmir, unpopular among his subjects, was reluctant to decide on accession to either dominion. He first signed agreements with both Pakistan and India that would provide for the continued flow of people and goods to Kashmir—as it is usually called—from both dominions. Alarmed by reports of oppression of fellow Muslims in Kashmir, armed groups from the North-West Frontier Province entered the maharaja's territory. The ruler requested military assistance from India but had to sign documents acceding to India before that country would provide aid in October 1947.

The government of Pakistan refused to recognize the accession and denounced it as a fraud even though the Indian government announced that it would require an expression of the people's will through a plebiscite after the invaders were driven back. Pakistan launched an active military and diplomatic campaign to undo the accession. The UN Security Council eventually brought about a cease-fire between Pakistani and Indian troops, which took place on January 1, 1949, thus ending the first Indo-Pakistani War, and directed that a plebiscite be held. The cease-fire agreement formalized the military status quo, leaving about 30 percent of Kashmir under Pakistani control (see India, ch. 4; The Formation of Pakistan, ch. 5).

Partition and its accompanying confusion also brought severe economic challenges to the two newly created and antagonistic countries. The partition plan ignored the principles of complementarity. West Pakistan, for example, traditionally produced more wheat than it consumed and had supplied the deficit areas in India. Cotton grown in West Pakistan was used in mills in Bombay and other west Indian cities. Commodities such as coal and sugar were in short supply in Pakistan—they had traditionally come from areas now part of India. Furthermore, Pakistan faced logistic problems for its commercial transportation because of the four major ports in British India, it was awarded only Karachi. But the problem that proved most intractable was defining relations between the two wings of Pakistan, which had had little economic exchange before partition.

The two dominions decided to allow free movement of goods, persons, and capital for one year after independence, but this agreement broke down. In November 1947, Pakistan levied export duties on jute; India retaliated with export duties of its own. The trade war reached a crisis in September 1949 when Britain devalued the pound, to which both the Pakistani rupee and the Indian rupee were pegged. India followed Britain's lead, but Pakistan did not, so India severed trade relations with Pakistan. The outbreak of the Korean War (1950–53), and the consequent price rises in jute, leather, cotton, and wool as a result of wartime needs, saved the economy of Pakistan. New trading relationships were formed, and the construction of cotton and jute mills in Pakistan was quickly undertaken.

Although India and Pakistan resumed trade in 1951, both the volume and the value of trade steadily declined; the two countries ignored bilateral trade for the most part and developed the new international trade links they had made.

The assets of British India were divided in the ratio of seventeen for India to five for Pakistan by decision of the Viceroy's Council in June 1947. Division was difficult to implement, however, and Pakistan complained of nondeliveries. A financial agreement was reached in December 1948, but the actual settlement of financial and other disputes continued until 1960 (see Structure of the Economy, ch. 3).

Division of the all-India services of the Indian Civil Service and the Indian Police Service was also difficult. Only 101 out of a total of 1,157 Indian officers were Muslim. Among these Muslim officers, ninety-five officers opted for Pakistan; they were joined by one Christian, eleven Muslim military officers transferring to civilian service, and fifty Britons, for a total of 157. But only twenty of them had had more than fifteen years of service, and more than half had had fewer than ten years. These men formed the core of the Civil Service of Pakistan, which became one of the most elite and privileged bureaucracies in the world. Members of the Civil Service of Pakistan were the architects of the administrative, judicial, and diplomatic services. They proved indispensable in running the government machinery during Pakistan's first two decades, and their contributions to government policy and economics were profound during the era of Mohammad Ayub Khan. The government of Zulfiqar Ali Bhutto in the 1970s precipitated a major reorganization and reorientation of the bureaucracy, however, which resulted in a noticeable decline in both the morale and the standards of the bureaucracy (see Zulfiqar Ali Bhutto and a New Constitutional System, this ch; Zulfiqar Ali Bhutto, 1971–77, ch. 4).

Constitutional Beginnings

At independence Jinnah was the supreme authority. An accomplished politician, he won independence for Pakistan within seven years of the Lahore Resolution and was hailed by his followers as the Quaid-i-Azam (Great Leader). As governor general, he assumed the ceremonial functions of head of state while taking on effective power as head of government, dominating his prime minister, Liaquat Ali Khan (the Quaid-i-Millet, or Leader of the Nation). To these roles, he added the leadership of the Muslim League and the office of president of the Constituent Assembly.

Although Jinnah had led the movement for Pakistan as a separate Muslim nation, he was appalled by the communal riots and urged equal rights for all citizens irrespective of religion. Jinnah died in September 1948—only thirteen months after independence—leaving his successors to tackle the problems of Pakistan's identity.

Jinnah's acknowledged lieutenant, Liaquat Ali Khan, assumed leadership and continued in the position of prime minister. Born to a Punjabi landed family, Liaquat used his experience in law to attempt to frame a constitution along the lines of the British Westminster system of parliamentary democracy. He failed in large part because neither the Muslim League nor the Constituent Assembly was equipped to resolve in a parliamentary manner the problems and conflicts of the role of Islam and the degree of autonomy for the provinces. Liaquat's term of office ended when he was assassinated in Rawalpindi in October 1951. He was replaced by Khwaja Nazimuddin, who stepped down as governor general; Nazimuddin was replaced as governor general by Ghulam Mohammad, the former minister of finance.

The Muslim League, unlike Congress, had not prepared itself for a postindependence role. Congress had constitutional, economic, social, and even foreign policy plans in place before independence and was ready to put them into effect when the time came. The Muslim League was so preoccupied with the struggle for Pakistan that it was poorly prepared for effective government. Its leaders were largely urban professionals whose political base was mainly in areas that were in India. In the areas that had become Pakistan, its base was weak. Landlords with ascriptive and inherited privileges were uncomfortable with procedures of decision making through debate, discussion, compromise, and majority vote. The Muslim League was a party with little grassroots support, a weak organizational structure, powerful factional leaders, and decisions made at the top. Although Ghulam Mohammad tried to exercise the "viceregal" power that Jinnah had used so powerfully as governor general, concern for office and the fruits of power were more important to most of the politicians than the evolution of ideology or the implementation of mass programs. The effect of this lack of direction was shown most clearly when the Muslim League was routed in the 1954 election in East Pakistan

Mohammad Ali Jinnah, the Quaid-i-Azam Courtesy Embassy of Pakistan, Washington

Liaquat Ali Khan, the Quaid-i-Millet Courtesy Embassy of Pakistan, Washington

by the United Front—mainly a coalition of the Awami League and the Krishak Sramik Party, led by two one-time Muslim League members, Hussain Shahid Suhrawardy and Fazlul Haq, who ran on an autonomist platform. Other parties established during this period included the leftist National Awami Party (a breakaway from the Awami League), which also supported provincial autonomy. Islamic parties also made their appearance on the electoral scene, most notably the Jamaat-i-Islami.

The Muslim League was held responsible for the deterioration of politics and society after independence and had to answer for its failure to fulfill people's high expectations. There was a rising level of opposition and frustration and an increasing use of repressive laws inherited from the British or enacted by Pakistan that included preventive detention and rules prohibiting the gathering of more than five persons. In 1949 the Public and Representative Office Disqualification Act

(PRODA) allowed the government to disqualify persons found guilty of "misconduct," a term that acquired a broad definition. In 1952 the Security of Pakistan Act expanded the powers of the government in the interests of public order.

The armed forces also posed a threat to Liaquat's government, which was less hostile toward India than some officers wished. In March 1951, Major General Mohammad Akbar Khan, chief of the general staff, was arrested along with fourteen other officers on charges of plotting a coup d'état. The authors of what became known as the Rawalpindi Conspiracy were tried in secret, convicted, and sentenced to imprisonment. All were subsequently released.

Pakistan's first Constituent Assembly was made up of members of the prepartition Indian Constituent Assembly who represented areas that had gone to Pakistan. The body's eighty members functioned as the legislature of Pakistan. As a constitution-making body, the assembly's only achievement was the Objectives Resolution of March 1949, which specified that Pakistan would be Islamic, democratic, and federal. But the assembly could not reach agreement on how these objectives would take form, raising fears among minorities and concern among East Bengalis. Other important matters remained equally problematic—the division of executive power between the governor general and the prime minister; the distribution of power between the center and the provinces; the balance of power, especially electoral, between the two wings; and the role of Islam in the government. With the 1951 assassination of Liaquat, resolution of these issues became unlikely.

During the years after Liaquat's assassination, none of these problems were resolved, and a major confrontation occurred between the governor general, Ghulam Mohammad, a Punjabi from the civil service, and the prime minister, Nazimuddin, a former chief minister of united Bengal and now chief minister of East Bengal. Ghulam Mohammad, who relished the trappings of dominance earlier held by Jinnah, asserted his power by declaring martial law in 1953 in Punjab during disturbances involving the Ahmadiyyas, a small but influential sect considered heterodox by orthodox Muslims. A year later, he imposed governor's rule after the Muslim League defeat in East Bengal, not permitting the United Front to take office. When Nazimuddin attempted to limit the power of the governor general through amendments to the Government of India Act of 1935—then still the basic law for Pakistan, as altered by the

India Independence Act of 1947—Ghulam Mohammad unceremoniously dismissed him in April 1953, and then the following year appointed his own "cabinet of talents," dismissing the Constituent Assembly.

The so-called cabinet of talents was headed by Mohammad Ali Bogra, a minor political figure from East Bengal who had previously been Pakistan's ambassador to the United States. Significantly, the cabinet also included both military and civil officials. Chaudhuri Mohammad Ali, who had been head of the Civil Service of Pakistan, became minister of finance. General Mohammad Ayub Khan became minister of defense while retaining his post as commander in chief of the army. Major General Iskander Mirza, a military officer who was seconded to civilian posts, including becoming governor of East Bengal when Ghulam Mohammad imposed governor's rule on that province, became minister of home affairs. The cabinet thus provided an opportunity for the military to take a direct role in politics. Ghulam Mohammad was successful in subordinating the prime minister because of the support of military and civil officers as well as the backing of the strong landed interests in Punjab. The facade of parliamentary government crumbled, exposing the military's role in Pakistan's political system to public view.

The revived Constituent Assembly convened in 1955. It differed in composition from the first such assembly because of the notable reduction of Muslim League members and the presence of a United Front coalition from East Bengal. Provincial autonomy was the main plank of the United Front. Also in 1955, failing health and the ascendancy of General Mirza forced Ghulam Mohammad to resign as governor general. He died the following year.

In 1956 the Constituent Assembly adopted a constitution that proclaimed Pakistan an Islamic republic and contained directives for the establishment of an Islamic state. It also renamed the Constituent Assembly the Legislative Assembly and changed the name of the head of state from governor general to president. The lawyer-politicians who led the Pakistan movement used the principles and legal precedents of a nonreligious British parliamentary tradition even while they advanced the idea of Muslim nationhood as an axiom. Many of them represented a liberal movement in Islam, in which their personal religion was compatible with Western technology and political institutions. They saw the basis for democratic processes and tolerance in the Islamic tradition of *ijma* (consensus of the community) and *ijtihad* (the concept of continuing interpretations of Islamic law). Most of Pakistan's intelligentsia and Westernized elites belonged to the group of *ijma* modernists (see Religious Life, ch. 2).

In contrast stood the traditionalist ulama, whose position was a legalistic one based on the unity of religion and politics in Islam. The ulama asserted that the Quran, the sunna (see Glossary), and the sharia provided the general principles for all aspects of life if correctly interpreted and applied. The government's duty, therefore, was to recognize the role of the ulama in the interpretation of the law. Because the ulama and the less-learned mullahs (Muslim clerics) enjoyed influence among the masses, especially in urban areas, and because no politician could afford to be denounced as anti-Islamic, none dared publicly to ignore them. Nevertheless, they were not given powers of legal interpretation until the Muhammad Zia ul-Haq regime of 1977–88 (see Zia ul-Haq and Military Domination, 1977–88, this ch; Early Political Development, ch. 4). The lawyer-politicians making decisions in the 1950s almost without exception preferred the courts and legal institutions they inherited from the British.

Another interpretation of Islam was provided by an Islamist movement in Pakistan, regarded in some quarters as fundamentalist. Its most significant organization was the Jamaat-i-Islami, which gradually built up support among the refugees, the urban lower middle class, and students (see Jamaat-i-Islami, ch. 4). Unlike the traditional ulama, the Islamist movement was the outcome of modern Islamic idealism. Crucial in the constitutional and political development of Pakistan, it forced politicians to face the question of Islamic identity. On occasion, definitions of Islamic identity resulted in violent controversy, as in Punjab during the early 1950s when agitation was directed against the Ahmadiyyas. In the mid-1970s, the Ahmadiyyas were declared non-Muslims by the government of Zulfiqar Ali Bhutto (1971–77) and the Organization of the Islamic Conference (OIC), based in Jiddah, Saudi Arabia.

During the 1950s, however, the fundamentalist movement led by Maulana Abul Ala Maududi, the founder and leader of the Jamaat-i-Islami, succeeded only in introducing Islamic principles into the 1956 constitution. A nonjudiciable section called the Directive Principles of State Policy attempted to define ways in which the Islamic way of life and Islamic moral standards could be pursued. The principles contained injunctions against the consumption of alcohol and the practice of usury. The substance of the 1956 clauses reappeared in the 1962 constitution, but the Islamist cause was undefeated. Sharia courts were established under Zia, and under Prime Minister Mian Nawaz Sharif in the early 1990s the sharia was proclaimed the basic law of the land.

Early Foreign Policy

Pakistan's early foreign policy espoused nonalignment. Despite disputes with India, the policies of the two countries were similar: membership in the Commonwealth of Nations; no commitment to either the United States or the Soviet Union; and a role in the UN.

Pakistan's foreign policy stance shifted significantly in 1953 when it accepted the United States offer of military and economic assistance in return for membership in an alliance system designed to contain international communism. When the administration of Dwight D. Eisenhower sought a series of alliances in the "Northern Tier"—Pakistan, Iran, and Turkey—and in East Asia, Pakistan became a candidate for membership in each. In 1954 Pakistan signed a Mutual Defense Assistance Agreement with the United States and became a member of the Southeast Asia Treaty Organization (SEATO). The following year, Pakistan joined Iran, Iraq, and Turkey in the Baghdad Pact, later renamed the Central Treaty Organization (CENTO) after Iraq's withdrawal in 1959. Pakistan also leased bases to the United States for intelligence-gathering and communications facilities. Pakistan saw these agreements not as bulwarks against Soviet or Chinese aggression, but as a means to bolster itself against India.

Collapse of the Parliamentary System

The parliamentary system outlined in the 1956 constitution required disciplined political parties, which did not exist. The Muslim League—the one political party that had appeared capable of developing into a national democratic party—continued to decline in prestige. In West Pakistan, Sindh and the North-West Frontier Province resented the political and economic dominance accorded Punjab and were hostile to the "One Unit Plan" introduced by the Constituent Assembly the year before. The One Unit Plan merged the western provinces of Balochistan, the North-West Frontier Province, Punjab, and Sindh into a single administrative unit named West Pakistan, which in the new Legislative Assembly was to have parity with the more populous province of East Pakistan.

In 1956 Suhrawardy formed a coalition cabinet at the center that included the Awami League and the newly formed Republican Party of the West Wing, which had broken off from the Muslim League. Suhrawardy was highly respected in East Pakistan, but he had no measurable political strength in West Pakistan. By taking a strong position in favor of the One Unit Plan, he lost support in Sindh, the North-West Frontier Province, and Balochistan.

Societal violence and ethnic unrest further complicated the growth and functioning of parliamentary government. In West Pakistan, chief minister Khan Sahib was assassinated. In the North-West Frontier Province, Khan Sahib's brother, Khan Abdul Ghaffar Khan, of the National Awami Party, turned his back on national politics and said he would work for the attainment of a separate homeland for the Pakhtuns. And in Balochistan, the khan of Kalat again declared his independence, but the Pakistan Army restored Pakistani control.

On October 7, 1958, President Mirza, with the support of the army, suspended the 1956 constitution, imposed martial law, and canceled the elections scheduled for January 1959. Mirza was supported by the civil service bureaucracy, which harbored deep suspicions of politicians. Nonetheless, on October 27 Mirza was ousted and sent into lifetime exile in London. General Ayub Khan, the army commander in chief, assumed control of a military government.

The Ayub Khan Era

In January 1951, Ayub Khan succeeded General Sir Douglas Gracey as commander in chief of the Pakistan Army, becoming the first Pakistani in that position. Although Ayub's military career was not particularly brilliant and although he had not previously held a combat command, he was promoted over several senior officers with distinguished careers. Ayub Khan probably was selected because of his reputation as an able administrator, his presumed lack of political ambition, and his lack of powerful group backing. Coming from a humble family of an obscure Pakhtun tribe, Ayub also lacked affiliation with major internal power blocks and was, therefore, acceptable to all elements.

Within a short time of his promotion, however, Ayub Khan had become a powerful political figure. Perhaps more than any other Pakistani, Ayub was responsible for seeking and securing military and economic assistance from the United States and for aligning Pakistan with it in international affairs. As army commander in chief and for a time as minister of defense in 1954, Ayub Khan was empowered to veto virtually any government policy that he felt was inimical to the interests of the armed forces.

By 1958 Ayub Khan and his fellow officers decided to turn out the "inefficient and rascally" politicians—a task easily accomplished without bloodshed. Ayub's philosophy was indebted to the Mughal and viceregal traditions; his rule was similarly highly personalized. Ayub justified his assumption of power by citing the nation's need for stability and the necessity for the army to play a central role. When internal stability broke down in the 1960s, he remained contemptuous of lawyer-politicians and handed over power to his fellow army officers.

Ayub Khan used two main approaches to governing in his first few years. He concentrated on consolidating power and intimidating the opposition. He also aimed to establish the groundwork for future stability through altering the economic, legal, and constitutional institutions.

The imposition of martial law in 1958 targeted "antisocial" practices such as abducting women and children, black marketeering, smuggling, and hoarding. Many in the Civil Service of Pakistan and the Police Service of Pakistan were investigated and punished for corruption, misconduct, inefficiency, or subversive activities. Ayub Khan's message was clear: he, not the civil servants, was in control.

Sterner measures were used against the politicians. The PRODA prescribed fifteen years' exclusion from public office for those found guilty of corruption. The Elective Bodies Disqualification Order (EBDO) authorized special tribunals to try former politicians for "misconduct," an infraction not clearly defined. Prosecution could be avoided if the accused agreed not to be a candidate for any elective body for a period of seven years. About 7,000 individuals were "EBDOed." Some people, including Suhrawardy, who was arrested, fought prosecution.

The Press and Publications Ordinance was amended in 1960 to specify broad conditions under which newspapers and other publications could be commandeered or closed down. Trade organizations, unions, and student groups were closely monitored and cautioned to avoid political activity, and imams (see Glossary) at mosques were warned against including political matters in sermons.

On the whole, however, the martial law years were not severe. The army maintained low visibility and was content to uphold the traditional social order. By early 1959, most army units had resumed their regular duties. Ayub Khan generally left administration in the hands of the civil bureaucracy, with some exceptions.

Efforts were made to popularize the regime while the opposition was muzzled. Ayub Khan maintained a high public profile, often taking trips expressly to "meet the people." He was also aware of the need to address some of the acute grievances of East Pakistan. To the extent possible, only Bengali members of the civil service were posted in the East Wing; previously, many of the officers had been from the West Wing and knew neither the region nor the language. Dhaka was designated the legislative capital of Pakistan, while the newly created Islamabad became the administrative capital. Central government bodies, such as the Planning Commission, were now instructed to hold regular sessions in Dhaka. Public investment in East Pakistan increased, although private investment remained heavily skewed in favor of West Pakistan. The Ayub Khan regime was so highly centralized, however, that, in the absence of democratic institutions, densely populated and politicized Bengal continued to feel it was being slighted.

Between 1958 and 1962, Ayub Khan used martial law to initiate a number of reforms that reduced the power of groups opposing him. One such group was the landed aristocracy. The Land Reform Commission was set up in 1958, and in 1959 the government imposed a ceiling of 200 hectares of irrigated land and 400 hectares of unirrigated land in the West Wing for a single holding. In the East Wing, the landholding ceiling was raised from thirty-three hectares to forty-eight hectares (see Farm Ownership and Land Reform, ch. 3). Landholders retained their dominant positions in the social hierarchy and their political influence but heeded Ayub's warnings against political assertiveness. Moreover, some 4 million hectares of land in West Pakistan, much of it in Sindh, were released for public acquisition between 1959 and 1969 and sold mainly to civil and military officers, thus creating a new class of farmers having medium-sized holdings. These farms became immensely important for future agricultural development, but the peasants benefited scarcely at all.

In 1955 a legal commission was set up to suggest reforms of the family and marriage laws. Ayub Khan examined its report and in 1961 issued the Muslim Family Laws Ordinance. Among other things, it restricted polygyny and "regulated" marriage and divorce, giving women more equal treatment under the law than they had had before. It was a humane measure supported by women's organizations in Pakistan, but the ordinance could not have been promulgated if the vehement opposition to it from the ulama and the fundamentalist Muslim groups had been allowed free expression. However, this law, which was similar to the one passed on family planning, was relatively mild and did not seriously transform the patriarchal pattern of society.

Ayub Khan adopted an energetic approach toward economic development that soon bore fruit in a rising rate of economic growth. Land reform, consolidation of holdings, and stern measures against hoarding were combined with rural credit programs and work programs, higher procurement prices, augmented allocations for agriculture, and, especially, improved seeds to put the country on the road to self-sufficiency in food grains in the process described as the Green Revolution.

The Export Bonus Vouchers Scheme (1959) and tax incentives stimulated new industrial entrepreneurs and exporters. Bonus vouchers facilitated access to foreign exchange for imports of industrial machinery and raw materials. Tax concessions were offered for investment in less-developed areas. These measures had important consequences in bringing industry to Punjab and gave rise to a new class of small industrialists.

Basic Democracies

Ayub Khan's martial law regime, critics observed, was a form of "representational dictatorship," but the new political system, introduced in 1959 as the "Basic Democracies" system, was an apt expression of what Ayub called the particular "genius" of Pakistan. In 1962 a new constitution was promulgated as a product of that indirect elective system. Ayub did not believe that a sophisticated parliamentary democracy was suitable for Pakistan. Instead, the Basic Democracies, as the individual administrative units were called, were intended to initiate and educate a largely illiterate population in the working of government by giving them limited representation and associating them with decision making at a "level commensurate with their ability." Basic Democracies were concerned with no more than local government and rural development. They were meant to provide a two-way channel of communication between the Ayub Khan regime and the common people and allow social change to move slowly.

The Basic Democracies system set up a multi-tiered system of institutions. The lowest but most important tier was composed of union councils, one each for groups of villages having an approximate total population of 10,000. Each union council comprised ten directly elected members and five appointed members, all called Basic Democrats. Union councils were responsible for local agricultural and community development and for rural law and order maintenance; they were empowered to impose local taxes for local projects. These powers, however, were more than balanced at the local level by the fact that the controlling authority for the union councils was the deputy commissioner, whose high status and traditionally paternalistic attitudes often elicited obedient cooperation rather than demands.

The next tier consisted of the *tehsil* (subdistrict) councils, which performed coordination functions. Above them, the *zilla* (district) councils, chaired by the deputy commissioners, were composed of nominated official and nonofficial members, including the chairmen of union councils. The district councils were assigned both compulsory and optional functions pertaining to education, sanitation, local culture, and social welfare. Above them, the divisional advisory councils coordinated the activities with representatives of government departments. The highest tier consisted of one development advisory council for each province, chaired by the governor and appointed by the president. The urban areas had a similar arrangement, under which the smaller union councils were grouped together into municipal committees to perform similar duties. In 1960 the elected members of the union councils voted to confirm Ayub Khan's presidency, and under the 1962 constitution they formed an electoral college to elect the president, the National Assembly (as the Legislative Assembly was renamed under the 1962 constitution), and the provincial assemblies.

The system of Basic Democracies did not have time to take root or to fulfill Ayub Khan's intentions before he and the system fell in 1969. Whether or not a new class of political leaders equipped with some administrative experience could have emerged to replace those trained in British constitutional law was never discovered. And the system did not provide for the mobilization of the rural population around institutions of national integration. Its emphasis was on economic development and social welfare alone. The authority of the civil service was augmented in the Basic Democracies, and the power of the landlords and the big industrialists in the West Wing went unchallenged.

The 1962 Constitution

In 1958 Ayub Khan had promised a speedy return to constitutional government. In February 1960, an eleven-member constitutional commission was established. The commission's recommendations for direct elections, strong legislative and judicial organs, free political parties, and defined limitations on presidential authority went against Ayub's philosophy of government, so he ordered other committees to make revisions.

The 1962 constitution retained some aspects of the Islamic nature of the republic but omitted the word *Islamic* in its original version; amid protests, Ayub Khan added that word later. The president would be a Muslim, and the Advisory Council of Islamic Ideology and the Islamic Research Institute were established to assist the government in reconciling all legislation with the tenets of the Quran and the sunna. Their functions were advisory and their members appointed by the president, so the ulama had no real power base.

Ayub Khan sought to retain certain aspects of his dominant authority in the 1962 constitution, which ended the period of martial law. The document created a presidential system in which the traditional powers of the chief executive were augmented by control of the legislature, the power to issue ordinances, the right of appeal to referendum, protection from impeachment, control over the budget, and special emergency powers, which included the power to suspend civil rights. As the 1965 elections showed, the presidential system of government was opposed by those who equated constitutional government with parliamentary democracy. The 1962 constitution relaxed martial law limitations on personal freedom and made fundamental rights justiciable. The courts continued their traditional function of protecting the rights of individual citizens against encroachment by the government, but the government made it clear that the exercise of claims based on fundamental rights would not be permitted to nullify its previous progressive legislation on land reform and family laws.

The National Assembly, consisting of 156 members (including six women) and elected by an electoral college of 80,000 Basic Democrats, was established as the federal legislature. Legislative powers were divided between the National Assembly and the provincial legislative assemblies. The National Assembly was to hold sessions alternatively in Islamabad and Dhaka; the Supreme Court would also hold sessions in Dhaka. The ban on political parties was operational at the time of the first elections to the National Assembly and the provincial legislative assemblies in January 1960, as was the prohibition on "EBDOed" politicians. Many of those elected were new and merged into factions formed on the basis of personal or provincial loyalties. Despite the ban, political parties functioned outside the legislative bodies as vehicles of criticism and formers of opinion. In late 1962, political parties were again legalized, and factions crystallized into government and opposition groups. Ayub Khan combined fragments of the old Muslim League and created the Pakistan Muslim League (PML) as the official government party.

The presidential election of January 1965 resulted in a victory for Ayub Khan but also demonstrated the appeal of the opposition. Four political parties joined to form the Combined Opposition Parties (COP). These parties were the Council Muslim League, strongest in Punjab and Karachi; the Awami League, strongest in East Pakistan; the National Awami Party, strongest in the North-West Frontier Province, where it stood for dissolving the One Unit Plan; and the Jamaat-i-Islami, surprisingly supporting the candidacy of a woman. The COP nominated Fatima Jinnah (sister of the Quaid-i-Azam and known as Madar-i-Millet, the Mother of the Nation) as their presidential candidate. The nine-point program put forward by the COP emphasized the restoration of parliamentary democracy. Ayub won 63.3 percent of the electoral college vote. His majority was larger in West Pakistan (73.6 percent) than in East Pakistan (53.1 percent).

Ayub Khan's Foreign Policy and the 1965 War with India

Ayub Khan articulated his foreign policy on several occasions, particularly in his autobiography, *Friends not Masters.* His objectives were the security and development of Pakistan and the preservation of its ideology as he saw it. Toward these ends, he sought to improve, or normalize, relations with Pakistan's immediate and looming neighbors—India, China, and the Soviet Union. While retaining and renewing the alliance with the United States, Ayub emphasized his preference for friendship, not subordination, and bargained hard for higher returns to Pakistan.

Other than ideology and Kashmir, the main source of friction between Pakistan and India was the distribution of the waters of the Indus River system. As the upper riparian power, India controlled the headworks of the prepartition irrigation canals. After independence India had, in addition, constructed several multipurpose projects on the eastern tributaries of the Indus. Pakistan feared that India might repeat a 1948 incident that curtailed the water supply as a means of coercion. A compromise that appeared to meet the needs of both countries was reached during the 1950s, but it was not until 1960 that a solution finally found favor with Ayub Khan and Jawaharlal Nehru.

The Indus Waters Treaty of 1960 was backed by the World Bank (see Glossary) and the United States. Broadly speaking, the agreement allocated use of the three western Indus rivers (the Indus itself and its tributaries, the Jhelum and the Chenab) to Pakistan, and the three eastern Indus tributaries (the Ravi, Beas, and Sutlej) to India. The basis of the plan was that irrigation canals in Pakistan that had been supplied by the eastern rivers would begin to draw water from the western Indus rivers through a system of barrages and link canals. The agreement also detailed transitional arrangements, new irrigation and hydroelectric power works, and the waterlogging and salinity problems in Pakistan's Punjab. The Indus Basin Development Fund was established and financed by the World Bank, the major contributors to the Aid-to-Pakistan Consortium, and India (see Foreign Aid, ch. 3).

Pakistan's tentative approaches to China intensified in 1959 when China's occupation of Tibet and the flight of the Dalai Lama to India ended five years of Chinese-Indian friendship. An entente between Pakistan and China evolved in step with the growth of Sino-Indian hostility, which climaxed in a border war in 1962. This informal alliance became a keystone of Pakistan's foreign policy and grew to include a border agreement in March 1963, highway construction connecting the two countries at the Karakoram Pass, agreements on trade, and Chinese economic assistance and grants of military equipment, which was later thought to have included exchanges in nuclear technology. China's diplomatic support and transfer of military equipment was important to Pakistan during the 1965 Indo-Pakistani War over Kashmir. China's new diplomatic influence in the UN was also exerted on Pakistan's behalf after the Indo-Pakistani War of 1971. Ayub Khan's foreign minister, Zulfiqar Ali Bhutto, is often credited for this China policy, which gave Pakistan new flexibility in its international relationships. The entente deepened during the Zia regime (1977–88).

The Soviet Union strongly disapproved of Pakistan's alliance with the United States, but Moscow was interested in keeping doors open to both Pakistan and India. Ayub Khan was able to secure Soviet neutrality during the 1965 Indo-Pakistani War.

Ayub Khan was the architect of Pakistan's policy of close alignment with the United States, and his first major foreign policy act was to sign bilateral economic and military agreements with the United States in 1959 (see The United States Alliance, ch. 5). Nevertheless, Ayub expected more from these agreements than the United States was willing to offer and thus remained critical of the role the United States played in South Asia. He was vehemently opposed to simultaneous United States support, direct or indirect, for India's military, especially when this assistance was augmented in the wake of the Sino-Indian War of 1962. Ayub maintained, as did many Pakistanis, that in return for the use of Pakistani military facilities, the United States owed Pakistan security allegiance in all cases, not merely in response to communist aggression. Especially troublesome to Pakistan was United States neutrality during the 1965 Indo-Pakistani War. The United States stance at this time was a contributing factor to Pakistan's closing of United States communications and intelligence facilities near Peshawar. Pakistan did not extend the ten-year agreement signed in 1959.

The 1965 war began as a series of border flare-ups along undemarcated territory at the Rann of Kutch in the southeast in April and soon after along the cease-fire line in Kashmir. The Rann of Kutch conflict was resolved by mutual consent and British sponsorship and arbitration, but the Kashmir conflict proved more dangerous and widespread. In the early spring of 1965, UN observers and India reported increased activity by infiltrators from Pakistan into Indian-held Kashmir. Pakistan hoped to support an uprising by Kashmiris against India. No such uprising took place, and by August India had retaken Pakistani-held positions in the north while Pakistan attacked in the Chamb sector in southwestern Kashmir in September. Each country had limited objectives, and neither was economically capable of sustaining a long war because military supplies were cut to both countries by the United States and Britain.

On September 23, a cease-fire was arranged through the UN Security Council. In January 1966, Ayub Khan and India's prime minister, Lal Bahadur Shastri, signed the Tashkent Declaration, which formally ended hostilities and called for a mutual withdrawal of forces. This objectively statesmanlike act elicited an adverse reaction in West Pakistan. Students as well as politicians demonstrated in urban areas, and many were arrested. The Tashkent Declaration was the turning point in the political fortunes of the Ayub Khan administration.

In February 1966, a national conference was held in Lahore, where all the opposition parties convened to discuss their differences and their common interests. The central issue discussed was the Tashkent Declaration, which most of the assembled politicians characterized as Ayub Khan's unnecessary capitulation to India. More significant, perhaps, was the noticeable underrepresentation of politicians from the East Wing. About 700 persons attended the conference, but only twenty-one were from the East Wing. They were led by Sheikh Mujibur Rahman (known as Mujib) of the Awami League, who presented his controversial six-point political and economic program for East Pakistani provincial autonomy. The six points consisted of the following demands: that the government be federal and parliamentary in nature, its members elected by universal adult suffrage with legislative representation on the basis of distribution of population; that the federal government have principal responsibility for foreign affairs and defense only; that each wing have its own currency and separate fiscal accounts; that taxation occur at the provincial level, with a federal government funded by constitutionally guaranteed grants; that each federal unit control its own earnings of foreign exchange; and that each unit raise its own militia or paramilitary forces.

Ayub Khan also lost the services of Minister of Foreign Affairs Bhutto, who resigned, became a vocal opposition leader, and founded the Pakistan People's Party (PPP—see Pakistan People's Party, ch. 4). By 1968 it was obvious that except for the military and the civil service, Ayub had lost most of his support. Ayub's illness in February 1968 and the alleged corruption of members of his family further weakened his position. In West Pakistan, Bhutto's PPP called for a "revolution"; in the east, the Awami League's six points became the rallying cry of the opposition.

In October 1968, the government sponsored a celebration called the Decade of Development. Instead of reminding people of the achievements of the Ayub Khan regime, the festivities highlighted the frustrations of the urban poor afflicted by inflation and the costs of the 1965 war. For the masses, Ayub Khan had become the symbol of inequality. Bhutto capitalized on this and challenged Ayub at the ballot box. In East Pakistan, dissatisfaction with the system went deeper than opposition to Ayub Khan. In January 1969, several opposition parties formed the Democratic Action Committee with the declared aim of restoring democracy through a mass movement.

Ayub Khan reacted by alternating conciliation and repression. Disorder spread. The army moved into Karachi, Lahore, Peshawar, Dhaka, and Khulna to restore order. In rural areas of East Pakistan, a curfew was ineffective; local officials sensed government control ebbing and began retreating from the incipient peasant revolt. In February, Ayub released political prisoners, invited the Democratic Action Committee and others to meet him in Rawalpindi, promised a new constitution, and said he would not stand for reelection in 1970. Still in poor health and lacking the confidence of his generals, Ayub Khan sought a political settlement as violence continued.

On March 25, 1969, martial law was again proclaimed; General Agha Mohammad Yahya Khan, the army commander in chief, was designated chief martial law administrator. The 1962 constitution was abrogated, Ayub Khan announced his resignation, and Yahya Khan assumed the presidency. Yahya soon promised elections on the basis of adult franchise to the National Assembly, which would draw up a new constitution. He also entered into discussions with leaders of political parties.

Yahya Khan and Bangladesh

The new administration formed a committee of deputy and provincial martial law administrators that functioned above the civil machinery of government. The generals held power and were no longer the supporting arm of the civilians—elected or bureaucratic—as they had been throughout much of the country's history. In the past, every significant change of government had relied, in large part, on the allegiance of the military. However, Yahya Khan and his military advisers proved no more capable of overcoming the nation's problems than their predecessors. The attempt to establish a military hierarchy running parallel to and supplanting the authority of the civilian administration inevitably ruptured the bureaucratic-military alliance, on which efficiency and stability depended. Little effort was made to promote a national program.

These weaknesses were not immediately apparent but became so as events moved quickly toward a crisis in East Pakistan. On November 28, 1969, Yahya Khan made a nationwide broadcast announcing his proposals for a return to constitutional government. General elections for the National Assembly were set for October 5, 1970, but were postponed to December as the result of a severe cyclone that hit the coast of East Pakistan. The National Assembly was obliged within 120 days to draw up a new constitution, which would permit maximum provincial autonomy. Yahya, however, made it clear that the federal government would require powers of taxation well beyond those contemplated by the six points of the Awami League. He also reserved the right to "authenticate" the constitution. On July 1, 1970, the One Unit Plan was dissolved into the four original provinces. Yahya Khan also determined that the parity of representation in the National Assembly between the East Wing and the West Wing that had existed under the 1956 and 1962 constitutions would end and that representation would be based on population. This arrangement gave East Pakistan 162 seats (plus seven reserved for women) versus 138 seats (plus six for women) for the new provinces of the West Wing.

An intense election campaign took place in 1970 as restrictions on press, speech, and assembly were removed. Bhutto campaigned in the West Wing on a strongly nationalist and leftist platform. The slogan of his party was "Islam our Faith, Democracy our Polity, Socialism our Economy." He said that the PPP would provide "*roti, kapra, aur makhan*" (bread, clothing, and shelter) to all. He also proclaimed a "thousand year war with India," although this pronouncement was played down later in the campaign. In the East Wing, the Awami League gained widespread support for the six-point program. Its cause was further strengthened because West Pakistani politicians were perceived as callously indifferent to the Bengali victims of the October cyclone and slow to come to their aid.

The first general election conducted in Pakistan on the basis of one person, one vote, was held on December 7, 1970; elections to provincial legislative assemblies followed three days later. The voting was heavy. Yahya Khan kept his promise of free and fair elections. The Awami League won a colossal victory in East Pakistan, for it was directly elected to 160 of the 162 seats in the east and thus gained a majority of the 300 directly elected seats in the National Assembly (plus the thirteen indirectly elected seats for women, bringing the total to 313 members) without winning a seat in the West Wing (see Yahya Khan, 1969–71, ch. 4). The PPP won a large majority in the West Wing, especially in Punjab and Sindh, but no seats in the East Wing. In the North-West Frontier Province and Balochistan, the National Awami Party won a plurality of the seats. The Muslim League and the Islamic parties did poorly in the west and were not represented in the east.

Any constitutional agreement clearly depended on the consent of three persons: Mujib of the East Wing, Bhutto of the West Wing, and Yahya Khan as the ultimate authenticator representing the military government. In his role as intermediary and head of state, Yahya tried to persuade Bhutto and Mujib to come to some kind of accommodation. This effort proved unsuccessful as Mujib insisted on his right as leader of the majority to form a government—a stand at variance with Bhutto, who claimed there were "two majorities" in Pakistan. Bhutto declared that the PPP would not attend the inaugural session of the assembly, thereby making the establishment of civilian government impossible. On March 1, 1971, Yahya Khan, who earlier had referred to Mujib as the "future prime minister of Pakistan," dissolved his civilian cabinet and declared an indefinite postponement of the National Assembly. In East Pakistan, the reaction was immediate. Strikes, demonstrations, and civil disobedience increased in tempo until there was open revolt. Prodded by Mujib, Bengalis declared they would pay no taxes and would ignore martial law regulations on press and radio censorship. The writ of the central government all but ceased to exist in East Pakistan.

Mujib, Bhutto, and Yahya Khan held negotiations in Dhaka in late March in a last-ditch attempt to defuse the growing crisis; simultaneously, General Tikka Khan, who commanded the Pakistani forces in East Pakistan, prepared a contingency plan for a military takeover and called for troop reinforcements to be flown in via Sri Lanka. In an atmosphere of distrust and suspicion, the talks broke down, and on March 25 Yahya Khan and Bhutto flew back to West Pakistan.

Tikka Khan's emergency plan went into operation. Roadblocks and barriers appeared all over Dhaka. Mujib was taken into custody and flown to the West Wing to stand trial for treason. Universities were attacked, and the first of many deaths occurred. The tempo of violence of the military crackdown during these first days soon accelerated into a full-blown and brutal civil war.

On March 26, Yahya Khan outlawed the Awami League, banned political activity, and reimposed press censorship in both wings. Because of these strictures, people in the West Wing remained uninformed about the crackdown in the east and tended to discount reports appearing in the international press as an Indian conspiracy.

Major Ziaur Rahman, a political unknown at the time, proclaimed the independence of Bangladesh from Chittagong, a city in the southeast of the new country. He would become president of Bangladesh in April 1977. A Bangladeshi government-in-exile was formed in Calcutta.

Ziaur Rahman and others organized Bengali troops to form the Mukti Bahini (Liberation Force) to resist the Pakistan Army. The East Pakistan Rifles, a paramilitary force, mutinied and joined the revolutionary forces. Nevertheless, the Pakistan Army pressed its heavy offensive and in early April controlled most of East Pakistan. More than 250,000 refugees crossed into India in the first few days of the war. The influx continued over the next six months and reached a total of about 10 million. No accurate estimate can be made of the numbers of people killed or wounded or the numbers of women raped, but the assessment of international human rights organizations is that the Pakistani crackdown was particularly alarming in its ferocity.

Relations between Pakistan and India, already tense, deteriorated sharply as a result of the crisis. On March 31, the Indian parliament passed a resolution in support of the "people of Bengal." The Mukti Bahini, formed around regular and paramilitary forces, received equipment, training, and other assistance from India. Superpower rivalries further complicated the situation, impinged on Pakistan's war, and possibly impeded its political resolution.

In the fall, military and guerrilla operations increased, and Pakistan and India reported escalation of border shelling. On the western border of East Pakistan, military preparations were also in evidence. On November 21, the Mukti Bahini launched an offensive on Jessore, southwest of Dhaka. Yahya Khan declared a state of emergency in all of Pakistan on November 23 and asked his people to prepare for war. In response to Indian military movements along and across the Indian-East Pakistani border, the Pakistan Air Force attacked military targets in northern India on December 3, and on December 4 India began an integrated ground, naval, and air invasion of East Pakistan. The Indian army launched a five-pronged attack and began converging on Dhaka. Indian forces closed in around Dhaka and received the surrender of Pakistani forces on December 16. Indian prime minister Indira Gandhi proclaimed a unilateral cease-fire on December 17.

Violent demonstrations against the military government soon broke out at the news of Pakistan's defeat. Yahya Khan resigned on December 20. Bhutto assumed power as president and chief martial law administrator of a disgraced military, a shattered government, and a bewildered and demoralized population. Formal relations between Pakistan and Bangladesh were not established until 1976.

Zulfiqar Ali Bhutto and a New Constitutional System

On assuming power on December 20, 1971, Bhutto promised to make a new Pakistan out of the West Wing and to restore national confidence. He conveniently laid the entire blame for the 1971 war and Pakistan's defeat on Yahya Khan and his junta. Asserting the principle of civilian leadership, Bhutto introduced a new constitution with a modified parliamentary and federal system. He attempted to control and reform the civil service and took steps to revitalize a stagnant economy and ameliorate conditions for the poor under the banner of Islamic socialism. Bhutto's most visible success, however, was in the international arena, where he employed his diplomatic skills. He negotiated a satisfactory peace settlement with India in 1972, built new links between Pakistan and the oil-exporting Islamic countries to the west, and generally was effective in repairing Pakistan's image in the aftermath of the war.

Bhutto's program appeared to be laudable but fell short in performance. His near-monopoly of decision-making power prevented democratic institutions from taking root, and his overreaching ambitions managed in time to antagonize all but his closest friends.

The PPP manifesto was couched in socialist terms. When Bhutto issued the Economic Reform Order on January 3, 1972, banking and insurance institutions were nationalized, and seventy other industrial enterprises were taken over by the government. The Ministry of Production, which incorporated the Board of Industrial Management, was established to oversee industry. Investment in the public sector increased substantially, and Bhutto maneuvered to break the power of the approximately twenty elite families who had dominated the nation's economy during the Ayub Khan period. Trade unions were strengthened, and welfare measures for labor were announced. Although Bhutto's initial zeal diminished as he came face-to-face with economic realities and the shortage of capital, he tried to refurbish his populist image with another spate of nationalizations in 1976.

Bhutto purged the military ranks of about 1,400 officers. He also created a paramilitary force called the Federal Security Force (which functioned almost as his personal bodyguard), a watchdog on the armed forces, and an internal security force. A white paper on defense issued in 1976 firmly subordinated the armed forces to civilian control and gave Bhutto, then also prime minister, the decisive voice in all matters relating to national security. In that role, Bhutto took credit for bringing home more than 90,000 prisoners of war without allowing any of them to come to trial in Bangladesh for war crimes. In 1976 Bhutto replaced Tikka Khan, whose term had expired, with General Mohammad Zia ul-Haq as chief of staff of the army. Like Ayub Khan, Zia was appointed over several more senior generals. Also like Ayub, Zia came from a community not heavily represented in the armed forces (the Arains from Punjab) and was thought to be without political ambition.

In April 1972, Bhutto lifted martial law and convened the National Assembly, which consisted of members elected from the West Wing in December 1970 (plus two from the East Wing who decided their loyalties were with a united Pakistan). The standing controversies about the role of Islam, provincial autonomy, and the form of government—presidential or parliamentary—remained on the agenda. There was much jostling for position among the three major political groups: the PPP, most powerful in Punjab and Sindh, and the National Awami

Party (NAP) and the Jamiat-ul-Ulama-i-Islam (JUI), both based in the North-West Frontier Province and Balochistan. The provincial assemblies were constituted from those elected in December 1970. There was much tension during the process of drafting a new constitution, especially from members from the North-West Frontier Province and Balochistan. Bhutto reached some accommodation with opposition leaders from those two provinces on the matter of gubernatorial appointment and constitutional principle.

Pakistan's third indigenous constitution was formally submitted on December 31, 1972, approved on April 10, 1973, and promulgated on independence day, August 14, 1973. Although Bhutto campaigned in 1970 for the restoration of a parliamentary system, by 1972 he preferred a presidential system with himself as president. However, in deference to the wishes of the opposition and some in his own cabinet, Bhutto accepted a formal parliamentary system in which the executive was responsible to the legislature. The unicameral parliament was changed to a bicameral legislature, consisting of the Senate, or upper house, and the National Assembly, or lower house. Purportedly in the interests of government stability, provisions were also included that made it almost impossible for the National Assembly to remove the prime minister. The 1973 constitution provided for a federal structure in which residuary powers were reserved for the provinces. However, Bhutto dismissed the coalition NAP-JUI ministries in Balochistan and the North-West Frontier Province, revealing his preference for a powerful center without opposition in the provinces.

Bhutto's power derived less from the 1973 constitution than from his charismatic appeal to the people and from the vigor of the PPP. Its socialist program and Bhutto's oratory had done much to radicalize the urban sectors in the late 1960s and were responsible for the popular optimism accompanying the restoration of democracy. The ideological appeal of the PPP to the masses sat uneasily with the compromises Bhutto reached with the holders of economic and political influence—the landlords and commercial elites. Factionalism and patrimonialism became rife in the PPP, especially in Punjab. The internal cohesion of the PPP and its standing in public esteem were affected adversely by the ubiquitous political and bureaucratic corruption that accompanied state intervention in the economy and, equally, by the rising incidence of political violence, which included beating, arresting, and even murdering opponents.

The PPP had started as a movement mobilizing people to overthrow a military regime, but in Bhutto's lifetime it failed to change into a political party organized for peaceful functioning in an open polity.

Bhutto's predilection for a strong center and for provincial governments in the hands of the PPP inevitably aroused opposition in provinces where regional and ethnic identity was strong. Feelings of Sindhi solidarity were maintained by Bhutto's personal connections with the feudal leaders (*wadera*) of Sindh and his ability to manipulate offices and officeholders. He did not enjoy the same leverage in the North-West Frontier Province or Balochistan.

A long-dormant crisis erupted in Balochistan in 1973 into an insurgency that lasted four years and became increasingly bitter. The insurgency was put down by the Pakistan Army, which employed brutal methods and equipment, including Huey-Cobra helicopter gunships, provided by Iran and flown by Iranian pilots. The deep-seated Baloch nationalism based on tribal identity had international as well as domestic aspects. Divided in the nineteenth century among Iran, Afghanistan, and British India, the Baloch found their aspirations and traditional nomadic life frustrated by the presence of national boundaries and the extension of central administration over their lands. Moreover, many of the most militant Baloch nationalists were also vaguely Marxist-Leninist and willing to risk Soviet protection for an autonomous Balochistan. As the insurgency wore on, the influence of a relatively small but disciplined liberation front seemed to increase.

Bhutto was able to mobilize domestic support for his drive against the Baloch. Punjab's support was most tangibly represented in the use of the army to put down the insurgency. One of the main Baloch grievances was the influx of Punjabi settlers, miners, and traders into their resource-rich but sparsely populated lands. Bhutto could also invoke the idea of national integration with effect in the aftermath of Bengali secession. External assistance to Bhutto was generously given by the shah of Iran, who feared a spread of the insurrection among the Iranian Baloch. Some foreign governments feared that an independent or autonomous Balochistan might allow the Soviet Union to develop and use the port at Gwadar, and no outside power was willing to assist the Baloch openly or to sponsor the cause of Baloch autonomy. During the mid-1970s, Afghanistan was preoccupied with its own internal problems and seemingly anxious to normalize relations with Pakistan. India was fearful of further balkanization of the subcontinent after Bangladesh, and the Soviet Union did not wish to jeopardize the leverage it was gaining with Pakistan. However, during the Bhutto regime hostilities in Balochistan were protracted. The succeeding Zia ul-Haq government took a more moderate approach, relying more on economic development to placate the Baloch.

Bhutto proceeded cautiously in the field of land reform and did not fulfill earlier promises of distributing land to the landless on the scale he had promised, as he was forced to recognize and to cultivate the sociopolitical influence of landowners. However, he did not impede the process of consolidation of tenancy rights and acquisition of mid-sized holdings by servicemen. Punjab was the vital agricultural region of Pakistan; it remained a bastion of support for the government.

Bhutto specifically targeted the powerful and privileged Civil Service of Pakistan (CSP) and introduced measures of administrative reform with the declared purpose of limiting the paternalistic power of the bureaucracy. The CSP, however, had played the role of guardian alongside the army since independence. Many of its members reacted badly to Bhutto's politicizing appointments, for which patronage seemed a more important criterion than merit or seniority.

Relations with India were, at best, uneven during the Bhutto period. He accomplished the return of the prisoners of war through the Simla Agreement of 1972, but no settlement of the key problem of Kashmir was possible beyond an agreement that any settlement should be peaceful. Bhutto reacted strongly to the detonation of a nuclear device by India in 1974 and pledged that Pakistan would match that development even if Pakistanis had to "eat grass" to cover the cost.

Bhutto claimed success for his economic policies. The gross national product (GNP—see Glossary) and the rate of economic growth climbed. Inflation fell from 25 percent in fiscal year (FY—see Glossary) 1972 to 6 percent in FY 1976, although other economic measures he introduced did not perform as well.

Bhutto pointed out that his foreign policy had brought Pakistan prestige in the Islamic world, peace if not friendship with India, and self-respect in dealings with the great powers. He felt assured of victory in any election. Therefore, with the commitment to a constitutional order at stake, in January 1977 he announced he would hold national and provincial assembly elections in March.

The response of the opposition to this news was vigorous. Nine political parties ranging across the ideological spectrum formed a united front—the Pakistan National Alliance (PNA). Fundamentalist Muslims were satisfied by the adoption of Nizam-i-Mustafa (see Glossary), meaning "Rule of the Prophet," as the front's slogan. Modern secular elements, however, respected the association of Air Marshal Asghar Khan. The PNA ran candidates for almost all national and provincial seats. As curbs on the press and political activity were relaxed for the election campaign, an apparently strong wave of support for the PNA swept Pakistan's cities. This prompted a whirlwind tour of the country by Bhutto, with all his winning charm in the forefront. In the background lurked indirect curbs on free expression as well as political gangsterism.

National Assembly election results were announced on March 7, proclaiming the PPP the winner with 155 seats versus thirty-six seats for the PNA. Expecting trouble, Bhutto invoked Section 144 of the Code of Criminal Procedure, which restricted assembly for political reasons. The PNA immediately challenged the election results as rigged and demanded a new election—not a recount. Bhutto refused, and a mass protest movement was launched against him. Religious symbols were used by both sides to mobilize agitation; for example, Bhutto imposed prohibitions on the consumption of alcoholic beverages and on gambling. Despite talks between Bhutto and opposition leaders, the disorders persisted as a multitude of frustrations were vented. The army intervened on July 5 and took all political leaders, including Bhutto, into custody.

Zia ul-Haq and Military Domination, 1977–88

General Mohammad Zia ul-Haq, chief of the army staff, took control of Pakistan by proclaiming martial law, beginning the longest period of rule by a single leader in Pakistan's history. It ended only with his death in a still-unexplained aircraft crash on August 17, 1988. President Fazal Elahi Chaudhry remained in office until his term expired in September 1978, when Zia assumed that office in addition to his role as chief martial law administrator.

In announcing his takeover of the government, Zia stated that he had taken action only in order to hold new elections for national and provincial assemblies within ninety days. Political parties were not banned, and nominations were filed for seats. The country expected that a new "free and fair" poll would take place. It did not. Zia canceled the elections because, he said, it was his responsibility first to carry out a program of "accountability"; he had "unexpectedly" found "irregularities" in the previous regime. As a result, a number of "white papers" on topics ranging from fraud in the 1977 elections, to abuses by the Federal Security Force, and to Bhutto's manipulation of the press were generated. The attacks on the Bhutto administration increased as time passed and culminated in the trial and the hanging in April 1979 of Bhutto for complicity in the murder of a political opponent.

After elections were canceled by decree on March 1, 1978, Zia banned all political activity, although political parties were not banned. The same month, some 200 journalists were arrested, and a number of newspapers were shut down. Zia, however, maintained that there would be elections sometime in 1979. Members of some of the PNA parties, including the Jamaat-i-Islami and the Pakistan Muslim League, joined Zia's cabinet as he tried to give a civilian cast to his government. But suppression of the PPP continued, and at times Bhutto's widow, Nusrat, and his daughter, Benazir, were placed under house arrest or jailed. Elections for local bodies were held in September 1979 on a nonparty basis, a system Zia continued in the 1985 national and provincial elections. Many of those elected locally identified themselves as Awami Dost (Friends of the People), a designation well known as a synonym for the PPP. Zia announced national and provincial elections for November 17 and 20, 1979, respectively, but these, too, were canceled. Many thought that the showing of the Awami Dost made him fear that a substantial number of PPP sympathizers would be elected. As further restrictions were placed on political activity, parties were also banned.

On February 6, 1981, the PPP—officially "defunct," as were the other parties—and several other parties joined to form the Movement for the Restoration of Democracy. Its demands were simple: an end to martial law and a call to hold elections under the suspended 1973 constitution. The Movement for the Restoration of Democracy demonstrated from time to time against Zia's government, especially in August 1983, but Zia was able to withstand its demands. Many of the leaders spent time in jail.

Nusrat Bhutto brought a suit protesting the martial law takeover. The Supreme Court ruled against her and invoked once again the "doctrine of necessity," permitting the regime to "perform all such acts and promulgate all measures, which [fall] within the scope of the law of necessity, including the power to amend the Constitution." After this ruling, Zia issued the Provisional Constitutional Order of 1980, which excluded all martial law actions from the jurisdiction of the courts. When the Quetta High Court ruled that this order was beyond the power of the martial law regime, the Provisional Constitutional Order of 1981 was issued. This order required all judges of the Supreme Court and high courts to take new oaths in which they swore to act in accordance with the orders. Several judges refused to do so and resigned.

In February 1982, in an unsatisfactory response to the demand for elections, Zia created an appointed Majlis-i-Shoora (Council of Advisers), claiming that this was the pattern of Islamic law. The body was clearly unrepresentative and had no powers of legislation. It served merely as a tame debating body.

The Islamization of Pakistan was another of Zia's goals. In 1978 he announced that Pakistani law would be based on Nizam-i-Mustafa, one of the demands of the PNA in the 1977 election. This requirement meant that any laws passed by legislative bodies had to conform to Islamic law and any passed previously would be nullified if they were repugnant to Islamic law. Nizam-i-Mustafa raised several problems. Most Pakistanis are Sunni, but there is a substantial minority of Shia whose interpretation of Islamic law differs in some important aspects from that of the Sunnis. Zia's introduction of state collection of *zakat* (see Glossary) was strongly protested by the Shia, and after they demonstrated in Islamabad, the rules were modified in 1981 for Shia adherents. There were also major differences in the views held by the ulama in the interpretation of what constituted nonconformity and repugnance in Islam (see Islam in Pakistani Society, ch. 2).

In 1979 Zia decreed the establishment of shariat courts to try cases under Islamic law. A year later, Islamic punishments were assigned to various violations (*hudood*—see Glossary), including drinking alcoholic beverages, theft, prostitution, fornication, adultery, and bearing false witness. Zia also began a process for the eventual Islamization of the financial system aimed at "eliminating that which is forbidden and establishing that which is enjoined by Islam." Of special concern to Zia was the Islamic prohibition on interest, or *riba* (sometimes translated as usury) (see Monetary Process, ch. 3).

Women's groups feared that Zia would repeal the Muslim Family Laws Ordinance of 1961, but he did not. The ordinance provided women critical access to basic legal protection, including, among other things, the right to divorce, support, and inheritance, and it placed limitations on polygyny. Still, women found unfair the rules of evidence under Islamic law by which women frequently were found guilty of adultery or fornication when in fact they had been raped. They also opposed rules that in some cases equated the testimony of two women with that of one man.

After the 1985 election, two members of the Senate from the Jamaat-i-Islami introduced legislation to make the sharia the basic law of Pakistan, placing it above the constitution and other legislation. The bill also would have added the ulama to the sharia courts and would have prohibited appeals from these courts from going to the Supreme Court. The bill did not pass in 1985, but after the dismissal of Prime Minister Junejo and the dissolution of the national and provincial assemblies in 1988, Zia enacted the bill by ordinance. The ordinance died when it was not approved by the parliament during the first prime ministership of Benazir Bhutto (December 1988–August 1990), but a revised Shariat Bill was passed by the government of Mian Nawaz Sharif (November 1990–July 1993) in May 1991.

Provincialism increased during Zia's tenure. He handled the problem of unrest in Balochistan more successfully than had Zulfiqar Ali Bhutto. Zia used various schemes of economic development to assuage the Baloch and was successful to a high degree. The North-West Frontier Province, alarmed at the presence of Soviet troops next door after the Soviet invasion of Afghanistan in December 1979, remained relatively quiet. But the long-festering division between Sindhis and non-Sindhis exploded into violence in Sindh. The *muhajirs* formed new organizations, the most significant being the Refugee People's Movement (Muhajir Qaumi Mahaz). The incendiary tensions resulted not only from Sindhi-*muhajir* opposition but also from Sindhi fear of others who had moved into the province, including Baloch, Pakhtuns, and Punjabis. The fact that Sindhi was becoming the mother tongue of fewer and fewer people of Sindh was also resented. The violence escalated in the late 1980s to the extent that some compared Karachi and Hyderabad to the Beirut of that period. The growth of the illicit drug industry also added to the ethnic problem.

The Badshahi Mosque, built by the Mughals in the seventeenth century, as seen from Lahore Fort
Courtesy Embassy of Pakistan, Washington

Pressure on Zia to hold elections mounted, and some of it came from overseas, including from the United States. In 1984 Zia announced that elections to legislative bodies would be held in 1985, and this time the schedule held.

Zia decided to restore the separate electorates, abandoned under Ayub Khan. In the National Assembly, ten of the 217 directly elected seats were set aside for minorities: four each for Hindus and Christians and one each for Ahmadiyyas and "others," including Parsis, Sikhs, and Buddhists. There were also twenty indirectly elected seats reserved for women, although women could run for directly elected seats. Zia decided that parties would not be permitted to participate. Each candidate, therefore, would be an "independent."

Before the general elections, Zia held a national referendum ostensibly seeking a mandate to continue in office as president.

The referendum, on December 19, 1984, focused on Pakistan's Islamization program. The electorate was asked simply if it felt the government was doing a good job of Islamizing the various social institutions of the state. Zia interpreted the positive results (98 percent voting "yes") to mean that he had received the right to a new five-year term as head of state. There was, however, little doubt that the vote was rigged.

After the "election," which most PPP supporters boycotted, Zia announced the appointment of Mohammad Khan Junejo as prime minister, subject to a vote of confidence in the National Assembly. Junejo, a Sindhi, took office on March 23, 1985. Zia issued the Revival of the Constitution of 1973 Order, which was a misnomer. The constitution was so vastly changed by various decrees that it was much different from the one enacted by the Bhutto regime. In the 1973 document, power had been in the hands of the prime minister; by 1985 it was in the hands of the president.

Zia promised to end martial law by the end of 1985, but he exacted a high price for this. The Eighth Amendment to the constitution confirmed and legalized all acts taken under martial law, including changes to the constitution. It affirmed the right of the president to appoint and dismiss the prime minister. With the amendment passed, Zia ended martial law in late 1985. Political parties were revived. In 1986 Junejo became president of a reconstituted Pakistan Muslim League. The PPP, although self-excluded from the National Assembly, also resumed activity under the leadership of Benazir Bhutto.

Junejo, however, was not able to accomplish all of Zia's agenda. For example, his government did not pass the Shariat Bill. It allowed the resumption of political parties, a step not welcomed by Zia, who saw parties as divisive in what should be a united Islamic community. Nonetheless, the dismissal of Junejo on May 29, 1988, and the dissolution of the national and provincial assemblies the next day, came as a surprise. In explaining his action, Zia pointed to the failure to carry Islamization forward and also to corruption, deterioration of law and order, and mismanagement of the economy. Another important reason for Junejo's dismissal was his interference in army promotions and his call for an investigation into an arsenal explosion near Islamabad; civilians were not expected to meddle in military affairs.

Zia procrastinated on calling new elections, which even his own version of the constitution required within ninety days. He finally set November 17, 1988, as the polling date for the National Assembly, with provincial elections three days later. His reasons for the delay were the holy month of Muharram, which fell in August during the hot weather, and the lack of current electoral registrations (a point he blamed on Junejo). Despite the open operation of political parties, Zia indicated that elections would again be on a nonparty basis. Before elections took place, Zia was killed in an explosion aboard his airplane near Bahawalpur, in Punjab, on August 17, 1988, along with the chairman of the joint chiefs committee, the United States ambassador, and twenty-seven others. A joint United States-Pakistani committee investigating the accident later established that the crash was caused by "a criminal act of sabotage perpetrated in the aircraft."

Court actions ended the nonparty basis for the elections, and parties were permitted to participate. A technicality—the failure to register as a political party—that would have prohibited the PPP from taking part was also voided. The election gave a plurality, not a majority, to the PPP. Its leader, Benazir Bhutto, was able to gain the assistance of other groups, and she was sworn in as prime minister on December 1, 1988, by acting President Ghulam Ishaq Khan. He in turn was elected to a five-year term as president by the National Assembly and the Senate.

Pakistan and the World During the Zia Regime

When Zia assumed power in mid-1977, Pakistan was out of the limelight and indeed was considered by some observers to be a political backwater. By the time of Zia's death in 1988, however, it had, because of the Soviet invasion of Afghanistan in 1979, become an important actor occupying a central position in the world arena.

Although Zulifqar Ali Bhutto had tried to redirect Pakistan's regional orientation toward West Asia and Zia continued this trend, the nation's geostrategic interests dictated a concentration on South Asia. Pakistan's foreign policy was very much centered on India. Less than two years after Zia's assumption of power, Congress, led by Indira Gandhi, was voted out of office and replaced by the Janata Party, whose foreign minister was Atal Behari Vajpayee of the Jana Sangh, long seen as anti-Pakistan. Nonetheless, relations between Pakistan and India may have reached their most cordial level during the almost three years Janata was in power. Vajpayee visited Pakistan in February 1978. There were exchanges on many issues, and agreements were signed on trade, cultural exchanges, and communications—but not on such key issues as Kashmir and nuclear development.

The nuclear issue was of critical importance to both Pakistan and India. In 1974 India successfully tested a nuclear "device." Bhutto reacted strongly to this test and said Pakistan must develop its own "Islamic bomb." Zia thus inherited a pledge that for domestic reasons he could not discard, and he continued the development program. He asked India to agree to several steps to end this potential nuclear arms race on the subcontinent. One of these measures was the simultaneous signing of the Nuclear Nonproliferation Treaty. The second step was a joint agreement for inspection of all nuclear sites by the International Atomic Energy Agency. Pakistan also proposed a pact between the two countries to allow for mutual inspection of sites. And, finally, Pakistan proposed a South Asian nuclear-free zone. It appeared that Zia was looking for a way to terminate the costly Pakistani program. But in order to sell this idea in Pakistan, he required some concessions from India. Termination would also get him out of difficulties the program was causing with the United States, including the curtailment of aid in 1979. These proposals were still on the table in the early 1990s and were supplemented by then Prime Minister Nawaz Sharif's call for a roundtable discussion among Pakistan, India, the United States, Russia, and China on nuclear weapons in South Asia (see The Armed Forces in a New World Order, ch. 5).

Not all relations within South Asia were negative. President Ziaur Rahman of Bangladesh proposed an organization for South Asian cooperation. Pakistan was at first reluctant, fearing Indian domination, but eventually agreed to join the group, along with Bangladesh, Bhutan, India, Maldives, Nepal, and Sri Lanka. The South Asian Association for Regional Cooperation (SAARC—see Glossary) was formally inaugurated at a summit meeting in Dhaka in 1985. There have been some positive steps toward cooperation, and regular rotating summits are held, although often with some delays.

Prime Minister Rajiv Gandhi of India (1984–89) came to Islamabad in 1988 to attend a SAARC summit, the first visit of an Indian prime minister since 1960, when Nehru signed the Indus Waters Treaty. Zia stopped briefly in New Delhi in December 1985, and in February 1987 he visited again, having invited himself to see a cricket match between the two countries. Zia's estimation was that he and Rajiv could meet quite cordially but could not agree on substantive issues.

Active and potential conflict continued to be a constant factor in Pakistan's relations with India. The dispute over the precise demarcation of the Line of Control, confirmed under the 1972 Simla Agreement, in Kashmir at the Siachen Glacier heated up periodically and over time caused substantial casualties on both sides because of numerous small skirmishes and the extreme cold in the remote area. Also, in the winter of 1986–87 the Indian army conducted Operation Brass Tacks, maneuvers close to the Pakistan border, and Pakistan mobilized its forces. However, the dangerous situation was defused, and no hostilities took place. India accused Pakistan of aiding Sikh insurgents in India's state of Punjab. Pakistan denied this accusation, but some people thought that Operation Brass Tacks might have been a means to strike at alleged bases in Pakistan's Punjab Province. Zia skillfully handled the diplomacy during the period of tension (see Pakistan Becomes a Frontline State, ch. 5).

Zia continued the process, begun by Bhutto, of opening Pakistan to the West and drew on Pakistan's Islamic, trade, and military ties to the Middle East. Military ties included stationing Pakistani troops in Saudi Arabia and training missions in several other countries. Remittances from Pakistanis employed as migrant workers in the Middle East, especially in the Persian Gulf area, increased during the Zia years and became an important factor in Pakistan's foreign-exchange holdings (see Labor, ch. 3).

Zia played a prominent role in the Organization of the Islamic Conference (OIC). A Pakistani was secretary general of the OIC, and Zia served on committees concerning the status of Jerusalem and the settlement of the Iran-Iraq War (1980–88), neither of which were successful. At the 1984 summit at Casablanca, Zia played a key role in the readmission of Egypt to the OIC and, in doing so, reminded his fellow heads of government that the organization was one for the entire Muslim community and not only for Arab states.

The United States under the administration of Jimmy Carter did not welcome the displacement of Bhutto by Zia; representative government, human rights, and nuclear nonproliferation were also of concern to Carter. The execution of Bhutto only added to the United States displeasure with Zia and Pakistan.

A number of United States laws—amendments to the Foreign Assistance Act of 1961—applied to Pakistan and its program of nuclear weapons development. The 1976 Symington Amendment stipulated that economic assistance be terminated to any country that imported uranium enrichment technology. The Glenn Amendment of 1977 similarly called for an end to aid to countries that imported reprocessing technology—Pakistan had from France. United States economic assistance, except for food aid, was terminated under the Symington Amendment in April 1979. In 1985 the Solarz Amendment was added to prohibit aid to countries that attempt to import nuclear commodities from the United States. In the same year, the Pressler Amendment was passed; referring specifically to Pakistan, it said that if that nation possessed a nuclear device, aid would be suspended. Many of these amendments could be waived if the president declared that it was in the national interests of the United States to continue assistance.

The Soviet Union invaded Afghanistan in December 1979, causing a sudden reversal of United States policy. Carter, who had described Pakistan as a "frontline state" in the Cold War, offered US$400 million in military and economic aid to Pakistan—an amount that Zia spurned and contemptuously termed "peanuts."

When Ronald Reagan took office in January 1981, the level of assistance increased substantially. Presidential waivers for several of the amendments were required. The initial package from the United States was for US$3.2 billion over six years, equally divided between economic and military assistance. A separate arrangement was made for the purchase of forty F-16 fighter aircraft. In 1986 a follow-on program of assistance over a further period of six years was announced at a total of more than US$4 billion, of which 57 percent was economic aid and the rest military aid.

The Soviet Union, meanwhile, under its new leader, Mikhail S. Gorbachev, was reassessing its role in Afghanistan. Indirect "proximity" negotiations in Geneva under the auspices of the UN were going on between Afghanistan and Pakistan, with the United States and the Soviet Union as observers. In April 1988, a series of agreements were signed among the United States, the Soviet Union, Pakistan, and Afghanistan that called for the withdrawal of Soviet forces by mid-February 1989. The withdrawal was completed on time.

Throughout the years of Soviet occupation of Afghanistan, relations between the United States and Pakistan were best characterized by close cooperation. Still, United States policy makers became increasingly concerned that Zia and his associates appeared to give preferential treatment to the Islamic fundamentalists, especially *mujahidin* leader Gulbaddin Hikmatyar. Other disagreements persisted, particularly over the failure of the Zia regime to convert to representative government. Documented Pakistani violations of human rights were another major issue; Pakistani involvement in narcotics trafficking was yet another. But the issue that after Zia's death led to another cutoff of aid was Pakistan's persistent drive toward nuclear development.

The events of the Zia period brought Pakistan to a leading position in world affairs. However, Pakistan's new visibility was closely connected to the supportive role it played for the anti-Soviet *mujahidin* in Afghanistan—and this decreased when the Soviet Union withdrew from Afghanistan. In the 1990s, Pakistan faced some major domestic problems—mounting ethnic and sectarian strife as well as widespread civil disorder. Pakistan will need to address these problems as it strives to improve its international standing as a maturing democratic nation and one aspiring to be the industrial and technological leader of the Muslim world.

* * *

For the study of the area of present-day Pakistan in the preindependence period, one must generally look to histories of India. The most recent survey is Stanley Wolpert's *A New History of India.* Published earlier, Percival Spear's Volume 1 and Romila Thapar's Volume 2 of *A History of India* also provide valuable information. Vincent Arthur Smith's *The Oxford History of India* gives a detailed account of the preindependence period. Two dictionaries that are difficult to obtain are helpful in looking up specific places and people: Sachchidananda Bhattacharya's *A Dictionary of Indian History* and Parshotam Mehra's *A Dictionary of Modern Indian History, 1707–1947.* Particularly valuable is the monumental *A Historical Atlas of South Asia,* edited by Joseph E. Schwartzberg. Two classic works on the Mughal period are Bamber Gascoigne's *The Great Moghuls* and Percival

Spear's *Twilight of the Mughals.* A more recent, standard work on the Mughals is *The Mughal Empire* by John F. Richards. Books that illuminate the Muslim movement include Peter Hardy's *The Muslims of British India*; Choudhry Khaliquzzaman's *Pathway to Pakistan*; Chaudri Muhammad Ali's *The Emergence of Pakistan*; Gail Minault's *The Khilafat Movement*; David Lelyveld's *Aligarh's First Generation*; and R.J. Moore's *The Crisis of Indian Unity, 1917–1940.* There is little biographic material except on Jinnah: the best sources are Stanley Wolpert's *Jinnah of Pakistan* and Ayesha Jalal's *The Sole Spokesman.*

Concerning independent Pakistan during the parliamentary period, Keith Callard's *Pakistan: A Political Study* and Richard S. Wheeler's *The Politics of Pakistan* are recommended. On Ayub Khan, Lawrence Ziring's *The Ayub Khan Era* is good. *Bangladesh: A Country Study*, edited by James Heitzman and Robert L. Worden, provides an analysis of the history of the East Wing of Pakistan (1947–71). The civil war is discussed in Craig Baxter's *Bangladesh: A New Nation in an Old Setting.* Bhutto's tenure is described in Shahid Javed Burki's *Pakistan under Bhutto, 1971–1977* and Stanley Wolpert's *Zulfi Bhutto of Pakistan: His Life and Times.* The Zia ul-Haq period is discussed in Shahid Javed Burki and Craig Baxter's *Pakistan under the Military: Eleven Years of Zia ul-Haq.* (For further information and complete citations, see Bibliography.)

Chapter 2. The Society and Its Environment

Artist's rendition of a tile mosaic composite of a man sitting, men with a camel, and geometric designs from the Pictured Wall, Lahore Fort, Punjab. Artwork represents seventeenth-century tile work of the Mughal period.

PAKISTANI SOCIETY IS ETHNICALLY DIVERSE yet overwhelmingly Muslim. It is largely rural yet beset by the problems of hyperurbanization. Since its independence in 1947, Pakistan has enjoyed a robust and expanding economy—the average per capita income in the early 1990s approached the transition line separating low-income from middle-income countries—but wealth is poorly distributed. A middle class is emerging, but a narrow stratum of elite families maintains extremely disproportionate control over the nation's wealth, and almost one-third of all Pakistanis live in poverty. It is a male-dominated society in which social development has lagged considerably behind economic change, as revealed by such critical indicators as sanitation, access to health care, and literacy, especially among females. Increasing population pressure on limited resources, together with this pattern of social and economic inequity, was causing increased disquietude within the society in the early 1990s.

Pakistan was created in 1947 as a homeland for Muslims in South Asia, and about 97 percent of Pakistanis are Muslim. The founders of Pakistan hoped that religion would provide a coherent focus for national identity, a focus that would supersede the country's considerable ethnic and linguistic differences. Although this aspiration has not been completely fulfilled, Islam has been a pervasive presence in Pakistani society, and debate continues about its appropriate role in national civic life. During the 1990s, Islamic discourse has been less prominent in political controversy, but the role that Islamic law should play in the country's affairs and governance remains an important issue.

There is immense regional diversity in Pakistan. Pakhtuns, Baloch, Punjabis, and Sindhis are all Muslim, yet they have diverse cultural traditions and speak different languages. Ethnic, regional, and—above all—family loyalties figure far more prominently for the average individual than do national loyalties. Punjabis, the largest ethnic group, predominate in the central government and the military. Baloch, Pakhtuns, and Sindhis find the Punjabi preponderance at odds with their own aspirations for provincial autonomy. Ethnic mixing within each province further complicates social and political relations.

Expectations had been raised by the return of democracy to Pakistan in 1988 after the death of Mohammad Zia ul-Haq, by the continued economic expansion in the early 1990s, and by some observable improvement in the volatile relations among ethnic groups that had so divided the country in years past. Also in the early 1990s, previously peripheralized social movements, particularly those concerning women and the environment, assumed a more central role in public life. As bilateral and multilateral development assistance has dwindled, nongovernmental organizations (NGOs) committed to economic and social development have emerged and have begun to take on important responsibilities (see Foreign Aid, ch. 3). Nonetheless, the problems that confront Pakistan pose a significant threat to its cohesion and future.

Sociologists speak of a loss of a sense of social contract among Pakistanis that has adversely affected the country's infrastructure: the economy, the education system, the government bureaucracy, and even the arts. As population pressure increases, the failure of the populace to develop a sense of publicly committed citizenship becomes more and more significant. The self-centeredness about which educator Ishtiaq Husain Qureshi complained soon after independence is increasingly noticeable in many areas of social life. Although many people once imagined that economic development would by itself improve the quality of life, few still believe this to be true.

Family or personal interest and status take precedence over public good in Pakistan. Thus traffic laws are often enforced solely according to a person's political clout rather than due process, and admission to school depends more upon connections or wealth than on ability. Salaries, as compared with bribes, are so inconsequential a privilege of employment that people often plead to be given appointments without pay.

Failure to develop civic-minded citizenship is also evident in public administration and imbalanced government spending. Military expenditures, for example, dwarf combined expenditures on health and education. Meanwhile, the bureaucracy—a legacy of the British colonial period—has not modernized sufficiently to incorporate new technologies and innovations despite efforts by the government staff colleges.

Although in the mid-1980s the World Bank (see Glossary) forecast the advancement of Pakistan to the ranks of middle-income countries, the nation had not quite achieved this transition in the early 1990s. Many blame this fact on Pakistan's failure to make significant progress in human development despite consistently high rates of economic growth. The annual population growth rate, which hovered between 3.1 and 3.3 percent in the early 1990s, threatens to precipitate increased social unrest as greater numbers of people compete for diminishing resources.

An anonymous Pakistani writer has said that three things symbolized Pakistan's material culture in the 1990s: videocassette recorders (for playing Hindi films), locally manufactured Japanese Suzuki cars, and Kalashnikov rifles. Although the majority of the people still reside in villages, they increasingly take social cues from cities. Videocassette tapes can be rented in many small villages, where residents also watch Cable News Network (CNN)—censored through Islamabad—on televisions that are as numerous as radios were in the 1970s. In many areas, tiny Suzuki automobiles have replaced the bicycles and motorcycles that were in great demand merely a decade earlier. Whereas urban violence was traditionally related to blood feuds, it has become more random and has escalated dramatically.

Physical Environment

Located in the northwestern part of the South Asian subcontinent, Pakistan became a state as a result of the partition of British India on August 14, 1947. Pakistan annexed Azad (Free) Kashmir after the Indo-Pakistani War of 1947–48. Initially, Pakistan also included the northeastern sector of the subcontinent, where Muslims are also in the majority. The East Wing and West Wing of Pakistan were, however, separated by 1,600 kilometers of hostile Indian territory. The country's East Wing, or East Pakistan, became the independent state of Bangladesh in December 1971 (see Yahya Khan and Bangladesh, ch. 1).

Boundaries

Pakistan occupies a position of great geostrategic importance, bordered by Iran on the west, Afghanistan on the northwest, China on the northeast, India on the east, and the Arabian Sea on the south (see fig. 1). The total land area is estimated at 796,095 square kilometers.

The boundary with Iran, some 800 kilometers in length, was first delimited by a British commission in 1893, separating Iran from what was then British Indian Balochistan. In 1957 Pakistan signed a frontier agreement with Iran, and since then the border between the two countries has not been a subject of serious dispute.

Pakistan's boundary with Afghanistan is about 2,250 kilometers long. In the north, it runs along the ridges of the Hindu Kush (meaning Hindu Killer) mountains and the Pamirs, where a narrow strip of Afghan territory called the Wakhan Corridor extends between Pakistan and Tajikistan. The Hindu Kush was traditionally regarded as the last northwestern outpost beyond which Hindus could not venture in safety. The boundary line with Afghanistan was drawn in 1893 by Sir Mortimer Durand, then foreign secretary in British India, and was acceded to by the amir of Afghanistan that same year. This boundary, called the Durand Line, was not in doubt when Pakistan became independent in 1947, although its legitimacy was in later years disputed periodically by the Afghan government as well as by Pakhtun tribes straddling the Pakistan-Afghanistan border. On the one hand, Afghanistan claimed that the Durand Line had been imposed by a stronger power upon a weaker one, and it favored the establishment of still another state to be called Pashtunistan or Pakhtunistan (see Independent Pakistan, ch. 1; Foreign Policy, ch. 4). On the other hand, Pakistan, as the legatee of the British in the region, insisted on the legality and permanence of the boundary. The Durand Line remained in effect in 1994.

In the northeastern tip of the country, Pakistan controls about 84,159 square kilometers of the former princely state of Jammu and Kashmir. This area, consisting of Azad Kashmir (11,639 square kilometers) and most of the Northern Areas (72,520 square kilometers), which includes Gilgit and Baltistan, is the most visually stunning of Pakistan. The Northern Areas has five of the world's seventeen highest mountains. It also has such extensive glaciers that it has sometimes been called the "third pole." The boundary line has been a matter of pivotal dispute between Pakistan and India since 1947, and the Siachen Glacier in northern Kashmir has been an important arena for fighting between the two sides since 1984, although far more soldiers have died of exposure to the cold than from any skirmishes in the conflict.

The Swat River valley in the North-West Frontier Province
Courtesy Sheila Ross

From the eastern end of the Afghanistan-Pakistan border, a boundary of about 520 kilometers runs generally southeast between China and Pakistan, ending near the Karakoram Pass. This line was determined from 1961 to 1965 in a series of agreements between China and Pakistan. By mutual agreement, a new boundary treaty is to be negotiated between China and Pakistan when the dispute over Kashmir is finally resolved between India and Pakistan.

The Pakistan-India cease-fire line runs from the Karakoram Pass west-southwest to a point about 130 kilometers northeast of Lahore. This line, about 770 kilometers long, was arranged with United Nations (UN) assistance at the end of the Indo-Pakistani War of 1947–48. The cease-fire line came into effect on January 1, 1949, after eighteen months of fighting and was last adjusted and agreed upon by the two countries in the Simla

Agreement of July 1972. Since then, it has been generally known as the Line of Control.

The Pakistan-India boundary continues irregularly southward for about 1,280 kilometers, following the line of the 1947 Radcliffe Award, named for Sir Cyril Radcliffe, the head of the British boundary commission on the partition of Punjab and Bengal in 1947. Although this boundary with India is not formally disputed, passions still run high on both sides of the border. Many Indians had expected the original boundary line to run farther to the west, thereby ceding Lahore to India; Pakistanis had expected the line to run much farther east, possibly granting them control of Delhi, the imperial capital of the Mughal Empire.

The southern borders are far less contentious than those in the north. The Thar Desert in the province of Sindh is separated from the desolate salt flats of the Rann of Kutch by a boundary that was first delineated in 1923–24. After partition, Pakistan contested this southeastern boundary. In early 1965, a series of border flare-ups and skirmishes occurred along the undemarcated territory of the Rann of Kutch. They were less dangerous and less widespread, however, than the conflict that erupted in Kashmir in the Indo-Pakistani War of August 1965. The Rann of Kutch dispute was ended by British mediation, and both sides accepted the award of the Indo-Pakistani Western Boundary Case Tribunal designated by the UN secretary general. The tribunal made its award on February 19, 1968, delimiting a line of 403 kilometers that was later demarcated by joint survey teams. Of its original claim of some 9,100 square kilometers, Pakistan was awarded only about 780 square kilometers. Beyond the western terminus of the tribunal's award, the final stretch of Pakistan's border with India is about eighty kilometers long, running west and southwest to an inlet of the Arabian Sea.

Topography and Drainage

Pakistan is divided into three major geographic areas: the northern highlands; the Indus River plain, with two major subdivisions corresponding roughly to the provinces of Punjab and Sindh; and the Balochistan Plateau. Some geographers designate additional major regions. For example, the mountain ranges along the western border with Afghanistan are sometimes described separately from the Balochistan Plateau, and on the eastern border with India, south of the Sutlej River, the Thar Desert may be considered separately from the Indus River plain. Nevertheless, the country may conveniently be visualized in general terms as divided in three by an imaginary line drawn eastward from the Khyber Pass and another drawn southwest from Islamabad down the middle of the country. Roughly, then, the northern highlands are north of the imaginary east-west line; the Balochistan Plateau is to the west of the imaginary southwest line; and the Indus River plain lies to the east of that line (see fig. 5).

The northern highlands include parts of the Hindu Kush, the Karakoram Range, and the Himalayas. This area includes such famous peaks as K2 (Mount Godwin Austen; 8,611 meters), the second highest peak in the world, and Nanga Parbat (8,126 meters), the twelfth highest. More than one-half of the summits are over 4,500 meters, and more than fifty peaks reach above 6,500 meters. Travel through the area is difficult and dangerous, although the government is attempting to develop certain areas into tourist and trekking sites. Because of their rugged topography and the rigors of the climate, the northern highlands and the Himalayas to the east have been formidable barriers to movement into Pakistan throughout history.

South of the northern highlands and west of the Indus River plain are the Safed Koh Range along the Afghanistan border and the Sulaiman Range and Kirthar Range, which define the western extent of the province of Sindh and reach almost to the southern coast. The lower reaches are far more arid than those in the north, and they branch into ranges that run generally to the southwest across the province of Balochistan. North-south valleys in Balochistan and Sindh have restricted the migration of peoples along the Makran coast on the Arabian Sea east toward the plains.

Several large passes cut through the ranges along the border with Afghanistan. Among them are the Khojak Pass, about eighty kilometers northwest of Quetta in Balochistan; the Khyber Pass, forty kilometers west of Peshawar and leading to Kabul; and the Baroghil Pass in the far north, providing access to the Wakhan Corridor.

Less than one-fifth of Pakistan's land area has the potential for intensive agricultural use. Nearly all of the arable land is actively cultivated, but outputs are low by world standards (see Agriculture, ch. 3). Cultivation is sparse in the northern mountains, the southern deserts, and the western plateaus, but the

Figure 5. Topography and Drainage

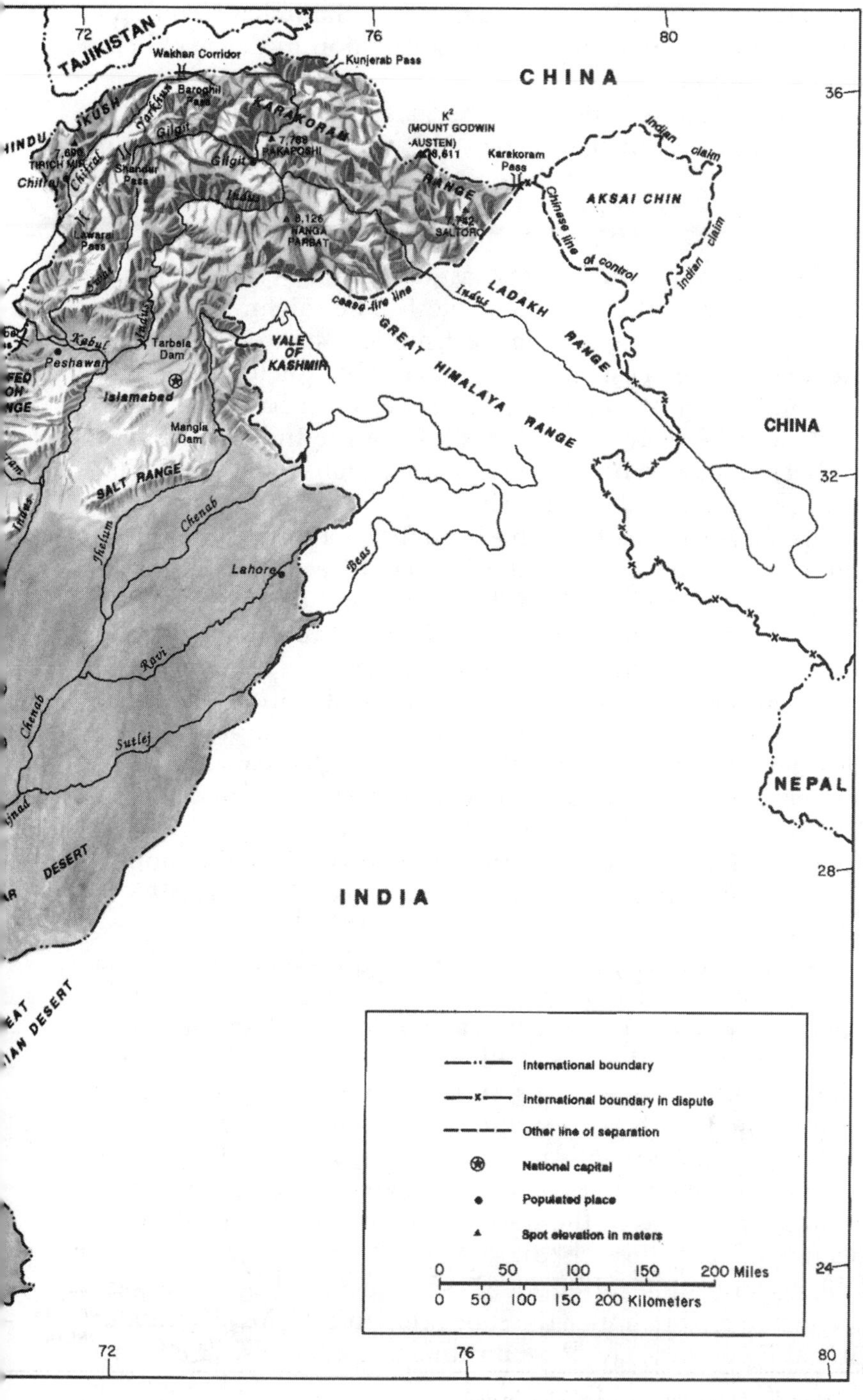
TAJIKISTAN
Wakhan Corridor
Kunjerab Pass
CHINA
Baroghil Pass
KARAKORAM
RANGE
K2 (MOUNT GODWIN AUSTEN)
Karakoram Pass
Indian claim
AKSAI CHIN
Chinese line of control
Gilgit
7,788 RAKAPOSHI
Shandur Pass
Chitral
Lawarai Pass
Swat
Indus
8,126 NANGA PARBAT
7,742 SALTORO
cease-fire line
LADAKH RANGE
GREAT HIMALAYA RANGE
Kabul
Peshawar
Tarbela Dam
VALE OF KASHMIR
Islamabad
Mangla Dam
SALT RANGE
CHINA
Jhelum
Chenab
Lahore
Beas
Ravi
Sutlej
NEPAL
DESERT
INDIA
International boundary
International boundary in dispute
Other line of separation
National capital
Populated place
Spot elevation in meters
0 50 100 150 200 Miles
0 50 100 150 200 Kilometers
72
76
80
36
32
28
24

Indus River basin in Punjab and northern Sindh has fertile soil that enables Pakistan to feed its population under usual climatic conditions.

The name *Indus* comes from the Sanskrit word *sindhu,* meaning ocean, from which also come the words *Sindh, Hindu,* and *India.* The Indus, one of the great rivers of the world, rises in southwestern Tibet only about 160 kilometers west of the source of the Sutlej River, which joins the Indus in Punjab, and the Brahmaputra, which runs eastward before turning southwest and flowing through Bangladesh. The catchment area of the Indus is estimated at almost 1 million square kilometers, and all of Pakistan's major rivers—the Kabul, Jhelum, Chenab, Ravi, and Sutlej—flow into it. The Indus River basin is a large, fertile alluvial plain formed by silt from the Indus. This area has been inhabited by agricultural civilizations for at least 5,000 years (see Early Civilizations, ch. 1).

The upper Indus River basin includes Punjab; the lower Indus River basin begins at the Panjnad River (the confluence of the eastern tributaries of the Indus) and extends south to the coast. In Punjab (meaning the "land of five waters") are the Indus, Jhelum, Chenab, Ravi, and Sutlej rivers. The Sutlej, however, is mostly on the Indian side of the border. In the southern part of the province of Punjab, the British attempted to harness the irrigation power of the water over 100 years ago when they established what came to be known as the canal colonies. The irrigation project, which facilitated the emergence of intensive cultivation despite arid conditions, resulted in important social and political transformations (see The British Raj, ch. 1).

Pakistan has two great river dams: the Tarbela Dam on the Indus, near the early Buddhist site at Taxila, and the Mangla Dam on the Jhelum, where Punjab borders Azad Kashmir. The Warsak Dam on the Kabul River near Peshawar is smaller. These dams, along with a series of headworks and barrages built by the British and expanded since independence, are of vital importance to the national economy and played an important role in calming the raging floodwaters of 1992, which devastated large areas in the northern highlands and the Punjab plains (see Irrigation, ch. 3).

Pakistan is subject to frequent seismic disturbances because the tectonic plate under the subcontinent hits the plate under Asia as it continues to move northward and to push the Himalayas ever higher. The region surrounding Quetta in Balochistan is highly prone to earthquakes. A severe quake in 1931 was followed by one of more destructive force in 1935. The small city of Quetta was almost completely destroyed, and the adjacent military cantonment was heavily damaged. At least 20,000 people were killed. Tremors continue in the vicinity of Quetta; the most recent major quake occurred in January 1991. Far fewer people were killed in the 1991 quake than died in 1935, although entire villages in the North-West Frontier Province were destroyed. A major earthquake centered in the North-West Frontier Province's Kohistan District in 1965 also caused heavy damage.

Climate

Pakistan lies in the temperate zone. The climate is generally arid, characterized by hot summers and cool or cold winters, and wide variations between extremes of temperature at given locations. There is little rainfall. These generalizations should not, however, obscure the distinct differences existing among particular locations. For example, the coastal area along the Arabian Sea is usually warm, whereas the frozen snow-covered ridges of the Karakoram Range and of other mountains of the far north are so cold year round that they are only accessible by world-class climbers for a few weeks in May and June of each year.

Pakistan has four seasons: a cool, dry winter from December through February; a hot, dry spring from March through May; the summer rainy season, or southwest monsoon period, from June through September; and the retreating monsoon period of October and November. The onset and duration of these seasons vary somewhat according to location.

The climate in the capital city of Islamabad varies from an average daily low of 2°C in January to an average daily high of 40°C in June. Half of the annual rainfall occurs in July and August, averaging about 255 millimeters in each of those two months. The remainder of the year has significantly less rain, amounting to about fifty millimeters per month. Hailstorms are common in the spring.

Pakistan's largest city, Karachi, which is also the country's industrial center, is more humid than Islamabad but gets less rain. Only July and August average more than twenty-five millimeters of rain in the Karachi area; the remaining months are exceedingly dry. The temperature is also more uniform in Karachi than in Islamabad, ranging from an average daily low of 13°C during winter evenings to an average daily high of 34°C on summer days. Although the summer temperatures do not get as high as those in Punjab, the high humidity causes the residents a great deal of discomfort.

Most areas in Punjab experience fairly cool winters, often accompanied by rain. Woolen shawls are worn by women and men for warmth because few homes are heated. By mid-February, the temperature begins to rise; springtime weather continues until mid-April, when the summer heat sets in. The onset of the southwest monsoon is anticipated to reach Punjab by May, but since the early 1970s, the weather pattern has been irregular. The spring monsoon has either skipped over the area or has caused it to rain so hard that floods have resulted. June and July are oppressively hot. Although official estimates rarely place the temperature above 46°C, newspaper sources claim that it reaches 51°C and regularly carry reports about people who have succumbed to the heat. Heat records were broken in Multan in June 1993, when the mercury was reported to have risen to 54°C. In August the oppressive heat is punctuated by the rainy season, referred to as *barsat*, which brings relief in its wake. The hardest part of the summer is then over, but cooler weather does not come until late October.

Pollution and Environmental Issues

Little attention was paid to pollution and environmental issues in Pakistan until the early 1990s. Related concerns, such as sanitation and potable water, received earlier scrutiny. In 1987 only about 6 percent of rural residents and 51 percent of urban residents had access to sanitary facilities; in 1990 a total of 97.6 million Pakistanis, or approximately 80 percent of the population, had no access to flush toilets. Greater success has been achieved in bringing potable water within reach of the people; nearly half the population enjoyed such access by 1990. However, researchers at the Pakistan Medical Research Council, recognizing that a large proportion of diseases in Pakistan are caused by the consumption of polluted water, have been questioning the "safe" classification in use in the 1990s. Even the 38 percent of the population that receives its water through pipelines runs the risk of consuming seriously contaminated water, although the problem varies by area. In Punjab, for example, as much as 90 percent of drinking water comes from groundwater, as compared with only 9 percent in Sindh.

The central government's Perspective Plan (1988–2003) and previous five-year plans do not mention sustainable development strategies (see Development Planning, ch. 3). Further, there have been no overarching policies focused on sustainable development and conservation. The state has focused on achieving self-sufficiency in food production, meeting energy demands, and containing the high rate of population growth, not on curtailing pollution or other environmental hazards.

In 1992 Pakistan's *National Conservation Strategy Report* attempted to redress the previous inattention to the nation's mounting environmental problem. Drawing on the expertise of more than 3,000 people from a wide array of political affiliations, the government produced a document outlining the current state of environmental health, its sustainable goals, and viable program options for the future (see National Conservation Goals, this ch.).

Of special concern to environmentalists is the diminishing forest cover in watershed regions of the northern highlands, which has only recently come under close scrutiny. Forest areas have been thoughtlessly denuded. Deforestation, which occurred at an annual rate of 0.4 percent in 1989–90, has contributed directly to the severity of the flooding problem faced by the nation in the early 1990s.

As industry has expanded, factories have emitted more and more toxic effluents into the air and water. The number of textile- and food-processing mills in rural Punjab has grown greatly since the mid-1970s, resulting in pollution of its rivers and irrigation canals. Groundwater quality throughout the country has also suffered from rapidly increasing use of pesticides and fertilizers aimed at promoting more intensive cropping and facilitating self-sufficiency in food production.

The *National Conservation Strategy Report* has documented how solid and liquid excreta are the major source of water pollution in the country and the cause of widespread waterborne diseases. Because only just over half of urban residents have access to sanitation, the remaining urban excreta are deposited on roadsides, into waterways, or incorporated into solid waste. Additionally, only three major sewage treatment plants exist in the country; two of them operate intermittently. Much of the untreated sewage goes into irrigation systems, where the wastewater is reused, and into streams and rivers, which become sewage carriers at low-flow periods. Consequently, the vegetables grown from such wastewater have serious bacteriological contamination. Gastroenteritis, widely considered in medical circles to be the leading cause of death in Pakistan, is transmitted through waterborne pollutants (see Health and Welfare, this ch.).

Low-lying land is generally used for solid waste disposal, without the benefit of sanitary landfill methods. The National Conservation Strategy has raised concerns about industrial toxic wastes also being dumped in municipal disposal areas without any record of their location, quantity, or toxic composition. Another important issue is the contamination of shallow groundwater near urban industries that discharge wastes directly into the ground.

Water in Karachi is so contaminated that almost all residents boil it before consumption. Because sewerage and water lines have been laid side by side in most parts of the city, leakage is the main cause of contamination. High levels of lead also have been found in water in Islamabad and Rawalpindi.

Air pollution has also become a major problem in most cities. There are no controls on vehicular emissions, which account for 90 percent of pollutants. The *National Conservation Strategy Report* claims that the average Pakistani vehicle emits twenty-five times as much carbon monoxide, twenty times as many hydrocarbons, and more than three and one-half times as much nitrous oxide in grams per kilometer as the average vehicle in the United States.

Another major source of pollution, not mentioned in the *National Conservation Strategy Report*, is noise. The hyperurbanization experienced by Pakistan since the 1960s has resulted in loose controls for heavy equipment operation in densely populated areas, as well as in crowded streets filled with buses, trucks, automobiles, and motorcycles, which often honk at each other and at the horse-drawn tongas (used for transporting people) and the horse-drawn *rehras* (used for transporting goods).

National Conservation Goals

The *National Conservation Strategy Report* has three explicit objectives: conservation of natural resources, promotion of sustainable development, and improvement of efficiency in the use and management of resources. It sees itself as a "call for action" addressed to central and provincial governments, businesses, nongovernmental organizations (NGOs), local communities, and individuals. The sustainable development of

Pakistan is viewed as a multigenerational enterprise. In seeking to transform attitudes and practices, the National Conservation Strategy recognizes that two key changes in values are needed: the restoration of the conservation ethic derived from Islamic moral values, called *qanaat*, and the revival of community spirit and responsibility, *haquq-ul-abad*.

The *National Conservation Strategy Report* recommends fourteen program areas for priority implementation: maintaining soils in croplands, increasing efficiency of irrigation, protecting watersheds, supporting forestry and plantations, restoring rangelands and improving livestock, protecting water bodies and sustaining fisheries, conserving biodiversity, increasing energy efficiency, developing and deploying renewable resources, preventing or decreasing pollution, managing urban wastes, supporting institutions to manage common resources, integrating population and environmental programs, and preserving the cultural heritage. It identifies sixty-eight specific programs in these areas, each with a long-term goal and expected outputs and physical investments required within ten years. Special attention has been paid to the potential roles of environmental NGOs, women's organizations, and international NGOs in working with the government in its conservation efforts. Recommendations from the *National Conservation Strategy Report* are incorporated in the Eighth Five-Year Plan (1993–98).

Population

In early 1994, the population of Pakistan was estimated to be 126 million, making it the ninth most populous country in the world. Its land area, however, ranks thirty-second among nations. Thus Pakistan has about 2 percent of the world's population living on less than 0.7 percent of the world's land. The population growth rate is among the world's highest, officially estimated at 3.1 percent per year, but privately thought to be closer to 3.3 percent per year by many planners involved in population programs. Pakistan's population is expected to reach 150 million by 2000 and to account for 4 percent of the world's population growth between 1994 and 2004. Pakistan's population is expected to double between 1994 and 2022.

These figures are estimates, however, because ethnic unrest led the government to postpone its decennial census in 1991. The government felt that tensions among Punjabis, Sindhis, *muhajirs* (immigrants or descendants of immigrants from

India), and Pakhtuns and between the Sunni Muslim majority and religious minorities were such that taking the census might provoke violent reactions from groups who felt they had been undercounted. The 1991 census had still not been carried out as of early 1994. The 1981 census enumerated 84.2 million persons (see table 2, Appendix).

Population Distribution and Density

Pakistan's people are not evenly distributed throughout the country. There is an average of 146 persons per square kilometer, but the density varies dramatically, ranging from scarcely populated arid areas, especially in Balochistan, to some of the highest urban densities in the world in Karachi and Lahore.

About 68 percent of the population lived in rural areas in 1994, a decrease of 7 percent since 1970. In contrast, the number of people living in urban areas has risen substantially, resulting in an urban growth rate of 4.6 percent between 1980 and 1991.

More than half of Pakistan's population is below the age of fifteen; nearly a third is below the age of nine (see fig. 6). For cultural reasons, enumerating the precise number of females has been difficult—and estimates of the percentage of females in the population range from 47.5 percent in the 1981 census to 48.3 percent in the 1987–88 Labour Force Survey. Pakistan is one of the few countries in the world with an inverse sex ratio: official sources claim there are 111 men for every 100 women. The discrepancy is particularly obvious among people over fifty: men in that age-group account for 7.1 percent of the country's total population and women for less than 5 percent. This figure reflects the secondary status of females in Pakistani society, especially their lack of access to quality medical care.

Population Planning Policies and Problems

Pakistan's extremely high rate of population growth is caused by a falling death rate combined with a continuing high birth rate. In 1950 the mortality rate was twenty-seven per 1,000 population; by 1990 the rate had dropped to twelve (estimated) per 1,000. Yet throughout this period, the birth rate was forty-four per 1,000 population. On average, in 1990 each family had 6.2 children, and only 11 percent of couples were regularly practicing contraception.

In 1952 the Family Planning Association of Pakistan, an NGO, initiated efforts to contain population growth. Three years later, the government began to fund the association and noted the need to reduce population growth in its First Five-Year Plan (1955–60). The government soon combined its population planning efforts in hospitals and clinics into a single program. Thus population planning was a dual effort led by the Family Planning Association and the public sector.

In the mid-1960s, the Ministry of Health initiated a program in which intrauterine devices (IUDs) were promoted. Payments were offered to hospitals and clinics as incentives, and midwives were trained to treat patients. The government was able to attract funding from many international donors, but the program lost support because the targets were overly ambitious and because doctors and clinics allegedly overreported their services to claim incentive payments.

The population planning program was suspended and substantively reorganized after the fall of Mohammad Ayub Khan's government in 1969. In late December 1971, the population was estimated at 65.2 million. In an attempt to control the population problem, the government introduced several new programs. First, the Continuous Motivation System Programme, which employed young urban women to visit rural areas, was initiated. In 1975 the Inundation Programme was added. Based on the premise that greater availability would increase use, shopkeepers throughout the country stocked birth control pills and condoms. Both programs failed, however. The unmarried urban women had little understanding of the lives of the rural women they were to motivate, and shopkeepers kept the contraceptives out of sight because it was considered tasteless to display them in an obvious way.

Following Zia ul-Haq's coup d'état in 1977, government population planning efforts were almost halted. In 1980 the Population Division, formerly under the direction of a minister of state, was renamed the Population Welfare Division and transferred to the Ministry of Planning and Economic Development. This agency was charged with the delivery of both family planning services and maternal and child health care. This reorganized structure corresponded with the new population planning strategy, which was based on a multifaceted community-based "cafeteria" approach, in cooperation with Family Welfare Centres (essentially clinics) and Reproductive Health Centres (mostly engaged in sterilizations). Community participation had finally became a cornerstone of the government's

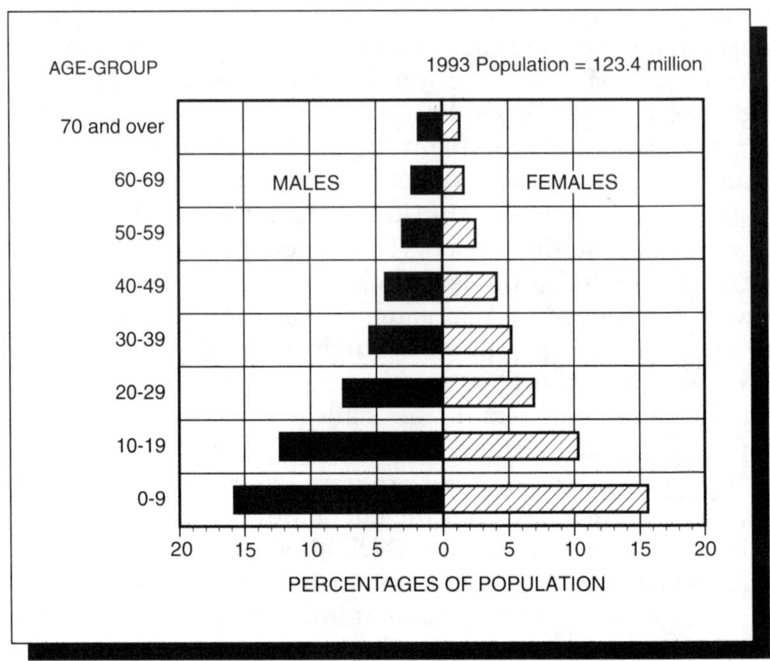

Source: Based on information from PC Globe 5.0: The New World Order, 1992, Tempe, Arizona, 1992.

Figure 6. Population by Age and Gender, 1993

policy, and it was hoped that contraceptive use would rise dramatically. The population by 1980 had exceeded 84 million.

In preparing the Sixth Five-Year Plan (1983–88), the government projected a national population of 147 million in the year 2000 if the growth rate were to remain at 2.8 percent per year, and of 134 million if the rate were to decline to the desired 2.1 percent per year by then. By the Seventh Five-Year Plan (1988–93) period, the multipronged approach initiated in the 1980s had increased international donor assistance and had begun to enlist local NGOs. Efforts to improve maternal and child health were coupled with education campaigns. Because of local mores concerning modesty, the government avoided explicit reference to contraceptive devices and instead focused its public education efforts on encouraging couples to limit their family size to two children.

The key to controlling population growth, according to activists in the women's movement, lies in raising the socioeconomic status of women. Until a woman's status is determined by something other than her reproductive capabilities, and especially by the number of sons she bears, severe impediments to lowering population growth rates will persist.

Migration and Growth of Major Cities

Pakistan's cities are expanding much faster than the overall population. At independence in 1947, many refugees from India settled in urban areas. In the 1950s, more than one-half of the residents of several cities in Sindh and Punjab were *muhajirs*. Some refugee colonies were eventually recognized as cities in their own right.

Between 1951 and 1981, the urban population quadrupled. The annual urban growth rate during the 1950s and 1960s was more than 5 percent. This figure dropped slightly in the 1970s to 4.4 percent. Between 1980 and early 1994, it averaged about 4.6 percent. By early 1994, about 32 percent of all Pakistanis lived in urban areas, with 13 percent of the total population living in three cities, each of which had over 1 million inhabitants—Karachi, Lahore, and Faisalabad.

The key reason for migration to urban areas has been the limited opportunity for economic advancement and mobility in rural areas. The economic and political control that local landlords exercise in much of the countryside has led to this situation.

The urban migrant is almost invariably a male. He retains his ties with his village, and his rights there are acknowledged long after his departure. At first, migration is frequently seen as a temporary expedient, a way to purchase land or pay off a debt. Typically, the migrant sends part of his earnings to the family he left behind and returns to the village to work at peak agricultural seasons. Even married migrants usually leave their families in the village when they first migrate. The decision to bring a wife and children to the city is thus a milestone in the migration process.

As cities have grown, they have engulfed surrounding villages, bringing agriculturists into the urban population. Many of these farmers commute to urban jobs from their original homes. The focus of these individuals' lives remains their family and fellow villagers. Similarly, migrants from rural areas who have moved to the cities stay in close touch with relatives and friends who have also moved, so their loyalties reflect earlier patterns. The Pakistani city tends to recreate the close ties of the rural community.

Pakistani cities are diverse in nature. The urban topology reflects the varied political history within the region. Some cities dating from the medieval era, such as Lahore and Multan, served as capitals of kingdoms or small principalities, or they were fortified border towns prior to colonial rule. Other precolonial cities, such as Peshawar, were trading centers located at strategic points along the caravan route. Some cities in Sindh and Punjab centered on cottage industries, and their trade rivaled the premier European cities of the eighteenth and early nineteenth centuries.

Under colonial rule, many of the older administrative cities declined. Where the British located a trading post (factory) near an existing administrative center, the city was typically divided into old and new, or European, sections. New towns and cities also emerged, especially in the expanding canal colonies; Faisalabad (formerly Lyallpur) is such a city. The town of Karachi expanded rapidly to become a center of rail and sea transport as a consequence of British rule and as a consequence of the opening of massive irrigation projects and the increase in agricultural exports. Pakistan's two largest cities, Karachi and Lahore, illustrate how differing regional and sociocultural histories have shaped the variations among Pakistan's cities.

Karachi absorbed tens of thousands of *muhajirs* following independence in 1947, grew nearly two and one-half times from 1941 to 1951, and nearly doubled again in the following decade. Karachi is by far Pakistan's largest city and is still rapidly growing. In the early 1990s, the population exceeded 10 million.

Karachi's rapid growth has been directly related to the overall economic growth in the country. The partition of British India into the independent states of Pakistan and India prompted an influx into Pakistan of Muslim merchants from various parts of the new, Hindu-majority India. These merchants, whom sociologist Hamza Alavi refers to as *salariat,* had money to invest and received unusual encouragement from the government, which wanted to promote the growth of the new state.

Karachi at first developed in isolation. Relatively few people from outlying areas were engaged in running its factories, and the city had little impact on Pakistan's cultural fabric. But when the economies of southern Sindh and parts of Punjab began to expand, large numbers of migrants flooded the city in search of work (generally low-paying jobs), and Karachi became the hub of the nation's commerce. The city, however, also has serious problems. It has the poorest slums in the country, and it suffers from serious interethnic conflict as a consequence of the influx of many competing groups. It was the site of considerable violence in the 1980s as *muhajirs* solidified their local power base vis-à-vis the Pakhtuns and native Sindhis (see Subversion and Civil Unrest, ch. 5).

Lahore, Pakistan's second largest city, contrasts markedly with Karachi. With just under half the population of Karachi, it is regarded as the cultural nucleus of Punjab. Residents of Lahore take special pride in their city's physical beauty, especially in its Mughal architecture, which includes the Badshahi Mosque, Shalimar Gardens, Lahore Fort, and the Mughal emperor Jahangir's tomb. In the earliest extant historical reference to the city, in A.D. 630 the Chinese traveler Xuan Zang described it as a large Brahmanical city. A center of learning by the twelfth century, Lahore reached its peak in the sixteenth century, when it became the quintessential Mughal city—the "grand resort of people of all nations and a center of extensive commerce."

The economy and the population expanded greatly in the 1980s in a number of other cities. The most important of these are Faisalabad, Gujranwala, Wazirabad, and Sialkot in Punjab; Hyderabad in Sindh; and Peshawar and Mardan in the North-West Frontier Province.

The nation's capital was situated in Karachi at independence. General Mohammad Ayub Khan, who assumed power in 1958, aspired, however, to build a new capital that would be better protected from possible attack by India and would reflect the greatness of the new country. In 1959 Ayub Khan decided to move the capital to the shadow of the Margalla Hills near Pakistan's third largest city, Rawalpindi. The move was completed in 1963, and the new capital was named Islamabad (abode of Islam). The population of Islamabad continues to increase rapidly, and the official 1991 estimate of just over 200,000 has probably been much exceeded.

Impact of Migration to the Persian Gulf Countries

Pakistan had a severe balance of payments deficit in the 1970s. To deal with this deficit, as well as to strengthen ties with the Islamic states in the Middle East, the government of Zulfiqar Ali Bhutto encouraged both skilled and unskilled men to work in the Persian Gulf countries. The government set up a program under the Ministry of Labour, Manpower, and Overseas Pakistanis to regulate this migration and also seconded military troops to many of the Gulf states.

By the mid-1980s, when this temporary migration was at its height, there were estimated to be more than 2 million Pakistanis in the Persian Gulf states remitting more than US$3 billion every year. At the peak, the remittances accounted for almost half of the country's foreign-exchange earnings. By 1990 new employment opportunities were decreasing, and the 1990–91 Persian Gulf War forced many workers to return quickly to Pakistan. Workers have only slowly returned to the Gulf since the war ended.

The majority of the emigrants are working-class men, who travel alone, leaving their wives and children behind with their extended families in Pakistan. These men are willing to sacrifice years with their families for what they see as their only chance to escape poverty in a society with limited upward mobility. A study in the old quarter (the inner walled city) of Lahore in 1987 suggested that half of all working-class families had at least one close relative working in the Gulf. Families generally use the remittances for consumer goods, rather than investing in industry. The wage earner typically returns after five to ten years to live at home.

Although this migration has had little effect on Pakistan demographically, it has affected its social fabric. While a man is away from his family, his wife often assumes responsibility for many day-to-day business transactions that are considered the province of men in this traditional male-dominated society. Thus for the women involved, there is a significant change in social role. Among the men, psychologists have identified a syndrome referred to as "*Dubai chalo*" ("let's go to Dubai"). This syndrome, which manifests itself as disorientation, appears to result from social isolation, culture shock, harsh working conditions, and the sudden acquisition of relative wealth. Men often feel isolated and guilty for leaving their families, and the resultant sociopsychological stress can be considerable.

Repercussions of the War in Afghanistan

The presence of large numbers Afghan refugees has had a weighty impact on the demographics of Pakistan. After the Soviet Union invaded Afghanistan in December 1979, refugees began streaming over the borders into Pakistan. By 1990

Street scene outside Lohari Gate, Lahore
Various forms of transportation as found in Lahore—tonga, rickshaw, automobiles, and carts
Courtesy Anita M. Weiss

approximately 3.2 million refugees had settled there, a decrease of about 90,000 from 1989. Previously uninhabited areas of the North-West Frontier Province and Balochistan had been settled by refugees during the 1980s. The United Nations High Commissioner for Refugees (UNHCR) estimated that in 1990 there were 345 Afghan refugee villages. Of these, 68.5 percent were in the North-West Frontier Province, 26.0 percent in Balochistan, and 5.5 percent in Punjab. Each village housed an average of 10,000 people, and women and children accounted for 75 percent of the refugee population.

The influx of refugees has had profound social consequences, and the refugee population in desert areas has placed a heavy burden on the environment. Initially, Pakistanis wanted to help their neighbors in a time of need, but difficulties slowly led many to think that their friendship had gone far enough. Among the problems were inflation, a dearth of low-paying jobs because these were taken by refugees, and a proliferation of weapons, especially in urban areas. The escalation of animosity between refugees and Pakistanis, particularly in Punjab, caused the government to restrict the refugees' free movement in the country in the mid-1980s.

To assist Pakistan in preventing conflict by keeping the refugees separate from the local population, the UNHCR placed restrictions on disbursements of food and other goods in its refugee camps in the North-West Frontier Province and in Balochistan. Since the end of the Soviet occupation of Afghanistan in February 1989, the UNHCR, the Pakistan government, and an array of NGOs have encouraged the refugees to return home, but until internecine fighting in Afghanistan stops, many will elect to remain in Pakistan. In early 1994, the number of Afghan refugees still residing in Pakistan was estimated at 1.4 million, according to Amnesty International.

Social Structure

Traditional Kinship Patterns

Pakistani social life revolves around family and kin. Even among members of the most Westernized elite, family retains its overarching significance. The family is the basis of social organization, providing its members with both identity and protection. Rarely does an individual live apart from relatives; even male urban migrants usually live with relatives or friends of kin. Children live with their parents until marriage, and sons often stay with their parents after marriage, forming a joint family.

The household is the primary kinship unit. In its ideal, or extended, form, it includes a married couple, their sons, their sons' wives and children, and unmarried offspring. Sons establish separate households upon their father's death. Whether or not an extended household endures depends on the preferences of the individuals involved. Quarrels and divisiveness, particularly among the women (mother-in-law and daughters-in-law), can lead to the premature dissolution of a joint household.

Descent is reckoned patrilineally, so only those related through male ancestors are considered relatives. The *biradari*, or group of male kin (the patrilineage), plays a significant role in social relations. Its members neither hold movable property in common nor share earnings, but the honor or shame of individual members affects the general standing of the *biradari* within the community. A common proverb expresses this view: "One does not share the bread, but one shares the shame."

In theory, members of a *biradari* are coresidents of a single village. In some areas, however, land fragmentation and generations of out-migration have led to the dispersal of many members of the *biradari* among various villages, regions, and cities. Patrilineal kin continue to maintain ties with their natal village and enjoy the legal right of first refusal in any *biradari* land sale.

Members of a *biradari* celebrate the major life events together. Patrilineal kin are expected to contribute food and to help with guests in the ceremonies accompanying birth, marriage, death, and major religious holidays. The *biradari* has traditionally served as a combined mutual aid society and welfare agency, arranging loans to members, assisting in finding employment, and contributing to the dowries of poorer families.

There is considerable pressure for patrilineal kin to maintain good relations with one another. *Biradari* members who quarrel will try to resolve their differences before major social occasions so that the patrilineage can present a united front to the village. People with sons and daughters of marriageable age keenly feel the necessity to maintain good relations because a person whose family is at odds with his or her *biradari* is considered a poor marriage prospect.

Although descent is reckoned patrilineally, women maintain relations with their natal families throughout life. The degree of involvement with maternal kin varies among ethnic groups and among regions of the country. The tie between brother and sister is typically strong and affectionate; a woman looks to her brothers for support in case of divorce or widowhood early in her marriage. In those regions where families maintain considerable contact with maternal kin, children, even though they are members of their father's patrilineage, are indulged by their mother's kin. Just as a family's relations with its *biradari* are considered in evaluating a potential spouse, so too are the mother's kin.

Marriage is a means of allying two extended families; romantic attachments have little role to play. The husband and wife are primarily representatives of their respective families in a contractual arrangement, which is typically negotiated between two male heads of household. It is fundamentally the parents' responsibility to arrange marriages for their children, but older siblings may be actively involved if the parents die early or if they have been particularly successful in business or politics. The terms are worked out in detail and are noted, by law, at the local marriage registry.

Marriage is a process of acquiring new relatives or reinforcing the ties one has with others. To participate fully in society, a person must be married and have children, preferably sons. Social ties are cemented by giving away daughters in marriage and receiving daughters-in-law. Marriage with one's father's brother's child is preferred, in part because property exchanged at marriage then stays within the patrilineage. The relationship between in-laws extends beyond the couple and well past the marriage event. Families related by marriage exchange gifts on important occasions in each others' lives. If a marriage is successful, it will be followed by others between the two families. The links thus formed persist and are reinforced through the generations. The pattern of continued intermarriage coupled with the occasional marriage of nonrelatives creates a convoluted web of interlocking ties of descent and marriage.

A woman's life is difficult during the early years of marriage. A young bride has very little status in her husband's household; she is subservient to her mother-in-law and must negotiate relations with her sisters-in-law. Her situation is made easier if she has married a cousin and her mother-in-law is also her aunt. The proper performance of all the elaborate marriage ceremonies and the accompanying exchange of gifts also serve to enhance the new bride's status. Likewise, a rich dowry serves as a trousseau; the household goods, clothing, jewelry, and furniture included remain the property of the bride after she has married.

Marriage also involves a dower, called *haq mehr* (see Glossary), established under Islamic law, the sharia (see Glossary). Although some families set a symbolic *haq mehr* of Rs32 (for value of the rupee—see Glossary) in accordance with the traditions of the Prophet Muhammad, others may demand hundreds of thousands of rupees.

A wife gains status and power as she bears sons. Sons will bring wives for her to supervise and provide for her in her old age. Daughters are a liability, to be given away in an expensive marriage with their virginity intact. Therefore, mothers favor their sons. In later life, the relationship between a mother and her son remains intimate, in all likelihood with the mother retaining far more influence over her son than his wife.

Linguistic and Ethnic Groups

Language is an important marker of ethnic identity. Among the more than twenty spoken languages in Pakistan, the most common ones—Punjabi, Sindhi, and Urdu—as well as Pakhtu or Pashto, Balochi, and others, belong to the Indo-Aryan branch of the Indo-European language family. Additional languages, such as Shina and other northern-area languages, are related to the Dardic branch of Indo-European and the early Dravidian language family. Brahui is one such language; it is spoken by a group in Balochistan.

The Indo-Aryan vernaculars stretch across the northern half of the Indian subcontinent in a vast range of related local dialects that change slightly from one village to the next. Residents of fairly distant communities typically cannot understand one another. Superimposed on this continuum are several types of more standardized literary or commercial languages. Although based on the vernaculars of their representative regions, these standardized languages are nonetheless distinct.

Nearly half of all Pakistanis (48 percent) speak Punjabi. The next most commonly spoken language is Sindhi (12 percent), followed by the Punjabi variant Siraiki (10 percent), Pakhtu or Pashto (8 percent), Urdu (8 percent), Balochi (3 percent), Hindko (2 percent), and Brahui (1 percent). Native speakers of other languages, including English, Burushaski, and various other tongues, account for 8 percent.

Although Urdu is the official national language, it is spoken as a native tongue by only 8 percent of the population. People who speak Urdu as their native language generally identify themselves as *muhajirs.* A large number of people from educated backgrounds (and those who aspire to upward mobility) speak Urdu, as opposed to their natal languages, in their homes, usually to help their children master it. The Punjabi elite in urban centers, for example, favor Urdu, although villagers in the Punjab speak a plethora of similar dialects.

The Urdu language originated during the Mughal period (1526–1858). It literally means "a camp language," for it was spoken by the imperial Mughal troops from Central Asia as they mixed with speakers of local dialects of northern India. Increasingly, elements of Persian, the official language of the Mughal administration, were incorporated until Urdu attained its stylized, literary form in the seventeenth and eighteenth centuries. The Devanagari script (used for Sanskrit and contemporary Hindi) was never adopted; instead, Urdu has always been written using the Persian script. These two literary languages, Urdu and Hindi, can be said to be dialects of colloquial Hindustani, the lingua franca of modern India before partition.

South Asian Muslims have long felt that Urdu symbolizes their shared identity. It has served as a link among educated Muslims and was stressed in the Pakistan independence movement. Christopher Schackle writes that "Urdu was the main literary vehicle of the Muslim elite of India." At independence, the Muslim League (as the All-India Muslim League was usually referred to) promoted Urdu as the national language to help the new Pakistani state develop an identity, even though few people actually spoke it. However, because many of the elite were fluent in English, English became the de facto national language. The push to elevate Urdu was unpopular in East Pakistan, where most of the population speaks Bengali (officially referred to as Bangla in Bangladesh since 1971) and identifies with its literary heritage. Language riots in Dhaka occurred in the early 1950s, leading to the elevation of Bengali as a second national language with Urdu until the secession of East Pakistan in 1971; when Bangladesh became independent, Bangla was designated the official language.

Instruction in the best schools continued to be in English until the early 1980s. Mastery of English was highly desirable because it facilitated admission to good universities in Britain, the United States, and Australia. Then, in a move to promote nationalism, the government of Zia ul-Haq declared Urdu to be the medium of instruction in government schools. Urdu was aggressively promoted via television, radio, and the education system. Private schools in urban centers (attended by children of the elite) were allowed to retain English, while smaller rural schools could continue to teach in the provincial languages (see Education, this ch.).

Punjabi, spoken by nearly half of the population, is an old, literary language whose early writings consist chiefly of folk tales and romances, the most famous being the eighteenth-century Punjabi poet Waris Shah's version of *Heer Ranjha* (the love story of Heer and Ranjha). Although Punjabi was originally written in the Gurmulki script, in the twentieth century it has been written in the Urdu script. Punjabi has a long history of being mixed with Urdu among Muslims, especially in urban areas. Numerous dialects exist, some associated with the Sikhs in India and others associated with regions in Pakistan. An example of the latter is the variant of Punjabi spoken in Sargodha in central Punjab.

The ethnic composition of Pakistan in the early 1990s roughly corresponded to the linguistic distribution of the population, at least among the largest groups: 66 percent of Pakistanis identify themselves as Punjabis, 13 percent as Sindhis, 9 percent as Pakhtuns, 8 percent as *muhajirs*, 3 percent as Baloch, and 1 percent as members of other ethnic groups. Each group is primarily concentrated in its home province, with most *muhajirs* residing in urban Sindh (see fig. 7).

Punjabis

Most Punjabis trace their ancestry to pre-Islamic Jat and Rajput castes. However, as they intermarried with other ethnic groups who came to the area, certain *qaums* (clan or tribal groups) came to predominate, especially Gujjars, Awans, Arains, and Khokkars in northern Punjab, and Gilanis, Gardezis, Qureshis, and Abbasis in the south. Other Punjabis trace their heritage to Arabia, Persia, Balochistan, Afghanistan, and Kashmir. Thus, in contrast with many other areas, where people often remained isolated, Punjabis had very diverse origins. The extent of this diversity facilitated their coalescence into a coherent ethnic community that has historically placed great emphasis both on farming and on fighting.

In censuses taken in British India, Punjabis were typically divided into "functional castes" or "agricultural tribes." The word *caste*, however, is grounded in the Hindu notions of reincarnation and karma; Muslims totally reject these religious connotations and use the term *qaum* instead. Tribal affiliation, based on descent and occupational specialization, tends to merge in Punjab into a *qaum* identity. An occupational group typically claims descent from a single ancestor, and many tribes traditionally followed a single occupation. The traditional occupation gives the group its name as well as its general position in the social hierarchy.

An important aspect of Punjabi ethnicity is reciprocity at the village level. A man's brother is his friend, his friend is his brother, and both enjoy equal access to his resources. Traditionally, a person has virtually free access to a kinsman's resources without foreseeable payback. This situation results in social networks founded on local (kinship-based) group needs as opposed to individual wants. These networks in turn perpetuate not only friendly relations but also the structure of the community itself. There is great social pressure on an individual to share and pool such resources as income, political influence, and personal connections. Kinship obligations continue to be central to a Punjabi's identity and concerns. Distinctions based on *qaum* remain significant social markers, particularly in rural areas.

Punjab, a region of fertile agricultural lands, is Pakistan's most populous province. Its landed elite remains a favored social stratum. Moreover, given the province's overwhelming importance, its landowners (in tandem with influential *muhajirs*) continue to predominate in the upper echelons of the military and civil service and in large part run the central government. This situation is resented by many Pakhtuns, Baloch, and, particularly, Sindhis, whose numbers and wealth are comparatively small and who are proportionately underrepresented in government and the military. Many Sindhis, alienated from the Punjabi-dominated central government, still resent the fact that the capital was moved from Karachi (in Sindh) to Islamabad (in northern Punjab). Sindhis also have bitter memories of the death of Zulfiqar Ali Bhutto, a champion of Sindhi regionalism, who was not only ousted but hanged. Of the three most prominent national politicians in the 1980s and early 1990s, two were Punjabis: President Zia ul-Haq and Prime Minister Mian Nawaz Sharif. Only Benazir

Bhutto, Pakistan People's Party leader and prime minister from October 1993, is Sindhi.

Pakhtuns

The North-West Frontier Province is closely identified with Pakhtuns, one of the largest tribal groups in the world. The Pakhtuns predominate in Balochistan and are also the major ethnic group in southern Afghanistan. The West has long been fascinated with the Pakhtuns, one of the few peoples able to defeat the advances of British imperialism. Authors as diverse as Rudyard Kipling and contemporary Pakistani anthropologist Akbar S. Ahmed wrote about them. More is written about Pakhtun norms, values, and social organization than any other ethnic group in Pakistan.

Central to identity as a Pakhtun is adherence to the male-centered code of conduct, the *pakhtunwali*. Foremost in this code is the notion of honor, *nang*, which is articulated in a starkly black-and-white, all-or-nothing manner. Without honor, life for a Pakhtun is not worth living. Honor demands the maintenance of sexual propriety. Complete chastity among female relatives is of the essence; only with the purity and good repute of his mother, daughters, sisters, and wife (or wives) does a man ensure his honor. Thus women are restricted to private, family compounds in much of the North-West Frontier Province. Census takers, invariably male, are constrained not to ask about the women in another man's home, and the number of men in a household is often overstated because sons and brothers are a source of strength. Hence, accurate enumeration of the population is not possible.

Closely related to the notion of honor is the principle of revenge, or *badal*. Offenses to one's honor must be avenged, or there is no honor. Although minor problems may be settled by negotiation, murder demands blood revenge, and partners in illicit sexual liaisons are killed if discovered. Even making lewd innuendos or, in the case of women, having one's reputation maligned may mean death. The men involved sometimes escape to other regions, where they may well be tracked down by the woman's kin. When a woman is killed, the assailant is, almost without exception, a close male relative. Killings associated with sexual misconduct are the only ones that do not demand revenge. Even the courts are accustomed to dealing leniently in such cases. Vendettas and feuds are an endemic feature of social relations and an index of individual and group identity.

Another major dimension of *pakhtunwali* is hospitality, or *melmastia*. Commensalism is a means of showing respect, friendship, and alliance. A complex etiquette surrounds the serving of guests, in which the host or his sons, when serving, refuse to sit with those they entertain as a mark of courtesy. Closely related to *melmastia* is the requirement of giving refuge to anyone, even one's enemy, for as long as the person is within the precincts of one's home. These codes, too, are related to the concept of honor, for the host gains honor by serving his guest, and the person who places himself under another's protection is weak, a supplicant. Refuge must extend to the point of being willing to sacrifice one's own life to defend one's guest, but a person who demeans himself so much as to plead for mercy should be spared.

Observers credit the relatively minimal tension that initially existed between Pakistani Pakhtuns and the large number of Pakhtun refugees from Afghanistan to the deeply felt obligation of Pakhtuns to obey the customary dictates of hospitality. However, Pakistani Pakhtuns' frustration with the refugees escalated after the Soviet army withdrew from Afghanistan in 1989. Many Pakistani Pakhtuns were upset that the internecine violence resulting from warring clans in conflict in Afghanistan was overflowing into Pakistan. In 1994 Pakistani Pakhtuns were as eager as other Pakistanis to see the refugees return to Afghanistan.

Pakhtuns are organized into segmentary clans (called *khels*), each named for a first migrant to their area to whom they trace their ancestry. Membership is tied to landownership as well as to descent. A person who loses his land is no longer treated as a full (adult) member of the community. He no longer may join or speak in the tribal *jirga*, or council of tribal leaders, at which issues of common interest are debated. But because brothers divide property among themselves, rivalry builds among the children of brothers who may need to subdivide increasingly unequal portions of an original estate. Hence, a man's greatest rival for women, money, and land (*zan*, *zar*, and *zamin*, respectively) is his first cousin—his father's brother's son—even though the same man may be his staunchest ally in the event of attack from the outside. Lineages themselves have a notable tendency to fragment; this tendency has contributed to the existence of a number of well-established clans among the

Pakhtuns. At every level of Pakhtun social organization, groups are split into a complex and shifting pattern of alliance and enmity.

Most Pakhtuns are pious Sunni (see Glossary) Muslims, and effective religious leaders often acquire a substantial following. However, there is a basic ambivalence on the whole toward mullahs (see Glossary), who have a formal role in leading prayers and in taking care of the mosque.

An intensely egalitarian ethos exists among Pakhtun men in a clan; the tribal leader is considered the first among equals. No man willingly admits himself less than any other's equal. Nor will he, unless driven by the most dire circumstances, put himself in a position of subservience or admit dependency on another. This sense of equality is evident in the structure of the men's council, composed of lineage elders who deal with matters ranging from disputes between local lineage sections to relations with other tribes or with the national government. Although the council can make and enforce binding decisions, within the body itself all are considered equals. To attempt or to appear to coerce another is to give grave insult and to risk initiating a feud.

To facilitate relations with Pakhtuns, the British appointed *maliks*, or minor chiefs. Agreements in which Pakhtuns have acceded to an external authority—whether the British or the Pakistani government—have been tenuous. The British resorted to a "divide and conquer" policy of playing various feuding factions against one another. British hegemony was frequently precarious: in 1937 Pakhtuns wiped out an entire British brigade. Throughout the 1930s, there were more troops stationed in Waziristan (homeland of the Wazirs, among the most independent of Pakhtun tribes) in the southern part of the North-West Frontier Province than in the rest of the subcontinent.

In tribal areas, where the level of wealth is generally limited, perennial feuding acts as a leveler. The killing, pillaging, and destruction keep any one lineage from amassing too much more than any other. In settled areas, the intensity of feuds has declined, although everyone continues to be loyal to the ideals of *pakhtunwali*. Government control only erratically contains violence—depending on whether a given government official has any relationship to the disputants. The proliferation of guns—including clones of Uzis and Kalashnikovs—has exacerbated much of the violence.

Since the 1980s, many Pakhtuns have entered the police force, civil service, and military and have virtually taken over the country's transportation network. A former president of Pakistan, Ghulam Ishaq Khan (1988–93), is a Pakhtun, as are many high-ranking military officers. The government of Pakistan has established numerous schools in the North-West Frontier Province—including ones devoted exclusively to girls—in an effort to imbue Pakhtuns with a sense of Pakistani nationalism.

A growing number of development projects in the North-West Frontier Province have provided diverse employment opportunities for Pakhtuns. Notably, the government has set up comprehensive projects such as building roads and schools as a substitution for cultivating opium poppies. Incentives for industrial investment have also been provided. However, the government lost much credibility when it proposed in 1991 (a proposal soon withdrawn) to build up the local infrastructure in the Gadoon-Amazai area of the North-West Frontier Province and to encourage it as a target for tax-free investment. Observers attributed the government's withdrawal of the incentive package to local unrest.

Sindhis

During the British Raj, Sindh, situated south of Punjab, was the neglected hinterland of Bombay. The society was dominated by a small number of major landholders (*waderas*). Most people were tenant farmers facing terms of contract that were a scant improvement over outright servitude; a middle class barely existed. The social landscape consisted largely of unremitting poverty, and feudal landlords ruled with little concern for any outside interference. A series of irrigation projects in the 1930s merely served to increase the wealth of large landowners when their wastelands were made more productive. Reformist legislation in the 1940s that was intended to improve the lot of the poor had little success. At the time of independence, the province had entrenched extremes of wealth and poverty.

There was considerable upheaval in Sindh in the years following partition. Millions of Hindus and Sikhs left for India and were replaced by roughly 7 million *muhajirs*, who took the places of the fairly well-educated emigrant Hindus and Sikhs in the commercial life of the province. Later, the *muhajirs* provided the political basis of the Refugee People's Movement

(Muhajir Qaumi Mahaz—MQM). As Karachi became increasingly identified as a *muhajir* city, other cities in Sindh, notably Thatta, Hyderabad, and Larkana, became the headquarters for Sindhi resistance.

In 1994 Sindh continued to be an ethnic battlefield within Pakistan. During the 1980s, there were repeated kidnappings in the province, some with political provocation. Fear of dacoits (bandits) gave rise to the perception that the interior of Sindh was unsafe for road and rail travel. Sectarian violence against Hindus erupted in the interior in 1992 in the wake of the destruction of the Babri Mosque in Ayodhya, India, by Hindu extremists who sought to rebuild a Hindu temple on the contested site. A travel advisory recommending that foreigners avoid the interior of the province remained in effect in early 1994.

Baloch

The final major ethnic group in Pakistan is the Baloch. A comparatively small group, the Baloch, like the Pakhtuns, are a tribal population whose original territory extends beyond the national borders. Over 70 percent of the Baloch live in Pakistan, with the remainder in Iran and Afghanistan. The Baloch trace their roots to tribes migrating eastward from around Aleppo, in Syria, before the Christian era. Sometime between the sixth century and the fourteenth century, they migrated to the region of present-day Balochistan.

Baloch speak Balochi, part of the Iranian group of Indo-European languages. Linguistic evidence indicates the origin of Balochi to be in the pre-Christian Medean or Parthian civilizations. The modern form has incorporated elements from Persian, Sindhi, Arabic, and a number of other languages. Beginning in the early nineteenth century, Baloch intellectuals used Persian and Urdu scripts to transcribe Balochi into written form. Since Pakistan's independence, and with the rise of Baloch nationalism, Baloch have favored the Nastaliq script, an adaptation of Arabic script.

The land of Balochistan is exceedingly inhospitable; geologists have even compared the landscape with Mars. A Pakhtu expression, reflecting on ethnic relations as well as on geography, describes Balochistan as "the dump where Allah shot the rubbish of creation." Subsistence is hard in this environment and is achieved by pastoral nomadism, dryland and irrigated agriculture, and fishing. Dryland farming is marginal, although it is a mainstay for many seminomadic herders. The Baloch plant drought-resistant grains in earthen embankments where scanty rainfall has accumulated.

Irrigated farming is concentrated near oases in two kinds of systems: open channels that bring water from a few riverbeds, and subsurface drains (*karez*) that channel groundwater downward to planted fields. However, such irrigation and cultivation are extremely limited, forcing most Baloch to eke out a living by herding or farming in the marginal hinterland.

Sheep and goats are the main herd animals. The herder typically consumes the dairy products these animals produce and sells the meat and wool. Pastoralists organize themselves around water sources; wells are the property of specific camps.

Kinship and social relations reflect the exigencies of dealing with the harsh physical environment. Like other Pakistanis, Baloch reckon descent patrilineally. Lineages, however, play a minimal role in the lives of most Baloch. They are notably flexible in arrangements with both family and friends. Ideally, a man should maintain close ties with relatives in his father's line, but in practice most relations are left to the discretion of the individual, and there is wide variation. It is typical for lineages to split and fragment, often because of disputes with close kin over matters such as inheritance and bad relations within marriages. Most Baloch treat both mother's and father's kin as a pool of potential assistance to be called on as the occasion demands. Again, the precariousness of subsistence favors having the widest possible circle of friends and relatives.

Marriage patterns embody this kind of flexibility. As in many parts of West Asia, Baloch say that they prefer to marry their cousins. Actually, however, marriage choices are dictated by pragmatic considerations. Residence, the complex means of access to agricultural land, and the centrality of water rights, coupled with uncertain water supply, all favor flexibility in the choice of in-laws. The plethora of land tenure arrangements tends to limit the value of marrying one's cousin, a marriage pattern that functions to keep land in the family in other parts of Pakistan.

The majority of Baloch are Hanafi Sunnis, but there is a community of an estimated 500,000 to 700,000 Zikri Baloch, who live in the coastal Makran area and in Karachi. The Zikris believe in the fifteenth-century teachings of a *madhi*, an Islamic messiah, named Nur Pak. These teachings, they believe, supersede those of the Prophet Muhammad—a violation of one of

Girl from Chitral
Courtesy Harvey Follender

Women and children in
Ziarat, Balochistan
Courtesy Anita M. Weiss

Islam's central tenets (see Basic Tenets of Islam, this ch.). Zikris have their own daily prayers and do not fast during Ramadan (known as Ramazan in Pakistan). By the Zikris' own self-estimation, they are devout Muslims. To the Sunni majority, however, their beliefs are heretical.

Only among the coastal Baloch is marriage between cousins common; there, nearly two-thirds of married couples are first cousins. The coastal Baloch are in greater contact with non-Baloch and manifest a concomitantly greater sense of group solidarity. For them, being "unified amongst ourselves" is a particularly potent cultural ideal. Because they are Zikris, they have a limited pool of eligible mates and do not generally marry outside of the group of Zikri Baloch.

Baloch society is stratified and has been characterized as "feudal militarism." The significant social tie is that between a leader, the *hakim*, and his retinue, consisting of pastoralists, agriculturists, lower-level leaders, and lower-level tenant farmers and descendants of former slaves (*hizmatkar*). Suprafamily groups formed through patrilineal descent are significant mostly for the elite *hakim,* whose concern for rivalry and politics is not shared by other groups.

The basic exchange traditionally underlying this elaborate system was the *hakim*'s offer of booty or property rights in return for support in battle. In more modern times, various favors are generally traded for votes, but the structure of the system—the participation of the lower-level leaders and the *hizmatkar* through patron-client ties—remains much the same.

In common with the neighboring Pakhtuns, Baloch are deeply committed to maintaining their personal honor, showing generous hospitality to guests, and giving protection to those who seek it of them. However, the prototypical relationship is that between the leader and his minions. A Baloch suffers no loss of status in submitting to another. Although competition for scarce water and land resources characterizes social relations between minor leaders and *hizmatkar,* competition coexists with a deeply held belief in the virtues of sharing and cooperation. Sharing creates networks of obligation among herders, mutual aid being an insurance policy in the face of a precarious livelihood.

Baloch tribal structure concentrates power in the hands of local tribal leaders. The British played local rivals against each other in a policy of indirect rule, as they did with the Pakhtun tribes to the north—and virtually throughout the subcontinent. In essence, the British offered local autonomy and subsidies to rulers in exchange for access to the border with Afghanistan. In the early 1990s, local leaders maintained this policy to a large extent, continuing to exploit the endemic anarchy, whether local, provincial, or national.

There have been sporadic separatist movements in Balochistan since independence. Baloch have long been accustomed to indirect rule, a policy that leaves local elites with a substantial measure of autonomy. The 1970s saw a precipitous deterioration in relations between Balochistan and the central government, however. The violent confrontation between Baloch insurgents and the Pakistani military in the mid-1970s was particularly brutal (see Zulfiqar Ali Bhutto and a New Constitutional System, ch. 1). The conflict touched the lives of most Baloch and politicized those long accustomed to accepting the status quo. Original demands for greater regional autonomy escalated into a full-scale movement aimed at restructuring the government along confederal lines. By the mid-1980s, traditional cleavages among *hakim,* minor leaders, and *hizmatkar* had declined in importance as the Baloch increasingly thought of themselves as a unified group in opposition to Pakistani, or Punjabi, hegemony.

Zia ul-Haq's overthrow of Zulfiqar Ali Bhutto in 1977 was welcomed by many in Balochistan, in contrast to popular sentiment in the rest of the country, which was appalled by the extraconstitutional act. As relations with the central government began to smooth out, however, the Soviet Union invaded Afghanistan in December 1979, placing nearly the entire northern border of Balochistan on alert as a frontline area.

Balochistan's landscape in the 1980s changed markedly as Afghan refugee camps were established throughout the northern parts of the province. In many instances, temporary mud housing eventually became transformed into concrete structures. The refugees also caused the demographic balance to change as ethnic Pakhtuns—many refugees from Afghanistan—came to settle in Balochistan.

Although social conditions in rural areas have changed little for most Baloch, two scandals in the early 1990s caused the region to receive much attention. The first grew out of reports that some owners of brick kilns in remote parts of the province had labor practices that resembled slavery, complete with indenturing workers to loans that were passed down through generations. The second was the charge that young boys were being recruited from the most remote parts of the province to be "camel boys" in races in the Persian Gulf states. The screaming of the young boys, who are tied to the backs of racing camels, supposedly scares the animals into running faster. The young boys often are maimed or killed in the process. Impoverished parents unwittingly accepted payment on the promise that their sons would be employed as apprentices.

Because of the area's limited population and its low population density levels, there has been little development in Balochistan except in Quetta, the capital of the province. The rural programs that exist stem mostly from the efforts of the Agha Khan Rural Support Development Project, an NGO that has expanded into rural Balochistan on the basis of its successes in the mountains around Gilgit, in the far north of the country. This project works on organizing disparate communities into local support groups and has had particular success in reaching women in remote areas of Balochistan.

Men, Women, and the Division of Space

Gender relations in Pakistan rest on two basic perceptions: that women are subordinate to men, and that a man's honor resides in the actions of the women of his family. Thus, as in other orthodox Muslim societies, women are responsible for maintaining the family honor. To ensure that they do not dishonor their families, society limits women's mobility, places restrictions on their behavior and activities, and permits them only limited contact with the opposite sex.

Space is allocated to and used differently by men and women. For their protection and respectability, women have traditionally been expected to live under the constraints of purdah (*purdah* is Persian for curtain), most obvious in veiling. By separating women from the activities of men, both physically and symbolically, purdah creates differentiated male and female spheres. Most women spend the major part of their lives physically within their homes and courtyards and go out only for serious and approved reasons. Outside the home, social life generally revolves around the activities of men. In most parts of the country, except perhaps in Islamabad, Karachi, and wealthier parts of a few other cities, people consider a woman—and her family—to be shameless if no restrictions are placed on her mobility.

Purdah is practiced in various ways, depending on family tradition, region, class, and rural or urban residence, but nowhere do unrelated men and women mix freely. The most extreme restraints are found in parts of the North-West Frontier Province and Balochistan, where women almost never leave their homes except when they marry and almost never meet unrelated men. They may not be allowed contact with male cousins on their mother's side, for these men are not classed as relatives in a strongly patrilineal society. Similarly, they have only very formal relations with those men they are allowed to meet, such as the father-in-law, paternal uncles, and brothers-in-law.

Poor rural women, especially in Punjab and Sindh, where gender relations are generally somewhat more relaxed, have greater mobility because they are responsible for transplanting rice seedlings, weeding crops, raising chickens and selling eggs, and stuffing wool or cotton into comforters (*razais*). When a family becomes more prosperous and begins to aspire to higher status, it commonly requires stricter purdah among its women as a first social change.

Poor urban women in close-knit communities, such as old cities of Lahore and Rawalpindi, generally wear eithe *burqa* (fitted body veil) or a chador (loosely draped cotto cloth used as a head covering and body veil) when they leave their homes. In these localities, multistory dwellings (*havelis*) were constructed to accommodate large extended families. Many *havelis* have now been sectioned off into smaller living units to economize. It is common for one nuclear family (with an average of seven members) to live in one or two rooms on each small floor. In less densely populated areas, where people generally do not know their neighbors, there are fewer restrictions on women's mobility.

The shared understanding that women should remain within their homes so neighbors do not gossip about their respectability has important implications for their productive activities. As with public life in general, work appears to be the domain of men. Rural women work for consumption or for exchange at the subsistence level. Others, both rural and urban, do piecework for very low wages in their homes. Their earnings are generally recorded as part of the family income that is credited to men. Census data and other accounts of economic activity in urban areas support such conclusions. For example, the 1981 census reported that 5.6 percent of all women were employed, as opposed to 72.4 percent of men; less than 4 percent of all urban women were engaged in some form of salaried work. By 1988 this figure had increased significantly, but still only 10.2 percent of women were reported as participating in the labor force.

Among wealthier Pakistanis, urban or rural residence is less important than family tradition in influencing whether women observe strict purdah and in determining the type of veil they wear. In some areas, women simply observe "eye purdah": they tend not to mix with men, but when they do, they avert their eyes when interacting with them. Bazaars in wealthier areas of Punjabi cities differ from those in poorer areas by having a greater proportion of unveiled women. In cities throughout the North-West Frontier Province, Balochistan, and the interior of Sindh, bazaars are markedly devoid of women, and when a woman does venture forth, she always wears some sort of veil.

The traditional division of space between the sexes is perpetuated in the broadcast media. Women's subservience is consistently shown on television and in films. And, although popular television dramas raise controversial issues such as women working, seeking divorce, or even having a say in family politics, the programs often suggest that the woman who strays from traditional norms faces insurmountable problems and becomes alienated from her family.

The Status of Women and the Women's Movement

Four important challenges confronted women in Pakistan in the early 1990s: increasing practical literacy, gaining access to employment opportunities at all levels in the economy, promoting change in the perception of women's roles and status, and gaining a public voice both within and outside of the political process.

There have been various attempts at social and legal reform aimed at improving Muslim women's lives in the subcontinent during the twentieth century. These attempts generally have been related to two broader, intertwined movements: the social reform movement in British India and the growing Muslim nationalist movement. Since partition, the changing status of women in Pakistan largely has been linked with discourse about the role of Islam in a modern state. This debate concerns the extent to which civil rights common in most Western democracies are appropriate in an Islamic society and the way these rights should be reconciled with Islamic family law.

Muslim reformers in the nineteenth century struggled to introduce female education, to ease some of the restrictions on women's activities, to limit polygyny, and to ensure women's rights under Islamic law. Sir Syed Ahmad Khan convened the Mohammedan Educational Conference in the 1870s to promote modern education for Muslims, and he founded the Muhammadan Anglo-Oriental College. Among the predominantly male participants were many of the earliest proponents of education and improved social status for women. They advocated cooking and sewing classes conducted in a religious framework to advance women's knowledge and skills and to reinforce Islamic values. But progress in women's literacy was slow: by 1921 only four out of every 1,000 Muslim females were literate.

Promoting the education of women was a first step in moving beyond the constraints imposed by purdah. The nationalist struggle helped fray the threads in that socially imposed curtain. Simultaneously, women's roles were questioned, and their empowerment was linked to the larger issues of nationalism and independence. In 1937 the Muslim Personal Law restored

People sleeping on rooftops, Lohari Gate, Lahore
Courtesy Anita M. Weiss

rights (such as inheritance of property) that had been lost by women under the Anglicization of certain civil laws. As independence neared, it appeared that the state would give priority to empowering women. Pakistan's founding father, Mohammad Ali Jinnah, said in a speech in 1944:

> No nation can rise to the height of glory unless your women are side by side with you; we are victims of evil customs. It is a crime against humanity that our women are shut up within the four walls of the houses as prisoners. There is no sanction anywhere for the deplorable condition in which our women have to live.

After independence, elite Muslim women in Pakistan continued to advocate women's political empowerment through legal reforms. They mobilized support that led to passage of the Muslim Personal Law of Sharia in 1948, which recognized a woman's right to inherit all forms of property. They were also behind the futile attempt to have the government include a Charter of Women's Rights in the 1956 constitution. The 1961 Muslim Family Laws Ordinance covering marriage and divorce, the most important sociolegal reform that they supported, is still widely regarded as empowering to women.

Two issues—promotion of women's political representation and accommodation between Muslim family law and democratic civil rights—came to dominate discourse about women and sociolegal reform. The second issue gained considerable attention during the regime of Zia ul-Haq (1977–88). Urban women formed groups to protect their rights against apparent discrimination under Zia's Islamization program. It was in the highly visible realm of law that women were able to articulate their objections to the Islamization program initiated by the government in 1979. Protests against the 1979 Enforcement of Hudood Ordinances focused on the failure of *hudood* (see Glossary) ordinances to distinguish between adultery (*zina*) and rape (*zina-bil-jabr*). A man could be convicted of *zina* only if he were actually observed committing the offense by other men, but a woman could be convicted simply because she became pregnant.

The Women's Action Forum was formed in 1981 to respond to the implementation of the penal code and to strengthen women's position in society generally. The women in the forum, most of whom came from elite families, perceived that many of the laws proposed by the Zia government were discriminatory and would compromise their civil status. In Karachi, Lahore, and Islamabad the group agreed on collective leadership and formulated policy statements and engaged in political action to safeguard women's legal position.

The Women's Action Forum has played a central role in heightening the controversy regarding various interpretations of Islamic law and its role in a modern state, and in publicizing ways in which women can play a more active role in politics. Its members led public protests in the mid-1980s against the promulgation of the Law of Evidence. Although the final version was substantially modified, the Women's Action Forum objected to the legislation because it gave unequal weight to testimony by men and women in financial cases. Fundamentally, they objected to the assertion that women and men cannot participate as legal equals in economic affairs.

Beginning in August 1986, the Women's Action Forum members and their supporters led a debate over passage of the

Shariat Bill, which decreed that all laws in Pakistan should conform to Islamic law. They argued that the law would undermine the principles of justice, democracy, and fundamental rights of citizens, and they pointed out that Islamic law would become identified solely with the conservative interpretation supported by Zia's government. Most activists felt that the Shariat Bill had the potential to negate many of the rights women had won. In May 1991, a compromise version of the Shariat Bill was adopted, but the debate over whether civil law or Islamic law should prevail in the country continued in the early 1990s.

Discourse about the position of women in Islam and women's roles in a modern Islamic state was sparked by the government's attempts to formalize a specific interpretation of Islamic law. Although the issue of evidence became central to the concern for women's legal status, more mundane matters such as mandatory dress codes for women and whether females could compete in international sports competitions were also being argued.

Another of the challenges faced by Pakistani women concerns their integration into the labor force. Because of economic pressures and the dissolution of extended families in urban areas, many more women are working for wages than in the past. But by 1990 females officially made up only 13 percent of the labor force. Restrictions on their mobility limit their opportunities, and traditional notions of propriety lead families to conceal the extent of work performed by women.

Usually, only the poorest women engage in work—often as midwives, sweepers, or nannies—for compensation outside the home. More often, poor urban women remain at home and sell manufactured goods to a middleman for compensation. More and more urban women have engaged in such activities during the 1990s, although to avoid being shamed, few families willingly admit that women contribute to the family economically. Hence, there is little information about the work women do. On the basis of the predominant fiction that most women do no work other than their domestic chores, the government has been hesitant to adopt overt policies to increase women's employment options and to provide legal support for women's labor-force participation.

The United Nations Children's Fund (UNICEF) commissioned a national study in 1992 on women's economic activity to enable policy planners and donor agencies to cut through the existing myths on female labor-force participation. The study addresses the specific reasons that the assessment of women's work in Pakistan is filled with discrepancies and underenumeration and provides a comprehensive discussion of the range of informal-sector work performed by women throughout the country. Information from this study was also incorporated into the Eighth Five-Year Plan (1993–98).

A melding of the traditional social welfare activities of the women's movement and its newly revised political activism appears to have occurred. Diverse groups, including the Women's Action Forum, the All-Pakistan Women's Association, the Pakistan Women Lawyers' Association, and the Business and Professional Women's Association, are supporting small-scale projects throughout the country that focus on empowering women. They have been involved in such activities as instituting legal aid for indigent women, opposing the gendered segregation of universities, and publicizing and condemning the growing incidents of violence against women. The Pakistan Women Lawyers' Association has released a series of films educating women about their legal rights; the Business and Professional Women's Association is supporting a comprehensive project inside Yakki Gate, a poor area inside the walled old city of Lahore; and the Orangi Pilot Project in Karachi has promoted networks among women who work at home so they need not be dependent on middlemen to acquire raw materials and to market the clothes they produce.

The women's movement has shifted from reacting to government legislation to focusing on three primary goals: securing women's political representation in the National Assembly; working to raise women's consciousness, particularly about family planning; and countering suppression of women's rights by defining and articulating positions on events as they occur in order to raise public awareness. An as yet unresolved issue concerns the perpetuation of a set number of seats for women in the National Assembly. Many women activists whose expectations were raised during the brief tenure of Benazir Bhutto's first government (December 1988–August 1990) now believe that, with her return to power in October 1993, they can seize the initiative to bring about a shift in women's personal and public access to power.

Religious Life

About 97 percent of all Pakistanis are Muslims. Official documentation states that Sunni Muslims constitute 77 percent of the population and that adherents of Shia (see Glossary) Islam make up an additional 20 percent. Christians, Hindus, and members of other religions each account for about 1 percent of the population.

Basic Tenets of Islam

The central belief in Islam is that there is only one God, Allah, and that the Prophet Muhammad was his final messenger. Muhammad is held to be the "seal of the prophets." Islam is derived from the Judeo-Christian tradition and regards Abraham (Ibrahim) and Jesus (Isa) as prophets and recognizes the validity of the Old Testament and New Testament.

Islam is held to be the blueprint for humanity that God has created. The word *Islam* comes from *aslama* (to submit), and the one who submits—a Muslim—is a believer who achieves peace, or *salaam.* God, the creator, is invisible and omnipresent; to represent God in any form is a sin.

The Prophet was born in A.D. 570 and became a merchant in the Arabian town of Mecca. At the age of forty, he began to receive a series of revelations from God transmitted through the angel Gabriel. His monotheistic message, which disdained the idolatry that was popularly practiced at the Kaaba (now in the Great Mosque and venerated as a shrine of Muslim pilgrimage) in Mecca at that time, was ridiculed by the town's leaders. Muhammad and his followers were forced to emigrate in 622 to the nearby town of Yathrib, later known as Medina, or "the city." This move, the hijra, marks the beginning of the Islamic era. In the ten years before his death in 632, the Prophet continued preaching and receiving revelations, ultimately consolidating both the temporal and the spiritual leadership of Arabia.

The Quran, the holy scripture of Islam, plays a pivotal role in Muslim social organization and values. The Quran, which literally means "reciting," is recognized by believers as truly the word of God, and as such it is eternal, absolute, and irrevocable. The fact that Muhammad was the last of the prophets and that no further additions to "the word" are allowed is significant; it closes the door to new revelations.

That there can be no authorized translation of the Quran in any language other than the original, Arabic, is crucial to its unifying importance. Cultural differences such as those that exist among various Muslim groups throughout the world cannot compromise the unifying role that the religion plays.

The Prophet's life is considered exemplary. His active engagement in worldly activities established precedents for Muslims to follow. These precedents, referred to as the hadith, include the statements, actions, and moods or feelings of the Prophet. Although many hadith are popularly accepted by most Muslims, there is no one canon accepted by all. Such things as the way in which Muhammad ran the state in Medina and the priority he placed on education remain important guidelines. The Quran and the hadith together form the sunna (see Glossary), a comprehensive guide to spiritual, ethical, and social living.

The five pillars of Islam consist of certain beliefs and acts to which a Muslim must adhere to affirm membership in the community. The first is the *shahada* (testimony), the affirmation of the faith, which succinctly states the central belief of Islam: "There is no god but God (Allah), and Muhammad is his Prophet." To become a Muslim, one needs only to recite this statement. Second is *salat*, the obligation for a Muslim to pray at five set times during the day. Muslims value prayers recited communally, especially the midday prayers on Friday, the Muslim sabbath. Mosques have emerged as important social and political centers as a by-product of this unifying value. The third pillar of Islam is *zakat*, the obligation to provide alms for the poor and disadvantaged (see *Zakat* as a Welfare System, this ch.). The fourth is *sawm*, the obligation to fast from sunrise to sunset during the holy month of Ramadan, in commemoration of the beginning of the Prophet's revelations from Allah. The final pillar is the expectation that every adult Muslim physically and financially able to do so perform the hajj, the pilgrimage to Mecca, at least once in his or her lifetime. The pilgrimage occurs during the last month of the Muslim lunar calendar, just over a month after the end of Ramadan. Its social importance as a unifier of the greater Muslim *umma* (community of believers) has led to the establishment of hajj committees for its regulation in every Muslim country. The pilgrimage of a Muslim to the sacred places at any other time of the year is referred to as *umra* (visitation). At various times of political crisis in Pakistan, almost every major leader has left for Saudi Arabia to perform *umra*. Performing *umra* may or may not increase the politician's reputation for moral standing.

A number of other elements contribute to a sense of social membership whereby Muslims see themselves as distinct from non-Muslims, including prohibition on the consumption of pork and alcohol, the requirement that animals be slaughtered in a ritual manner, and the obligation to circumcise sons. Another element is jihad, the "striving." Jihad is often misunderstood in the West, where people think of it as a fanatical holy war. There are two kinds of jihad: the far more important inner one is the battle each Muslim wages with his or her lower self; the outer one is the battle that each Muslim must wage to preserve the faith and its followers. People who fight the outer jihad are *mujahidin.* The Afghan rebels waging an insurrection against the Soviet-backed government in the 1980s deftly used this term to identify themselves and hence infused their struggle with a moral dimension.

The concept of predestination in Islam is different from that in Christianity. Islam posits the existence of an all-powerful force (Allah) who rules the universe and knows all things. Something will happen—*inshaallah*—if it is God's will. The concept is not purely fatalistic, for although people are responsible to God for their actions, these actions are not predestined. Instead, God has shown the world the right way to live as revealed through the Quran; then it is up to individual believers to choose how to live.

There are two major sects in Islam—the Sunnis and the Shia. They are differentiated by Sunni acceptance of the temporal authority of the Rashudin Caliphate (Abu Bakr, Omar, Usman, and Ali) after the death of the Prophet and the Shia acceptance solely of Ali, the Prophet's cousin and husband of his daughter, Fatima, and his descendants. Over time, the Sunni sect divided into four major schools of jurisprudence; of these, the Hanafi school is predominant in Pakistan. The Shia sect split over the matter of succession, resulting in two major groups: the majority Twelve Imam Shia believe that there are twelve rightful imams, Ali and his eleven direct descendants. A second Shia group, the numerically smaller Ismaili community, known also as Seveners, follows a line of imams that originally challenged the Seventh Imam and supported a younger brother, Ismail. The Ismaili line of leaders has been continuous down to the present day. The current leader, Sadr ad Din Agha Khan, who is active in international humanitarian efforts, is a direct descendant of Ali.

Islam in Pakistani Society

Islam was brought to the South Asian subcontinent in the eighth century by wandering Sufi (see Glossary) mystics known as *pir* (see Glossary). As in other areas where it was introduced by Sufis, Islam to some extent syncretized with pre-Islamic influences, resulting in a religion traditionally more flexible than in the Arab world. Two Sufis whose shrines receive much national attention are Data Ganj Baksh in Lahore (ca. eleventh century) and Shahbaz Qalander in Sehwan, Sindh (ca. twelfth century).

The Muslim poet-philosopher Sir Muhammad Iqbal first proposed the idea of a Muslim state in the subcontinent in his address to the Muslim League at Allahabad in 1930. His proposal referred to the four provinces of Punjab, Sindh, Balochistan, and the North-West Frontier Province—essentially what would became post-1971 Pakistan. Iqbal's idea gave concrete form to the "Two Nations Theory" of two distinct nations in the subcontinent based on religion (Islam and Hinduism) and with different historical backgrounds, social customs, cultures, and social mores.

Islam was thus the basis for the creation and the unification of a separate state, but it was not expected to serve as the model of government. Mohammad Ali Jinnah made his commitment to secularism in Pakistan clear in his inaugural address when he said, "You will find that in the course of time Hindus would cease to be Hindus and Muslims would cease to be Muslims, not in the religious sense, because that is the personal faith of each individual, but in the political sense as citizens of the State." This vision of a Muslim majority state in which religious minorities would share equally in its development was questioned shortly after independence. The debate continued into the 1990s amid questions of the rights of Ahmadiyyas (a small but influential sect considered by orthodox Muslims to be outside the pale of Islam), issuance of identity cards denoting religious affiliation, and government intervention in the personal practice of Islam (see Constitutional Beginnings, ch. 1; Islamic Provisions, ch. 5).

Politicized Islam

From the outset, politics and religion have been intertwined both conceptually and practically in Islam. Because the Prophet established a government in Medina, precedents of governance and taxation exist. Through the history of Islam, from the Ummayyad (661–750) and Abbasid empires (750–1258) to the Mughals (1526–1858) and the Ottomans (1300–1923), religion and statehood have been treated as one.

Indeed, one of the beliefs of Islam is that the purpose of the state is to provide an environment where Muslims can properly practice their religion. If a leader fails in this, the people have a right to depose him.

In 1977 the government of Zulfiqar Ali Bhutto outlawed alcohol and changed the "day off" from Sunday to Friday, but no substantive Islamic reform program was implemented prior to General Zia's Islamization program. Starting in February 1979, new penal measures based on Islamic principles of justice went into effect. These carried considerably greater implications for women than for men. A welfare and taxation system based on *zakat* and a profit-and-loss banking system were also established in accordance with Islamic prohibitions against usury (see Policy Developments since Independence, ch. 3).

Zia's Islamization program was pursued within a rather complicated ideological framework. His stance was in contrast to the popular culture, in which most people are "personally" very religious but not "publicly" religious. An unexpected outcome was that by relying on a policy grounded in Islam, the state fomented factionalism: by legislating what is Islamic and what is not, Islam itself could no longer provide unity because it was then being defined to exclude previously included groups. Disputes between Sunnis and Shia, ethnic disturbances in Karachi among Pakhtuns, Sindhis, and *muhajirs*, increased animosity toward Ahmadiyyas, and the revival of Punjab-Sindh tensions can all be traced to the loss of Islam as a common vocabulary of public morality. More profoundly, in a move that reached into every home, the state had attempted to dictate a specific ideal image of women in Islamic society, an ideal that was largely antithetical to that existing in popular sentiment and in everyday life.

A major component of the Islamization program, the Shariat Bill, was passed in May 1991. This bill required that all laws in the country conform to Islam. Women's groups in particular were concerned that the reforms in the Muslim Family Laws Ordinance of 1961 could be jeopardized by the new bill.

A controversial law, Section 295–C of the Pakistan Penal Code, drew a great deal of attention from critics associated with the Human Rights Commission in 1993–94. Introduced in 1986 by Zia, the law, referred to as "the blasphemy trap," states that "whoever by words, either spoken or written, or by visible representation or by any imputation, innuendo, or insinuation, directly or indirectly, defiles the sacred name of the Prophet

Muhammad shall be punished with death or imprisoned for life and shall be liable to fine." The law extends to Muslims and non-Muslims alike, but it has been indiscriminately used against members of minorities. According to Amnesty International, several dozen people had been charged under Pakistan's blasphemy laws by early 1994. In all cases, these charges appear to have been arbitrarily brought and to have been based on an individual's minority religious beliefs or on malicious accusations. The current government of Benazir Bhutto, sensitive to Pakistan's image in the world community, has attempted to approve changes in the blasphemy law in order to "curb abuses of the law"—especially those involving false accusations and fabricated cases. Critics claim, however, that Benazir, constantly under attack for being too liberal by the religious right, has been overly cautious and slow to introduce amendments to the law.

Non-Muslim Minorities

The most visible groups of non-Muslim minorities are Hindus and Christians. Hindus are found largely in the interior of Sindh and in the vicinity of Quetta in Balochistan. Christians, representing almost all West European dominations, are found throughout the country; many are engaged in menial work. Other minorities include Zoroastrians (also called Parsis), largely concentrated in Karachi, and members of groups relatively recently designated as non-Muslim, notably the Ahmadiyyas.

The Ahmadiyyas are followers of Mirza Ghulam Ahmad (ca. 1840–1908), who founded the sect in Qadian, India, in 1901. Ahmad's adherents are often called Qadianis. Mirza Ghulam Ahmad claimed to have received a revelation from God, and such a claim, argue orthodox Muslims, violates a central tenet of Islam that Muhammad is the final prophet. Orthodox ulama therefore consider the Ahmadiyyas apostates.

As a group, the Ahmadiyyas are highly organized and have a marked degree of community spirit. They are characteristically ascetic in their personal lives; they bring to their vision of Islam the reforming zeal of some of the fundamentalists. They seek to re-create the glories of the early caliphs. Ahmadiyyas strictly adhere to purdah. They are accustomed to running their own schools and welfare institutions.

The Ahmadiyyas' high literacy rate, as well as their general industriousness, has won them a substantial measure of economic success and public prominence. As a result, they frequently have been the object of envy. In 1953 there were anti-Ahmadiyya riots, which resulted in the first imposition of martial law, albeit local and temporary. Sunnis called for the firing of prominent Ahmadiyya officeholders and demanded that the sect be declared non-Muslim. Anti-Ahmadiyya sentiment stirred again in the mid-1970s. Prime Minister Zulfiqar Ali Bhutto capitulated to popular demands, and the sect was declared non-Muslim. In 1984 President Zia ul-Haq, reacting to calls for violence against the Ahmadiyyas by disaffected ulama, placed additional legal restrictions on the community. The Ahmadiyya question is likely to persist in the Islamic state of Pakistan, where the question of who is a Muslim is of such crucial importance.

The various religious minority groups have secured separate representation in national and provincial assemblies but still have limited influence on national policy. They finally united around a common issue in October 1992 when the government of Mian Nawaz Sharif decreed that religious affiliation would be indicated on identity cards. These cards were needed for a range of activities, including attending school, opening a bank account, registering to vote, casting a vote, and obtaining a passport. Members of minority groups organized demonstrations to protest this discrimination, which they argued would demote them to the ranks of second-class citizens. They argued that safeguards existed for them both within Islamic law and in the promises that had been made to them in 1947 at independence. The government soon rescinded the decree.

Education

At independence, Pakistan had a poorly educated population and few schools or universities. Although the education system has expanded greatly since then, debate continues about the curriculum, and, except in a few elite institutions, quality remained a crucial concern of educators in the early 1990s.

Adult literacy is low, but improving. In 1992 more than 36 percent of adults over fifteen were literate, compared with 21 percent in 1970. The rate of improvement is highlighted by the 50 percent literacy achieved among those aged fifteen to nineteen in 1990. School enrollment also increased, from 19 percent of those aged six to twenty-three in 1980 to 24 percent in 1990. However, by 1992 the population over twenty-five had a mean of only 1.9 years of schooling. This fact explains the minimal criteria for being considered literate: having the ability to both read and write (with understanding) a short, simple statement on everyday life.

Relatively limited resources have been allocated to education, although there has been improvement in recent decades. In 1960 public expenditure on education was only 1.1 percent of the gross national product (GNP—see Glossary); by 1990 the figure had risen to 3.4 percent. This amount compared poorly with the more than 30 percent being spent on defense in 1993. In 1990 Pakistan was tied for fourth place in the world in its ratio of military expenditures to health and education expenditures. Although the government enlisted the assistance of various international donors in the education efforts outlined in its Seventh Five-Year Plan (1988–93), the results did not measure up to expectations.

Structure of the System

Education is organized into five levels: primary (grades one through five); middle (grades six through eight); high (grades nine and ten, culminating in matriculation); intermediate (grades eleven and twelve, leading to an F.A. diploma in arts or an F.S. in science); and university programs leading to undergraduate and advanced degrees. Preparatory classes (*kachi*, or nursery) were formally incorporated into the system in 1988 with the Seventh Five-Year Plan.

Academic and technical education institutions are the responsibility of the federal Ministry of Education, which coordinates instruction through the intermediate level. Above that level, a designated university in each province is responsible for coordination of instruction and examinations. In certain cases, a different ministry may oversee specialized programs. Universities enjoy limited autonomy; their finances are overseen by a University Grants Commission, as in Britain.

Teacher-training workshops are overseen by the respective provincial education ministries in order to improve teaching skills. However, incentives are severely lacking, and, perhaps because of the shortage of financial support to education, few teachers participate. Rates of absenteeism among teachers are high in general, inducing support for community-coordinated efforts promoted in the Eighth Five-Year Plan (1993–98).

In 1991 there were 87,545 primary schools, 189,200 primary school teachers, and 7,768,000 students enrolled at the primary level, with a student-to-teacher ratio of forty-one to one. Just over one-third of all children of primary school age were enrolled in a school in 1989. There were 11,978 secondary schools, 154,802 secondary school teachers, and 2,995,000 students enrolled at the secondary level, with a student-to-teacher ratio of nineteen to one.

Primary school dropout rates remained fairly consistent in the 1970s and 1980s, at just over 50 percent for boys and 60 percent for girls. The middle school dropout rates for boys and girls rose from 22 percent in 1976 to about 33 percent in 1983. However, a noticeable shift occurred in the beginning of the 1980s regarding the postprimary dropout rate: whereas boys and girls had relatively equal rates (14 percent) in 1975, by 1979—just as Zia initiated his government's Islamization program—the dropout rate for boys was 25 percent while for girls it was only 16 percent. By 1993 this trend had dramatically reversed, and boys had a dropout rate of only 7 percent compared with the girls' rate of 15 percent.

The Seventh Five-Year Plan envisioned that every child five years old and above would have access to either a primary school or a comparable, but less comprehensive, mosque school. However, because of financial constraints, this goal was not achieved.

In drafting the Eighth Five-Year Plan in 1992, the government therefore reiterated the need to mobilize a large share of national resources to finance education. To improve access to schools, especially at the primary level, the government sought to decentralize and democratize the design and implementation of its education strategy. To give parents a greater voice in running schools, it planned to transfer control of primary and secondary schools to NGOs. The government also intended to gradually make all high schools, colleges, and universities autonomous, although no schedule was specified for achieving this ambitious goal.

Female Education

Comparison of data for men and women reveals a significant disparity in educational attainment. By 1992, among people older than fifteen years of age, 22 percent of women were literate, compared with 49 percent of men. The comparatively slow rate of improvement for women is reflected in the fact that between 1980 and 1989, among women aged fifteen to twenty-four, 25 percent were literate. United Nations sources say that in 1990 for every 100 girls of primary school age there were only thirty in school; among girls of secondary school age, only thirteen out of 100 were in school; and among girls of the third level, grades nine and ten, only 1.5 out of 100 were in school. Slightly higher estimates by the National Education Council for 1990 stated that 2.5 percent of students—3 percent of men and 2 percent of women—between the ages of seventeen and twenty-one were enrolled at the degree level. Among all people over twenty-five in 1992, women averaged a mere 0.7 year of schooling compared with an average of 2.9 years for men.

The discrepancy between rural and urban areas is even more marked. In 1981 only 7 percent of women in rural areas were literate, compared with 35 percent in urban areas. Among men, these rates were 27 and 57 percent, respectively. Pakistan's low female literacy rates are particularly confounding because these rates are analogous to those of some of the poorest countries in the world.

Pakistan has never had a systematic, nationally coordinated effort to improve female primary education, despite its poor standing. It was once assumed that the reasons behind low female school enrollments were cultural, but research conducted by the Ministry for Women's Development and a number of international donor agencies in the 1980s revealed that danger to a woman's honor was parents' most crucial concern. Indeed, reluctance to accept schooling for women turned to enthusiasm when parents in rural Punjab and rural Balochistan could be guaranteed their daughters' safety and, hence, their honor.

Reform Efforts

Three initiatives characterized reform efforts in education in the late 1980s and early 1990s: privatization of schools that had been nationalized in the 1970s; a return to English as the medium of instruction in the more elite of these privatized schools, reversing the imposition of Urdu in the 1970s; and continuing emphasis on Pakistan studies and Islamic studies in the curriculum.

Until the late 1970s, a disproportionate amount of educational spending went to the middle and higher levels. Education in the colonial era had been geared to staffing the civil service and producing an educated elite that shared the values of and was loyal to the British. It was unabashedly elitist, and contemporary education—reforms and commissions on reform notwithstanding—has retained the same quality. This fact is evident in the glaring gap in educational attainment between the country's public schools and the private schools, which were nationalized in the late 1970s in a move intended to facilitate equal access. Whereas students from lower-class backgrounds did gain increased access to these private schools in the 1980s and 1990s, teachers and school principals alike bemoaned the decline in the quality of education. Meanwhile, it appears that a greater proportion of children of the elites are traveling abroad not only for university education but also for their high school diplomas.

The extension of literacy to greater numbers of people has spurred the working class to aspire to middle-class goals such as owning an automobile, taking summer vacations, and providing a daughter with a once-inconceivable dowry at the time of marriage. In the past, Pakistan was a country that the landlords owned, the army ruled, and the bureaucrats governed, and it drew most of its elite from these three groups. In the 1990s, however, the army and the civil service were drawing a greater proportion of educated members from poor backgrounds than ever before.

One of the education reforms of the 1980s was an increase in the number of technical schools throughout the country. Those schools that were designated for females included hostels nearby to provide secure housing for female students. Increasing the number of technical schools was a response to the high rate of underemployment that had been evident since the early 1970s. The Seventh Five-Year Plan aimed to increase the share of students going to technical and vocational institutions to over 33 percent by increasing the number of polytechnics, commercial colleges, and vocational training centers. Although the numbers of such institutions did increase, a compelling need to expand vocational training persisted in early 1994.

Health and Welfare

In 1992 some 35 million Pakistanis, or about 30 percent of the population, were unable to afford nutritionally adequate food or to afford any nonfood items at all. Of these, 24.3 million lived in rural areas, where they constituted 29 percent of the population. Urban areas, with one-third of the national population, had a poverty rate of 26 percent.

Between 1985 and 1991, about 85 percent of rural residents and 100 percent of urban dwellers had access to some kind of Western or biomedical health care; but 12.9 million people had no access to health services. Only 45 percent of rural people had safe water, as compared with 80 percent of urbanites, leaving 55 million without potable water. Also in the same period, only 10 percent of rural residents had access to modern sanitation while 55 percent of city residents did; a total of 94.9 million people hence were without sanitary facilities.

In the early 1990s, the leading causes of death remained gastroenteritis, respiratory infections, congenital abnormalities, tuberculosis, malaria, and typhoid. Gastrointestinal, parasitic, and respiratory ailments, as well as malnutrition, contributed substantially to morbidity. The incidence of communicable childhood diseases was high; measles, diphtheria, and pertussis took a substantial toll among children under five years of age. Although the urban poor also suffered from these diseases, those in rural areas were the principal victims.

Despite these discouraging facts, there has been significant improvement in some health indicators. For example, in 1960 only 25 percent of the population had purportedly safe water (compared with 56 percent in 1992). In addition, average life expectancy at birth was 43.1 years in 1960; in 1992 it had reached 58.3 years.

Maternal and Child Health

The average age of marriage for women was 19.8 between 1980 and 1990, and, with the rate of contraception use reaching only 12 percent in 1992, many women delivered their first child about one year later. Thus, nearly half of Pakistani women have at least one child before they complete their twentieth year. In 1988–90 only 70 percent of pregnant women received any prenatal care; the same proportion of births was attended by health workers. A study covering the years 1975 to 1990 found that 57 percent of pregnant women were anemic and that many suffered from vitamin deficiencies. In 1988 some 600 of every 100,000 deliveries resulted in the death of the mother. Among women who die between ages fifteen and forty-five, a significant portion of deaths are related to childbearing.

The inadequate health care and the malnutrition suffered by women are reflected in infant and child health statistics. About 30 percent of babies born between 1985 and 1990 were of low birth weight. During 1992 ninety-nine of every 1,000 infants died in their first year of life. Mothers breast-feed for a median of twenty months, according to a 1986–90 survey, but generally withhold necessary supplementary foods until weaning. In 1990 approximately 42 percent of children under five years of age were underweight. In 1992 there were 3.7 million malnourished children, and 652,000 died. Poor nutrition contributes significantly to childhood morbidity and mortality.

Progress has been made despite these rather dismal data. The infant mortality rate dropped from 163 per 1,000 live births in 1960 to ninety-nine per 1,000 in 1992. Immunization has also expanded rapidly in the recent past; 81 percent of infants had received the recommended vaccines in 1992. A network of immunization clinics—virtually free in most places—exists in urban areas and ensures that health workers are notified of a child's birth. Word of mouth and media attention, coupled with rural health clinics, seem to be responsible for the rapid increase in immunization rates in rural areas. By 1992 about 85 percent of the population had access to oral rehydration salts, and oral rehydration therapy was expected to reduce child mortality.

Health Care Policies and Developments

National public health is a recent innovation in Pakistan. In prepartition India, the British provided health care for government employees but rarely attended to the health needs of the population at large, except for establishing a few major hospitals, such as Mayo Hospital in Lahore, which has King Edward Medical College nearby. Improvements in health care have been hampered by scarce resources and are difficult to coordinate nationally because health care remains a provincial responsibility rather than a central government one. Until the early 1970s, local governing bodies were in charge of health services.

National health planning began with the Second Five-Year Plan (1960–65) and continued through the Eighth Five-Year Plan (1993–98). Provision of health care for the rural populace has long been a stated priority, but efforts to provide such care continue to be hampered by administrative problems and difficulties in staffing rural clinics. In the early 1970s, a decentralized system was developed in which basic health units provided primary care for a surrounding population of 6,000 to 10,000 people, rural health centers offered support and more comprehensive services to local units, and both the basic units and the health centers could refer patients to larger urban hospitals.

In the early 1990s, the orientation of the country's medical system, including medical education, favored the elite. There has been a marked boom in private clinics and hospitals since the late 1980s and a corresponding, unfortunate deterioration in services provided by nationalized hospitals. In 1992 there was only one physician for every 2,127 persons, one nurse for every 6,626 persons, and only one hospital for every 131,274 persons. There was only one dentist for every 67,757 persons.

Medical schools have come under a great deal of criticism from women's groups for discriminating against females. In some cities, females seeking admission to medical school have even held demonstrations against separate gender quotas. Males can often gain admission to medical schools with lower test scores than females because the absolute number for males in the separate quotas is much greater than that for females. The quota exists despite the pressing need for more physicians available to treat women.

The government has embarked on a major health initiative with substantial donor assistance. The initial phase of an estimated US$140 million family health project, which would eventually aid all four provinces, was approved in July 1991 by the government of Pakistan and the World Bank, the latter's first such project in Pakistan. The program is aimed at improving maternal health care and controlling epidemic diseases in Sindh and the North-West Frontier Province. It will provide help for staff development, particularly in training female paramedics, and will also strengthen the management and organization of provincial health departments. The estimated completion date is 1999. The second stage of the project will include Punjab and Balochistan.

In addition to public- and private-sector biomedicine, there are indigenous forms of treatment. *Unani-Tibb* (Arabic for Greek medicine), also called *Islami-Tibb,* is Galenic medicine resystematized and augmented by Muslim scholars. Herbal treatments are used to balance bodily humors. Practitioners, *hakims,* are trained in medical colleges or learn the skill from family members who pass it down the generations. Some manufactured remedies are also available in certain pharmacies. Homeopathy, thought by some to be "poor man's Western medicine," is also taught and practiced in Pakistan. Several forms of religious healing are common too. Prophetic healing is based largely on the hadith of the Prophet pertaining to hygiene and moral and physical health, and simple treatments are used, such as honey, a few herbs, and prayer. Some religious conservatives argue that reliance on anything but prayer suggests lack of faith, while others point out that the Prophet remarked that Allah had created medicines in order that humans should avail themselves of their benefits. Popular forms of religious healing, at least protection from malign influences, are common in most of the country. The use of *tawiz*, amulets containing Quranic verses, or the intervention of a *pir*, living or dead, is generally relied upon to direct the healing force of Allah's blessing to anyone confronted with uncertainty or distress.

Special Problems: Smoking, Drugs, and AIDS

Smoking is primarily a health threat for men. Nearly half of all men smoked in the 1970s and 1980s, whereas only 5 percent of women smoked. Twenty-five percent of all adults were estimated to be smokers in 1985, with a marked increase among women (who still generally smoke only at home). The national airline, Pakistan International Airlines (PIA), instituted a no-smoking policy on all its domestic flights in the late 1980s. In an unusual departure from global trends, PIA reversed this policy in mid-1992, claiming public pressure—despite no evident public outcry in newspapers or other media (see Transportation, ch. 3). Men also take *neswar*, a tobacco-based ground mixture including lime that is placed under the tongue. Both men and women chew *pan*, betel nut plus herbs and sometimes tobacco wrapped in betel leaf; the dark red juice damages teeth and gums. Both *neswar* and *pan* may engender mild dependency and may contribute to oral cancers or other serious problems.

Opium smuggling and cultivation, as well as heroin production, became major problems after the Soviet invasion of Afghanistan in 1979. The war interrupted the opium pipeline from Afghanistan to the West, and Ayatollah Ruhollah Khomeini's crackdown on drug smuggling made shipment through Iran difficult. Pakistan was an attractive route because corrupt officials could easily be bribed. Although the government cooperated with international agencies, most notably the United States Agency for International Development, in their opium poppy substitution programs, Pakistan became a major center for heroin production and a transshipment point for the international drug market.

Opium poppy cultivation, already established in remote highland areas of the North-West Frontier Province by the late nineteenth century, increased after World War II and expanded again to become the basis of some local economies in the mid-1980s. Harvesting requires intensive labor, but profits are great, and storage and marketing are easy. The annual yield from an entire village can be transported from an isolated area on a few donkeys. Opium poppy yields, estimated at 800 tons in 1979, dropped to between forty and forty-five tons by 1985 but dramatically rose to 130 tons in 1989 and then 180 tons in 1990. Yields then declined slowly to 175 tons in 1992 and 140 tons in 1993. The area under opium poppy cultivation followed the same pattern, from 5,850 hectares in 1989 to 8,215 hectares in 1990. It reached 9,147 hectares in 1992 but dropped to 6,280 the following year. The caretaker government of Moeen Qureshi (July to mid-October 1993) was responsible for the reductions in production and area under cultivation; the succeeding government of Benazir Bhutto has perpetuated his policies and declared its intent to augment them.

Use of heroin within Pakistan has expanded significantly. The Pakistan Narcotics Control Board estimates that although there were no known heroin addicts in Pakistan in 1980, the figure had reached 1.2 million by 1989; there were more than 2 million drug addicts of all types in the country in 1991. This dramatic increase is attributed to the ready availability of drugs. There were only thirty drug treatment centers in Pakistan in 1991, with a reported cure rate of about 20 percent.

Acquired immune deficiency syndrome (AIDS) has not yet been much of a problem in Pakistan, probably as a result of cultural mores opposing premarital, extramarital, and openly homosexual relations. The effect of poor quality control on blood supplies and needle sharing among addicts is undetermined. The government has been slow to respond to the threat posed by AIDS. Cultural and religious restrictions prevent official policies encouraging "safe-sex" or other programs that would prevent the spread of the disease. State-run radio and television stations have made no attempt to educate the public about AIDS. In fact, the government has minimized the problem of AIDS in the same way that it has dealt with potentially widespread alcoholism by labeling it as a "foreigners' disease."

The Ministry of Health, however, has established the National AIDS Control Programme to monitor the disease and to try to prevent its spread. During 1993 twenty-five AIDS screening centers were established at various hospitals, including the Agha Khan University Hospital in Karachi, the National Institute of Health in Islamabad, and the Jinnah Postgraduate Medical Centre. AIDS screening kits and materials are provided free at these facilities. By early 1994, approximately 300,000 people in Pakistan had been tested.

A center for AIDS testing has also been established at the Port Health Office in Keamari Harbor in Karachi. Another is expected to open during 1994 at Quaid-i-Azam Karachi International Airport. Beginning in 1994, all foreigners and sailors arriving in Pakistan are required to have certificates stating that they are AIDS-free. Certificates of inspection are already required of Pakistani sailors. All imported blood, blood products, and vaccines must also be certified.

Zakat as a Welfare System

Social security plans were first introduced in the 1960s but have never achieved much success. Traditionally, the family and *biradari* have functioned as a welfare system that can be relied on in times of need based on reciprocal obligations.

In 1980, as a part of his Islamization program, Zia introduced a welfare system, known as the Zakat and Ushr Ordinance. Based on the Islamic notion of *zakat*, the aim was to forge a national system to help those without kin. The Zakat and Ushr Ordinance combined elements of the traditional Islamic welfare institution with those of a modern public welfare system. The ordinance's moral imperative and much of its institutional structure were directly based on the Quran and the sharia.

As a traditional religious institution, *zakat* involves both the payment and the distribution of an alms tax given by Muslims who enjoy some surplus to certain kinds of deserving poor Muslims (*mustahaqeen*—see Glossary). The traditional interpretation by the Hanafi school of religious law stipulates that *zakat* is to be paid once a year on wealth held more than one year. The rate varies, although it is generally 2.5 percent. *Ushr* is another form of almsgiving, a 5 percent tax paid on the produce of land, not on the value of the land itself. Both *zakat* and *ushr* are paid to groups as specified in the Quran, such as the poor, the needy, recent converts to Islam, people who do the good works of God, and those who collect and disburse *zakat.*

The Zakat and Ushr Ordinance set broad parameters for eligibility for *zakat,* which is determined by local *zakat* committees. Priority is given to widows, orphans, the disabled, and students in traditional religious schools. Eligibility is broad and flexible and presumes great trust in the integrity, fairness, and good sense of the local *zakat* committees. Although the program initially focused on providing cash payments, it gradually has moved into establishing training centers, especially sewing centers for women. By 1983 the *zakat* program had disbursed more than Rs2.5 billion to some 4 million people. The program, however, has come under a great deal of criticism for the uneven manner in which funds are disbursed.

Shia have vociferously criticized the program on the basis that its innate structure is built around Sunni jurisprudence. Shia leaders have successfully championed the right to collect *zakat* payments from members of their community and to distribute them only among Shia *mustahaqeen.*

Prospects for Social Cohesion

Pakistan has been struggling to develop an all-encompassing identity since the founding of the state in 1947. The nation was created by Western-oriented professionals and bureaucrats as a homeland for Muslims, a place where they would no longer be a minority community in the Hindu-majority state of India. Enthusiasm and a sense of profound moral renaissance for Muslims in South Asia accompanied independence. Expectations were high that Pakistan would flourish and that its citizens would be unified by their sense of social contract. It was hoped that Pakistanis would freely and vigorously engage in parliamentary debate, while creating new industries, all under the umbrella of Islam.

This vision of promise and unity soon encountered the realities of state building. Islamists and secularists disputed the centrality of Islam in the government. Pakhtun and Baloch tribes resisted relinquishing their autonomy to the new centralized state, which they regarded as an outside power. Partition also created new ethnic communities. The Urdu-speaking entrepreneurs and industrialists who migrated to Karachi created a new self-identifying group, the *muhajirs.* Unlike the majority of Pakistanis, who are tied emotionally and politically to a specific locality in the country, *muhajirs* did not have these ties. When the new state granted housing and land to the *muhajirs* to compensate them for what they had left behind in India, indigenous Punjabis and Sindhis clashed with the newcomers. Also during the 1950s, language riots in East Pakistan and anti-Ahmadiyya protests in Punjab cast doubt on the unity of Pakistanis under the rubric of Muslim brotherhood.

In the 1950s and 1960s, Pakistan emphasized building its industrial base to ensure both economic and political survival. Western-educated professionals and industrialists, as well as forward-looking feudal landlords who valued education, were increasingly influential; more traditional leaders saw their power deteriorate. A fairly liberal interpretation of Islam was supported by the state, resulting in the passage of the Muslim Family Laws Ordinance in 1961.

Zulfiqar Ali Bhutto promoted "Islamic Socialism" in his 1971 electoral campaign, raising the material expectations of the masses to an unprecedented level. Many people believed that life would improve significantly under Bhutto and the Pakistan People's Party (PPP), but from 1971 to 1977 there was little change in the standard of living.

Intergroup tensions grew as members of the lower and middle classes became disillusioned, as upper-class industrialists were alienated by the government's nationalization policies, and as wealthy landlords were threatened by Bhutto's land reform program.

Ethnic groups in Balochistan and the North-West Frontier Province pressed for increased autonomy, while *muhajirs*, not yet organized as a political group, ran the city of Karachi and as non-Muslim minorities worried about the state's increasingly formal identification with Islam.

Bhutto restructured the civil bureaucracy while increasing his personal authority, alienating many people at the highest echelons of power while creating opportunities for others. Under the first democratically elected government in twenty years, Bhutto made full use of his power by giving jobs and privileges to supporters of the PPP.

Under Zia ul-Haq, who governed from 1977 to 1988, nepotism continued: who one knew was much more important than what one knew. The leadership gave jobs, contracts, and privileges to its allies as it sought to undermine the PPP. Traditional markers of ascribed identity, such as mother tongue, area of family origin, and kinship ties, increasingly dictated individuals' opportunities as competition continued to block the development of citizenship based on shared, nationwide concerns. The common expression in Urdu and Punjabi, "the whole world knows (or believes) that . . .," reflects the small (usually family or neighborhood) social reference group of many Pakistanis. This way of constructing a social world is not conducive to setting aside one's own kinship identity and ties in favor of a more abstract national one based on citizenship.

In February 1979, Zia decreed that Islam—or, rather, a certain interpretation of Islam—was to be the basis of Pakistan's legal system. Fearing discrimination, some non-Muslim minorities, especially Zoroastrians, began to emigrate from Karachi in unprecedented numbers. Shia Muslims marched on Islamabad in 1982 to protect their right to maintain their own system of social welfare.

Zia employed his rhetoric of Islamic state building to disguise his political opportunism. He also exploited the Soviet invasion of Afghanistan to build his arsenal of weapons by diverting some that were shipped through Pakistan for the Afghans. Some experts have even argued that the massive explosion at the Ojhri munitions camp on the outskirts of Rawalpindi in April 1988 was deliberately planned to justify "replacement" purchases in excess of the quantity actually lost.

In the 1980s, Pakistan continued to place little emphasis on social programming despite growing problems, including a rapid rise in heroin addiction. The country has been criticized by international development organizations for ignoring social and human development. In the 1980s, the government's priorities were instead political, and it strengthened those regional political leaders who could contain the PPP in their localities. In addition, the central government declared that democratic principles would have to remain in abeyance while the state searched for the right Islamic guidelines. The government's decision allowed local officials to continue corrupt practices, such as hiring and firing people within the bureaucracy at will and making significant commissions from contracts on projects they approved.

To many Pakistanis already disillusioned with the economic and political functioning of the state, the fundamental social weaknesses of the nation came to the fore in the early 1990s. The most obvious of these—uneven distribution of wealth; the self-centeredness, nepotism, and greed of the privileged; and rapid population growth among the nation's poorest people—made the institutionalization of a nationwide concept of citizenship problematic. The failure to forge a widely understood social contract is reflected in increased tensions among ethnic groups, social classes, extended families, and religious factions.

The way people interrelate with one another, the way they perceive national issues and their role in affecting them, and the priority they assign to personal ties and group identification are all parts of the matrix of a society and indicators of its social cohesion. Until Pakistanis can come up with an inner commitment to a cause—which in Pakistan's history has been fairly rare outside of kinship circles—little can be done or will be done to serve the wider society impartially, be it a national conservation strategy, education reform, opium poppy substitution programs, or the promotion of industrial growth.

* * *

General works pertaining to social change in Pakistan include Sabeeha Hafeez's *The Changing Pakistan Society*, Akbar S. Ahmed's *Discovering Islam*, Anita M. Weiss's *Culture, Class, and Development in Pakistan*, Hastings Donnan and Pnina Werbner's *Economy and Culture in Pakistan*, and Myron Weiner and Ali Banuazizi's *The State and the Restructuring of Society in Afghanistan, Iran, and Pakistan*. Shahid Javed Burki examines Pakistan's social development in *Pakistan: A Nation in the Making*, and Naseem Jaffer Quddus addresses education issues in *Problems of Education in Pakistan*.

Khawar Mumtaz and Farida Shaheed's *Women of Pakistan* gives an overview of the Pakistan women's movement. The controversial report by the Pakistan Commission on the Status of Women became available in 1991, five years after it was published. For a composite of statistical information on women based on all four of Pakistan's official censuses, the Pakistan government's Federal Bureau of Statistics' Women's Division's *Women in Pakistan: A Statistical Profile* and Ann Duncan's *Women in Pakistan: An Economic and Social Strategy* are helpful. A recent study of women's lives, drawing on women's own words and views in the context of wider social changes, is Anita M. Weiss's *Walls Within Walls*. Islamic issues in Pakistan are analyzed in Anita M. Weiss's *Islamic Reassertion in Pakistan* and John L. Esposito's *Islam and Politics*.

Environmental issues are addressed in the Pakistan government's *National Conservation Strategy Report*. Geographic information can be found in Ashok K. Dutt and M.M. Geib's *Atlas of South Asia* and in K.U. Kureshy's *A Geography of Pakistan*. The works of Frederick Barth and Akbar S. Ahmed analyze Pakhtun society, and an in-depth look at the Baloch is provided in A.H. Siddiqi's *Baluchistan.*

The most important English-language magazines providing useful accounts of current social issues are the *Herald* and *Newsline,* both based in Karachi. Travel narratives that capture cultural features of Pakistani life include Geoffrey Moorhouse's *To the Frontier,* Richard Reeves's *Passage to Peshawar,* and Christina Lamb's controversial *Waiting for Allah.* (For further information and complete citations, see Bibliography.)

Chapter 3. The Economy

Artist's rendition of tile mosaic of lion chasing deer from the Pictured Wall, Lahore Fort, Punjab. Artwork represents seventeenth-century tile work of the Mughal period.

PAKISTAN'S CULTIVATION of the rich alluvial soil of the Indus River basin is its single most important economic activity. Because of extensions and improvements of the irrigation system, waters of the Indus River and its tributaries flow to the fields, a necessity because of scant rainfall. The Indus irrigation system is the world's largest, but there are many problems because of inadequate water management and use. Farmers continue to employ traditional cultivation practices, and support services, such as research and development, are inadequate, although high-yield seeds and fertilizers are fairly widely used. Yields of most crops, with the significant exception of cotton, are low by international standards and substantially below the area's potential. Many farms are too small to support a family using existing agricultural practices. The landless often sharecrop or work as agricultural laborers. A flood in September 1992 temporarily displaced as many as 3 million people and destroyed many irrigation networks. Its effects are expected to limit agricultural production, particularly cotton, in the 1990s.

Since Pakistan became independent in 1947, its leaders have generally sought to increase the role of industry in the nation's economy. They have achieved a remarkable degree of success toward this end. A broad industrial base is now in place, producing a wide range of products for both consumer and industrial use. Industrialization, however, has failed to create sufficient jobs for the rapidly expanding urban population. Construction and service-sector activities, especially in trade, transportation, and government, have expanded and now provide more employment than industry. Nonetheless, underemployment remains prevalent throughout the economy. An outdated infrastructure is another problem facing the economy. Frequent electricity shortages, for example, hamper industrial development and production.

Most central government administrations have sought to raise the majority of the population's low standard of living through economic growth rather than through the redistribution of wealth. The gross domestic product (GDP—see Glossary) in constant prices increased an average of 5.3 percent per year between 1950 and 1993, roughly 2 percent per year more than population growth. In fiscal year (FY—see Glossary) 1993,

GDP amounted to the equivalent of US$50.8 billion, or roughly US$408 on a per capita basis. Income, however, has never been evenly distributed. Furthermore, the unequal income distribution pattern has been a political issue since the late 1960s and is expected to remain controversial throughout the 1990s. Social development indicators reflect long-standing problems in providing basic health and education services. Only just over-one third of all children of primary school age attended school in 1989, a rate well below the average for low-income countries (see Education, ch. 2). It was estimated in 1992 that 28 percent of the population lived below the official poverty line, which is based on the government's estimate of an income sufficient to provide basic minimum needs.

A pressing problem facing the economy is the government's chronically high budget deficit, which has adverse implications for the nation's balance of payments, inflation and exchange rates, capital formation, and overall financial stability. The government has been attempting to restore fiscal balance through a multiyear structural adjustment program designed to increase revenues, control spending, and stabilize monetary growth. In addition, the government has privatized public-sector industrial enterprises, financial institutions, and utilities; eliminated state monopolies in banking, insurance, shipping, telecommunications, airlines, and power generation; and liberalized investment and foreign-exchange regulations. As of early 1994, not all these programs had been implemented as quickly as planned, however, and the deficit and the associated structural problems persisted.

Structure of the Economy

Pakistan attained nationhood under difficult circumstances (see Problems at Independence, ch. 1). At the partition of British India in 1947 resulting in the creation of the independent nations of India and Pakistan, Pakistan was an agrarian economy in which a small number of powerful landowners with large holdings dominated the countryside. The majority of the population consisted of tenant farmers who cultivated small plots for a meager existence. Scant rainfall in West Pakistan (present-day Pakistan) forced farmers to rely on the extensive irrigation system developed by the British. The headwaters of the Indus River and its main tributaries, however, were under Indian control. Disputes arose between the two nations and were not settled until the Indus Waters Treaty of 1960 was signed (see Irrigation, this ch.).

At partition Pakistan had almost no industry. Under British rule, the area had supplied agricultural products for processing to the territory that became independent India. Energy sources were rudimentary, with wood and animal dung furnishing the bulk of the energy consumed. Ports, transportation, and other services, such as banking and government, were underdeveloped. More than 1,600 kilometers of Indian territory separated the East Wing and West Wing of Pakistan until the former became independent Bangladesh in 1971 (see Yahya Khan and Bangladesh, ch. 1). In 1949 a dispute over exchange rates halted the flow of goods between Pakistan and India, disrupting the complementary nature of their economies that had developed under British colonial rule.

Despite formidable problems, Pakistan achieved rapid economic expansion. From FY 1951 to FY 1986, the GDP growth rate measured at a constant FY 1960 factor averaged 5.2 percent. Rates of growth averaged 3.1 percent in the 1950s—when agriculture stagnated—but rose to 6.8 percent in the 1960s. They fell to 3.8 percent between FY 1971 and FY 1977 but rebounded to 6.8 percent between FY 1978 and FY 1986. From FY 1987 to FY 1991, growth averaged 5.8 percent, and a rate of 7.8 percent was achieved in FY 1992. Provisional data indicate that GDP grew only 2.6 percent in FY 1993. This decline is mainly a result of the floods in September 1992, which reduced agricultural output.

Rapid growth substantially altered the structure of the economy. Agriculture's share (including forestry and fishing) declined from 53 percent of GDP in FY 1950 to 25 percent in FY 1993 (see table 3, Appendix). A substantial industrial base was added as industry (including mining, manufacturing, and utilities) became the fastest growing sector of the economy. Industry's share of GDP rose from 8 percent in FY 1950 to 21.7 percent in FY 1993. Various services (including construction, trade, transportation and communications, and other services) accounted for the rest of GDP.

Pakistan has an important "parallel," or "alternative," economic sector, but it is not well documented in official reports or most academic studies. This sector includes a thriving black market, a large illicit drug industry, and illegal payments to politicians and government officials to ensure state contracts. Corruption rose in the 1980s, partly as a result of the difficulty in monitoring the massive infusion of United States aid that flowed to Pakistan as a result of the Soviet occupation of neighboring Afghanistan. Some aid went to the Pakistani government to help defray the costs of supporting several million Afghan refugees. Other aid bolstered Pakistan's military capability, necessary because Pakistan had become a "frontline" state. Finally, large amounts of aid were also funneled directly to Afghan resistance movements based in Pakistan. It was much of this money that reportedly was delivered illegally and invested in arms and drug enterprises.

General allegations of corruption are routinely made in the Pakistani press, and politicians often accuse their opponents of corrupt practices. Asif Ali Zardari, the husband of Prime Minister Benazir Bhutto, was accused of corruption after the fall of Benazir's first government in 1990, and former President Ghulam Ishaq Khan accused the government of former Prime Minister Mian Nawaz Sharif and especially its privatization program of corruption when dismissing his government in April 1993. In 1994 allegations of corruption were routinely traded between Benazir's government and the opposition headed by Nawaz Sharif. Political maneuvering aside, corruption has an altogether real and pervasive effect on Pakistani society. Industrialists consider bribery and other handouts a routine cost of production, and contractors and businessmen interviewed on television openly state that a significant percentage of their revenue is paid to government officers who allocate their contracts. Corruption is alleged to be prevalent in almost all official institutions, including the police, the judiciary, the revenue department, the passport office, customs and excise offices, telecommunications organizations, and electricity and gas boards. In each of these departments, the personnel involved range from low-level employees to top management. Some scholars believe that the low salaries of civil servants, compared with earnings from jobs of similar status in business and industry, explain the magnitude of corruption. In the mid-1980s, Mahbubul Haq, a former minister of finance, estimated that illegal payments to government officials were equivalent to about 60 percent of the total taxes collected by the government.

The Role of Government

Policy Developments since Independence

Since 1947 Pakistani officials have sought a high rate of eco-

Quaid-i-Azam Karachi International Airport
Courtesy Embassy of Pakistan, Washington

nomic growth in an effort to lift the population out of poverty. Rapid industrialization was viewed as a basic necessity and as a vehicle for economic growth. For more than two decades, economic expansion was substantial, and growth of industrial output was striking. In the 1960s, the country was considered a model for other developing countries. The rapid expansion of the Pakistani economy, however, did not alleviate the widespread poverty. In the 1970s and 1980s, although a high rate of growth was sought, greater attention was given to income distribution. In the early 1990s, a more equitable distribution of income remained an important but elusive goal of government policy.

At partition in 1947, the new government lacked the personnel, institutions, and resources to play a large role in developing the economy. Exclusive public ownership was reserved for military armaments, generation of hydroelectric power, and manufacture and operation of railroad, telephone, telegraph, and wireless equipment—fields that were unattractive, at least in the early years of independence, to private investors. The rest of the economy was open to private-sector development, although the government used many direct and indirect measures to stimulate, guide, or retard private-sector activities.

The disruptions caused by partition, the cessation of trade with India, the strict control of imports, and the overvalued exchange rate necessitated the stimulation of private industry. Government policies afforded liberal incentives to industrialization, while public development of the infrastructure complemented private investment. Some public manufacturing plants were established by government holding companies. Manufacturing proved highly profitable, attracting increasing private investments and reinvestment of profits. Except for large government investments in the Indus irrigation system, agriculture was left largely alone, and output stagnated in the 1950s. The broad outline of government policy in the 1950s and early 1960s involved squeezing the peasants and workers to finance industrial development.

Much of the economy, and particularly industry, was eventually dominated by a small group of people, the *muhajirs* (see Glossary), who were largely traders who migrated to Pakistan's cities, especially Karachi, at partition. These refugees brought modest capital, which they initially used to start trading firms. Many of these firms moved into industry in the 1950s as a response to government policies. Largely using their own resources, they accounted for the major part of investment and ownership in manufacturing during the first two decades after independence.

By the late 1960s, there was growing popular dissatisfaction with economic conditions and considerable debate about the inequitable distribution of income, wealth, and economic power—problems that had always plagued the country. Studies by economists in the 1960s indicated that the forty big industrial groups owned around 42 percent of the nation's industrial assets and more than 50 percent of private domestic assets. Eight of the nine major commercial banks were also controlled by these same industrial groups. Concern over the concentration of wealth was dramatically articulated in a 1968 speech by Mahbubul Haq, then chief economist of the Planning Commission. Haq claimed that Pakistan's economic growth had done little to improve the standard of living of the common person and that the "trickle-down approach to development" had only concentrated wealth in the hands of "twenty-two industrial families." He argued that the government needed to intervene in the economy to correct the natural tendency of free markets to concentrate wealth in the hands of those who already possessed substantial assets.

Although Haq exaggerated the extent of the concentration of wealth, his speech struck a chord with public opinion. In response, the government enacted piecemeal measures between 1968 and 1971 to set minimum wages, promote collective bargaining for labor, reform the tax structure toward greater equity, and rationalize salary structures. However, implementation was weak or nonexistent, and it was only when the government of Zulfiqar Ali Bhutto (father of Benazir) came to power in 1971 that there was a major shift in government policy.

Bhutto promised a new development strategy more equitable than previous policies. Yet he downplayed economic analysis and planning and relied instead on ad hoc decisions that created many inconsistencies. In May 1972, he promulgated a major act that devalued the rupee (R or Re, pl., Rs; for value of the rupee—see Glossary) by 57 percent and abolished the multiple exchange-rate system. This act greatly stimulated exports and indicated that the removal of price distortions could spur the economy. But devaluation also completely altered the cost and price structure for industry and affected the level and composition of industrial investment and the terms of trade between the industrial and agricultural sectors. Devaluation helped agriculture, particularly larger farms that had marketable surpluses. Mechanization increased but had the adverse side effect of displacing farm laborers and tenants, many of whom migrated to cities seeking industrial jobs.

In 1972 Bhutto's government nationalized thirty-two large manufacturing plants in eight major industries. The industries affected included iron and steel, basic metals, heavy engineering, motor vehicle and tractor assembly and manufacture, chemicals, petrochemicals, cement, and public utilities. Subsequently, domestically owned life insurance companies, privately owned banks, domestic shipping companies, and firms engaged in oil distribution, vegetable oil processing, grain milling, and cotton ginning were nationalized. The result was a drop of nearly 50 percent in private investment in large-scale manufacturing between FY 1970 and FY 1973. By FY 1978 such investments were little more than one-third (in constant prices) of those in FY 1970. Private capital fled the country or went into small-scale manufacturing and real estate. Between 1970 and 1977, industrial output slowed considerably.

The public sector expanded greatly under the Bhutto government. In addition to the nationalization of companies, plants were built by the government and additional public companies were created for various functions, such as the export of cotton and rice. Able managers and technicians were scarce, a situation that became worse after 1974, when many persons left to seek higher salaries in Middle East oil-producing states. Labor legislation set high minimum wages and fringe benefits, which boosted payroll costs for both public and private firms. Efficiency and profits in public-sector enterprises fell. Public industrial investment rose, surpassing private industrial investment in FY 1976.

Many of the other economic measures undertaken by the Bhutto government were largely ineffective because of the power of vested interests and the inefficiency of the civil administration. Ceilings on the size of landholdings were lowered, tenants were given greater security of tenure, and measures were enacted to tax farm income (see Agriculture, this ch.). Bhutto also supported large, but inadequately planned, long-term projects that tied up the country's development resources for long periods. The largest projects were an integrated iron and steel plant, a major highway on the west bank of the Indus River, and a highway tunnel in the mountainous north.

After 1977 the government of Mohammad Zia ul-Haq (1977–88) began a policy of greater reliance on private enterprise to achieve economic goals, and successive governments continued this policy throughout the late 1980s and early 1990s. Soon after Zia came to power, the government instituted constitutional measures to assure private investors that nationalization would occur only under limited and exceptional circumstances and with fair compensation. A demarcation of exclusive public ownership was made that excluded the private sector from only a few activities. Yet government continued to play a large economic role in the 1980s. Public-sector enterprises accounted for a significant portion of large-scale manufacturing. In FY 1991, it was estimated that these enterprises produced about 40 percent of industrial output.

Islamization of the economy was another policy innovation of the Zia government. In 1977 Zia asked a group of Islamic scholars to recommend measures for an Islamic economic system. In June 1980, the Zakat and Ushr Ordinance was promulgated. *Zakat* is a traditional annual levy, usually 2.5 percent, on wealth to help the needy (see *Zakat* as a Welfare System, ch. 2). *Ushr* is a 5 percent tax on the produce of land, allowing some deductions for the costs of production, to be paid in cash by the landowner or leaseholder. *Ushr* replaced the former land tax levied by the provinces. Self-assessment by farmers is checked by local groups if a farmer fails to file or makes a very low estimate. Proceeds of *ushr* go to *zakat* committees to help local needy people.

The government of Prime Minister Nawaz Sharif (1990–93) introduced a program of privatization, deregulation, and economic reform aimed at reducing structural impediments to sound economic development. Top priority was given to denationalizing some 115 public industrial enterprises, abolishing the government's monopoly in the financial sector, and selling utilities to private interests. Despite resistance from officials and labor unions and criticism that the government was moving too quickly, by March 1992, control of twenty industrial units and two banks had been sold to private investors, and plans were under way to begin denationalizing several utilities. As of early 1994, proposals to end state monopolies in insurance, telecommunications, shipping, port operations, airlines, power generation, and road construction were also in various stages of implementation. Private investment no longer requires government authorization, except in sensitive industries. Investment reforms eliminated government sanction requirements, eased restrictions on repatriable direct and portfolio investment from abroad, enabled foreign firms to issue shares in enterprises in Pakistan, and authorized foreign banks to underwrite securities on the same basis as Pakistani banks.

Although the Nawaz Sharif government made considerable progress in liberalizing the economy, it failed to address the problem of a growing budget deficit, which in turn led to a loss of confidence in the government on the part of foreign aid donors. The caretaker government of July–October 1993 led by Moeen Qureshi, a former World Bank (see Glossary) vice president, asserted that the nation was near insolvency and would require a number of measures to impose fiscal discipline. The caretaker government thus responded with sharp increases in utility prices, new taxes, stiffer enforcement of existing taxes, and reductions in government spending. In early 1994, the government of Benazir Bhutto, elected in October 1993, announced its intention to continue the policies of both deregulation and liberalization carried out by Nawaz Sharif and the tighter fiscal policies put in place by Qureshi. The government also said it intended to devote a greater proportion of the nation's resources to health and education, especially for women (see The Status of Women and the Women's Movement, ch. 2; Benazir Bhutto Returns, ch. 4).

Development Planning

Pakistan's economic development planning began in 1948. By 1950 a six-year plan had been drafted to guide government investment in developing the infrastructure. But the initial effort was unsystematic, partly because of inadequate staffing. More formal planning—incorporating overall targets, assessing resource availability, and assigning priorities—started in 1953 with the drafting of the First Five-Year Plan (1955–60). In practice, this plan was not implemented, however, mainly because political instability led to a neglect of economic policy, but in 1958 the government renewed its commitment to planning by establishing the Planning Commission.

The Second Five-Year Plan (1960–65) surpassed its major goals when all sectors showed substantial growth. The plan encouraged private entrepreneurs to participate in those activities in which a great deal of profit could be made, while the government acted in those sectors of the economy where private business was reluctant to operate. This mix of private enterprise and social responsibility was hailed as a model that other developing countries could follow. Pakistan's success, however, partially depended on generous infusions of foreign aid, particularly from the United States. After the Indo-Pakistani War of 1965 over Kashmir, the level of foreign assistance declined. More resources than had been intended also were diverted to defense. As a result, the Third Five-Year Plan (1965–70), designed along the lines of its immediate predecessor, produced only modest growth.

When the government of Zulfiqar Ali Bhutto came to power in 1971, planning was virtually bypassed. The Fourth Five-Year Plan (1970–75) was abandoned as East Pakistan became independent Bangladesh. Under Bhutto, only annual plans were prepared, and they were largely ignored.

The Zia government accorded more importance to planning. The Fifth Five-Year Plan (1978–83) was an attempt to stabilize the economy and improve the standard of living of the poorest segment of the population. Increased defense expenditures and a flood of refugees to Pakistan after the Soviet invasion of Afghanistan in December 1979, as well as the sharp increase in international oil prices in 1979–80, drew resources away from planned investments (see Pakistan Becomes a Frontline State, ch. 5). Nevertheless, some of the plan's goals were attained. Many of the controls on industry were liberalized or abolished, the balance of payments deficit was kept under control, and Pakistan became self-sufficient in all basic foodstuffs with the exception of edible oils. Yet the plan failed to stimulate substantial private industrial investment and to raise significantly the expenditure on rural infrastructure development.

The Sixth Five-Year Plan (1983–88) represented a significant shift toward the private sector. It was designed to tackle some of the major problems of the economy: low investment and savings ratios; low agricultural productivity; heavy reliance on imported energy; and low spending on health and education. The economy grew at the targeted average of 6.5 percent during the plan period and would have exceeded the target if it had not been for severe droughts in 1986 and 1987.

The Seventh Five-Year Plan (1988–93) provided for total public-sector spending of Rs350 billion. Of this total, 38 percent was designated for energy, 18 percent for transportation and communications, 9 percent for water, 8 percent for physical infrastructure and housing, 7 percent for education, 5 percent for industry and minerals, 4 percent for health, and 11 percent for other sectors. The plan gave much greater emphasis than before to private investment in all sectors of the economy. Total planned private investment was Rs292 billion, and the private-to-public ratio of investment was expected to rise from 42:58 in FY 1988 to 48:52 in FY 1993. It was also intended that public-sector corporations finance most of their own investment programs through profits and borrowing.

In August 1991, the government established a working group on private investment for the Eighth Five-Year Plan (1993–98). This group, which included leading industrialists, presidents of chambers of commerce, and senior civil servants, submitted its report in late 1992. However, in early 1994 the eighth plan had not yet been announced, mainly because the successive changes of government in 1993 forced ministers to focus on short-term issues. Instead, economic policy for FY 1994 was being guided by an annual plan.

Finance

Budget

The federal budget has two main parts: the ordinary budget, which covers current expenditures, and the development budget (Public-Sector Development Programme), which covers capital investment and development programs (see table 4, Appendix). Current expenditures accounted for 78 percent of planned spending in the FY 1994 budget. Defense accounted for 26 percent of all expenditures, and debt service took up another 36 percent. About 25 percent of federal income was earmarked to be transferred to the provinces as statutory and discretionary grants. The provinces have their own budgets and limited powers to impose taxes. In 1991 the National Finance Commission, which includes the prime minister and the four provincial chief ministers, agreed to raise the proportion of funds going to the provinces. In return, the federal government is no longer responsible for financing provincial budget deficits.

Tax collections historically have constituted a smaller proportion of GDP than that of many other countries—between FY 1984 and FY 1992, they averaged 13.8 percent. The 1993 budget estimates called for an increase to 15.1 percent, up from 13.9 percent in FY 1992. Income and corporation taxes provided 12.9 percent of tax revenues in FY 1993. Tax evasion, however, is thought to be widespread. The agricultural sector was exempt from income tax until 1993, when a temporary levy on large landowners was introduced by the Qureshi government. In early 1994, it appeared unlikely that this tax would be reimposed by the new government led by Benazir, herself a large landowner in Sindh.

Indirect taxes are the main source of revenue. They provided 84 percent of tax revenues in FY 1991 and an estimated 83 percent in FY 1992 and FY 1993. Customs duties were expected to account for 35.0 percent of all government taxes in FY 1993. Excise duties made up 17 percent of revenues, and sales taxes made up 10 percent. Potential foreign aid donors consider the heavy reliance on indirect taxes regressive and inflationary and an impediment to the general policy of trade liberalization. Under pressure from the International Monetary Fund (IMF—see Glossary), the government reduced import duty rates in the FY 1992 and FY 1993 budgets.

In a three-year (FY 1992–94) policy statement made in agreement with the World Bank and IMF in December 1991, the government committed itself to important changes in the fiscal system. New measures extended the narrow base of both direct and indirect taxes, and administrative steps were taken to increase receipts of income and wealth taxes as well as general sales and federal excise taxes as a proportion of GDP. In FY 1993, however, the Nawaz Sharif government failed to meet its fiscal targets, and relations with the World Bank and IMF became strained. After the Qureshi caretaker government came to power in July 1993, fiscal discipline was restored, and in November 1993, the World Bank and IMF made substantial aid commitments to the new government of Benazir Bhutto.

Fiscal Administration

Government tax and nontax receipts fell far short of total expenditures in the 1980s and early 1990s. Many economists believe that the increasing government debt is a growing threat to Pakistan's future economic growth. The overall deficit, as a percentage of GDP, was around 5.3 percent in the early 1980s and averaged 7.5 percent between FY 1984 and FY 1990. It reached 8.8 percent in FY 1991, but the provisional figure for FY 1992 was 6.5 percent. The FY 1993 budget forecast a deficit of 4.8 percent of GDP, but spending was higher and revenues lower than anticipated, and provisional data indicate that the deficit exceeded 9 percent. The continued gap between government revenues and spending is a major concern to potential donors of foreign aid, and in 1993 Qureshi's caretaker government raised taxes and cut spending. In 1994 the Benazir Bhutto government aimed to reduce the budget deficit to 4.5 percent of GDP by FY 1996. The government relies on bond sales and on borrowing from the banking system to finance its deficit. Internal public debt was estimated at 49.9 percent of GDP in FY 1992. By contrast, in FY 1981 internal public debt had constituted 20.9 percent of GDP.

Monetary Process

The State Bank of Pakistan was established in 1948 and remains the country's central bank and financial adviser. It is the sole bank of issue, holder of gold and currency reserves, banker to the government, lender of last resort to other banks, supervisor of other banks, and overseer of national credit policy. In October 1993, legislation reduced government control of the bank, but without giving it complete autonomy.

From 1974, when all Pakistani banks were nationalized, until 1991, all local banks were in the state sector. In 1991, as part of the government's general program of economic liberalization and the privatization of state enterprises, two small banks—the Muslim Commercial Bank and the Allied Bank—were privatized. In 1991 the government also instructed the State Bank of Pakistan to approve proposals for new private commercial banks. In early 1994, there were twenty-four commercial banks, including ten private banks that had opened since 1991, two privatized banks, and twelve banks that remained in the state sector. One of the new private banks, Mehran Bank, was closed in early 1994 amidst allegations of massive fraud. The number of new private banks was expected to increase in 1994. In March 1993, the total assets of all Pakistani banks amounted to Rs1,090 billion. Pakistani banks had 119 foreign branches and operated joint banking ventures in Malaysia, Oman, Saudi Arabia, and the United Arab Emirates.

Twenty-one foreign banks operated in Pakistan in early 1994. They had sixty-one branches, most of which were located in Karachi. United States banks with branches in Pakistan included Citibank, Chase Manhattan Bank, American Express Bank, and Bank of America.

In the 1970s and 1980s, the Bank of Credit and Commerce International (BCCI) was an important foreign bank in Pakistan. The bank had many close links with the Pakistani political and commercial elite. It was founded in 1972 by Agha Hasan Abedi, a leading Pakistani banker. Prime Minister Nawaz Sharif's family company, Ittefaq Industries, was a major borrower. BCCI's international operations were run from London, but there were three important branches in Pakistan. Abedi resigned as president of BCCI in 1990, when the ruling Al Nuhayyan family of Abu Dhabi obtained a majority share in the company. BCCI collapsed in July 1991 when the Bank of England closed BCCI's operations amid allegations of massive losses, fraud, racketeering, and laundering of drug money. The Pakistani branches continued to operate for some time after BCCI had been closed elsewhere, and there were many allegations that Pakistani businessmen and politicians had profited from the bank's illegal activities. Abedi was later indicted in the

United States for fraud and racketeering. In 1992 Pakistani operations of BCCI were amalgamated with Habib Bank.

In 1991 four Punjab-based financial cooperatives, together known as the Pakistan Cooperative Societies, failed amidst allegations of misappropriation of public funds. Estimates of money lost by depositors ranged from Rs10 billion to Rs23 billion, with up to 2.6 million accounts affected. Two of the four cooperatives were owned by relatives of then Prime Minister Nawaz Sharif, but an official inquiry cleared him and his family of any wrongdoing.

From independence until the mid-1970s, the commercial banks were poor providers of long-term capital because the interest rate structure favored short-term over long-term financing and long-term deposits over long-term loans. As a result, the government encouraged the growth of nonbanking financial institutions to act as sources of long-term credit and equity finance. These institutions continued to play an important role in the early 1990s.

The Industrial Development Bank, established in 1961, provides medium- and long-term credit, primarily to small and medium-sized firms in the private sector, while the Pakistan Industrial Credit and Investment Corporation provides long-term assistance in local or foreign currency to private companies in the industrial sector, arranging foreign loans for large projects. The National Development Finance Corporation, founded in 1973, provides similar services for the public sector and in the early 1990s also began to provide financing for the private sector. The Agricultural Development Bank gives credit to agriculture and to cottage industries, while the House Building Finance Corporation provides interest-free housing finance, taking a percentage of the property's rental income. Other specialized financial institutions include the Investment Corporation of Pakistan, the Small Business Finance Corporation, the National Investment Trust, and Bankers Equity. All these organizations, with the exception of the Pakistan Industrial Credit Corporation, which is 35 percent foreign owned, are government owned, although they often act as channels for foreign aid.

In the 1980s, three new financing corporations—Pakistan-Libya Holding, Pakistan-Kuwait Investment, and Saudi-Pak Industrial and Agricultural Investment—were established. These three institutions are jointly owned by the Pakistan government and the respective foreign governments; most of their funding comes from the foreign governments.

The adoption of Zia's policy of Islamization led to changes in the practices of financial institutions because of the Islamic prohibition against usury. In July 1979, the Investment Corporation of Pakistan, the National Investment Trust, and the House Building Finance Corporation opened interest-free accounts that operate on a profit-and-loss-sharing basis. In 1981 the commercial banks followed suit. Under this system, profits and losses on projects financed with deposit sums are shared in an agreed-on proportion between lender and borrower. In 1985 regulations prohibited new interest-bearing loans and interest-bearing rupee deposits. These regulations cover rupee deposits in foreign banks but not deposits made in foreign currencies. In 1990 more than 63 percent of funds on deposit were held in profit-and-loss-sharing schemes.

In addition to the profit-and-loss-sharing system, lending takes two other forms. Banks make interest-free loans but assess service charges at rates determined by the State Bank of Pakistan. Banks also provide financing for the purchase of goods or real estate according to a system whereby the bank purchases the item and agrees to resell it to the client at an increased price. All these modes of finance are subject to criticism by some advocates of Islamization on the grounds that they contain a provision for a guaranteed rate of return that can be construed as the equivalent of interest.

In November 1991, the Federal Shariat Court declared all laws pertaining to the payment or receipt of interest and markup contrary to Islam. It also ruled against the indexation of financial assets for inflation. The federal and provincial governments were ordered to amend all relevant laws by June 30, 1992, but appeals by banks and the central government rendered the deadline inoperative. As of early 1994, no higher court decision had been announced (see Politicized Islam, ch. 2).

The National Credit Consultative Council formulates annual credit plans. The council includes members from government, financial institutions, and the private sector. The credit plan sets a limit on the expansion of the money supply, taking into account the targets of the development plan and the government's fiscal objectives, as well as prevailing rates of growth and projections for GDP. In the late 1980s and early 1990s, money growth tended to run well ahead of plan targets.

Rapid expansion of the money supply, coupled with the impact of the 1991 Persian Gulf War on domestic energy prices, pushed up the consumer price index by 13 percent during FY 1991. Although energy prices fell in FY 1992, heavy government borrowing from the central bank kept inflation relatively high in FY 1992 and FY 1993, at around 9 percent. Some independent observers, including the World Bank, believed that the official inflation statistics understated the real rate in FY 1993, which they put at about 13 percent.

The principal stock market is the Karachi Stock Exchange, although there are also small stock markets in Lahore and Islamabad. The stock market expanded greatly during the 1980s. In 1991 there were almost 550 companies listed, with a market capitalization of US$4.3 billion. The turnover ratio was 12.6 percent, which represented a traded value of US$542 million. In 1991, as part of the government's deregulation policies, restrictions on foreign investment in shares of listed Pakistani companies were lifted, as were constraints on the repatriation of investment proceeds, gains, and dividends. Initially, most foreign investment was carried out by portfolio managers and institutional investors based in Hong Kong and Singapore.

Foreign Economic Relations

Foreign Aid

Since independence Pakistan has had to depend on foreign assistance in its development efforts and to balance its international debt payments. In 1960 the World Bank organized the Aid-to-Pakistan Consortium to facilitate coordination among the major providers of international assistance. The consortium held 92 percent of Pakistan's outstanding disbursed debt at the end of June 1991. The consortium's members include the United States, Canada, Japan, Britain, Germany, France, and international organizations such as the World Bank and the Asian Development Bank (ADB). The World Bank accounted for 26 percent of the outstanding debt, and the ADB, which was the largest lender in the early 1990s, accounted for 15 percent. Most nonconsortium funding comes from Saudi Arabia and other oil-producing Middle Eastern countries. Most aid is in the form of loans, although the proportion of grants increased from around 12 percent in the late 1970s to around 25 percent in the 1980s, mainly because of food aid and other funds directed toward Afghan refugees.

With the decline in this aid after 1988, the proportion of grants decreased to 16 percent in FY 1992.

The United States has been a major provider of aid since independence and was the largest donor in the 1980s (see Foreign Policy, ch. 4). All United States military aid and all new civilian commitments, however, ended in October 1990 after the United States Congress failed to receive the required annual presidential certification that Pakistan was not developing a nuclear bomb. As of early 1994, United States aid had not resumed, but Agency for International Development projects already under way in October 1990 continued to receive funds (see The Armed Forces in a New World Order, ch. 5).

Foreign Trade

Foreign trade is important to the economy because of the country's need to import a variety of products. Imports have exceeded exports in almost every year since 1950, and Pakistan had a deficit in its balance of trade each year from FY 1973 through FY 1992 (see table 5, Appendix). In FY 1991, exports were US$5.9 billion, compared with imports of US$8.4 billion, which resulted in a deficit of US$2.5 billion. In FY 1992, exports rose to an estimated US$6.9 billion, but imports reached an estimated US$9.3 billion, resulting in a trade deficit of US$2.4 billion. Economists forecast a trade deficit of around US$2.5 billion for FY 1993. Pakistan's terms of trade, expressed in an index set at 100 in FY 1981, were 78.0 in FY 1991 and 82.7 in FY 1992.

Crude oil and refined products are significant imports (see table 6, Appendix). Their value varies with internal demand and changes in the world oil price. In FY 1982, oil products accounted for around 30 percent of Pakistan's imports, falling to an annual average of 15 percent from FY 1987 to FY 1990, rising to over 21 percent in FY 1991, but dropping back to 15 percent in FY 1992. Other important categories of imports in FY 1992 included nonelectrical machinery (24 percent), chemicals (10 percent), transportation equipment (9 percent), and edible oils (4 percent).

Although import-substitution industrialization policies favored domestic manufacturing of substitutes for imports, officials also encouraged manufactured exports in the 1950s and 1960s. In the early 1980s, incentives were again provided to industrialists to increase manufactured exports. Nonetheless, in the early 1990s the export base remained primarily dependent on two agricultural products, cotton and rice, which are subject to great variations in output and demand. In FY 1992, raw cotton, cotton yarn, cotton cloth, and cotton waste accounted for 37 percent of all exports (see table 7, Appendix). Other important exports were ready-made garments (15 percent), synthetic textiles (6 percent), and rice (6 percent). There was some diversification during the late 1980s as the share of manufactured goods rose. The share of primary goods fell from 35 percent to 16 percent between FY 1986 and FY 1993. During the same period, the share of semimanufactures rose from 16 percent to 20 percent, and that of manufactured goods rose from 49 percent to 64 percent.

In the early 1990s, Pakistan's balance of trade remained particularly vulnerable to changes in the world economy and bad weather. Sharp increases in crude oil prices, such as those of 1979–81 and 1990, raised the nation's import bill significantly.Total exports, on the other hand, are more sensitive to agricultural production. The decline in cotton production in FY 1993, for instance, seriously affected the export level.

Sources for imports and markets for exports are widely scattered, and they fluctuate from year to year. In the early 1990s, the United States and Japan were Pakistan's most important trading partners. In FY 1993, the United States accounted for 13.7 percent of Pakistan's exports and 11.2 percent of its imports. Japan accounted for 6.6 percent of exports and 14.2 percent of imports. Germany, Britain, and Saudi Arabia are also important trading partners. Hong Kong is an important export market and China a significant supplier of imports. Trade with the Republic of Korea (South Korea) and Malaysia is small but not unimportant. Trade with India is negligible.

Because of Pakistani fears of protectionism in developed countries and the increasing importance of regional blocs in international trade, the government in the 1980s and early 1990s placed new importance on developing trade links with nearby nations. In the early 1990s, new trading initiatives were being pursued through membership in two regional organizations, the Economic Co-operation Organization (ECO) and the South Asian Association for Regional Cooperation (SAARC—see Glossary).

The ECO was formed in 1985 with Pakistan, Iran, and Turkey as its only members, but Afghanistan, Azerbaijan, Kyrgyzstan, Tajikistan, Turkmenistan, and Uzbekistan joined in 1992. Some politicians in the member nations see the ECO as a potential Muslim common market, but political rivalries, especially between Iran and Turkey, limit its effectiveness. In 1994 most of the concrete measures being taken by the ECO concerned the improvement of transportation and communications among the member nations, including the construction of a highway from Turkey to Pakistan through Iran.

SAARC was founded in the mid-1980s, primarily as a vehicle to increase trade within South Asia by delinking the region's political conflicts from economic cooperation. Its seven member states—Bangladesh, Bhutan, India, Maldives, Nepal, Pakistan, and Sri Lanka—adopted the principle of unanimity in selecting multilateral questions for debate. Despite frequent consultative committee meetings, progress toward increased trade remained limited in 1994. At the annual SAARC summit in April 1993, members agreed to negotiate a South Asian Preferential Trade Agreement by 1996 that would lower or abolish tariffs among members.

During the first four decades after independence, controls on imports were used to ensure priority use of foreign exchange and to assist industrialization. In the 1980s, the government maintained lists of permissible imports and also used quantitative restrictions and regulations on foreign exchange to control imports. The most extensive list covers consumer goods as well as raw materials and capital goods that can be imported by commercial and industrial users. A second list, mostly of raw materials, can only be imported by industrial users. A third list covers commodities only the public sector can import.

In 1991 and 1992, the government announced various measures to liberalize trade. Import licensing was ended for most goods, many products were removed from the lists of restricted imports, and import duties were cut. In addition, foreign companies were allowed into the export trade. The government also promised to convert the remaining nontariff barriers into tariffs, incorporate various ad hoc import taxes into customs duties, and reduce the numerous exemptions and concessions on duties.

External Debt

Pakistan frequently encounters balance of payments difficulties, requiring emergency funding and rescheduling of debt payments (see table 8, Appendix). The main reason for the negative balance of payments is the chronic trade deficit. How-

Cinema in Karachi
Courtesy Sheila Ross
A craftsman creating beautiful patterns on Namdas
Courtesy Embassy of Pakistan, Washington

ever, remittances from Pakistanis employed overseas have compensated for a portion of the trade deficit. Remittances sent home from these workers increased from US$339 million in FY 1976 to US$2.9 billion in FY 1983, when they exceeded total commodity export earnings. After FY 1983, remittances gradually declined, although they averaged US$2.3 billion between FY 1984 and FY 1990. Remittances totaled US$1.8 billion in FY 1991 but then fell to US$1.5 billion in FY 1992, in part because of the disruption caused by the Persian Gulf War. In FY 1992, Pakistanis in the Middle East accounted for 67.1 percent of all remittances; 45.3 percent came from Saudi Arabia alone. Workers in Kuwait provided around 9 percent in the late 1980s, but that proportion fell to 3.6 percent in FY 1992. Pakistanis also send significant remittances from the United States (10.2 percent) and Britain (9.3 percent).

At the end of June 1993, Pakistani officials estimated the public and publicly guaranteed external debt at US$18.4 billion. The World Bank, however, estimated the total external debt at US$24.1 billion at the end of 1992, up from US$16.7 billion at the end of 1987. Total external debt was 48 percent of the gross national product (GNP—see Glossary). Commercial borrowing is a small proportion of debt; at the end of 1992, it accounted for only 0.4 percent of long-term debt.

Labor

Between independence and the early 1990s, the labor force grew rapidly, reflecting the high population growth and the subsequently burgeoning proportion of the population under twenty years of age. The data available concerning employment are only estimates because few concrete facts are available. Official labor force figures represent orders of magnitude and are not precise. Observers agree, however, that relatively few women participate in the formal nonagricultural labor force.

In FY 1992, the civilian labor force was estimated at 33.8 million, compared with 26.3 million in FY 1982 and only 10.4 million in 1951 (see table 9, Appendix). In FY 1993, about 48 percent of the civilian labor force was engaged in agriculture, 13 percent in industry, 7 percent in construction, 13 percent in trade, 5 percent in transportation and communications, and 14 percent in other services. Only about 25 percent of the official labor force are wage earners, which reflects the high levels of casual enterprise, family businesses, and self-employment.

Agricultural employment, although increasing, has expanded at a slower rate than the total labor force for most of the period since independence. In the 1960s and 1970s, owners of mid-sized farms turned increasingly to managing their own holdings, displacing former tenants. Increased mechanization displaced agricultural laborers. Industry, the major growth sector of the economy, was unable to absorb sufficient workers. From the early 1960s until the early 1990s, the proportion of the labor force employed in the industrial sector remained steady, while the proportion working in trade, construction, and transportation rose. Official estimates placed unemployment at around 3 percent in the late 1980s, but this rate rose in the early 1990s to around 6 percent. Underemployment is a greater problem and is particularly evident in agriculture, construction, and trade.

Overseas employment partially compensates for the insufficient job market. Since the mid-1970s, a growing number of Pakistanis, both skilled and unskilled men, have gone to labor-deficient, oil-exporting countries in the Middle East, where wages are much higher than at home. By the mid-1980s, this exodus of manpower had reached more than 2 million. Pakistanis working in the Persian Gulf states sent back remittances of more than US$3 billion a year through official channels. An equal amount may have come in through unofficial channels. Significantly, these remittances meant that for the first time, wealth flowed directly to ordinary Pakistanis rather than to bankers, landlords, or army officers.

Employment opportunities in the Persian Gulf states were reduced in the early 1990s. The Persian Gulf War forced many workers to return abruptly to Pakistan. Workers only slowly returned to the Gulf after the war. Remittances, however, although below the peak levels of the mid-1980s, nonetheless accounted for between US$1.5 billion and US2.0 billion a year, or over 30 percent of Pakistan's foreign-currency earnings and almost 5 percent of GNP.

Over 1 million Pakistanis (some estimates are much higher) continued to work in the Middle East in the early 1990s, mostly in Saudi Arabia and the United Arab Emirates. These workers range from unskilled laborers to highly skilled professionals such as engineers, accountants, teachers, physicians, and nurses. In addition, significant numbers of Pakistanis live and work in other countries, especially Britain and the United States.

Agriculture

Farming is Pakistan's largest economic activity. In FY 1993, agriculture and small-scale forestry and fishing contributed 25 percent of GDP and employed 48 percent of the labor force. Agricultural products, especially cotton yarn, cotton cloth, raw cotton, and rice, are important exports. Although there is agricultural activity in all areas of Pakistan, most crops are grown in the Indus River plain in Punjab and Sindh. Considerable development and expansion of output have occurred since the early 1960s; however, the country is still far from realizing the large potential yield that the well-irrigated and fertile soil from the Indus irrigation system could produce. The floods of September 1992 showed how vulnerable agriculture is to weather; agricultural production dropped dramatically in FY 1993.

Land Use

Pakistan's total land area is about 803,940 square kilometers. About 48 million hectares, or 60 percent, is often classified as unusable for forestry or agriculture consists mostly of deserts, mountain slopes, and urban settlements (see Topography and Drainage, ch. 2). Some authorities, however, include part of this area as agricultural land on the basis that it would support some livestock activity even though it is poor rangeland. Thus, estimates of grazing land vary widely—between 10 percent and 70 percent of the total area. A broad interpretation, for example, categorizes almost all of arid Balochistan as rangeland for foraging livestock. Government officials listed only 3 million hectares, largely in the north, as forested in FY 1992. About 21.9 million hectares were cultivated in FY 1992. Around 70 percent of the cropped area was in Punjab, followed by perhaps 20 percent in Sindh, less than 10 percent in the North-West Frontier Province, and only 1 percent in Balochistan.

Since independence, the amount of cultivated land has increased by more than one-third. This expansion is largely the result of improvements in the irrigation system that make water available to additional plots. Substantial amounts of farmland have been lost to urbanization and waterlogging, but losses are more than compensated for by the addition of new land. In the early 1990s, more irrigation projects were needed to increase the area of cultivated land.

The scant rainfall over most of the country makes about 80 percent of cropping dependent on irrigation (see Climate, ch.

2). Fewer than 4 million hectares of land, largely in northern Punjab and the North-West Frontier Province, are totally dependent on rainfall. An additional 2 million hectares of land are under nonirrigated cropping, such as plantings on floodplains as the water recedes. Nonirrigated farming generally gives low yields, and although the technology exists to boost production substantially, it is expensive to use and not always readily available.

Irrigation

In the early 1990s, irrigation from the Indus River and its tributaries constituted the world's largest continuous irrigation system, capable of watering over 16 million hectares. The system includes three major storage reservoirs and numerous barrages, headworks, canals, and distribution channels. The total length of the canal system exceeds 58,000 kilometers; there are an additional 1.6 million kilometers of farm and field ditches.

Partition placed portions of the Indus River and its tributaries under India's control, leading to prolonged disputes between India and Pakistan over the use of Indus waters. After nine years of negotiations and technical studies, the issue was resolved by the Indus Waters Treaty of 1960. After a ten-year transitional period, the treaty awarded India use of the waters of the main eastern tributaries in its territory—the Ravi, Beas, and Sutlej rivers. Pakistan received use of the waters of the Indus River and its western tributaries, the Jhelum and Chenab rivers.

After the treaty was signed, Pakistan began an extensive and rapid irrigation construction program, partly financed by the Indus Basin Development Fund of US$800 million contributed by various nations, including the United States, and administered by the World Bank. Several immense link canals were built to transfer water from western rivers to eastern Punjab to replace flows in eastern tributaries that India began to divert in accordance with the terms of the treaty. The Mangla Dam, on the Jhelum River, was completed in 1967. The dam provided the first significant water storage for the Indus irrigation system. The dam also contributes to flood control, to regulation of flows for some of the link canals, and to the country's energy supply. At the same time, additional construction was undertaken on barrages and canals.

A second phase of irrigation expansion began in 1968, when a US$1.2 billion fund, also administered by the World Bank, was established. The key to this phase was the Tarbela Dam on the Indus River, which is the world's largest earth-filled dam. The dam, completed in the 1970s, reduced the destruction of periodic floods and in 1994 was a major hydroelectric generating source. Most important for agriculture, the dam increases water availability, particularly during low water, which usually comes at critical growing periods.

Despite massive expansion in the irrigation system, many problems remain. The Indus irrigation system was designed to accommodate the availability of water in the rivers, to supply the largest area with minimum water needs, and to achieve these objectives at low operating costs with limited technical staff. This system design has resulted in low yields and low cropping intensity in the Indus River plain, averaging about one crop a year, whereas the climate and soils could reasonably permit an average of almost 1.5 crops a year if a more sophisticated irrigation network were in place. The urgent need in the 1960s and 1970s to increase crop production for domestic and export markets led to water flows well above designed capacities. Completion of the Mangla and Tarbela reservoirs, as well as improvements in other parts of the system, made larger water flows possible. In addition, the government began installing public tube wells that usually discharge into upper levels of the system to add to the available water. The higher water flows in parts of the system considerably exceed design capacities, creating stresses and risks of breaches. Nonetheless, many farmers, particularly those with smallholdings and those toward the end of watercourses, suffer because the supply of water is unreliable.

The irrigation system represents a significant engineering achievement and provides water to the fields that account for 90 percent of agricultural production. Nonetheless, serious problems in the design of the irrigation system prevent achieving the highest potential agricultural output.

Water management is based largely on objectives and operational procedures dating back many decades and is often inflexible and unresponsive to current needs for greater water use efficiency and high crop yields. Charges for water use do not meet operational and maintenance costs, even though rates more than doubled in the 1970s and were again increased in the 1980s. Partly because of its low cost, farmers often waste water.

Powerhouse of Tarbela Dam, the largest earth-filled dam in the world
Courtesy Embassy of Pakistan, Washington

Good water management is not practiced by government officials, who often assume that investments in physical aspects of the system will automatically yield higher crop production. Government management of the system does not extend beyond the main distribution channels. After passing through these channels, water is directed onto the fields of individual farmers, whose water rights are based on long-established social and legal codes. Groups of farmers voluntarily manage the watercourses between main distribution channels and their fields. In effect, the efficiency and effectiveness of water management rely on the way farmers use the system.

The exact amounts of water wasted have not been determined, but studies suggest that losses are considerable and perhaps amount to one-half of the water entering the system. Part of the waste results from seepages in the delivery system. Even greater amounts are probably lost because farmers use water whenever their turn comes even if the water application is detrimental to their crops. The attitude among almost all farmers is that they should use water when available because it may not be available at the next scheduled turn. Moreover, farmers have little understanding of the most productive applications of water during crop-growing cycles because of the lack of research and extension services. As a result, improvements in the irrigation system have not raised yields and output as expected. Some experts believe that drastic changes are needed in government policies and the legal and institutional framework of water management if water use is to improve and that effective changes can result in very large gains in agricultural output.

Drainage

The continuous expansion of the irrigation system over the past century significantly altered the hydrological balance of the Indus River basin. Seepage from the system and percolation from irrigated fields caused the water table to rise, reaching crisis conditions for a substantial area. Around 1900 the water table was usually more than sixteen meters below the surface of the Indus Plain. A 1981 survey found the water table to be within about three meters of the surface in more than one-half the cropped area in Sindh and more than one-third the area in Punjab. In some locations, the water table is much closer to the surface. Cropping is seriously affected over a wide area by poor drainage—waterlogging—and by accumulated salts in the soil.

Although some drainage was installed before World War II, little attention was paid to the growing waterlogging and salinity problems. In 1959 a salinity control and reclamation project was started in a limited area, based on public tube wells, to draw down the water table and leach out accumulated salts near the surface, using groundwater for irrigation. By the early 1980s, some thirty such projects had been started that when completed would irrigate nearly 6.3 million hectares. By 1993 the government had installed around 15,000 tube wells. Private farmers, however, had installed over 200,000 mostly small tube wells, mainly for irrigation purposes but also to lower the water table. Private wells probably pumped more than five times as much water as public wells.

Officials were aware of the need for additional spending to prevent further deterioration of the existing situation. Emphasis in the 1980s and early 1990s was on rehabilitation and maintenance of existing canals and watercourses, on improvements on the farms themselves (including some land leveling to conserve water), and on drainage and salinity in priority areas. Emphasis was also placed on short-term projects, largely to improve the operation of the irrigation system in order to raise yields. Part of the funding would come from steady increases in water use fees; the intention is to gradually raise water charges to cover operation and maintenance costs. Considerable time and money are needed to realize the full potential of the irrigation system and bring it up to modern standards.

Farm Ownership and Land Reform

At independence Pakistan was a country with a great many small-scale farms and a small number of very large estates. Distribution of landownership was badly skewed. Less than 1 percent of the farms consisted of more than 25 percent of the total agricultural land. Many owners of large holdings were absentee landlords, contributing little to production but extracting as much as possible from the sharecroppers who farmed the land. At the other extreme, about 65 percent of the farmers held some 15 percent of the farmland in holdings of about two hectares or less. Approximately 50 percent of the farmland was cultivated by tenants, including sharecroppers, most of whom had little security and few rights. An additional large number of landless rural inhabitants worked as agricultural laborers. Farm laborers and many tenants were extremely poor, uneducated, and undernourished, in sharp contrast to the wealth, status, and political power of the landlord elite.

After independence the country's political leaders recognized the need for more equitable ownership of farmland and security of tenancy. In the early 1950s, provincial governments attempted to eliminate some of the absentee landlords or rent collectors, but they had little success in the face of strong opposition. Security of tenancy was also legislated in the provinces, but because of their dependent position, tenant farmers benefitted only slightly. In fact, the reforms created an atmosphere of uncertainty in the countryside and intensified the animosity between wealthy landlords and small farmers and sharecroppers.

In January 1959, accepting the recommendations of a special commission on the subject, General Mohammad Ayub Khan's government issued new land reform regulations that aimed to boost agricultural output, promote social justice, and ensure security of tenure (see The Ayub Khan Era, ch. 1). A ceiling was placed on individual landownership; compensation was paid to owners for land surrendered. Numerous exemptions, including title transfers to family members, limited the impact of the ceilings. Slightly fewer than 1 million hectares of land were surrendered, of which a little more than 250,000 hectares were sold to about 50,000 tenants. The land reform regulations made no serious attempt to break up large estates or to lessen the power or privileges of the landed elite. However, the measures attempted to provide some security of tenure to tenants, consolidate existing holdings, and prevent fragmentation of farm plots. An average holding of about five hectares was considered necessary for a family's subsistence, and a holding of about twenty to twenty-five hectares was pronounced as a desirable "economic" holding.

In March 1972, the Bhutto government announced further land reform measures, which went into effect in 1973 (see Zulfiqar Ali Bhutto and a New Constitutional System, ch. 1). The landownership ceiling was officially lowered to about five hectares of irrigated land and about twelve hectares of nonirrigated land; exceptions were in theory limited to an additional 20 percent of land for owners having tractors and tube wells. The ceiling could also be extended for poor-quality land. Owners of expropriated excess land received no compensation, and beneficiaries were not charged for land distributed. Official statistics showed that by 1977 only about 520,000 hectares had been surrendered, and nearly 285,000 hectares had been redistributed to about 71,000 farmers.

The 1973 measure required landlords to pay all taxes, water charges, seed costs, and one-half of the cost of fertilizer and other inputs. It prohibited eviction of tenants as long as they cultivated the land, and it gave tenants first rights of purchase. Other regulations increased tenants' security of tenure and prescribed lower rent rates than had existed.

In 1977 the Bhutto government further reduced ceilings on private ownership of farmland to about four hectares of irrigated land and about eight hectares of nonirrigated land. In an additional measure, agricultural income became taxable, although small farmers owning ten hectares or fewer—the majority of the farm population—were exempted. The military regime of Zia ul-Haq that ousted Bhutto neglected to implement these later reforms. Governments in the 1980s and early

1990s avoided significant land reform measures, perhaps because they drew much of their support from landowners in the countryside.

Government policies designed to reduce the concentration of landownership had some effect, but their significance was difficult to measure because of limited data. In 1993 the most recent agricultural census was that of 1980, which was used to compare statistics with the agricultural census of 1960. Between 1960 and 1980, the number of farms declined by 17 percent, and farms decreased in area by 4 percent, resulting in slightly larger farms. This decline in the number of farms was confined to marginal farms of two hectares or fewer, which in 1980 represented 34 percent of all farms, constituting 7 percent of the farm hectarage. At the other extreme, the number of very large farms of sixty hectares or more was 14,000—both in 1960 and in 1980—although the average size of the biggest farms was smaller in 1980. The number of farms between two and ten hectares increased during this time. Greater use of higher-yielding seeds requiring heavier applications of fertilizers, installation of private tube wells, and mechanization accounted for much of the shift away from very small farms toward mid-sized farms, as owners of the latter undertook cultivation instead of renting out part of their land. Observers believed that this trend had continued in the 1980s and early 1990s.

In early 1994, land reform remained a controversial and complex issue. Large landowners retain their power over small farmers and tenants, especially in the interior of Sindh, which has a feudal agricultural establishment. Tenancy continues on a large scale: one-third of Pakistan's farmers are tenant farmers, including almost one-half of the farmers in Sindh. Tenant farmers typically give almost 50 percent of what they produce to landlords. Fragmented holdings remain a substantial and widespread problem. Studies indicate that larger farms are usually less productive per hectare or unit of water than smaller ones.

Cropping Patterns and Production

In the early 1990s, most crops were grown for food (see table 10; table 11, Appendix). Wheat is by far the most important crop in Pakistan and is the staple food for the majority of the population. Wheat is eaten most frequently in unleavened bread called chapati. In FY 1992, wheat was planted on 7.8 million hectares, and production amounted to 14.7 million tons.

Output in FY 1993 reached 16.4 million tons. Between FY 1961 and FY 1990, the area under wheat cultivation increased nearly 70 percent, while yields increased 221 percent. Wheat production is vulnerable to extreme weather, especially in nonirrigated areas. In the early and mid-1980s, Pakistan was self-sufficient in wheat, but in the early 1990s, more than 2 million tons of wheat were imported annually.

Rice is the other major food grain. In FY 1992, about 2.1 million hectares were planted with rice, and production amounted to 3.2 million tons, with 1 million tons exported. Rice yields also have increased sharply since the 1960s, following the introduction of new varieties. Nonetheless, the yield per hectare of around 1.5 tons in FY 1991 was low compared with many other Asian countries. Pakistan has emphasized the production of rice in order to increase exports to the Middle East and therefore concentrates on the high-quality basmati variety, although other grades also are exported. The government has increased procurement prices of basmati rice disproportionately to encourage exports and has allowed private traders into the rice export business alongside the public-sector Rice Export Corporation.

Other important food grains are millet, sorghum, corn, and barley. Corn, although a minor crop, gradually increased in area and production after independence, partly at the expense of other minor food grains. Chick-peas, called *gram* in Pakistan, are the main nongrain food crop in area and production. A number of other foods, including fruits and vegetables, are also grown.

In the early 1990s, cotton was the most important commercial crop. The area planted in cotton increased from 1.1 million hectares in FY 1950 to 2.1 million hectares in FY 1981 and 2.8 million hectares in FY 1993. Yields increased substantially in the 1980s, partly as a result of the use of pesticides and the introduction in 1985 of a new high-yielding variety of seed. During the 1980s, cotton yields moved from well below the world average to above the world average. Production in FY 1992 was 12.8 million bales, up from 4.4 million bales ten years earlier. Output fell sharply, however, to 9.3 million bales in FY 1993 because of the September 1992 floods and insect infestations.

Other cash crops include tobacco, rapeseed, and, most important, sugarcane. In FY 1992, sugarcane was planted on 880,000 hectares, and production was 35.7 million tons. Except for some oil from cottonseeds, the country is dependent on imported vegetable oil. By the 1980s, introduction and experimentation with oilseed cultivation was under way. Soybeans and sunflower seeds appear to be suitable crops given the country's soil and climate, but production was still negligible in the early 1990s.

Livestock

Livestock provides the draft power available to most farmers as well as food, fuel, manure, wool, and hides. Livestock contributed about 30 percent of the value added by agriculture in FY 1993. In Balochistan raising sheep and goats on the arid rangeland is an important source of cash to a considerable part of the population, although many areas are overgrazed.

In FY 1993, the livestock population was estimated at 17.8 million cattle, 18.7 million water buffalo, 27.7 million sheep, 40.2 million goats, and 5.4 million other animals, including camels, horses, and mules. Production of animal products in FY 1993 was estimated to include 17 million tons of milk, 844,000 tons of beef, 763,000 tons of mutton, 50,500 tons of wool, and 42.6 million tons of hides and skins. Despite substantial increases in livestock production in the 1980s, the country faces shortages because of the limited amount of feed and grazing areas. In the 1980s, the government increased the size of cross-breeding programs and took other measures to increase productivity, but production still fell short of demand.

Commercial chicken farming has shown exceptional promise because production using modern methods has expanded rapidly since the 1960s. Although many farmers raise some poultry, the commercial chicken farms account for most of the increased availability of eggs and poultry. Poultry meat production increased from 14,000 tons in FY 1972 to 75,000 tons in FY 1983 and 188,000 tons in FY 1993. Egg production increased from 14 million in FY 1972, to 4.2 billion in FY 1983, and 5.4 billion in FY 1992.

Forestry

Forests cover about 3 million hectares, less than 4 percent of the country. Many forests are in the Northern Areas and Azad Kashmir, where coniferous trees predominate, but the management and exploitation of these forests are hampered by the remoteness of the land. Elsewhere, most of the native forest was destroyed before independence by population pressure, overcultivation, and overgrazing. The lack of tree cover contributes to many of the problems the agricultural sector has experienced since independence, including soil erosion, the silting of streams, flooding, and a shortage of timber and firewood.

In the mid-1990s, government efforts to increase the extent of forests have had little success, but tree-planting programs continue. Many of the nation's forests, including some irrigated tree plantations in the Indus River basin, are under government control. These forests produced 321,000 cubic meters of timber and 534,000 cubic meters of firewood in FY 1993, but production was far short of demand. Imports filled part of the requirement for timber, while cutting trees and shrubs on private land met part of the need for firewood. In October 1993, however, the government imposed a two-year nationwide ban on the private felling of trees. This action was taken because of concerns that Pakistan was fast losing the little tree cover that existed (see Pollution and Environmental Issues, ch. 2).

Fishing

Fishing is a small sector of the economy, accounting for around 0.6 percent of GDP in FY 1992. Nevertheless, fishing had increased sharply in the 1970s and 1980s and seemed well-positioned for further expansion in the 1990s. The fish catch was 173,000 tons in FY 1970, approximately 301,000 tons in FY 1982, and 510,000 tons in FY 1992. The bulk of the catch is taken offshore in the Arabian Sea. Much of the catch, especially prawns and shrimp, is exported to the Middle East. Fish accounted for 1.7 percent of export earnings in FY 1992. The country is considered to have a large potential in fishing, reportedly as high as 14 million tons a year if sufficient investment and market expansion occur.

Industry

In 1947 only 5 percent of the large-scale industrial facilities in British India were located in what became Pakistan. The country started with virtually no industrial base and no institutional, financial, or energy resources. Three small hydroelectric power stations provided limited electricity to a few urban areas. Firewood and dung were the main sources of energy; commercial energy sources supplied only about 30 percent of the energy consumed. Further, there was a shortage of management personnel and skilled labor.

Manufacturing

The pace of industrialization since independence has been rapid, although it has fluctuated in response to changes in government policy and to world economic conditions. During the 1950s, manufacturing expanded at about 16 percent annually; during the first half of the 1960s, it expanded at around 11 percent a year. The pace slowed to under 7 percent a year in the second half of the 1960s. Between FY 1970 and FY 1977, the index of manufacturing output increased an average of only 2.3 percent a year. Between FY 1977 and FY 1982, the index rose an average of 9.9 percent a year. Growth averaged 7.7 percent during the Sixth Five-Year Plan (1983–88) and 5.4 percent from FY 1989 through FY 1992. In FY 1993, manufacturing accounted for 17.3 percent of GDP at current factor cost, of which large-scale manufacturing accounted for 61 percent and small-scale manufacturing for 39 percent. Manufactured goods accounted for 64 percent of all exports by value in FY 1993, but the bulk of these exports came in the relatively low-technology areas of cotton textiles and garments.

Total fixed capital formation in manufacturing was estimated at Rs57 billion in FY 1993. During the 1980s, private investment became much more important than public investment. In FY 1982, private investment was 53.9 percent of the total, but in FY 1993 the proportion was 96.1 percent. Total investment in manufacturing was 5.1 percent of GNP in FY 1993.

In the early 1990s, the manufacturing sector was dominated by food processing and textiles (see table 12, Appendix). Provisional figures for FY 1992 indicated that sugar production was 2.1 million tons, vegetable ghee 819,000 tons, cotton yarn 862,000 tons, and cotton cloth 234 million square meters. Other industrial products included motor tires (647,000 units), cycle tires (2.2 million units), cement (6.1 million tons), urea (1.4 million tons), soda ash (147,000 tons), bicycles (364,000 units), and paperboard (13,000 tons).

Pakistan has one steel mill, located near Karachi, with a production capacity of 1.1 million tons per year. A major undertaking, the mill required the bulk of public industrial investment in the late 1970s and early 1980s, although the plant was designed and partly financed by the Soviet Union. It produced at 81 percent of capacity in FY 1993, and it was dependent on imports of iron ore and coking coal. As of early 1994, the mill had not achieved sustained profitability, but there were plans to expand it.

Public-sector firms produced about 40 percent of the total manufacturing value added in FY 1991, and they absorbed about 48 percent of gross fixed investment. The total value of public-sector industrial output in FY 1991 was Rs36 billion (in constant FY 1988 prices), but pretax profits were only Rs1.3 billion, reflecting the inefficiencies and overstaffing prevalent in these enterprises.

To improve the efficiency and competitiveness of public-sector firms and end federal subsidies of their losses, the government launched a privatization program in FY 1991. Majority control in nearly all public-sector enterprises will be auctioned off to private investors, and foreign investors are eligible buyers. In March 1992, twenty units had been privatized, but by 1993 only about 30 percent of the government's target number of firms had been sold because some of the enterprises were unattractive for private investors. In 1994 the government led by Benazir Bhutto was committed to continuing the policy of privatization.

Construction

Construction is one of the more vigorous sectors of the economy, growing at a rate of 5.9 percent in FY 1992. Construction of houses and the associated infrastructure was a major element in the Seventh Five-Year Plan (1988–93), which proposed the provision of 650,000 urban housing sites and 2.2 million plots for the rural poor to construct their own houses. The plan also sought to provide a rural water supply to an additional 31.2 million people and sanitation facilities for 17 million people. Total planned construction expenditure was Rs29.7 billion over the five-year period. Much of the investment in housing came from the remittances of Pakistani workers in the Middle East. Some economists felt that this investment distorted the market for land on which to build in some areas and made the position of poor people more difficult.

Energy

From 1947 to the early 1990s, the economy made considerable progress in the transformation from a wood-burning base

The Pak-Arab Fertilizer Factory in Multan
Courtesy Embassy of Pakistan, Washington

to modern energy sources. The process remains incomplete. Bagasse (the woody residue left over from crushed sugarcane), dung, and firewood furnished about 32 percent of all energy in FY 1988. Some localities had been denuded of firewood, forcing the local population to use commercial energy sources, such as kerosene or charcoal. Domestic sources of commercial energy accounted for 77 percent of all commercial energy in FY 1990. The major domestic energy resources are natural gas, oil, and hydroelectric power. The remainder of energy requirements are met by imports of oil and oil products.

Crude oil production increased sharply in the 1980s, from almost 4.0 million barrels in FY 1982 to 22.4 million barrels in FY 1992. This increase was the result of the discovery and development of new oil fields. Despite this expanded production, however, about 28 million barrels of crude oil were imported annually in the early 1990s. The production from domestic oil refineries also rose in the 1980s, reaching 42 million barrels annually in the early 1990s. However, oil products imports accounted for about 30 percent of the value of all oil imports.

Pakistan vigorously pursued oil exploration in the 1980s and early 1990s and made a number of new discoveries. In the early 1990s, the most productive oil field was at Dhurnal in Punjab, accounting for 21 percent of total output in FY 1993. The Badin area in southern Sindh was the site of a number of discoveries in the 1980s, and its proportion of total output has continued to increase over the years. In the early 1990s, more favorable terms on pricing and repatriation of profits stimulated the interest of foreign oil companies. About twenty foreign companies are engaged in oil exploration, but poor security for workers and property in remote areas of Balochistan and Sindh remains a significant constraint on foreign investment.

The large Sui natural gas field in Balochistan was discovered after independence. Production at Sui began in 1955 and peaked in 1985. In the early 1990s, it remained the nation's most productive gas field, accounting for 46 percent of production in FY 1993. The second largest gas field, also located in Balochistan at Mari, accounted for 20 percent of all production. Twenty-five gas fields were operational in FY 1993. Natural gas recoverable reserves were estimated at 662.0 billion cubic meters, with an extraction rate in the early 1990s of around 14.0 billion cubic meters, up from 9.3 billion cubic meters in FY 1982 and 1.3 billion cubic meters in FY 1970.

Natural gas pipelines, in which the government owns controlling shares, link the Sui gas field and a few others to the main population centers and the major crude oil production areas. The southern pipeline leads from Sui to Hyderabad and Karachi, and a spur supplies Quetta. The northern pipeline branches at Faisalabad. One branch goes a little farther north of Lahore; the other branch is connected to the crude oil fields and supplies gas to Islamabad and Peshawar. There are plans for a new gas pipeline through which Iran would export natural gas to Pakistan.

Coal reserves were boosted substantially in May 1992 when a large coal field was discovered in the Thar Desert in Sindh. In early 1993, these reserves were estimated at 17 billion tons. However, much of Pakistan's coal has a low calorific value and a high ash and sulfur content, which limits its value. Output was 1.3 million tons in FY 1992, down from 1.8 million tons in FY

1982. The bulk of production is from small, privately owned mines whose owners generally lack funds, expertise, and interest in expanding output. A public-sector firm, the Pakistan Mineral Development Corporation, accounted for about one-fifth of output in the early 1990s. The corporation has six operational mines—at Degari, Sor Range, and Sharigh in Balochistan; Lakhra and Meting in Sindh; and the Makerwal/ Gullakhel complex straddling the border between Punjab and the North-West Frontier Province.

Hydroelectric power is an important domestic primary energy resource, and hydroelectric potential is estimated at around 10,000 megawatts. A large number of additional sites with major potential exist in the mountainous north, but the difficulty of access and the high cost of transmission to the populous south make development a distant prospect. A large proportion of hydrogenerators are located at two large multipurpose dams. The Tarbela Dam located on the Indus River in the North-West Frontier Province has an installed capacity of 2,164 megawatts, and the Mangla Dam situated on the Jhelum River in Azad Kashmir has an installed capacity of 800 megawatts.

In 1965 Pakistani officials contracted with the Canadian government for the supply of a 125-megawatt pressurized, heavy-water nuclear reactor, which in 1972 became operational near Karachi. This was Pakistan's only nuclear power plant in 1994, and its operating record is poor. In 1983 plans for a nuclear plant at Chashma, on the Indus River in Punjab, about 240 kilometers south of Islamabad, were announced. The construction of this plant was delayed, in part because of the reluctance of foreign governments to supply needed fuel and technology because of concern over possible military use of the atomic energy program. In 1993 Pakistani officials expected the plant to open in 1997 with a capacity of 300 megawatts. China is providing the necessary technology and materials for the Chashma plant. Pakistani officials expect that fuel for the plant will be provided by the uranium enrichment plant at Kahuta near Islamabad. Some observers, however, believe it is unlikely that the plant will be ready in 1997.

In FY 1992, the country had a total installed generating capacity of 9,293 megawatts, of which approximately 62.7 percent was thermal, 35.9 percent hydroelectric, and 1.5 percent nuclear. In FY 1991, industry consumed 34.2 percent of electricity, households 31.7 percent, agriculture 21.4 percent, commercial businesses 4.3 percent, and other users 8.3 percent. A rural electrification program increased the number of villages having electricity from around 14,000 in FY 1983 to nearly 41,000 in FY 1992, leaving only about 5,000 villages without electricity. Beginning in the 1980s, considerable improvements were made in transmission facilities. By 1983 a grid connected generators and urban centers of the more populous areas, largely in Punjab and Sindh. Installations of high-voltage transmission lines and other facilities helped reduce power losses. Nonetheless, in 1993 the World Bank estimated that 28 percent of electricity generated in Pakistan was diverted illegally in transmission and distribution, and even the government puts this figure at 12 percent.

In 1993 the government planned a rapid increase of generating capacity, in part through the expansion of existing hydroelectric and thermal units and in part through the construction of new plants. Nonetheless, observers expected shortages of electricity to continue in the early 1990s and probably longer. In much of 1993, both urban and rural areas experienced three power cuts a day, lasting a total of around two hours. Industrial and commercial users are required to reduce consumption by an even greater amount, and they risk being disconnected if they violate "agreed-on levels." Peak demand for electricity is estimated to exceed the supply by around 30 percent.

In 1991 the power sector was opened to private capital, both foreign and domestic. In that year, a World Bank consortium that included investors from Britain, Saudi Arabia, and the United States agreed to finance a project for a new US$1.3 billion, 1,292-megawatt oil-fired power station at Hub Chowki in Balochistan, forty-eight kilometers west of Karachi. Construction began in September 1992, and the station is scheduled to go into operation in 1996. The consortium is responsible for the construction and operation of the power station, while its output is sold to the national grid. In 1992 the government announced plans to privatize the Water and Power Development Authority's thermal plants and area electricity boards, but in 1994 legal and political obstacles prevented implementation of this policy.

Some development of renewable energy sources has been undertaken, primarily for rural areas so isolated they would not otherwise have electricity in the foreseeable future. The aim is to upgrade village life while lowering urban migration, reducing reliance on firewood, and providing power to pump water for irrigation where possible. For example, a small family-owned biogas plant uses human and animal waste (from three or four water buffalo, for example) to produce around 2.8 to 4.2 cubic meters of gas a day for heating and lighting. Larger biogas plants serve a number of homes or a village. Construction costs are too high for most villagers unless the government underwrites installation.

Mining and Quarrying

Through the 1980s, development of mining was discouraged by the absence of venture capital and the limited demand for many minerals from domestic industries. The slow development of mining was due in part to the remoteness of the areas where most minerals are found, which adds greatly to the costs of exploration, production, and transportation. Moreover, some of these areas have a poor reputation for law and order. By the early 1990s, mining was of little importance to the economy, despite the presence of fairly extensive mineral resources. Foreign companies have been invited to bid for concessions for mineral extraction.

Minerals include antimony, bauxite, chromite, copper, gypsum, iron ore, limestone, magnesite, marble, molybdenum, rock salt, and sulfur. Much of the mineral wealth is found in Balochistan. In FY 1992, mineral production included 8.5 million tons of limestone, 833,000 tons of rock salt, 471,000 tons of gypsum, and 6,333 tons of magnesite. Some iron-ore deposits are of good enough quality for use in the country's steel plant, but in FY 1992 production was only 937,000 tons.

The Saindak Integrated Mineral Project, managed by the state-owned Resource Development Corporation, was developed in the 1980s and early 1990s, but in 1993 there were as yet few results. Located in Balochistan, the project area contains three separate large deposits of copper ore, gold, iron ore, molybdenum, silver, and sulfur.

Services

Transportation

The domestic transportation system was not well developed at independence. Railroads were the main means of transportation, but the network in West Pakistan had been constructed under the assumption that the area formed part of a larger sub-

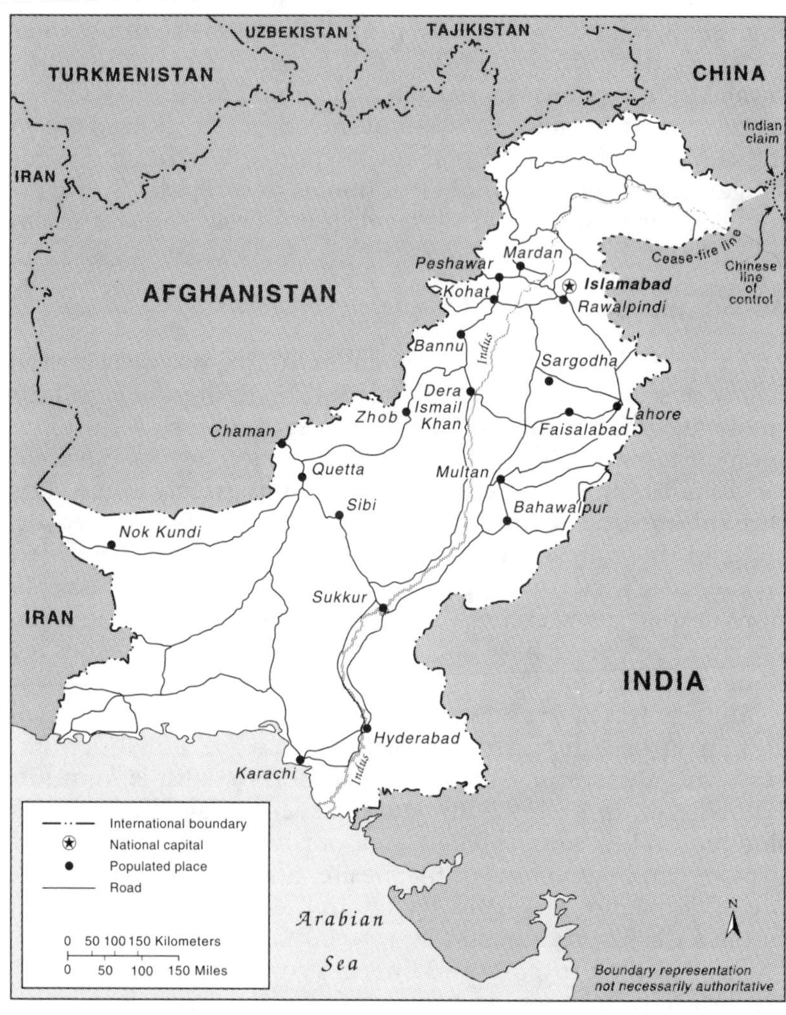

Figure 8. Transportation System: Roads, 1994

continental economic and political entity and was not suited to the needs of the new nation. Considerable development was necessary to improve links between Karachi, Pakistan's first capital and the country's principal port and commercial center, and Punjab, where Islamabad was established as the new administrative capital in 1962.

In the 1970s and 1980s, road and air networks grew considerably faster than the railroads. Between FY 1978 and FY 1992,

Figure 9. Transportation System: Railroads, Airports, and Ports, 1994

the volume of freight and the number of passengers carried by rail increased only slightly, whereas road-borne freight and the number of air passengers more than doubled. In 1994 transportation policy was aimed at shifting more of the traffic back to the rail system, with a long-term goal of a rail-to-road freight traffic ratio of 33:67 by 2000. However, it appears unlikely that this target will be met.

In June 1992, the road system covered 179,752 kilometers, of which asphalt roads made up 51.2 percent (see fig. 8). The number of motor vehicles more than doubled during the 1980s. Their number was estimated at nearly 2 million in 1992, including 932,000 motorcycles, 454,000 automobiles, 220,000 tractors, 157,000 trucks and vans, and 37,000 buses. In March 1992, the government approved a five-year Rs73 billion program of road construction and rehabilitation. This plan included building a four-lane 339-kilometer highway between Lahore and Islamabad, scheduled for completion in mid-1995. Road transport is mostly in the private sector, but some passenger and freight services are provided by public-sector corporations.

The railroad system is government owned and covers 8,775 kilometers (see fig. 9). In FY 1992 there were 753 locomotives and 34,851 freight wagons. The system usually runs at a loss. In mid-1992, the most profitable route, that between Lahore and Faisalabad, was privatized. It is expected that the government will attempt to privatize other rail routes, but the Lahore-Faisalabad line was renationalized in September 1993 when the private operator failed to make a profit.

Shipping capacity decreased in the 1980s. The merchant fleet, almost all operated by the Pakistan National Shipping Corporation (PNSC), consisted in 1992 of twenty-two vessels, down from fifty vessels in 1982. Approximately half the fleet is more than fifteen years old and is unsuited to present needs. The PNSC handled 2.74 million tons of cargo in the last six months of 1991, compared with 2.77 million tons during the corresponding period in 1990. In 1992, in line with its privatization policy, the government invited applications for setting up a private shipping sector and promised to operate the PNSC on a commercial basis.

There are two international ports—Karachi and Port Muhammad bin Qasim. In the early 1990s, Karachi handled the bulk of the maritime traffic. During the nine months ending in March 1992, Karachi handled 14.7 million tons of cargo, of which 11.0 million tons were imports and 3.7 million tons exports. This was 4.2 percent more cargo than was handled during the corresponding period of 1990–91. Port Qasim, which is fifty-three kilometers south of Karachi, handled 5.8 million tons of cargo in the first nine months of FY 1992.

In early 1994, the major airline was Pakistan International Airlines (PIA), controlled by the government. PIA had a fleet of forty-seven aircraft in March 1993, of which fifteen were

Motorized rickshaw stand on Circular Road, Lahore
Courtesy Anita M. Weiss
Truck in the North-West Frontier Province
Courtesy Harvey Follender

wide-bodied Boeing 747s and A300–B4s. The PIA network includes forty-five international and thirty-five domestic airports. There are international airports at Karachi, Islamabad, Lahore, Peshawar, and Quetta. Several small private airlines began operating domestic routes in 1993. One of these carriers, Shaheen Air International, also operates international cargo routes and plans to provide international passenger service in 1994 or 1995.

Telecommunications

In the 1980s, considerable effort was made to upgrade the telecommunications system. The Sixth Five-Year Plan, for instance, called for a public-sector investment of Rs10.1 billion to improve and expand the telephone and telex systems. In the mid-1990s, all overseas telecommunications used the Intelsat-VI satellite of the International Telecommunications Satellite Organization. There were also plans to launch a Pakistani satellite based on very small aperture earth stations, which would provide nationwide coverage for domestic telecommunications. The number of telephone connections increased from 461,000 in June 1984 to 1.6 million in March 1993, when the government announced that the Pakistan Telecommunications Corporation would be privatized. A new entity, the National Telecommunications Network, was planned to assume responsibility for the government's own network.

Radio and television are dominated by government corporations. The Pakistan Broadcasting Corporation (PBC) has a monopoly on radio broadcasting. In March 1992, there were 705,000 licensed radios, but the actual number of radios in use was estimated at 10 million. The PBC operates twenty-four medium-wave and three short-wave transmitters for its domestic programs and two medium-wave and eight short-wave transmitters for its external service. There are six networks for domestic service—one national network and regional networks for Balochistan, the Islamabad Capital Territory, the North-West Frontier Province, the Northern Areas, Punjab, and Sindh. The external service broadcasts in fifteen languages—Arabic, Burmese, Bengali, Dari, English, Farsi, French, Gujarati, Hindi, Indonesian, Swahili, Tamil, Turkmen, Turkish, and Urdu. An important target audience is Pakistanis working in the Middle East. Azad Kashmir Radio, a separate government-run organization, broadcasts in Azad Kashmir.

In early 1994, the government-controlled Pakistan Television Corporation (PTV) carried programs produced in five centers—Islamabad, Karachi, Lahore, Peshawar, and Quetta. Programming comes under the purview of the Ministry of Information and Broadcasting, and goals include providing wholesome entertainment, promoting national solidarity, and projecting an Islamic way of life. In November 1992, PTV began broadcasting on a second channel made possible by Japanese financing and technology. This channel is intended mainly for educational purposes. A commercial station was also established in the early 1990s and competes with PTV. In 1993 it was estimated that there were over 2 million television sets, and the number is expected to climb steeply in the 1990s. The main PTV channel is capable of reaching 87 percent of the population, while the second channel is accessible to 56 percent of the population.

Tourism

As of early 1994, foreign tourism remained relatively undeveloped. Annual tourist arrivals averaged 442,136 for the period 1985–89 but fell to 284,779 in 1990 because of uncertainties generated by the Persian Gulf War. The number of tourist arrivals rose to 415,529 in 1991. Many of the arrivals are visitors of Pakistani origin who have settled in Europe and North America. Pakistan has considerable tourist potential, but the generally poor law and order situation in the late 1980s and early 1990s discouraged rapid growth. Hotels meeting international standards are concentrated in the larger cities, especially Islamabad, Karachi, Lahore, Peshawar, and Rawalpindi.

In early 1994, the immediate future of the economy appeared uncertain. Although the economy is responding well to the government's liberalization program, and many sectors appear poised to achieve healthy rates of growth, economic prospects are constrained by the government's large budget deficits, the continued absorption of public expenditures by defense and interest payments, and the perception of widespread corruption. Pakistan remains heavily dependent on foreign aid donors. The failure to address more adequately the nation's low levels of education and health is also likely to act as a constraint on economic growth in the remainder of the 1990s.

* * *

Two publications from the Economist Intelligence Unit, the annual *Country Profile: Pakistan, Afghanistan* and the quarterly *Country Report: Pakistan, Afghanistan*, provide up-to-date information on the economy. More detailed analysis is found in two annual publications of Pakistan's Ministry of Finance, the *Economic Survey* and the *Economic Survey: Statistical Supplement.* Two monthly periodicals, the *National Bank of Pakistan Monthly Economic Letter* and the *Economic Outlook* are also useful. Shahid Javed Burki deserves special mention as one of the most astute writers on the Pakistani economy, especially as it relates to the nation's historical and social legacy. His *Pakistan: A Nation in the Making* and *Pakistan: The Continuing Search for Nationhood* include important essays pertinent to the economy, as does *Pakistan under the Military*, coauthored by Craig Baxter. Other recent general accounts of the economy include Nadeem Qasir's *Pakistan Studies*, B.M. Bhatia's *Pakistan's Economic Development, 1948–88*, and Anita M. Weiss's *Culture, Class, and Development in Pakistan.* (For further information and complete citations, see Bibliography.)

Chapter 4. Government and Politics

Artist's rendition of tile mosaic of man with jezail *(musket) from the Pictured Wall, Lahore Fort, Punjab. Artwork represents seventeenth-century tile work art of the Mughal period.*

NATION BUILDING REMAINS a difficult process in Pakistan. But although the country has undergone a succession of traumatic sociopolitical experiences since achieving independence in 1947, it continues to demonstrate its resilience and its capacity to survive and adapt to changing circumstances. Joining the community of nations as a bifurcated state, with its two wings separated by 1,600 kilometers of foreign soil, Pakistan was faced with the immediate task of absorbing large numbers of refugees from India in the months immediately following partition. The new nation struggled with severe economic disadvantages made acutely painful by a shortage of both administrative personnel and the material assets necessary to establish and sustain its fledgling government. With the death of Mohammad Ali Jinnah—the revered Quaid-i-Azam (Great Leader)—only thirteen months after independence, the nation was dealt another severe blow.

Created to provide a homeland for the Muslims of the Indian subcontinent, Pakistan was heir to a government structure and a political tradition that were essentially Western and secular. From its inception, Pakistan has worked to synthesize Islamic principles with the needs of a modern state. The young nation was immediately challenged by a host of other factors affecting national development, including ethnic and provincial tensions, political rivalries, and security considerations. The country subsequently survived civil war and the resultant loss of its East Wing, or East Pakistan, which became the independent nation of Bangladesh in December 1971, and has accommodated an influx of refugees resulting from the Soviet occupation of Afghanistan (December 1979–February 1989), which over the course of the conflict exceeded 3.2 million people.

Pakistan has had difficulty in establishing stable, effective political institutions. The country has experimented with a variety of political systems, has endured periods of martial law, and has had five constitutions, one inherited from the British and four indigenous ones since independence. Its political parties have suffered from regionalism, factionalism, and lack of vision. Power has shifted between the politicians and the civil-military establishment, and regional and ethnic forces have threatened national unity. However, the impulse toward cohesion has been stronger than the impetus toward division, and the process of nation building has continued. The return to democracy in 1988, and the peaceful, constitutional transfer of power to new governments in 1990 and 1993 testify to Pakistan's progress in the quest for political stability.

Constitutional and Political Inheritance

Independence

Pakistan, in its comparatively short history, has tried various forms of parliamentary, military, and presidential governments in its efforts to achieve political stability. At independence Pakistan was governed by the Government of India Act of 1935 as amended by the authority of the India Independence Act of 1947. The amended act provided at the center for a governor general (as successor to the British viceroy) as head of state and for a Constituent Assembly with two separate functions—to prepare a constitution and to be a federal legislature until the constitution came into effect.

At the outset, however, this structure of governor general and parliamentary legislature took on singular characteristics tailored to the personality, prestige, and unique position occupied by Jinnah, Pakistan's first governor general (see table 13, Appendix). At independence, he was the supreme authority, the founder of the state, and the chief political leader. As head of the All-India Muslim League, in 1940 he mobilized the political effort that in just seven years won Pakistan's independence. His ultimate authority came not from military power, not from the support of the bureaucracy, and not from constitutional prerogatives but from the political support of the people. In these circumstances, Jinnah chose to unite in himself the functions of head of state and the power of chief executive and party boss. In addition to his position as governor general, he was elected president of the Constituent Assembly.

For the office of governor general to be held by an active party politician who continued as political leader was an innovation. Initially, the arrangement may have seemed necessary to preserve national unity after independence and to facilitate the work of the new government. When Jinnah died, the prime minister, Liaquat Ali Khan, and the cabinet assumed increased power, in more traditional roles, and Khwaja Nazimuddin, as the new governor general, became a more traditional, nonpolitical head of state. Liaquat, however, found it difficult to establish his political authority. Whether the transfer of effective power to Liaquat while Jinnah was still alive might have created a precedent for future political stability in Pakistan is a moot point. Liaquat's assassination, three years later in October 1951, was the catalyst for a series of constitutional and political crises that over the years seemed almost endemic.

Role of Islam

Pakistan has provided a unique setting for experiments in synthesizing Islamic principles with the needs of a modern state. Although Pakistan's independence movement was articulated in Western terminology and centered on the right of national self-determination, it was also rooted in the Islamic concept of society and of what constitutes legitimate political authority for a Muslim. The basis of the ideal Muslim polity is the sharia (see Glossary), the sacred law of Islam as embodied in the Quran. Efforts to apply Quranic law in a modern political context have had a direct impact on Pakistan's political history and have also complicated the nation's constitutional evolution (see Politicized Islam, ch. 2).

Regional and Ethnic Factors

Government and politics bear the imprint of Pakistan's diversity. Despite the loss of the country's East Wing in 1971, the body politic remains a varied and volatile mix of ethnic, linguistic, and regional groups, and provincialism and ethnic rivalries continue to impede the progress of national integration. Although Islam is a unifying force, and the majority of Pakistanis are Sunni (see Glossary) Muslims, there is considerable cultural diversity within and among the country's four provinces, and coreligionists' identification as Sindhis, Punjabis, Baloch, or Pakhtuns (see Glossary) is strong.

Added to the indigenous human mosaic are the more than 7 million *muhajirs* (refugees or immigrants from India and their descendants) from various parts of India. Economic and political rivalries persist between the *muhajirs* and the indigenous populations of the provinces of Pakistan. These contests often turn violent and have contributed significantly to national unrest and instability (see Subversion and Civil Unrest, ch. 5). Ethnic riots have cost hundreds of lives and destroyed millions of dollars worth of property. A further challenge to national stability results from the approximately 1.4 million Afghan refugees who in early 1994 still had not returned to their country.

Linguistic diversity is also a divisive force. Some twenty languages are spoken, and although Urdu is the official language, it is not the native tongue of the majority of the population. Islam provides a tenuous unity in relation to such diversity. Efforts to build national consensus in the face of these obstacles remains central to effective government in Pakistan.

The Civil Service

The bureaucracy, particularly the higher civil service, has been a continuing source of stability and leadership and a counterweight to political upheaval and government instability. This cadre originated in the prepartition Indian Civil Service, whose members were well educated, well trained, and dedicated to a tradition of efficiency and responsibility. In time, the British recruited indigenous people, who were among India's best and brightest, into the Indian Civil Service ranks.

At partition, out of more than 1,100 Indian Civil Service officers, scarcely 100 were Muslims, and eighty-three of them opted to go to Pakistan. Because none of them held a senior rank equivalent to that of a secretary (and administrators were urgently needed to staff senior posts in the new state), this initial group was augmented by quick promotions in the Civil Service of Pakistan (CSP) through ad hoc appointments from other services and through retention, for a time, of some British officers. The CSP prided itself on being the backbone of the nation, the "steel frame" as it was sometimes called, and played a key role in Pakistan's survival in the difficult years following independence. Although Jinnah commended its contribution, he also warned CSP cadres to stay out of politics and to discharge their duties as public servants. After Jinnah's death, however, in the subsequent absence of strong political leadership, members of the CSP assumed an extraordinary role in the country's policy-making process. When the CSP was disbanded in 1973 and the various services were amalgamated into one administrative system, the expertise of its former members was much valued, and they continued to hold critical positions in the country's administrative apparatus through subsequent transitions in government. It is not surprising, then, that a later president of Pakistan, Ghulam Ishaq Khan (1988–93) was once a member of the CSP.

The Military

Another significant aspect of Pakistan's political legacy is its military forces and, in particular, the role of the largest of these forces, the army (see Role and Structure of the Security Forces, ch. 5). The military remains one of the country's most cohesive national institutions. Since independence it has oscillated between indirect and direct political control, remaining a major power. The military's sense of mission in defending and preserving the Islamic state of Pakistan has always been strong. For Muslim members of the British Indian Army, the transfer of loyalties from the colonial to the ideological state was not difficult. Successors to the historical legacy of the Muslim armies of the once powerful Mughal Empire, Muslim soldiers could relate to a new role of protecting the faith and the state embodied in Pakistan. The military also provided alternative political leadership in times of crisis. Military regimes in Pakistan have legitimized their actions by the doctrine of necessity, stepping in temporarily when political crises have reached a deadlock and threatened the state (see Constitutional Basis and Missions, ch. 5).

Early Political Development

Early Constitution Building, 1947–58

The path to the current constitution and government was often tortuous and accompanied by successive upheavals in the nation's political life. The years between 1947 and 1958 were marked by political chaos moderated by the administrative power and acumen of the CSP. They were also years in which the armed forces, especially the army, expanded its mission and assumed political influence alongside the CSP. Initially, the country was governed by a Constituent Assembly (see Independent Pakistan, ch. 1). The Constituent Assembly had dual functions: to draft a constitution and to enact legislation until the constitution came into effect. It was nine years before Pakistan adopted its first constitution in 1956. Conflicts in the Constituent Assembly included the issues of representation to be given to major regional groups (particularly the East Wing) and religious controversy over what an Islamic state should be.

The first major step in framing a constitution was the passage by the Constituent Assembly of the Objectives Resolution of March 1949, which defined the basic principles of the new state. It provided that Pakistan would be a state "wherein the principles of democracy, freedom, equality, tolerance and social justice, as enunciated by Islam, shall be fully observed; wherein the Muslims shall be enabled to order their lives in the individual and collective spheres in accordance with the teachings and requirements of Islam as set out in the Holy Quran and Sunna; [and] wherein adequate provision shall be made for the minorities freely to progress and practice their religions and develop their cultures." Seven years of debate, however, failed to produce agreement on fundamental issues such as regional representation or the structure of a constitution. This impasse prompted Governor General Ghulam Mohammad to dismiss the Constituent Assembly in 1954. The Supreme Court of Pakistan upheld the action of the governor general, arguing that he had the power to disband the Constituent Assembly and veto legislation it passed. This preeminence of the governor general over the legislature has been referred to as the viceregal tradition in Pakistan's politics.

The revived Constituent Assembly promulgated Pakistan's first indigenous constitution in 1956 and reconstituted itself as the national legislature—the Legislative Assembly—under the constitution it adopted. Pakistan became an Islamic republic. The governor general was replaced by a president, but despite efforts to create regional parity between the East Wing and the West Wing, the regional tensions remained. Continuing regional rivalry, ethnic dissension, religious debate, and the weakening power of the Muslim League—the national party that spearheaded the country's founding—exacerbated political instability and eventually led President Iskander Mirza to disband the Legislative Assembly on October 7, 1958, and declare martial law. General Mohammad Ayub Khan, Pakistan's first indigenous army commander in chief, assisted Mirza in abrogating the constitution of 1956 and removing the politicians he believed were bringing Pakistan to the point of collapse. Ayub Khan, as Mirza's chief martial law administrator, then staged another coup also in October 1958, forced Mirza out of power, and assumed the presidency, to the relief of large segments of the population tired of the politicians' continued machinations.

Ayub Khan, 1958–69

Although Ayub Khan viewed himself as a reformer, he was predisposed to the benevolent authoritarianism of the Mughal

Field Marshal Mohammad Ayub Khan
Courtesy Embassy of Pakistan, Washington

General Agha Mohammad Yahya Khan
Courtesy Embassy of Pakistan, Washington

and viceregal traditions. He also relied heavily on the country's civilian bureaucrats, who formed the majority of his advisers and cabinet ministers. Ayub Khan initiated a plan for Basic Democracies, a measure to create a system of local government from the grass roots (see Basic Democracies, ch. 1). The Basic Democracies system consisted of a mulitiered pyramidal hierarchy of interlocking tiers of legislative councils from the village to the provincial level. The lowest but most important tier was composed of union councils, one each for groups of villages having an approximate population of 10,000. The members of these union councils were called Basic Democrats. The union councils were responsible for local government, including agricultural and community development, maintaining law and order through rural police, and trying minor cases in conciliation courts.

In 1960 the Basic Democrats were asked to endorse Ayub Khan's presidency and to give him a mandate to frame a new constitution. Ayub's constitution, promulgated in 1962, ended martial law, established a presidential form of government with a weak legislature (now called the National Assembly), and gave the president augmented executive, legislative, and financial powers. Adult franchise was limited to the election of Basic Democrats, who constituted an electoral college for the president and members of the national and provincial assemblies. This constitution was abrogated in 1969 when Ayub, who by then had lost the people's confidence, resigned, handing over the responsibility for governing to the army commander in chief, General Agha Mohammad Yahya Khan (see The Ayub Khan Era, ch. 1). Yahya Khan assumed the title of president and also became chief martial law administrator.

Yahya Khan, 1969–71

Although Yahya Khan established a semi-military state, he also introduced changes that led to the return of parliamentary democracy. These changes ultimately resulted in the division of the country in two. Yahya held national elections in December 1970 for the purpose of choosing members of the new National Assembly who were to be elected directly by the people. However, the results of these elections, which brought the politicians once more to the fore, led to the secession of East Pakistan and the creation of an independent Bangladesh in 1971.

Yahya accepted the demand of East Pakistan for representation in the new assembly on the basis of population. As a result, Bengali leader Sheikh Mujibur ("Mujib") Rahman's Awami League won all but two of the 162 seats allotted East Pakistan out of the 300 directly elected seats in the assembly (thirteen indirectly elected seats for women were added), and Mujib wanted considerable regional autonomy for East Pakistan. Zulfiqar Ali Bhutto and his Pakistan People's Party (PPP) emerged as the political victors in West Pakistan in the 1970 elections. Bhutto's intransigence—he refused to participate in the discussions to frame the new constitution—led to the continuation of martial law and the eventual political and military confrontation between East Pakistan and West Pakistan, which precipitated civil war and the country's dismemberment in December 1971. With Pakistan's military in disarray, Yahya resigned, and Bhutto was appointed president and civilian chief martial law administrator of a truncated Pakistan.

Zulfiqar Ali Bhutto, 1971–77

Bhutto lifted martial law within several months, and after an "interim constitution" granting him broad powers as president, a new constitution was promulgated in April 1973 and came into effect on August 14 of that year, the twenty-sixth anniversary of the country's independence. This constitution represented a consensus on three issues: the role of Islam; the sharing of power between the federal government and the provinces; and the division of responsibility between the president and the prime minister, with a greatly strengthened position for the latter. Bhutto stepped down as president and became prime minister. In order to allay fears of the smaller provinces concerning domination by Punjab, the constitution established a bicameral legislature with a Senate, providing equal provincial representation, and a National Assembly, allocating seats according to population. Islam was declared the state religion of Pakistan.

Bhutto had the opportunity to resolve many of Pakistan's political problems. But although the country finally seemed to be on a democratic course, Bhutto lost this opportunity because of a series of repressive actions against the political opposition that made it appear he was working to establish a one-party state. In a final step, he suddenly called national elections in March 1977, hoping to catch the opposition unprepared and give his party total control of the National Assembly. When Bhutto's party overwhelmingly won the election, the opposition charged voting irregularities and launched mass disturbances requiring action by the army to restore law and order. Bhutto was ousted by the military, which again took control. This action resulted not solely from sheer political ambition but from the military's belief that the law and order situation had dangerously deteriorated.

Zia ul-Haq, 1977–88

General Zia ul-Haq, chief of the army staff, became chief martial law administrator in July 1977 and president in September 1978. He suspended the constitution, with the army's stated objective being to create an environment in which fair elections could be held. However, Bhutto, his primary opponent, was tried and sentenced to death in 1978 on the charge of conspiring to murder a political opponent. The Supreme Court upheld the sentence, and Bhutto was hanged in April 1979. Zia cancelled the elections that had been promised and kept the country under martial law until 1985. During this time, Zia pressed the policy that Pakistan's survival and progress were dependent on building an Islamic state. A number of measures were taken to implement this policy, including the introduction of the Federal Shariat Court. A referendum held in 1984 confirmed Zia's policy of Islamization. In this referendum, a "yes" vote agreeing with Zia's Islamization policy was also interpreted as a vote for Zia to remain in office as president for another five years. According to the results reported by the government but contested by the opposition, Zia obtained 98 percent of total votes cast.

Zia's government also adapted Ayub's Basic Democracies structure to institute a new system of local government. Local councils were organized into tiers with union councils at the base, *tehsil* (subdistrict) councils above them, and *zilla* (district) councils at the apex. The system also included municipal committees and municipal corporations in the larger metropolitan centers. Councillors were elected for four-year terms and could stand for reelection. The councils were designed to meet a need for grass-roots expression. Elections were conducted without formal political party affiliation or involvement. The councils were to concentrate on improving local development, including agricultural production, education, health, roads, and water supply.

In 1985 elections were held for both the national and the provincial assemblies, an amended version of the 1973 constitution was reinstated, and martial law was ended. Zia remained president, and the amended constitution, including the controversial Eighth Amendment passed by the National Assembly in November 1985, gave predominant political authority to the president (see President, this ch.). The president could appoint and dismiss the prime minister and the provincial governors and could dissolve both the national and the provincial assemblies. A significant feature of the 1973 constitution as amended in 1985, insofar as the Islamization process was concerned, was that the Objectives Resolution, adopted by the first Constituent Assembly in 1949 and made a preamble to the 1956, 1962, and 1973 constitutions, was incorporated as a substantive part (Article 2–A) of this restored constitution. The Objectives Resolution provided, in part, that Pakistan would be a state "wherein the Muslims shall be enabled to order their lives in the individual and collective spheres in accordance with

Zulfiqar Ali Bhutto
Courtesy Embassy of Pakistan, Washington

General Mohammad Zia ul-Haq
Courtesy Embassy of Pakistan, Washington

the teachings and requirements of Islam as set out in the Holy Quran and the Sunna."

Political parties were not allowed to participate in the 1985 elections, and the PPP, led by Benazir Bhutto (Zulfiqar Ali Bhutto's daughter), boycotted them. After the elections, Zia picked Mohammad Khan Junejo, a politician from Sindh and a minister in one of his earlier cabinets, as his prime minister. The Zia-Junejo period lasted three years until Zia dismissed the prime minister and dissolved the National Assembly and the four provincial assemblies. Zia cited incompetence, corruption, and failure to further the Islamization process as reasons for his actions. In addition, Zia came to regard Junejo as too independent, and the two men clashed on a number of issues including differences on policy relating to Afghanistan and promotions in the armed services. Zia also announced that new elections would be held.

Zia's sudden death in an airplane crash in August 1988 near Bahawalpur, a town in central Punjab, left Pakistan without a president, prime minister, or national or provincial assemblies. In a demonstration of the country's resilience, Ghulam Ishaq Khan, the chairman of the Senate—which had not been dissolved by Zia—and next in the constitutional line of succession, became interim president in December. Elections were held, Benazir became prime minister, and Ishaq Khan was subsequently elected president.

Constitution and Government Structure

Pakistan's independence was won through a democratic and constitutional struggle. Although the country's record with parliamentary democracy has been mixed, Pakistan, after lapses, has returned to this form of government. The constitution of the Islamic Republic of Pakistan adopted in 1985 provides for a federal parliamentary system with a president as head of state and a popularly elected prime minister as head of government.

President

The president, in keeping with the constitutional provision that the state religion is Islam, must be a Muslim. Elected for a five-year term by an electoral college consisting of members of the Senate and National Assembly and members of the provincial assemblies, the president is eligible for reelection. No individual may hold the office for more than two consecutive terms. The president may resign or be impeached and may be removed from office for incapacity or gross misconduct by a two-thirds vote of the members of the parliament. The president generally acts on the advice of the prime minister but has important residual powers. One of the most important—a legacy of Zia—is contained in the Eighth Amendment, which gives the president the power to dissolve the National Assembly "in his discretion where, in his opinion . . . a situation has arisen in which the Government of the Federation cannot be carried on in accordance with the provisions of the Constitution and an appeal to the electorate is necessary."

Parliament and Federal Government

The bicameral federal legislature is the Majlis-i-Shoora (Council of Advisers), consisting of the Senate (upper house) and National Assembly (lower house) (see fig. 10). Members of the National Assembly are elected by universal adult suffrage (over twenty-one years of age in Pakistan). Seats are allocated to each of the four provinces, the Federally Administered Tribal Areas, and Islamabad Capital Territory on the basis of population. National Assembly members serve for the parliamentary term, which is five years, unless they die or resign sooner, or unless the National Assembly is dissolved. Although the vast majority of the members are Muslim, about 5 percent of the seats are reserved for minorities, including Christians, Hindus, and Sikhs. Elections for minority seats are held on the basis of separate electorates at the same time as the polls for Muslim seats during the general elections.

The prime minister is appointed by the president from among the members of the National Assembly. The prime minister is assisted by the Federal Cabinet, a council of ministers whose members are appointed by the president on the advice of the prime minister. The Federal Cabinet comprises the ministers, ministers of state, and advisers. As of early 1994, there were thirty-three ministerial portfolios: commerce; communications; culture; defense; defense production; education; environment; finance and economic affairs; food and agriculture; foreign affairs; health; housing; information and broadcasting; interior; Kashmiri affairs and Northern Areas; law and justice; local government; minority affairs; narcotics control; parliamentary affairs; petroleum and natural resources production; planning and development; railroads; religious affairs; science and technology; social welfare; special education; sports; state and frontier regions; tourism; water and power; women's development; and youth affairs.

The Senate is a permanent legislative body with equal representation from each of the four provinces, elected by the members of their respective provincial assemblies. There are representatives from the Federally Administered Tribal Areas and from Islamabad Capital Territory. The chairman of the Senate, under the constitution, is next in line to act as president should the office become vacant and until such time as a new president can be formally elected. Both the Senate and the National Assembly can initiate and pass legislation except for finance bills. Only the National Assembly can approve the federal budget and all finance bills. In the case of other bills, the president may prevent passage unless the legislature in joint sitting overrules the president by a majority of members of both houses present and voting.

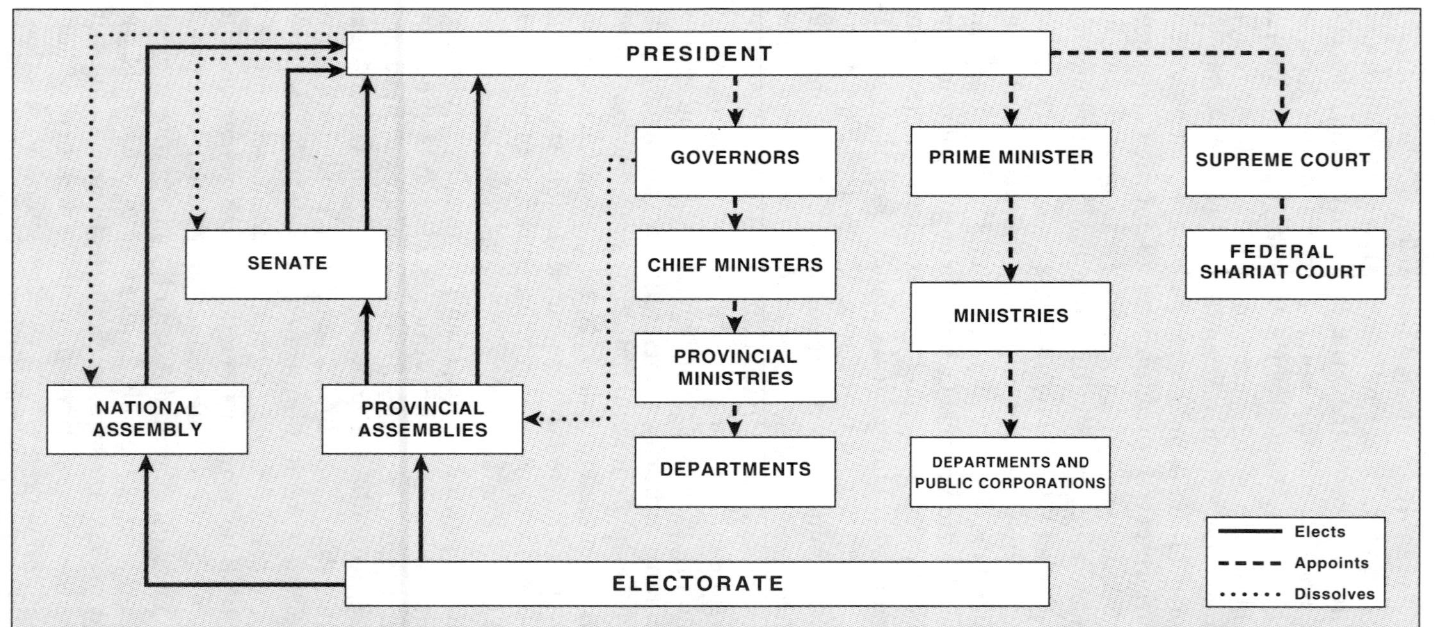

Source: Based on information from Pakistan, Ministry of Justice and Parliamentary Affairs, *The Constitution of the Islamic Republic of Pakistan (as Modified up to 19th March 1985)*, Islamabad, 1985; and Craig Baxter et al., *Government and Politics in South Asia*, Boulder, Colorado, 1993, 210.

Figure 10. Structure of the Government, 1994

Other offices and bodies having important roles in the federal structure include the attorney general, the auditor general, the Federal Land Commission, the Federal Public Service Commission, the Central Election Commission, and the Wafaqi Mohtasib (Ombudsman).

Provincial Governments

Pakistan's four provinces enjoy considerable autonomy. Each province has a governor, a Council of Ministers headed by a chief minister appointed by the governor, and a provincial assembly. Members of the provincial assemblies are elected by universal adult suffrage. Provincial assemblies also have reserved seats for minorities. Although there is a well-defined division of responsibilities between federal and provincial governments, there are some functions on which both can make laws and establish departments for their execution. Most of the services in areas such as health, education, agriculture, and roads, for example, are provided by the provincial governments. Although the federal government can also legislate in these areas, it only makes national policy and handles international aspects of those services.

Judiciary

The judiciary includes the Supreme Court, provincial high courts, and other lesser courts exercising civil and criminal jurisdiction. The chief justice of the Supreme Court is appointed by the president; the other Supreme Court judges are appointed by the president after consultation with the chief justice. The chief justice and judges of the Supreme Court may remain in office until age sixty-five. The Supreme Court has original, appellate, and advisory jurisdiction. Judges of the provincial high courts are appointed by the president after consultation with the chief justice of the Supreme Court, as well as the governor of the province and the chief justice of the high court to which the appointment is being made. High courts have original and appellate jurisdiction.

There is also a Federal Shariat Court consisting of eight Muslim judges, including a chief justice appointed by the president. Three of the judges are ulama, that is, Islamic Scholars, and are well versed in Islamic law. The Federal Shariat Court has original and appellate jurisdiction. This court decides whether any law is repugnant to the injunctions of Islam. When a law is deemed repugnant to Islam, the president, in the case of a federal law, or the governor, in the case of a provincial law, is charged with taking steps to bring the law into conformity with the injunctions of Islam. The court also hears appeals from decisions of criminal courts under laws relating to the enforcement of *hudood* (see Glossary) laws, that is, laws pertaining to such offenses as intoxication, theft, and unlawful sexual intercourse (see Islamic Provisions, ch. 5).

In addition, there are special courts and tribunals to deal with specific kinds of cases, such as drug courts, commercial courts, labor courts, traffic courts, an insurance appellate tribunal, an income tax appellate tribunal, and special courts for bank offenses. There are also special courts to try terrorists (see Courts and Criminal Procedure, ch. 5). Appeals from special courts go to high courts except for labor and traffic courts, which have their own forums for appeal. Appeals from the tribunals go to the Supreme Court.

A further feature of the judicial system is the office of Wafaqi Mohtasib (Ombudsman), which is provided for in the constitution. The office of Mohtasib was established in many early Muslim states to ensure that no wrongs were done to citizens. Appointed by the president, the Mohtasib holds office for four years; the term cannot be extended or renewed. The Mohtasib's purpose is to institutionalize a system for enforcing administrative accountability, through investigating and rectifying any injustice done to a person through maladministration by a federal agency or a federal government official. The Mohtasib is empowered to award compensation to those who have suffered loss or damage as a result of maladministration. Excluded from jurisdiction, however, are personal grievances or service matters of a public servant as well as matters relating to foreign affairs, national defense, and the armed services. This institution is designed to bridge the gap between administrator and citizen, to improve administrative processes and procedures, and to help curb misuse of discretionary powers.

Political Dynamics

Pakistan has had considerable difficulty developing stable, cohesive political organizations because they have suffered long periods of repression. Further, political parties, with few exceptions, have been founded as vehicles for one person or a few individuals, or to achieve specifically defined goals. When these individuals die or abandon their parties, or after party goals have been met, many organizations have lost their raison d'être and have lacked the ability to carry on. In addition, political parties have been handicapped by regional and ethnic factors that have limited their national appeal and have also been torn by personal and class rivalries.

Muslim League

The Muslim League was founded in 1906 as the All-India Muslim League to protect the interests of Muslims in British India and to counter the political growth of the Indian National Congress, founded in 1885. Under the leadership of Mohammad Ali Jinnah, the Muslim League adopted the Lahore Resolution (often referred to as the "Pakistan Resolution") in March 1940 and successfully spearheaded the movement for the creation of an independent homeland for Indian Muslims. At independence the Muslim League was the only major party in Pakistan and claimed the allegiance of almost every Muslim in the country. However, with the deaths of its two principal leaders, Jinnah and Liaquat Ali Khan, shortly after independence and its central goal of creating Pakistan achieved, the party failed to develop a coherent, postindependence ideology. The Muslim League gradually came under the influence of West Pakistani, and particularly Punjabi, landlords and bureaucrats more concerned with increasing their personal influence than with building a strong national organization.

The Muslim League was further weakened by the constitutional impasse in the 1950s resulting from difficulties in resolving questions of regional representation as well as the problem of reaching a consensus on Islamic issues. Regional loyalties were intensified during the constitutional debates over the respective political representation of the country's west and east wings. In addition, East Pakistan had a larger Hindu population, and some strong provincial leaders believed their power depended on developing broad-based secular institutions. The Muslim League, however, pressed for provisions to establish Pakistan as an Islamic state.

Two powerful Bengali leaders and former Muslim League members, Hussain Shahid Suhrawardy and Fazlul Haq, used their own parties, the Awami League and the Krishak Sramik Party (Workers and Peasants), respectively, in a joint effort in 1954 to defeat the Muslim League in the first election held in East Pakistan after partition. Fazlul Haq had made the motion to adopt the historic "Pakistan Resolution" in 1940, and

Suhrawardy, subsequently the last chief minister of undivided Bengal, had seconded it. But both men were alienated by West Pakistani domination of the Muslim League. Suhrawardy was elected leader of the opposition in the second Constituent Assembly and in 1956 was appointed prime minister, a further loss for the Muslim League because he was the first non-Muslim League politician to hold this position. By this time, the Muslim League had lost its influence in both East Pakistan and West Pakistan, having also lost its majority in the West Pakistan Legislative Assembly to the Punjab-centered Republican Party. The promulgation of martial law in 1958 and the dissolution of all political parties finally resulted in the demise of the Muslim League after its fifty-two-year existence.

General Ayub Khan formed a party called the Pakistan Muslim League (PML) in 1962, and Junejo established a party with the same name (PML-J) in 1986, but these two parties had little in common with the 1906–58 Muslim League in terms of their objectives and composition. After Junejo died in March 1993, Mian Nawaz Sharif took over the party and it became the Pakistan Muslim League (PML-N) for Nawaz Sharif. The death of Junejo signified the end to an uneasy coalition that had existed between the feudal lobby under Junejo and the representatives of the new business and industrialist classes who, under the guidance of Nawaz Sharif, were running the Islamic Democratic Alliance (Islami Jamhoori Ittehad—IJI) government of 1990–93.

Islami Jamhoori Ittehad

The Islami Jamhoori Ittehad (IJI) was formed in September 1988 to oppose the PPP in elections that year. The alliance comprised nine parties, of which the major components were the PML and the Islamic Organization (Jamaat-i-Islami—JI). The IJI won only fifty-three seats in the National Assembly, compared with ninety-two won by the PPP. Most IJI seats were won in Punjab. Nawaz Sharif emerged from the 1988 elections as the most powerful politician outside the PPP. In December 1988, he succeeded in forming an IJI administration in Punjab and became the province's chief minister. It was from this power base that he waged the political battles that eventually led to his becoming prime minister in 1990. In the supercharged atmosphere of the 1990 elections, the electorate surprised observers. Neither the IJI nor the PPP was expected to come up with a firm mandate to rule. Yet the IJI received a strong mandate to govern, winning 105 seats versus forty-five seats for the Pakistan Democratic Alliance (PDA)—of which the PPP was the main component in the National Assembly.

In the 1993 national elections, the IJI coalition no longer existed to bring together all the anti-PPP forces. The religious parties expended most of their energies trying to form a workable electoral alliance rather than bolstering the candidacy of Nawaz Sharif, the only person capable of challenging Benazir.

Jamaat-i-Islami

The Jamaat-i-Islami (JI), the largest and most articulate of Pakistan's religious parties, was founded in 1941 by Maulana Abul Ala Maududi as an ideological movement to promote Islamic values and practices in British India. It initially opposed the Pakistan movement, arguing that Islam was a universal religion not subject to national boundaries. It changed its position, however, once the decision was made to partition India on the basis of religion. In 1947 Maududi redefined the JI's purpose as the establishment of an Islamic state in Pakistan. In order to achieve this objective, the JI believed it was necessary to purge the community of deviant behavior and to establish a political system in which decision making would be undertaken by a few pious people well versed in the meaning of Islam. Maududi's writings also gained a wide audience. He retired as head of the party in 1972.

In order to rid the community of what it considered to be deviant behavior, the JI waged a campaign in 1953 against the Ahmadiyya community in Pakistan that resulted in some 2,000 deaths, brought on martial law rule in Punjab, and led Governor General Ghulam Mohammad to dismiss the Federal Cabinet. The anti-Ahmadiyya movement resulted in 1974 in a bill successfully piloted through the National Assembly by then Prime Minister Zulfiqar Ali Bhutto declaring the Ahmadiyyas a non-Muslim minority.

The JI's views on Islamization and limited political participation were opposed by those people who saw the party's platform as advocating religious dictatorship. The question of whether the JI was a political party or an organization working to subvert legitimate political processes was raised in the courts. The Supreme Court ultimately decided in favor of the JI as a lawful political organization. Prominent in political life since independence, the JI was the dominant voice for the interests of the ulama in the debates leading to the adoption of

Pakistan's first constitution. The JI participated in opposition politics from 1950 to 1977.

Under party chief Mian Tufail Muhammad, the JI supported the Zia regime's Islamization program, but it clashed with him over the 1984 decision to ban student unions because this ban affected the party's student wing, the Jamiat-i-Tulaba-i-Islam (Islamic Society of Students). The Jamiat-i-Tulaba-i-Islam had become increasingly militant and had been involved in clashes with other student groups on Pakistani campuses. Aspiring student activists, supportive of religious issues, have flocked to the Jamiat-i-Tulaba-i-Islam as a means of having an impact on national politics. The Jamiat-i-Tulaba-i-Islam also has been a major source of new recruits for the JI; it is thought that one-third of JI leaders come from the Jamiat-i-Tulaba-i-Islam. The JI envisions a state governed by Islamic law and opposes Westernization—including capitalism, socialism, and such practices as bank interest, birth control, and relaxed social mores.

The JI's influence has been far greater than its showing at the polls suggests. In 1986, for example, two JI senators successfully piloted the controversial Shariat Bill through the Senate, although it did not become law at that time. In addition, the movement of student recruits from the Jamiat-i-Tulaba-i-Islam into the JI has created a new bloc of Islamist voters. Through the Jamiat-i-Tulaba-i-Islam, the JI is working to leave a permanent mark on the political orientation of the country's future leaders. However, the Pakistani electorate has been resistant to making religion a central factor in determining statecraft. In 1990 the JI was an important component of the IJI but nevertheless won only four seats. Furthermore, in the 1993 national elections, the Islamization factor was even more muted because the religious parties—spearheaded by the JI—were not aligned with the two main contenders, the PML-N and the PPP. The JI and its political umbrella group, the Pakistan Islamic Front, captured only three seats in the National Assembly.

Pakistan People's Party

The Pakistan People's Party (PPP) represents another part of Pakistan's political spectrum. The PPP was a vehicle for the political ambitions of Zulfiqar Ali Bhutto. His immediate aim was to bring down the government of his former political mentor, Ayub Khan. The party's inaugural convention was held in Lahore in 1967. The PPP adopted the slogan "Islam our Faith, Democracy our Polity, Socialism our Economy." The party, like

Pakistan People's Party sign in Karachi
Courtesy Sheila Ross

Former prime minister and leading politician, Mian Nawaz Sharif
Courtesy Embassy of Pakistan, Washington

its founder, was enigmatic and full of contradictions. A left-leaning populist movement, the PPP attempted to blend Islam with socialism. The PPP espoused such policies as land reform to help the peasants; nationalization of industries to weaken the industrialists; and administrative reforms to reduce the power of the bureaucrats. The party, however, was built on the foundations of the wealthy, landed elite, Pakistan's traditional ruling class.

The PPP came to power in December 1971 after the loss of East Pakistan, when Bhutto was sworn in as president and chief martial law administrator. Bhutto lifted martial law in April 1972 and in 1973 stepped down as president and became prime minister. The PPP did little to advance the first two tenets of its platform, Islam and democracy, but promoted socialism with a vengeance. Bhutto nationalized large-scale industries, insurance companies, and commercial banks, and he set up a number of public corporations to expand the role of the government in commerce, construction, and transportation. The heavy hand with which Bhutto and the PPP exerted their power aroused widespread resentment. Matters came to a head in 1977 when the PPP won 155 of the 200 seats in the National Assembly with 58 percent of the total votes cast. The Pakistan National Alliance (PNA), a coalition of nine opposition parties and with 35 percent of the votes, won only thirty-six seats. The PNA charged widespread electoral fraud, and the resulting PPP-PNA confrontation and the accompanying civil unrest precipitated the imposition of martial law.

The survival of Bhutto's party after his execution in 1979 was facilitated by dynastic politics. His widow Nusrat and his daughter Benazir led the party as cochairpersons. During martial law, the PPP joined with ten other parties in the Movement for the Restoration of Democracy (MRD) to pressure the Zia government to hold free elections under the 1973 constitution. Four of the MRD's component parties were members of the PNA, which had been formed to oppose the PPP in the 1977 elections. The PPP joined the MRD coalition, hoping the military would be prepared to negotiate with the MRD if it were part of a larger political alliance.

The MRD campaign launched in February 1981 appeared to gain momentum. In March 1981, however, a Pakistan International Airlines aircraft was hijacked by terrorists demanding the release of political prisoners. The hijacking was the work of an organization—Al-Zulfiqar—allegedly run by Bhutto's son, Murtaza. Although the PPP dissociated itself from the episode, the hijacking was a major setback for both the PPP and the MRD. Another MRD agitation failed in 1983. After Zia's death in 1988, the MRD was dissolved, and the PPP, the largest party in the alliance, contested the 1988 elections on its own. Although the PPP emerged as the single largest party in the National Assembly as a result of the 1988 elections, it won a narrow plurality, and only with the support of the Refugee People's Movement (Muhajir Qaumi Mahaz—MQM) and other parties was it able to form a government. After a troubled period in power, the PPP government was dismissed by President Ishaq Khan in 1990. The PPP was the principal member of the PDA, which lost the 1990 elections to the IJI. The PDA blamed its defeat on alleged tampering with the vote. The National Democratic Institute for International Affairs, an international observer team, did note irregularities in the election but declared that the ultimate outcome was in general accordance with the popular will.

In the October 1993 general elections that returned Benazir to power, the PPP won eighty-six of the 217 seats in the National Assembly, while Nawaz Sharif's PML-N won seventy-two. The PPP was successful in forming a coalition with other parties to control a block of 121 seats.

Muhajir Qaumi Mahaz

The Muhajir Qaumi Mahaz (MQM), a party formed to represent the interests of the *muhajir* community in Pakistan, had a meteoric rise in the political life of the country. Founded by Altaf Hussain in 1984, the MQM won thirteen (out of 207) seats in the National Assembly in the 1988 elections, making it the third largest party in the assembly after the PPP and the IJI. MQM support of the PPP made it possible for Benazir to form a government and become prime minister. Shortly after the election, however, the coalition between the PPP and the MQM broke down, and the two parties' subsequently troubled relations contributed greatly to the instability of Benazir's first government. In the 1990 general elections, the MQM won fifteen seats in the National Assembly, remaining the third largest party. The MQM boycotted the 1993 National Assembly elections but won twenty-seven seats in the provincial assembly of Sindh.

The MQM had its origin in the All-Pakistan Muhajir Students Organization at Karachi University. At a large public meeting in Karachi in 1986, the MQM expressed the political and economic demands of the *muhajir* community. The MQM's political strength came primarily from the urban areas of Sindh, and its main emphasis was on securing better job opportunities for *muhajirs*. The MQM played an active role in the ethnic riots in Karachi in the winter of 1986–87. These disturbances brought prominence and notoriety to the MQM and its leader, Altaf Hussain. It was after these riots that the MQM leadership converted the movement into a political party. The MQM's full political weight was first felt in the 1988 elections.

Awami National Party

The Awami National Party (*awami* means "people's"), which depends on Pakhtuns of the North-West Frontier Province and northern Balochistan as its political base, won six seats in the National Assembly in the 1990 elections. In the 1993 national elections, the party won three seats in the National Assembly. The Awami National Party was formed in 1986 by the merger of several left-leaning parties including the Awami Tehrik and the National Democratic Party. Khan Abdul Wali Khan was appointed its first president. Wali Khan's political career had been built on the tradition of intense Pakhtun nationalism inherited from his father, Khan Abdul Ghaffar Khan. Both men were opposed to the creation of Pakistan, and after partition they were imprisoned. In 1956 Wali Khan joined the National Awami Party (NAP), led by a charismatic Bengali socialist, Maulana Bhashani. In 1965 the NAP split into two factions, with Wali Khan becoming president of the pro-Moscow faction. In 1972 the party was strong enough to form coalition provincial governments, with its partner the Jamiat-ul-Ulama-i-Islam (JUI) in the North-West Frontier Province and Balochistan. These governments were short-lived. Wali Khan was again jailed, and his party was barred from politics when the Supreme Court upheld the finding of Bhutto that the NAP was conspiring against the state of Pakistan. General Zia subsequently withdrew the charges against the NAP. Wali Khan was released, joined the National Democratic Party, and ultimately formed the Awami National Party.

Jamiat-ul-Ulama-i-Islam

The Jamiat-ul-Ulama-i-Islam (JUI), led by Maulana Fazlur Rahman, had its origins in the Jamiat-ul-Ulama-i-Hind (JUH), founded by a group of ulama of the Deoband Movement in prepartition India. The JUH argued that Muslims could coexist with other religions in a society where they were not the majority. In 1945, however, a group of JUH ulama, led by Maulana Shabir Ahmad Usmani, split off from the JUH, formed the JUI, and gave their support to the movement for an independent Pakistan. Since 1947 the JUI has undergone a number of organizational and program changes. It developed strong support in the North-West Frontier Province and Balochistan. In 1972 it joined the NAP to form governments in those two provinces. In 1977 the JUI contested the National Assembly elections as a component of the Pakistan National Alliance. The JUI did not sympathize with General Zia's Islamization program, and in 1981 the JUI joined the MRD to pressure Zia to hold free elections. The JUI won six seats in the National Assembly in the 1990 elections. In the 1993 national elections, the JUI was the main component of the Islami Jamhoori Mahaz, which won four seats in the National Assembly.

Tehrik-i-Istiqlal

The Tehrik-i-Istiqlal (Solidarity Movement) was founded by retired Air Marshal Asghar Khan in 1969. The party's aim was to provide a vehicle, in the center of the political spectrum, for the growing middle class. Although the party acquired sizable support among the professional classes, including lawyers and doctors, it did not develop significant grassroots strength. In an effort to gain increased status, in 1981 the Tehrik-i-Istiqlal joined a number of other parties in the MRD, but it left the movement in 1986. The Tehrik-i-Istiqlal did not fare well in the elections of 1988, and Asghar Khan resigned as the party's chairman in 1989. In the elections of 1990, the Tehrik-i-Istiqlal allied itself with the PPP in the Pakistan Democratic Alliance. In the elections of 1993, the Tehrik-i-Istiqlal did not win any seats.

Political Developments since Zia

The First Government of Benazir Bhutto

Benazir Bhutto, the first woman prime minister of a modern Muslim state, is clearly the beneficiary of dynastic politics and of the emotional ties of a large section of the electorate to her charismatic family. However, this legacy as the daughter of Zulfiqar Ali Bhutto has proven to be a mixed political blessing.

Although she inherited her father's party, the PPP, and has led it to victory, the party won a very narrow plurality in the 1988 elections and was therefore forced to enter into a coalition with the MQM (representing Pakistan's *muhajir* community) and several other parties in order to form a government. Benazir wanted to repeal the Eighth Amendment in order to strengthen her position as prime minister but could not muster sufficient political support and soon abandoned the effort. Benazir also had to address several long-standing problems: how to cope with an intrusive and politicized military; how to resolve the power play between the central and provincial governments; and how to fashion an appropriate role for Islam in government. In addition to these problems, Benazir had to face pressing new ones, including a large budget deficit and growing ethnic violence.

Several early actions appeared to strengthen Benazir's ability to deal with these problems. In choosing her cabinet, for example, Benazir kept the portfolios of finance and defense for herself but appointed a seasoned bureaucrat, Wasim Jafari, as her top adviser on finance and economic affairs. Her retention of Zia's foreign minister, Sahibzada Yaqub Khan, signaled continuity in the country's policy on Afghanistan. Also, when working out their political coalition, the MQM agreed to support the PPP government at both federal and provincial levels. The agreement, signed by the Sindh-based MQM and the head of the PPP in Sindh, pledged to protect and safeguard the interests of all the people of Sindh, regardless of language, religion, or origin of birth, as well as to stamp out violence and to support the rule of law. The agreement—short-lived, as it turned out—was an effort to achieve peace and cooperation between the indigenous population and the *muhajirs* in Benazir's troubled home province.

Benazir's assumption of office brought great expectations from inside as well as outside Pakistan. In her first address to the nation, Benazir pledged to work for a progressive and democratic Pakistan—one guided by Islamic principles of brotherhood, equality, and tolerance. At the same time, she invoked the Quaid-i-Azam's vision for a Pakistan that would grow as a modern state. Benazir's rhetoric promised much to an expectant nation: strengthened relations with the United States, the Soviet Union, and China; protected minority rights; increased provincial autonomy; improvement of education; introduction of a comprehensive national health policy; enhanced rights for women, with equal pay for equal work; and so on. When faced with the hard realities of government, however, most of Benazir's rhetoric did not translate into action. Although she was successful in advancing the democratization process in Pakistani politics and was able to achieve warmer relations with the United States and, for a short while, with India as well, Benazir's first term in office is usually looked upon, by both foreign and domestic observers, as ineffectual—a period of governmental instability. Within months she had lost much of her political support.

The scion of the feudal elite of Sindh, the Harvard- and Oxford-educated Benazir was often described as autocratic during her first term. Although she spoke of healing wounds and putting an end to the past, she was inexorably tied to her father's political legacy, which included harsh repression of political opposition. Further, her appointment of her mother, Nusrat, as a senior minister without portfolio, followed by the selection of her father-in-law as chairman of the parliamentary Public Accounts Committee, was viewed in some quarters as ill-advised nepotism. Benazir's government also set up the controversial Placement Bureau, which made political appointments to the civil bureaucracy, although the bureau was later abolished. Benazir let the political legacy of her family intrude, for example, when able public servants, who had earlier harbored disagreements with her father, were dismissed for reasons other than job performance.

Benazir also had to contend with growing political opposition. As a political power broker, she was in the late 1980s no match for her main rival, then chief minister of Punjab, Nawaz Sharif. In the 1988 elections that brought Benazir to power, her party had won the largest number of seats in the National Assembly but controlled only one of the four provinces. Punjab, the most populous province, with over half of Pakistan's population, came under the control of the opposition IJI and of its leader, Nawaz Sharif, who was the only major political figure from the Zia era to survive the reemergence of the PPP. To maintain her power and implement her programs, Benazir would have needed to maneuver successfully between a powerful president and the military elite and to reach a political accommodation with Nawaz Sharif. Instead, she pursued a course of confrontation, including unsuccessful efforts to overthrow him in the provincial assembly. In addition, the failure of the PPP to share power and spoils with its coalition partners caused further alienation, including the withdrawal of the MQM from the government in October 1989.

The public's sense of disillusionment deepened as the government failed to deliver its promised employment and economic development programs. Inflation and unemployment were high, and the country's burgeoning population put increased pressure on already overburdened education and health systems. The government also failed to deal with the country's growing drug abuse problem, and there was opposition from religious conservatives who distrusted the degree of Benazir's commitment to the state's Islamic principles. Despite tensions, disagreements, and mutual misgivings, however, Benazir continued to be supported by the armed forces. The chief of the army staff, General Mirza Aslam Beg, publicly stated his intention to maintain a politically neutral army.

Benazir narrowly survived a no-confidence motion in the National Assembly. Her government did not compile a record of accomplishment that might have offset her other difficulties. Instead, she found herself constrained by the military and by the constitutional structure her government inherited. During her tenure, no significant legislation was passed. Fewer than a dozen bills—all minor amendments to existing legislation—passed the National Assembly. Benazir complained that legislation was stymied because the Senate was dominated by her opposition.

Benazir's problems were further accentuated in February 1990 when an MQM-directed strike in Karachi escalated into rioting that virtually paralyzed the city. The strike had been called to protest the alleged abduction of MQM supporters by the PPP. The resulting loss of life and property forced Benazir to call in the army to restore order. In addition to the violence in Sindh and elsewhere, she had to cope with increasing charges of corruption leveled not only at her associates, but at her husband, Asif Ali Zardari, and father-in-law. On the international front, Pakistan faced heightened tensions with India over Kashmir and problems associated with the unresolved Afghan war.

Finally, on August 6, 1990, President Ghulam Ishaq Khan dismissed Benazir's government, dissolved the National Assembly as well as the Sindh and North-West Frontier Province provincial assemblies, and appointed a caretaker government headed by Ghulam Mustafa Jatoi, the leader of the Combined Opposition Parties in the National Assembly. In accordance with the constitution, the president scheduled national and provincial elections for October 1990. Ishaq Khan said his actions were justified because of corruption, incompetence, and inaction; the release of convicted criminals under the guise of freeing political prisoners; a failure to maintain law and order in Sindh; and the use of official government machinery to promote partisan interests. A nationwide state of emergency was declared, citing both "external aggression and internal disturbance." Benazir called her dismissal "illegal, unconstitutional, and arbitrary" and implied that the military was responsible. She added that the PPP would not take to the streets to avoid giving Ghulam Ishaq Khan's regime any pretext for not holding scheduled elections. The military proclaimed that its only interest was in maintaining order.

The Caretaker Government of Ghulam Mustafa Jatoi

Ironically, Benazir's successor, the caretaker prime minister, was one of Pakistan's largest landowners, also from Benazir's Sindh Province. Jatoi had joined the PPP when Zulfiqar Ali Bhutto had founded it in the late 1960s, was in Bhutto's first cabinet, and was later chief minister of Sindh until Zia overthrew Bhutto in 1977. Jatoi had remained supportive of the PPP during the martial law period and had spearheaded the campaign organized by the MRD against Zia's government. Following Benazir's return to Pakistan in 1986, however, Jatoi was removed as chairman of the Sindh PPP and subsequently formed his own political organization, the National People's Party. Known as a moderate, Jatoi said that his party's objective was to make Pakistan a modern, democratic, and progressive Islamic welfare state.

Jatoi's caretaker government instituted accountability proceedings against persons charged with corruption and, under the authority of laws enacted by both the Zulfiqar Ali Bhutto and the Zia regimes, set up special courts to handle accountability cases. The accountability process had traditionally been used to disqualify from public office those found guilty of corruption and wrongdoing. It had also been used as a weapon by politicians in power against their opponents. The period for accountability defined by the Jatoi government was limited to the twenty months of Benazir's regime. The PPP demand that Nawaz Sharif's Punjab government during that same time be subjected to similar scrutiny was rejected. Nevertheless, the Jatoi government defended the proceedings as fair and neutral. Although several charges were brought against Benazir, and her appearance before the accountability tribunals was required, she remained free and was able to lead her party in the October 1990 elections.

The Central Election Commission, consisting of three members of the senior judiciary, supervised preparation of the electoral rolls and the conduct of the 1990 elections as well as processing complaints and issuing reports. Although Pakistan has a large number of political parties, the two main contenders in the elections were both broad-based coalitions. One contender was the PDA, established during the campaign by Benazir's dominant PPP, together with the Tehrik-i-Istiqlal, headed by Asghar Khan, and two smaller parties. Asghar Khan had been Pakistan's first commander in chief of the air force and later became chairman of Pakistan International Airlines, before entering the political arena in 1969 and founding his own party. In the 1970s, Asghar Khan was one of Zulfiqar Ali Bhutto's harshest critics. Having helped to oust Bhutto, however, he did not benefit from the Zia military government, and in 1989 he resigned as Tehrik-i-Istiqlal's chairman. Political observers were surprised when the party joined the PDA.

The other major contender in opposition to the PDA was the IJI, the coalition that had also competed with the PPP in the 1988 elections. The Pakistan Muslim League was a major component of the IJI, as was the JI. The three chief competitors for leadership in the IJI and specifically in the Pakistan Muslim League were Nawaz Sharif, former Prime Minister Mohammad Khan Junejo, and Ejaz ul-Haq, son of the late President Zia ul-Haq. These three men represented key groups in Pakistan's political culture. Junejo belonged to a major Sindhi landowning family and represented the feudal classes. Ejaz appealed particularly to Zia's Islamic fundamentalist supporters. His candidacy was weakened, however, by his relative lack of political experience. Nawaz Sharif, the ultimate victor, represented the country's growing business classes. The caretaker prime minister also aspired to remain in power, but his party was not a member of the IJI, and so he lacked sufficient political strength.

Other important parties included Altaf Hussain's MQM, representing the refugee community in urban Sindh, and Khan Abdul Wali Khan's Awami National Party, based in the North-West Frontier Province and northern Balochistan. Although in 1990 the PDA and the IJI were the major election contenders in Pakistan's largest provinces (Punjab, Sindh, and the North-West Frontier Province), they had only a limited presence in Balochistan, compared with regional and religious parties, such as the JUI and the Jamhoori Watan Party.

The central campaign issue in 1990 for the IJI was the Benazir government's alleged corruption and wrongdoing in office. The principal issue for the PDA was the alleged unconstitutionality of her dismissal from office and the subsequent treatment of her, and her family and associates, by the caretaker government. The campaign was heated and included incidents of violence, harassment, and political kidnappings. Media coverage played an active role. During the campaign, the government no longer held a monopoly on television news because a second network, People's Television Network (PTN), had been started, to compete with Pakistan Television Corporation (PTV). The new network introduced Cable News Network (CNN) in Pakistan. The PPP filed a complaint against PTV, charging biased network election coverage, but the complaint was rejected by the Lahore High Court. Print media coverage offered more variety. Although government-controlled newspapers tended to be anti-Benazir, the larger private sector of print media provided more diversity of opinion. Both the PDA and the IJI predicted victory, but at least one detailed public opinion poll gave the edge to the PDA.

The election results were disastrous for the PDA, as the IJI won 105 of the 207 contested seats in the National Assembly. The PDA won only forty-five seats. The IJI attributed its success to holding its coalition together as well as establishing electoral alliances nationwide to ensure that PDA candidates would not run unopposed. The PDA blamed the defeat on alleged rigging of the elections. Although the elections were certainly not free of irregularities, observation teams both from inside the country and from outside, including a team from member countries of the South Asian Association for Regional Cooperation (SAARC—see Glossary), concluded that the elections had been generally free and fair. Despite their problems, the 1990 elections were another step forward in the quest for political stability and democratic government. The constitutional transfer of power was achieved without direct military intervention.

The Government of Nawaz Sharif

When Nawaz Sharif became prime minister in November 1990, his political coalition, the IJI, had more than a two-thirds majority in the National Assembly. The IJI alliance, a grouping of parties whose chief components were the PML and the JI, had been formed in 1988 to oppose the PPP in the elections of that year. In the 1988 elections, the PPP emerged as the single largest group in the National Assembly, and its leader, Benazir, became prime minister. At the same time, however, Nawaz Sharif emerged as the most powerful politician outside the PPP. Just two years later, the IJI under Nawaz Sharif's leadership achieved victory at the polls, and Nawaz Sharif took over in a peaceful, constitutional transfer of power—the third prime minister since Zia's death in 1988—and ushered in a return to democracy. Nawaz Sharif's ascendancy also marked a transition in the political culture of Pakistan—a power shift from the traditional feudal aristocracy to a growing class of modern entrepreneurs. This transition mirrored the socioeconomic changes that had been at work in Pakistan, moving the country gradually from a feudal to an industrial society.

Nawaz Sharif, born in Lahore in 1949, belongs to a postindependence generation of politicians. Scion of a leading industrial family, he is a practicing Muslim, an ardent capitalist, and a political moderate. A graduate of the Government College Lahore, with a degree from Punjab University Law College, also in Lahore, he rose to prominence representing an urban constituency seeking its own political identity. His family, along with other major industrial families, had suffered from the nationalization of large industrial enterprises during Bhutto's regime (1971–77). Nawaz Sharif had worked to build a political constituency that would favor private industrial and commercial entrepreneurship. He served in Punjab, first as finance minister and then as chief minister, before coming to national office. As finance minister, he presented development-oriented budgets. As chief minister, he stressed welfare and development activities and the maintenance of law and order.

In his first address to the nation after taking office as prime minister, Nawaz Sharif announced his government's comprehensive national reconstruction plan and said that its implementation would ensure the successful march of Pakistan into the twenty-first century. He stressed that proper use of the country's natural resources would be made, the pace of industrialization expedited, and the best use of talented manpower identified. Under his development policy, investment would be encouraged, and restrictions on setting up new industries would be lifted.

Early assessments of Nawaz Sharif and his government noted his initiative, youthful energy, and already proven ability and popularity in his home province, the country's power base. The newspaper *Dawn* pointed out, however, that his Punjab connection was both an asset and a liability and that "to acquire a genuinely all-Pakistan stature, he will have to have ingenuity, and acumen, magnanimity and vision, and the strength to take bold decisions."

Nawaz Sharif's cabinet initially included eighteen ministers: nine from Punjab, two from the Islamabad Capital Territory, six from Sindh, and one from Balochistan. His cabinet was later expanded to include representation from the North-West Frontier Province. Of paramount importance to the new government was implementation of Nawaz Sharif's program for strengthening the economy. Goals of the program included self-reliance, deregulation and denationalization, tax reform, foreign-exchange and payment reform, administrative and law reform, and increases in agricultural productivity and exports. The government's economic strategy rested on streamlining the institutional framework for industrialization and on starting a new partnership with the private sector in order to promote common objectives. Nawaz Sharif regarded unemployment as Pakistan's major problem and believed it could be solved only by rapid industrialization. He said his government was considering special incentives for rural industrialization and agro-based industries and was fully committed to a policy of deregulation.

The IJI government was third in a line representing a dyarchical arrangement of shared power between Pakistan's civil-military and political forces. Nawaz Sharif and his predecessors, Junejo and Benazir, came to power under a constitutional framework in which, under the controversial Eighth Amendment introduced by Zia, the president was empowered to dissolve the parliament and dismiss the government. Both Junejo and Benazir had earlier been unceremoniously dismissed from office, and the constitutional framework limited Nawaz Sharif's ability to govern despite the support of a majority in the parliament. He, too, would be dismissed under the constitutional framework in 1993.

Pakistan's emerging two-party system was strengthened by the 1988 and 1990 elections and the constitutional transfer of power in 1990 from Benazir to Nawaz Sharif. In these elections, the two political alliances, the IJI and the PDA (headed by the

PPP), became the main contenders for power. Although both alliances agreed on Pakistan's need for a liberal democracy and a market economy, the PDA opposition represented a real political challenge to the government, and Benazir conducted a relentless campaign to oust Nawaz Sharif.

From the outset, the Nawaz Sharif government's record was mixed. On the one hand, it achieved passage in May 1991 of the Shariat Bill, which declared the Quran and the sunna (see Glossary) to be the law of the land. Islamic fundamentalists, on the other hand, did not think the bill went far enough. The more secular-minded Pakistanis feared that a theocracy was being established. A working group was set up to monitor and make recommendations for enforcing Islamic laws in the country. The working group adopted a nineteen-point plan that included calls for the implementation of all Islamic legislation, especially the laws creating sharia courts; transformation of the education system to reflect Islamic teaching; controls on the print and electronic media designed to ensure Islamic moral values; uniform and enforced prayer schedules; and the establishment of an Islamic banking system and the total abolition of interest.

Additionally, in November 1991, the Federal Shariat Court, Pakistan's supreme religious court, declared the provisions of some twenty federal and provincial laws repugnant to Islam. A particular problem was the ruling that payment of interest (*riba*) was prohibited by Islam even if the loan involved was for productive purposes. Although the government had publicly committed itself to Islamization, its major domestic policy initiative was the liberalization of the economy. If the ruling on *riba* were fully implemented, this new economic policy likely would fail. With no consensus in Pakistan regarding either the content or the pace of Islamic reform, Nawaz Sharif sought to strike an acceptable balance to enable his government to remain in power.

The government also had to contend with rampant crime and terrorism, which continued to be a cause for alarm in the country, particularly in Sindh. Kidnappings, bombings, and murders persisted despite concerted efforts by the police and the military to stem lawlessness. Pakistanis called this state of affairs the "Kalashnikov culture" because the flood of available automatic weapons gave long-standing ethnic and political rivalries a deadly new significance (see Prospects for Social Cohesion, ch. 2). The arms were largely a legacy from the war in neighboring Afghanistan. The police were increasingly outgunned, and even foreigners were not immune from attack. In the summer of 1991, the prime minister was forced to cancel an important trip to Japan in quest of investment in order to calm a population shaken by a particularly savage string of murders in Punjab. In an effort to stem the violence, the government decreed that Pakistanis turn in their weapons, but, predictably, few of them did. The government also passed the Twelfth Amendment to the constitution, which provided for the further jurisdictional authority of Speedy Trial Courts to dispense summary justice. The opposition, however, criticized the law as suppressing fundamental rights.

Nawaz Sharif held to his conviction that the solution to Pakistan's political problems was free-market reform and economic growth, so he liberalized foreign-exchange regulations and denationalized public-sector industrial enterprises and financial institutions. Furthermore, government approval was no longer required for the establishment of new industrial enterprises (with some exceptions, particularly in relation to arms and explosives). A number of important industries such as electricity generation, shipping, airlines, highway construction, and telecommunications were opened up to the private sector. Although there was support for liberalizing and privatizing the economy, there was considerable criticism of the process of implementation. Some critics feared that moving too fast could produce turmoil, with the resultant demand for renationalization. Other critics asked for protection for the more vulnerable groups in society who would not be able to compete in a free market. The government's ability to focus effectively on and deal with these problems was weakened by its involvement with the Pakistan Cooperative Societies and the Bank of Credit and Commerce International (BCCI) financial scandals (see Finance, ch. 3).

In keeping with his goals of consolidating economic growth and overcoming the country's regional divisions, Nawaz Sharif was convinced of the need for a modern national infrastructure, regardless of cost. As a result, he launched the construction of a US$1 billion highway project, which National Highway Authority chairman Hidayat Niazi described as a step toward building a nation (see Transportation, ch. 3).

Nawaz Sharif's government continued to be under pressure from within and without, and his ruling coalition, the IJI, was plagued by internal dissention. Tensions, disagreements, and political rivalries were present within the IJI's largest component, the Pakistan Muslim League. In May 1992, the fundamentalist JI, the second largest member of the coalition, formally left the IJI. Since its inception, the IJI had been an alliance of varied right-of-center and Islamic parties in a marriage of convenience to oppose the PPP. However, the PML and the JI had long been antagonists, and their disagreements mounted over a number of issues. The JI was unhappy with the IJI government's support of Saudi Arabia and the United States during the Persian Gulf War (1990–91), fearing that the defeat of Iraq would transform Shia (see Glossary) Iran into a major regional power. The JI also criticized the mainstream PML for what it perceived to be foot-dragging on Islamization, including the matter of *riba*, as well as its abandonment of support for the Afghan *mujahidin* in favor of efforts to establish a neutral, United Nations-sponsored government in Kabul. The JI also criticized the government's policy on Kashmir as not evidencing sufficient commitment to Islamic "freedom fighters" there.

The government's chief opposition, Benazir and the PPP, criticized Nawaz Sharif's efforts at privatization, calling them the "loot and plunder" of Pakistan and saying his plan favored large investors and ran roughshod over labor. Benazir was also critical of the government's Islamization policies and continued to allege that the 1990 elections, which brought Nawaz Sharif's government to power, were fraudulent. In late 1992, she tried to organize widespread protest marches against the government. In response, Nawaz Sharif banned Benazir from two of the country's largest cities and ordered police measures against her supporters.

Benazir ultimately did not muster enough demonstrators throughout the country to threaten the government. However, Nawaz Sharif's actions, in the eyes of some, made him appear too willing to espouse repressive measures rather than adhere to democratic principles. Subsequently, relations between Nawaz Sharif and Benazir appeared to soften somewhat. He reportedly ceased calling her an "enemy of Pakistan," and Benazir abandoned her demonstrations designed to topple Nawaz Sharif's government through street power.

The ruling coalition appeared to weaken by early 1993. The four major powers in Pakistan continued to be the president, the military, Nawaz Sharif's IJI government, and the PPP opposition led by Benazir. Reports of a growing rift between Nawaz Sharif and Ishaq Khan became more commonplace. The military—which never had an overt constitutional role in the government but which had historically been a key player in the formation and dismissal of governments—was closely and nervously monitored by observers.

President Ghulam Ishaq Khan as Power Broker

A powerful player in the political equation was President Ishaq Khan. The president, under the constitution, is elected by a majority of the members of the national and provincial assemblies. Ishaq Khan was a seasoned senior bureaucrat-turned politician who had been a key figure in Pakistan for more than three decades. Born in 1915 in the North-West Frontier Province, he was appointed to the prestigious Civil Service of Pakistan after independence in 1947. After holding various regional posts, including being chairman of the West Pakistan Water and Power Development Authority (1961–66), he was appointed to several positions in the central government—first as secretary, Ministry of Finance (1966–70) and later as governor of the State Bank of Pakistan (1971–75). In the latter position, he questioned the wisdom of a number of the economic policies of then Prime Minister Zulfiqar Ali Bhutto. He was subsequently moved from the bank and made secretary general at the Ministry of Defence. Although an unusual post for a senior economics expert, it proved to be fortuitous in that it brought him into close contact with the senior officers of the armed forces. Among them was General Zia, who later ousted Bhutto and turned the management of the economy over to Ishaq Khan. During the martial law period (1977–85), Ishaq Khan's titles changed, but he was responsible for all important economic decisions (see Zia ul-Haq and Military Domination, 1977–88, ch. 1). Among other things, he supported the Zia government's efforts to Islamize the economy through changes in the fiscal and banking systems.

In 1985 Ishaq Khan was elected to the Senate and later became chairman of the Senate. The death of Zia in 1988 thrust Ishaq Khan to the center of the political stage. When the military decided to use the constitution to handle the issue of succession, Ishaq Khan, as chairman of the Senate and therefore next in the line of succession, became acting president. He and the emergency council he instituted decided to hold general elections and to allow political parties to participate. Thus, the country was guided back to democracy, Benazir became prime minister, and Ishaq Khan was subsequently elected president by the national and provincial assemblies.

Ishaq Khan's position was considerably strengthened by the Eighth Amendment to the constitution, introduced by President Zia, which allows the president to dismiss the government and to override the government's choice of army chief. When the previous army chief died unexpectedly, President Ishaq Khan reportedly turned down the government's choice and named General Abdul Waheed to head the army. General Waheed, who is not known to have any political ambitions, is from the same ethnic group as Ishaq Khan—the Pakhtuns of the North-West Frontier Province (see Linguistic and Ethnic Groups, ch. 2).

Intermittent and conflicting signals of rapprochement, realignment, and behind-the-scenes alliances among the various political players heightened the political tension in late 1992 and early 1993. There was speculation that the opposition and the government might join forces to muster a two-thirds majority in the parliament to repeal the Eighth Amendment or even that they might field a candidate against the president. However, it was also noticeable that Benazir had stopped openly attacking the president, and some observers considered that she might be playing for time, hoping to use the differences between the president and the prime minister to her own advantage. The army, however, always a key ingredient in the mix, continued to support the president as well as the continuation of the Eighth Amendment. Against this backdrop, Pakistan's developing democracy continued to be tested by economic problems, persistent violence, and corruption, as well as the power struggles of its leaders.

The "Silent Revolution": A Year of Political Struggle

In 1993 a protracted power struggle between Prime Minister Nawaz Sharif and President Ishaq Khan played out as Pakistan's two leading politicians maneuvered each other out of power. This period of behind-the-scenes struggle was described by a Pakistani daily as a "Silent Revolution" and was watched with some concern by the international community, which feared that Pakistan could once again fall under military rule.

On April 18, 1993, the power struggle seemed to be resolved when President Ishaq Khan, exercising the extraordinary constitutional powers afforded the president by the Eighth Amendment, dismissed the government of Prime Minister Nawaz

Sharif. Once again Ishaq Khan had invoked the Eighth Amendment to bring down an elected government. The charges of corruption and mismanagement of the economy that he leveled against Nawaz Sharif were almost identical to those he had earlier brought against Benazir in 1990. President Ishaq Khan appointed Balakh Sher Mazari as caretaker prime minister and announced a new timetable for elections.

On May 26, 1993, the Supreme Court voted that Ishaq Khan's dissolution of the National Assembly and his dismissal of the prime minister were unconstitutional. The Supreme Court's action was a sharp rebuke of Ishaq Khan's heavy-handed exercise of presidential powers and was widely hailed as a victory for the advocates of democratization. Yet, although the Supreme Court was able to reinstate the Nawaz Sharif government, the status quo ante was not restored, and the struggle between the president and the prime minister continued unabated, making the pursuit of regular government workings impossible. Noting the mounting impatience of the Pakistani military with the endless machinations of the country's politicians, the United States and the European Community communicated their concern, warning against a military takeover.

The continuing political crisis in Pakistan came to an abrupt halt when the prime minister and president both resigned after two weeks of intense negotiations among the Nawaz Sharif government, Benazir, and the army. The resolution of the crisis was unique because for the first time in the nation's history a government had voluntarily stepped down in order to avoid a possible military intervention. Interestingly, the negotiations had been mediated by General Waheed, the chief of the army staff. The resultant agreement and its implementation followed strict constitutional procedure. Ishaq Khan was replaced by the chairman of the Senate, Wasim Sajjad, who functioned as acting president until the elections. More important, Moeen Qureshi, a former civil servant and senior World Bank (see Glossary) official, agreed to serve as caretaker prime minister. Qureshi, a Pakistani national, had left the World Bank in 1992, obtained permanent residence status in the United States, and established his own company, Emerging Markets Corporation.

The Caretaker Government of Moeen Qureshi

During his three-month tenure as caretaker prime minister, Moeen Qureshi initiated a substantial number of strong reform measures. He devalued the currency and cut farm subsidies, while raising the prices of wheat, electricity, and gasoline—strategies to reduce Pakistan's huge budget deficit—7.5 percent of the gross national product (GNP—see Glossary). Qureshi also cut public-sector expenditures by instituting austerity measures, including closing down ten embassies and abolishing fifteen ministries. Qureshi's most daring innovation, however, was a temporary levy on agricultural output—a measure resisted by powerful landed interests (see Farm Ownership and Land Reform, ch. 3).

Qureshi next proceeded to single out those politicians who had outstanding loans obtained from state banks and institutions—loans received under easy terms in return for past political favors—a total estimated at US$2 billion. In a move calculated to shame these individuals, Qureshi added their names to a published list of 5,000 individuals who had not fulfilled their loan obligations. Approximately 15 percent of the individuals on the list had planned to run for office in the coming elections. These candidates included Benazir, Benazir's husband, and Nawaz Sharif's brother. Most candidates quickly repaid their loans; those who did not were barred from contesting the October 1993 elections. Drug-trafficking barons, a small but powerful group including some members of the parliament, were permanently barred from running in the elections. Anticipating a further crackdown, several of the drug barons fled the country.

In his three months in power, Qureshi exhibited an admirable degree of technocratic efficiency tempered by dogged determination. Yet it remained to be seen whether his achievements would be accepted without reversal by the subsequent administration. Indeed, some argue that the Qureshi caretaker government, because of its temporary nature, was not much constrained by the realpolitik of Pakistani society that the succeeding government would have to face. The Qureshi government had, nonetheless, set a standard—one with which past governments and the succeeding government of Benazir would no doubt be compared.

Benazir Bhutto Returns

In the National Assembly elections of October 6–7, 1993, Benazir's PPP won a plurality—eighty-six seats—but not the absolute majority needed to immediately form a government in the 217-seat National Assembly. Nawaz Sharif's Pakistan Muslim League ran a close second in gaining seventy-two seats.

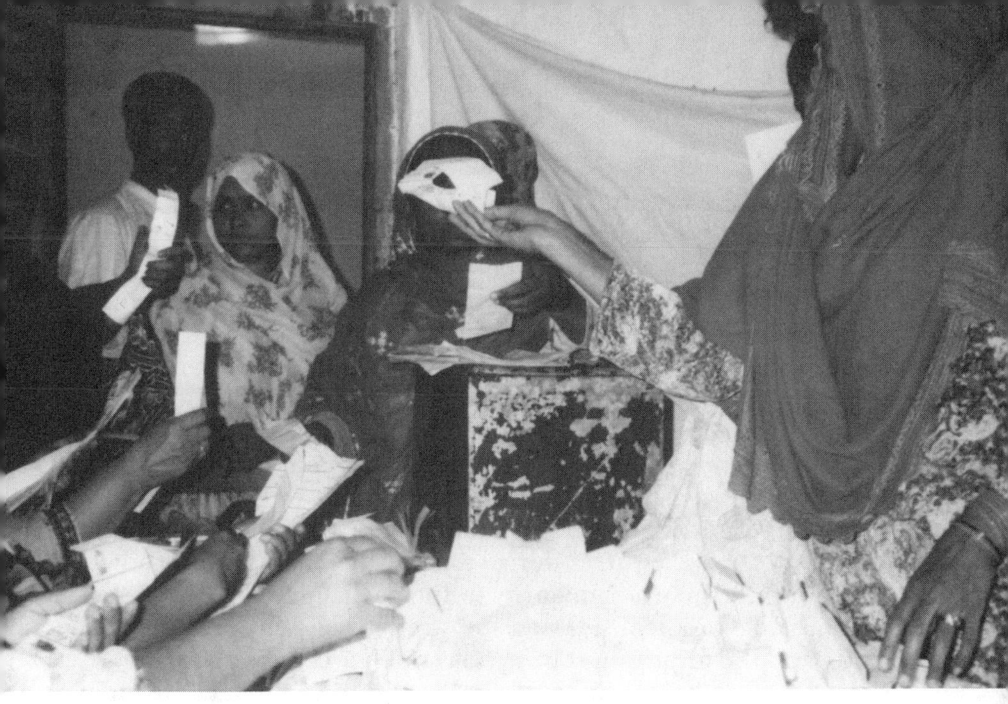

Women voters at poll in Pishin, Balochistan, during national elections of October 1993
Courtesy Anita M. Weiss

Over the next two weeks, Benazir was successful in mustering the allegiance of a number of small regional parties and independent members of the assembly and on October 19, 1993, was able to reclaim power with 121 seats in her coalition government. The October elections were hailed as the fairest in Pakistan's history and were, according to international observers, held "without hindrance or intimidation." Voter turnout, however, was lower than usual, as only about 40 percent of registered voters participated.

Benazir benefitted in the 1993 national elections from the MQM's boycott. In the 1990 national elections, the MQM, which had captured fifteen seats, supported Nawaz Sharif's IJI coalition. Benazir also benefitted by the poor showing of the religious parties.

After only one month in office, Benazir was able to strengthen her position considerably. On November 13, 1993, Benazir's candidate for president, Farooq Leghari, an Oxford-educated PPP stalwart, easily defeated acting President Wassim Sajjad, who was backed by Nawaz Sharif. In a vote by the two parliamentary chambers—the National Assembly and the Senate—and the four provincial assemblies, Leghari won 273 votes to Sajjad's 167. Bhutto hailed Leghari's election as a triumph for democracy and predicted that he would contribute to the country's stability.

Although the new president retained the constitutional authority vested in the Eighth Amendment to dismiss the popularly elected National Assembly as well as the prime minister, he appeared willing to support Benazir in curbing the power of his office. Leghari promised not only to support a constitutional amendment to annul the extraordinary presidential powers granted by the Eighth Amendment but also to challenge restrictive laws that related to Islamic religious courts and to women's rights. In order to amend the constitution, however, a three-quarters majority in the parliament is needed—a formidable task, considering the strength of Benazir's opposition and the unproven staying power of her coalition. Leghari's victory, nonetheless, was expected to end the pattern of disruptive power struggles between prime minister and president that had so undermined previous governments.

Early in her term, Benazir declared that she would end Pakistan's isolation and, in particular, that she would strive to improve her country's troubled relations with the United States. At the same time, however, she vowed to maintain Pakistan's nuclear program and not allow the "national interest to be sacrificed." Relations between the United States and Pakistan had deteriorated sharply during 1992 when the former threatened to classify the latter as a terrorist state because of its aid to militants fighting in Indian-controlled Kashmir. Although the United States withdrew its threat in mid-July 1993, the Kashmir issue still loomed large and threatened to complicate Pakistan's relations with both India and the United States (see the United States and the West, this ch.).

Benazir faced another, personal challenge. As her administration settled into office, a bitter Bhutto family feud played out on the front pages of the Pakistani press. The feud pitted Benazir against her younger brother Murtaza and her mother, Nusrat, over dynastic control of the PPP. Nusrat organized Murtaza's election campaign for the Sindh provincial assembly, in which her son contested (in absentia) more than twenty constituencies as an anti-Benazir candidate. Although he could only occupy one seat in the assembly, Murtaza contested multiple seats because if he had won more than one, his political stature would have risen. The electorate gave Murtaza only one victory, however, and as he returned to Pakistan from years in

Prime Minister Benazir Bhutto
Courtesy Embassy of Pakistan, Washington

exile in Damascus, he was jailed by the government on long-standing terrorist charges. In retaliation for her mother's championing of Murtaza's political ambitions over her own, Benazir ousted Nusrat from her position as cochairperson of the PPP, further deepening the family rift. These family squabbles were a distraction for the new government, but Benazir was expected to make progress on a wide variety of social, educational, and cultural issues.

The Media

The press, television, and radio are vital forces in Pakistan's political life. The importance of the press was evident even before independence. In prepartition India, Muslim journalism flourished until the Sepoy Rebellion of 1857–58, when many Muslim newspapers were shut down (see The Seeds of Muslim Nationalism, ch. 1). Between 1857 and the Government of India Act of 1935, which gave a large measure of self-government to Indians, none of the major newspapers were owned or edited by Muslims. However, when Indian Muslims began to organize and rally to the political platform of the All-India Muslim League, concerted efforts were made to develop a strong press to support the Muslim national cause. A number of Muslim-owned newspapers were established, including *Azad,* a Bengali-language daily founded in Calcutta in 1936. Two English-language newspapers, *Morning News* in Calcutta and *Dawn* in Delhi, began publishing in 1942. In the late 1930s, the first Indian Muslim news agency, the Orient Press of India, was founded.

On the eve of independence, however, only four major Muslim-owned newspapers existed in the area constituting the new state of Pakistan: *Pakistan Times, Zamindar, Nawa-i-Waqt,* and *Civil and Military Gazette,* all located in Lahore. A number of Muslim newspapers moved to Pakistan. *Dawn* began publication as a daily in Karachi, then the federal capital, on the day of independence in 1947. Other publications were also shifted to Pakistan including the *Morning News* and the Urdu-language dailies, *Jang* and *Anjam.*

In the early 1990s, there were over 1,500 newspapers and journals in the country, including publications in Urdu, English, and in regional languages. The major national daily newspapers in Urdu are *Jang, Nawa-i-Waqt, Jasarat, Masawat, Mashriq,* and *Hurriyat.* The major national dailies in English are *Dawn, Pakistan Times, Muslim, Morning News, Nation, Frontier Post,* and *News. Herald* is an important English-language magazine.

Newspapers and periodicals are owned by either private individuals, joint-stock companies, or trusts. The National Press Trust, a nonprofit organization that is a major newspaper publisher, was established by businessmen in 1964 and taken over by the government in 1972. There are several other large newspaper and journal publishers. The two major news agencies in Pakistan are the Associated Press of Pakistan and Pakistan Press International. The Associated Press of Pakistan was taken over by the government in 1960. Pakistan Press International is a private joint-stock company.

Radio also has been an effective method of communication because the literacy rate is low and other methods of communication are sometimes not available. The Pakistan Broadcasting Corporation has played a key role in disseminating information and transmitting government policies as well as promoting Islamic principles and their application. Another state-run organization, Azad Kashmir Radio, broadcasts in Azad Kashmir. Television, although newer, has also been effective, with coverage in the mid-1990s reaching more than 80 percent of the population. Until August 1990, the only television channel was the government-owned Pakistan Television Corporation

(PTV). At that time, however, another television channel, People's Television Network was established (see Telecommunications, ch. 3). People's Television Network brought Cable News Network (CNN) to Pakistan.

The media played an active role in all three national elections from the late 1980s to the mid-1990s. Although the government-owned radio and PTV presented a progovernment line, the establishment of People's Television Network ended the government monopoly of television news. In the case of the print media, government-controlled newspapers tended to express the government's viewpoint, but the large private sector of print journalism furnished a much greater variety of opinion.

The imposition of regulations based on the sharia was also reflected in the media. For example, the government required all women to wear *dupattas,* or scarves, over their heads on newscasts and other PTV programs. Such restrictions, for instance, prevented the women's swimming events of the 1992 Barcelona Olympic Games from being telecast in Pakistan because the swimsuits were regarded as immodest. Radio censors also ordered a number of controversial songs dropped from broadcasting.

Foreign Policy

Pakistan's foreign policy has been marked by a complex balancing process—the result of its history, religious heritage, and geographic position. The primary objective of that policy has been to preserve Pakistan's territorial integrity and security, which have been in jeopardy since the state's inception.

A new era began with the partition of British India in 1947 and the formation of two independent, sovereign states—India and Pakistan. Both nations searched for their place in the world order and aspired to leadership roles beyond the subcontinent.

India and Pakistan became adversaries at independence and have so remained. The two countries fought each other shortly after partition, in 1965, and in 1971, causing the dismemberment of Pakistan and the creation of still another new sovereign entity—Bangladesh. India-Pakistan rivalry intensified rather than diminished after the Cold War, and the Kashmir territorial dispute remains dangerous and recurrent.

Pakistan sought security through outside alliances. The new nation painstakingly worked on building a relationship with the United States, in which the obligations of both sides were clearly defined. The Western-oriented, anticommunist treaties and alliances Pakistan joined became an important part of its foreign policy. Pakistan also saw itself as a vanguard of independent Muslim states.

India

A major focus in Pakistan's foreign policy is the continuing quest for security against India, its larger, more powerful, and generally hostile neighbor. Pakistan was created despite the opposition of the most powerful political party in prepartition India, the Hindu-dominated Indian National Congress, and the suspicion remains among Pakistanis that India has never reconciled itself to the existence of an independent Pakistan. Several events further soured the relationship. One of these was the massive transfer of population between the two countries at partition, with its attendant bloodshed as Muslims left India and Hindus and Sikhs left Pakistan. There was also bitterness over the distribution of financial assets left by the British, with India initially blocking payments to Pakistan from the joint sterling account. An even more complex issue was the sovereignty of Kashmir, a concern arising from the accession of the princely states to India or Pakistan at partition. Although almost all of these states made the choice quickly, based on geographic location and the religious majority of their population, several delayed. One of these was Hyderabad, with a predominantly Hindu population and a Muslim ruler who did not want to accede to India. Hyderabad was a landlocked state in the south of India, and Indian military intervention was used to incorporate it into India.

The princely state of Jammu and Kashmir (usually referred to as Kashmir), however, had a Hindu ruler and boundaries with both Pakistan and India. Although Muslims constituted a majority of the state's population, the Hindu-Sikh community made up the majority in the province of Jammu, and Buddhists predominated around Ladakh. After a popular uprising against the Hindu ruler in late 1947, supported by Pakistani tribesmen and some military units, the ruler panicked and acceded to India. The subsequent Indo-Pakistani War of 1947–48 over control of Kashmir concluded with a cease-fire brokered by the United Nations (UN), which took effect on January 1, 1949. Kashmir was divided by a UN line between the areas held by the two countries, and a 1949 UN Security Council resolution provided for a plebiscite to be held under UN auspices to decide the issue of accession. India has refused to hold the plebiscite, and the dispute has continued. In 1965 war broke out again between the two countries over Kashmir, ending in another cease-fire in September. The Tashkent Declaration, signed on January 10, 1966, under the auspices of the Soviet Union, provided for restoration of the India-Pakistan international boundary and the Kashmir cease-fire line but did not result in a permanent solution to the problem.

Relations between the two countries reached a new low in 1971, when India intervened militarily in support of secessionist forces in East Pakistan, thus playing an instrumental role in the creation of independent Bangladesh. Although the Indo-Pakistani War of 1971 was fought over East Pakistan, heavy fighting also occurred along the Kashmir cease-fire line. Consequently, under the Simla Agreement of 1972 following the end of that war, the cease-fire line in Kashmir was redefined (it is now usually referred to as the Line of Control), and India and Pakistan agreed not to use force in Kashmir. The agreement also improved relations sufficiently for India to release some 90,000 prisoners of war taken when Pakistan's army had surrendered in East Pakistan (see Yahya Khan and Bangladesh, ch. 1).

The circumstances surrounding the conflict over Kashmir have changed considerably over the years, as have the levels of UN involvement in the dispute. The military balance between India and Pakistan after the latter's defeat in the 1971 war heavily favored India. Another changed circumstance is that beginning in 1989, India has had to face a virtual "Kashmiri intifada" in its repressive efforts to keep a sullen and predominantly Muslim Kashmiri populace under control. This insurrection, India claims, is supported by the "hidden hand" of Pakistan. Furthermore, the situation became even more complex with a growing movement among certain factions of Kashmiri militants for an independent Kashmiri state, precluding accession to either India or Pakistan. The volatile and potentially explosive situation in Kashmir continued to be monitored in 1994 by a team of UN observers, who operate under significant constraints. The Kashmir dispute remains the major deterrent to improved relations between the two countries.

Pakistan's suspicions of Indian intentions were further aroused by India's entry into the nuclear arena. India's explosion of a nuclear device in 1974 persuaded Pakistan to initiate its own nuclear program. The issue has subsequently influenced the direction of Pakistan's relations with the United States and China. United States-Pakistan relations over the nuclear issue are particularly prickly. Pakistan's relations with China on this issue, however, have been influenced by both countries' suspicions of India. In 1991 China called on India to accept Pakistan's proposal of a nuclear-free weapons zone in South Asia. In the same year, Pakistan and China signed a nuclear cooperation treaty reportedly intended for peaceful purposes. This agreement included provision by China of a nuclear power plant to Pakistan.

An added source of tension in Indo-Pakistani relations concerned the Soviet Union's invasion of Afghanistan in December 1979 (see Other South Asian Countries, this ch.). India refused to condemn the Soviet action, while Pakistan provided sanctuary for Afghan refugees and was a conduit for supplying arms from the United States and others to the Afghan *mujahidin.* During the Soviet Union's military intervention in Afghanistan, therefore, Pakistan felt an increased threat on both its eastern and northwestern borders. The rise of militant Hinduism in India, and the accompanying violence against Muslims there, is a further source of uneasiness between the two countries.

Other South Asian Countries

Pakistan seeks to expand its relations with other South Asian states, particularly Bangladesh. After an initial period of understandable coolness following the civil war that created Bangladesh in 1971, relations between the two countries have improved considerably. Although Pakistan initially refused to recognize Bangladesh, formal relations between the two countries were established in 1976. Trade revived between Pakistan and its former East Wing, and air links were reestablished. The presidents of the two countries have exchanged visits. Both countries often agree on international issues, sometimes in opposition to India's views. Pakistan also joined the South Asian Association for Regional Cooperation (SAARC), which was founded through the efforts of Bangladesh's President Ziaur Rahman. SAARC generally avoids political issues, instead addressing social, economic, technological, and environmental matters. However, SAARC's annual summit meetings provide an opportunity for private discussions among the heads of government.

Pakistan's relations with Afghanistan, its Muslim neighbor to the northwest, have never been easy. When Pakistan was admitted to the UN, only Afghanistan cast a negative vote, the result of Afghanistan's refusal to accept the Durand Line as its border with Pakistan. This border, established in 1893, divides the Pakhtu or Pashto-speaking people of the region. Afghanistan promoted secessionist movements among the Pakhtuns in Pakistan, calling for the creation of an independent Pakhtunistan or, alternatively, for Pakistan's North-West Frontier Province to join Afghanistan.

The Soviet invasion of Afghanistan, however, had a profound effect on Pakistan's geopolitical situation. Pakistan became a frontline state in the Cold War. Altogether more than 3 million Afghan refugees fled to Pakistan, and the country became a base for *mujahidin* fighting against the Soviet forces and the Afghan communists. Pakistan also became a conduit for military assistance by the United States and others to the *mujahidin.*

After the Soviet Union completed its troop withdrawal from Afghanistan in February 1989, warfare continued between the *mujahidin* and the Afghan communist government in Kabul. The demise of the Soviet Union and the end of the Cold War, however, resulted in a reassessment of Pakistan's foreign policy, particularly in light of the sweeping restructuring of central and southwest Asia. The Afghan resistance had been unable to unseat the Kabul regime. The heavy burden of the Afghan refugees continued, and Pakistan wanted to be in a position to establish linkages with the newly emerging Central Asian republics of the former Soviet Union. Pakistan decided in early 1992 to press for a political settlement. The communist government in Kabul was ousted in May 1992 and replaced by a fragile coalition of various *mujahidin* factions. But the coalition did not include the most radical of the Islamist *mujahidin* leaders, Gulbaddin Hikmatyar.

In March 1993, the government of Nawaz Sharif brokered an agreement between President Burhanuddin Rabbani of Afghanistan and Hikmatyar, Rabbani's longtime enemy, to share power in Afghanistan for eighteen months and then hold elections. Under the agreement, Rabbani would remain president, Hikmatyar would become prime minister, and they would choose government ministers together. A cease-fire was also to be implemented. It remains, however, for the agreement to be ratified by the leaders of all Muslim groups involved in the war.

In 1994 fighting between *mujahidin* groups escalated in Kabul, and a flood of refugees moved toward the Pakistani border.

The Former Soviet Union

In November 1992, Pakistan, Iran, Turkey, Afghanistan, and the five former Soviet republics of Kazakhstan, Azerbaijan, Kyrgyzstan, Turkmenistan, and Uzbekistan created an extended Muslim economic block linking Asia and Europe. As a result, the expanded Economic Co-operation Organization (ECO), in terms of geographic territory covered, became the largest economic bloc after the European Community. Then Prime Minister Nawaz Sharif noted in a speech marking the occasion that the ECO "now corresponds to the boundaries of the ancient area, which brought prosperity and civilization . . . through fruitful exchanges along the historic silk route. The people of these lands have a shared history and common spiritual and cultural values." Nawaz Sharif added his belief that extensive investment in infrastructure and encouragement of the private sector were the most important immediate objectives. He noted that Pakistan was building a major highway network to link Central Asia to the Arabian Sea and that its railroads were "poised to link not only member states but also [the] ECO with Europe, Russia, and South Asia." He added that "peace in Afghanistan is essential for political harmony and fruitful cooperation in our entire region."

China

Pakistan's desire for maximum balance and diversification in its external relations has also led to close relations with China—a valuable geopolitical connection. In 1950 Pakistan recognized the People's Republic of China, the third noncommunist state and the first Muslim country to do so. The deterioration in Sino-Indian relations that culminated in the 1962 border war provided new opportunities for Pakistan's relations with China. The two countries reached agreement on the border between them, and a road was built linking China's Xinjiang-Uygur Autonomous Region with the Northern Areas of Pakistan. China supported Pakistan diplomatically in both its 1965 and 1971 wars with India and provided Pakistan with economic and military assistance. Pakistan's China connection enabled it to facilitate the 1971 visit of United States secretary of state Henry Kissinger to that country, and in the 1980s China and the United States supplied military and economic assistance through Pakistan to the Afghan *mujahidin* fighting the Soviet occupation forces. Pakistan's ties with China remain strong, and friendly relations between the two countries continue to be an important factor in Pakistan's foreign policy.

Middle East

Pakistan also maintains close relations with the Islamic countries of the Middle East. These ties are important for religious, strategic, political, and economic reasons. In 1955 Pakistan, together with Iran, Iraq, and Turkey, joined the Baghdad Pact, a security arrangement later called the Central Treaty Organization (CENTO) after Iraq's withdrawal. CENTO was buttressed in 1964 by a regional arrangement among Pakistan, Iran, and Turkey called the Regional Cooperation for Development (RCD), and economic cooperation activities overshadowed the security aspects of the countries' relations. CENTO was disbanded in 1979 with the overthrow of Shah Muhammad Reza Pahlavi's government in Iran, and the RCD was dissolved. The RCD was effectively revived in 1985 as the ECO.

Pakistan's foreign policy fostered stronger ties with the Middle East through expanded trade. In addition, Pakistani workers employed in the Persian Gulf states, Libya, and Iran provided remittances to Pakistan that were a major source of foreign-exchange earnings. The loss of remittances caused by the 1991 Persian Gulf War was a serious concern to Pakistan. During the war, Pakistani units were sent to Saudi Arabia as components of the multinational forces. Pakistan has also contributed to the defense systems of several Arab states, supplying both officers and enlisted personnel. Pakistan has strengthened its Islamic ties by playing a leading role in the Organization of the Islamic Conference (OIC) and has also supported the Palestinian cause by withholding recognition of Israel.

Pakistan's ties with Saudi Arabia and the Persian Gulf states were strained during the 1990–91 crisis in the gulf. Although a member of the United States-led international coalition, Pakistan played only a limited role, sending a force of 11,000 troops tasked with "protecting" religious sites in Saudi Arabia. Nevertheless, during the war a vocal segment of public opinion in Pakistan supported ousting the Kuwaiti monarch and approved of Saddam Husayn's defiance of the United States-led coalition. The then chief of the army staff, General Mirza Aslam Beg, openly expressed support for Iraq, resulting in further embarrassment for Pakistan's government. Following the Persian Gulf

War, Pakistan undertook diplomatic efforts to recover its position in the region. In addition, many Pakistani expatriate workers returned to their jobs, and cooperative defense training activities continued. As a result, Pakistan largely restored its position as an influential player in the region.

The United States and the West

Although Pakistan's foreign policy has been dominated by problems with India as well as by efforts to maximize its own external support, its relationship with the West, particularly Britain and the United States, is of major importance. At independence in 1947, Pakistan became a member of the British Commonwealth of Nations. After independence Pakistan retained Britons in high administrative and military positions. Britain also was the primary source of military supplies and officer training. Many of Pakistan's key policy makers, including the nation's founding father, Mohammad Ali Jinnah, had studied in Britain and had great faith in the British sense of justice. Over the years, however, there was disillusionment at what Pakistanis perceived as Britain's indifference toward Pakistan and its failure to treat Pakistan fairly in dealings where India was involved. Nevertheless, Pakistan remained in the Commonwealth even after the country became a republic under the constitution of 1956. Pakistan withdrew its membership in the Commonwealth in 1972 to protest the recognition of Bangladesh by Britain, Australia, and New Zealand, but rejoined in October 1989 under Benazir's first government.

Pakistan's relations with the United States developed against the backdrop of the Cold War. Pakistan's geostrategic position made it a valuable partner in Western alliance systems to contain the spread of communism. In 1954 Pakistan signed a Mutual Defense Assistance Agreement with the United States and subsequently became a member of the Southeast Asia Treaty Organization (SEATO) and CENTO. These agreements placed Pakistan in the United States sphere of influence. Pakistan was also used as a base for United States military reconnaissance flights over Soviet territory. During the Cold War years, Pakistan was considered one of Washington's closest allies in Asia.

Pakistan, in return, received large amounts of economic and military assistance. The program of military assistance continued until the 1965 Indo-Pakistani War when President Lyndon B. Johnson placed an embargo on arms shipments to Pakistan and India. The United States embargo on arms shipments to Pakistan remained in place during the Indo-Pakistani War of 1971 and was not lifted until 1975, during the administration of President Gerald R. Ford.

United States-Pakistani relations preceding the 1971 war were characterized by poor communications and much confusion. The administration of President Richard M. Nixon was forced to formulate a public stance on the brutal crackdown on East Pakistanis by West Pakistani troops that began in March 25, 1971, and it maintained that the crackdown was essentially an internal affair of Pakistan in which direct intervention of outside powers was to be avoided. The Nixon administration expressed its concern about human rights violations to Pakistan and restricted the flow of assistance—yet it stopped short of an open condemnation.

Despite the widely publicized United States "tilt" toward Pakistan during the 1971 war, Pakistan's new leader, Zulfiqar Ali Bhutto, felt betrayed. In his opinion, the United States could have prevented India from intervening in Pakistan's civil war, thereby saving his country the trauma of defeat and dismemberment. Bhutto strove to lessen Pakistan's dependence on the United States.

The foreign policy Bhutto envisioned would place Pakistan at the forefront of Islamic nations. Issues central to the developing world would take precedence in foreign affairs over those of the superpowers. Bhutto called this policy "bilateralism," which implied neutrality in the Cold War with equal treatment accorded both superpowers. Bhutto's distancing of Islamabad from Washington and other Western links was accompanied by Pakistan's renewed bid for leadership in the developing world.

Following the loss of the East Wing, Pakistan withdrew from SEATO. Pakistan's military links with the West continued to decline throughout Bhutto's tenure in power and into the first years of the Zia regime. When CENTO was disbanded in March 1979, Pakistan joined the Nonaligned Movement. Zia also continued Bhutto's policy of developing Pakistan's nuclear capability. This policy had originated as a defensive measure in reaction to India's explosion of a nuclear device in 1974. In April 1979, President Jimmy Carter cut off economic assistance to Pakistan, except for food assistance, as required under the Symington Amendment to the Foreign Assistance Act of 1961. This amendment called for ceasing economic assistance to nonnuclear weapon countries that imported uranium-enrichment technology. Relations between the United States and Pakistan were further strained in November 1979 when protesters sacked the United States embassy in Islamabad, resulting in the death of four persons. The violence had been sparked by a false report that the United States was involved in a fire at the Grand Mosque in Mecca.

The Soviet invasion of Afghanistan in December 1979 revived the close relationship between Pakistan and the United States. Initially, however, the Carter administration's offer the following month of US$400 million in economic and military aid to Pakistan was spurned by Zia, who termed it "peanuts." Under President Ronald Reagan, the United States agreed in 1981 to provide US$3.2 billion to Pakistan over a period of six years, equally divided between economic and military assistance. However, although the Symington Amendment was waived, the amount was subject to the annual appropriation process. A second economic and military assistance program was announced in 1986, this time for over US$4.0 billion, with 57 percent for economic assistance. The continuation of the war in Afghanistan led to waivers—in the case of Pakistan—of legislative restrictions on providing aid to countries with nuclear programs. The Pressler Amendment of 1985 required that if the United States president could not certify to Congress on an annual basis that Pakistan did not possess a nuclear weapon, United States assistance to that country would be cut off. For several years, the United States president, with Pakistan's assurances that its nuclear program was for peaceful uses, was able to make this certification. However, with the Soviet withdrawal from Afghanistan in 1989 and the end of the Cold War, the United States took a harder position on the nuclear weapons issue. In 1990 President George Bush refused to make the certification required under the Pressler Amendment, and assistance to Pakistan was subsequently terminated.

After 1990 Pakistan's retention of the nuclear option became a defining issue in its relations with the United States. Pakistan, like India, considered the Nuclear Nonproliferation Treaty to be discriminatory—allowing the five acknowledged nuclear states to keep their weapons while banning others from joining the club. Pakistan declared that it would sign the treaty only in the unlikely event that India did so first. India refused to join any regional accord as long as China possessed nuclear weapons. Although the United States government continued to push both India and Pakistan for a regional solution to the threat of nuclear weapons proliferation, Pakistan complained that it bore the brunt of United States antiproliferation policies.

The long and close security relationship between the United States and Pakistan persisted in 1994, although the 1954 Mutual Defense Assistance Agreement on which the relationship was based was increasingly regarded by some in the United States government as outdated—and thus less pertinent to the post-Cold War period. Moreover, despite Pakistan's differences with the position of the United States on nuclear and other issues, both countries were determined to maintain friendly relations.

International Organizations

Pakistan joined the UN on September 30, 1947, and since then has been an active participant in the UN and its specialized agencies and other bodies, as well as in various specialized UN conferences. In 1993 Pakistan was elected to a two-year term on the UN Security Council. In addition, Pakistani nationals have contributed their skills within the UN itself. For example, in 1987 Nafis Sadik, a Pakistani woman physician, became executive director of the United Nations Population Fund (UNFPA) with the rank of undersecretary general. Pakistan has also been the recipient of assistance from UN development organizations, including the United Nations Development Programme (UNDP) and the Food and Agriculture Organization (FAO) in a variety of fields such as agriculture, water and sanitation, national planning, and human development. The UNDP, for example, allocated more than US$87 million for assistance to Pakistan for the 1992–96 program period.

Pakistan's view of the UN has necessarily been conditioned by its own needs and experience. Although recognizing the shortcomings and powerlessness of the UN in many situations, Pakistan has seen no alternative to the UN as a forum where weaker countries could appeal to the world's conscience against the actions of stronger powers. Consequently, Pakistan has called for solutions to international problems through UN auspices, most notably for resolution of the Kashmir issue. Pakistan also has played a highly visible role in UN peacekeeping efforts, contributing more than 7,000 troops to the United Nations Operation in Somalia (UNOSOM)—the largest single national contingent to any peacekeeping force in 1994. Pakistan had troops serving with the United Nations Protection Force in Bosnia and Herzegovina (UNPROFOR BH) and had participating observers in a number of other UN missions (see Foreign Security Relationships, ch. 5).

Pakistan's participation in other international organizations, including SAARC and the ECO, reflects its desire to be an influential player in the geographic region of which it is a part. In addition, Pakistan has played a leading role in the OIC, and President Zia was instrumental in revitalizing the OIC as a forum for periodic meetings of the heads of Islamic states. Pakistan thus appears firmly committed to the utility of broad-based international cooperation.

* * *

Political developments are examined in considerable detail in Lawrence Ziring's *Pakistan: The Enigma of Political Development.* For studies of Islam in Pakistan, Leonard Binder's *Religion and Politics in Pakistan* and Hafeez Malik's *Moslem Nationalism in India and Pakistan* are useful. For Pakistan's formative period, Richard Symonds's *The Making of Pakistan,* Khalid B. Sayeed's *Pakistan: The Formative Phase,* and Wayne Ayres Wilcox's *Pakistan: The Consolidation of a Nation* are excellent.

Pakistan's first ten years or so are expertly covered in Keith Callard's *Political Forces in Pakistan, 1947–1959* and G.W. Choudhury's *Constitutional Development in Pakistan.* The Pakistani bureaucracy is described by Ralph Braibanti in *Bureaucracy and Political Development,* edited by Joseph LaPalombara.

The Pakistani army and its political role are described in Fazal Muqeem Khan's *The Story of the Pakistan Army.* The dismemberment of Pakistan is investigated in G.W. Choudhury's *The Last Days of United Pakistan.* Useful accounts of Pakistan's foreign policy are Latif Ahmed Sherwani's *Pakistan, China, and America* and S.M. Burke and Lawrence Ziring's *Pakistan's Foreign Policy.* An overview of politics and government in Pakistan from independence through 1990 is provided in Craig Baxter et al., *Government and Politics in South Asia.* An analysis of political developments in the early 1990s is provided by *Pakistan: 1992,* edited by Charles H. Kennedy. (For further information and complete citations, see Bibliography.)

Chapter 5. National Security

Artist's rendition of tile mosaic of horseman with lance from the Pictured Wall, Lahore Fort, Punjab. Artwork represents seventeenth-century tile work of the Mughal period.

THE ARMED FORCES OF PAKISTAN have traditionally played a distinctive role in the life of the nation. As in many other developing countries, they are an important modernizing force in society and a key tool of national integration. As defenders of the nation's interests in Pakistan's troubled and volatile geopolitical neighborhood, the armed forces are accorded a particularly high status in public opinion. Less welcome, however, has been the repeated interference of the armed forces in the internal affairs and politics of the country. The military has frequently been called in to gain control of unrest that has gone beyond the ability of the police to cope; some of these intrusions have had a major impact and have been of fairly long duration. The military has assumed control of the entire country three times under proclamations of martial law. Indeed, since it became an independent state in 1947, Pakistan has been under military control for much of its existence.

At the same time, however, democracy has always been seen as the "natural" state of the Pakistani polity, and the military has ultimately returned power to civilian hands. Thus, although the armed forces have dominated the country to a certain extent, they have not perpetuated a military dictatorship. The military has been a permanent factor in the life of the country, but in a role that has ranged from complete control to vigilant observer. As political scientist Leonard Binder has observed, "Even [Pakistan's] dependence upon the military does not necessarily make of it a praetorian state, because there is little evidence that the state works in the sole interest of the military. Rather, it was the military which intervened in order to prevent the breakdown of the patrimonial system." Much of the political history of Pakistan has been set in this drama of contending influences, and the military in early 1994 was still searching for a role that would reconcile its interests and the broader needs of a country whose politicians were struggling to establish a credible authority of their own.

The Armed Services: A Historical Perspective

The Colonial Background

At its creation in 1947, Pakistan looked back on two traditions while seeking to reject a third. One was the more than

100 years of British colonial rule that radically reshaped the superstructure of the subcontinent and was the door to modernity. The other inheritance, the Muslim conquest and dominance from the thirteenth century to the nineteenth century, provided the Islamic factor that led to the partition of India and shaped modern-day Pakistan. The Muslim conquest also offered a useful mythology of exaggerated Islamic military prowess and dominance. The tradition that the new nation rejected and sought to leave behind was that of largely Hindu India. Indeed, differentiation from that heritage was the raison d'être of Pakistan; yet it remains important, for much of Pakistan's cultural heritage is shared with India. India also remains the primary preoccupation of Pakistan's foreign policy and security concerns.

The country's British heritage has played the greatest role in transforming the often amorphous military tradition of the Muslim period into streamlined modern forces. Beginning in the earliest days of the East India Company (chartered in 1600), native guards were hired by the British to protect trading posts. As time went by, these troops were given additional training and were organized under British officers into the armies of the company's presidencies at Calcutta (Fort William), Madras (Fort St. George), and Bombay. In 1748 the presidency armies were brought under the command of Major Stringer Lawrence, who subsequently became known as the father of the British Indian Army. A series of military reforms, first undertaken by Robert Clive in the mid-eighteenth century, continued through the first half of the nineteenth century as the British Parliament asserted increasing control over the East India Company and its military arm. Part of the legacy that shaped the British Indian Army was the growing understanding that civil and military spheres of activity were distinct, that each must respect the other, but that ultimate control rested with the civilian power, whether in later times the governor general or the local district magistrate. The role of the military was to give "aid-to-the-civil power."

The critical event in the evolution of the British Indian Army was the uprising of 1857–58—known as the Indian Mutiny or Sepoy Rebellion by British historians and sometimes as the First War of Independence by later Indian nationalists—when troops in north-central India, Muslim and Hindu alike, rose up against the British (see The Seeds of Muslim Nationalism, ch. 1). Some bonds of loyalty held, but many Indian troops slaughtered both their British leaders and hapless civilians. With the help of Indian troops who did not join the rebellion—especially Sikhs and Muslims from the Punjab—the mutineers were put down with a violence that matched the atrocities that they had committed.

The bond between Indian and Briton had been broken, and a rethinking of British military policy in India was set in motion. East India Company rule was abolished, and direct British rule—the British Raj—was instituted in 1858. Emphasis was put on recruiting in areas where disaffection was least and where the British discerned the existence of "martial races" (ethnic groups) noted for their military tradition, lack of political sophistication, and demonstrated loyalty. By these criteria, the most fertile area for recruitment was in the Punjab region of northwestern India. The Punjabization of the British Indian Army and the assumptions that underlay it would weigh heavily on both the international and the domestic politics of Pakistan once it was created as an independent entity.

Pakistan's military structure in the early 1990s in many ways bore a close resemblance to the British Indian Army structure at the end of the nineteenth century. During that period, recruitment into individual, homogeneous regiments depended on class and caste, rather than on territory. Over time, these regiments became sources of immense pride to the men who served in them and to the ethnic group from which they were frequently recruited. Service in a specific regiment passed from father to son; the eventual shift from British to Pakistani rule went with hardly a ripple in the structure except for the change in nationality of the senior officer corps.

The British experimented with various forms of recruitment and of elevation to officer rank. During the period between the two world wars (1919–39), the British trained Indian officers to command Indian troops, and training establishments were set up to produce an indigenous officer corps. A small number of officer candidates were sent to Britain to the Royal Military Academy at Sandhurst; after 1932 the majority of candidates were trained at the Indian Military Academy at Dehra Dun.

A rank that predated that of the native officer was the viceroy's commissioned officer—an Indian who had risen from the ranks and performed officer functions (except for commanding officer), especially at the company level. The viceroy's commissioned officer came from the same social background as did the troops in his unit and performed a dual function: for the troops, he was a role model and figure of respect to whom they could turn for advice; he was also an invaluable intermediary between the troops and the British officer who commanded them.

The British Indian Army came under immense stress during both world wars, when it was rapidly expanded and deployed abroad to wherever the British Empire appeared threatened. During World War I, nearly 750,000 Indian troops were recruited for service; some 36,000 were killed, and twice as many were wounded. The troops generally acquitted themselves well, and their contribution was used as an arguing point by Indian nationalist politicians who sought greater autonomy for their country.

The army encountered a different kind of stress during the interwar period and beyond, when it was called on to suppress the growing wave of nationalist resistance. This use of Indian personnel alienated the nationalist leaders, especially those of the Indian National Congress, who would become the leaders of India in 1947. The problem was much less serious in what was to become Pakistan. Indeed, during the "Quit India" movement during World War II, when the British sought to crush Congress with special vigor because of its resistance to the war, the All-India Muslim League and the army supported the British cause (see Toward Partition, ch. 1).

During World War II, the British Indian Army (together with the small Royal Indian Navy and Royal Indian Air Force) grew to meet imperial requirements, expanding from essentially a constabulary force of 175,000 to a mass army of more than 2 million. This growth meant appointing many Indians as officers, who received only short training courses, and general recruitment in areas of the country where "martial" spirit had not been discerned before. Once again, Indian troops performed loyally and effectively, even while the country was in political turmoil.

The Formation of Pakistan

The Indian military had no role in the relinquishment of control by the British and the division of India into two parts—India and Pakistan. Under their British commanders, the Indian military had resisted the nationalist tide, and then, when London changed its course, Indian military personnel obediently shifted their allegiance to new masters. After partition and independence, the relationship between the military

Soldiers on parade
Courtesy Embassy of Pakistan, Washington

and the new nationalist government in India was at first problematic. India's first prime minister, Jawaharlal Nehru, deliberately limited the expansion and modernization of his country's armed forces, fearing that an excessive emphasis on the military would lead to the militarization of society and undermine the nation's fledgling democratic institutions.

The Pakistani military, however, immediately became a central part of the national consciousness. Unlike their Indian counterparts, Pakistani soldiers did not bear the stigma of being antinational. The main base of army recruitment, Punjab, was at the heart of Pakistan, and the army was immediately called upon to defend the interests of the nation against a perceived security threat from "Hindu India."

The Pakistani army was fortunate in its political position, but less so in regard to the experience and technical expertise required to field an effective military force. Muslims had been significantly underrepresented in the Indian officer corps, and when partition occurred, there was a severe shortage of personnel. To lead the planned army of 150,000 men, 4,000 officers were needed, but there were only 2,500, and many of those, especially in the technical services, were underqualified. Only one major general, two brigadiers, and six colonels were available, and in the middle officer ranks the situation was equally bad. The first two commanders in chief of the army were British. The first Pakistani commander in chief—General Mohammad Ayub Khan—did not become commander in chief of the army until 1951. In the small Pakistani navy and air force, the situation was even worse: there were only nine regular officers in the navy and sixty-five pilots in the air force. Both forces had to be commanded by British officers: the navy until 1953 and the air force until 1957. Overall, some 500 British officers were retained on contract to ease the transition of the armed forces until Pakistanis could be qualified and promoted. In the interim, training underqualified officers for rapid promotion was a matter of top priority.

The lack of equipment presented further problems. Most of the depots and virtually all of the military production facilities were located in areas that became India, which was less than forthcoming in handing over the share of military matériel that was due Pakistan under the partition agreement. Pakistan received little or nothing in the way of ships and only two of the ten squadrons of the former Royal Indian Air Force. Pakistani military historian Fazl Muqeem Khan records: "It is no exaggeration to say that for its first few months the infant state of Pakistan was without an organized army."

Units with a majority of Muslims (as well as individual Muslims in other units who opted for Pakistan) that were located in India had to find their way to Pakistan. These men formed new units based on common traditions and class affiliation; the remaining service gaps were gradually filled by recruitment. Intercommunal violence at partition took a huge toll of lives, and the role played by the army in protecting the citizens of the new Pakistan created an important initial bond between army and people.

The crucial challenge to the new Pakistani military was the outbreak of hostilities with India over the disputed state of Jammu and Kashmir immediately after partition (see Problems at Independence, ch. 1). Unlike most of the rulers of the other princely states of India, the Hindu ruler of Kashmir (as it is usually called) hesitated in declaring the allegiance of his largely Muslim realm to one or the other of the new nations. Bands of Muslim tribesmen from Pakistan—together with "volunteers" from the Pakistani army—entered the state in early October 1947 to force the issue and, after joining up with insurgents within Kashmir, were soon threatening to overwhelm the Kashmiri forces. As the price for protection, the ruler acceded to India, and elements of the Indian army arrived on October 27. They soon routed the Pakistani irregulars and moved westward to consolidate control over all of the state. Pakistan committed regular military formations to combat in May 1948 to ensure its borders and stabilize the situation. Fighting continued until January 1, 1949, when a United Nations (UN)-sponsored cease-fire took effect. The cease-fire did not, however, settle the underlying conflict. The dispute flared up several times again, most notably in 1965, and remained unresolved as of early 1994. The Indian and Pakistani armies remained deployed along much the same line as they had in 1949. The Pakistani army, however, performed credibly in the Indo-Pakistani War of 1947–48 and won immense admiration and support among Pakistanis, on which it drew heavily as Pakistan began to pay the price of developing a military capability to offset that of India.

Pakistan's Evolving Security Dilemma

Survival in a Harsh Environment

Pakistan is located in a critical and historically contentious part of the world. At the time of independence, it was the world's fifth largest nation. Yet three of its close neighbors (China, India, and the Soviet Union) were larger, more populous, and not necessarily well-intentioned. Pakistan was divided into two wings, East Pakistan (renamed Bangladesh when it became independent in 1971) and West Pakistan. It would soon become apparent that the country, divided by 1,600 kilometers of a hostile India, was also divided by competing ethnic groups with only Islam serving as a tenuous link. Furthermore, West Pakistan was geographically a fairly narrow country, lacking in strategic depth—its main cities and communications arteries lay close to the border with India and thus were vulnerable to attack. Additionally, the headwaters of Pakistan's rivers and vital irrigation systems were largely controlled by India. East Pakistan, except for its Bay of Bengal coast, was also virtually surrounded by India.

There were other security complications. Pakistan's borders with India were new and hence were totally unfortified and, in most places, were drawn in ways that made them almost indefensible. Because the borders were also undemarcated, there was ample opportunity for conflict. Although the military gave border control over to paramilitary forces, the armed forces remained ready for deployment in case of emergency.

Almost all of Pakistan's ethnic groups extended into neighboring countries. This situation caused particular problems with the Afghans, who did not recognize the border as valid and hoped that their new neighbor would be unable to assert its interests.

Security concerns were not limited to the outside world. Despite the euphoria of nationhood, Pakistan was increasingly subject to the same kinds of internal stresses that had characterized British India—fractious tribesmen, *dacoits* (armed gangs of robbers), and restive cities—and required the army to render aid-to-the-civil power. Even the need to repress nationalist movements recurred as regional groups within Pakistan sought greater autonomy from central control.

Although Pakistan perceived in India a threat to its security, initially it was not able to defend itself against that perceived threat because of limited personnel and matériel. Pakistan therefore had to develop a comprehensive military strategy that would offset at least some of its weaknesses. High hopes were placed on support from other Muslim nations, some of which could help financially and others of which would provide through alliances some of the geostrategic territorial depth that Pakistan lacked. But the emergence of the first state created on the basis of Islam was of relatively little interest to the nations of the Arab world. Britain helped significantly in supplying officers and equipment, but it was itself in an economic crisis and would not alienate India.

In 1951, during a period of heightened tension with India along the frontier, Mohammad Ayub Khan was appointed the first Pakistani commander in chief of the army. Ayub Khan immediately concentrated on reshaping the Pakistani military, putting special emphasis on training and operational planning, two critical areas in which Pakistan did not depend completely on foreign resources. These tasks, plus reorganization, occupied the attention of the army well into the 1950s. Critical shortages of equipment, however, remained, requiring that Pakistan look abroad for its provisioning. The selection of Ayub Khan as the commander in chief of the army was of seminal importance. Perhaps more than any other Pakistani, he was responsible for seeking and securing military and economic assistance from the United States and for aligning Pakistan with the United States in international affairs.

The United States Alliance

In the immediate aftermath of World War II, it was natural for Pakistan to covet the wealth and surplus military equipment of the United States. United States-Pakistan relations were cordial, and throughout the late 1940s, Pakistan sought to nurture those close relations and gain access to United States military support; initially, these attempts were rebuffed.

As the new decade opened, however, a series of events put new hope into the possibility of United States-Pakistan cooperation. First was the reassessment of Pakistan's military position undertaken by Ayub Khan. The second event was the outbreak of the Korean War (1950-53), which drew United States attention toward Asia and marked the point of no return of the globalization of United States security policy. The third factor was the advent of the Eisenhower-Dulles team, which set to work building a ring of containment around the Sino-Soviet bloc. India, committed to nonalignment, had come into sharp disagreement with the United States in the UN when it refused to censure China as an aggressor in the Korean War and thus was viewed by the United States as a voice for communist appeasement. India's refusal to join the United States-sponsored 1951 Treaty of Peace with Japan—a pact among nations designed, among other purposes, to recruit Japan as an ally against communist inroads in Asia—further divided the two countries. India was not available as an ally; Pakistan was the inevitable alternative (see Foreign Policy, ch. 4).

Pakistan and the United States drew closer together, high-level visits were exchanged, and the groundwork was laid for a security relationship that seemed to meet Pakistan's political needs and equipment deficit. At United States prompting, Pakistan and Turkey concluded a security treaty in 1954—the Turko-Pakistan Pact—which immediately enabled United States military assistance to Pakistan under the Mutual Defense Assistance Agreement signed the same year. Pakistan also became a member of the Southeast Asia Treaty Organization (SEATO) in 1954 and joined the Baghdad Pact, later renamed the Central Treaty Organization (CENTO) in 1959. Pakistan had little interest in SEATO and discerned no danger to its interests from China, joining mainly to oblige Washington. Even CENTO, which offered the advantage of a new approach to the Muslim world, was problematic because it drove a wedge between Pakistan and the Arab countries that remained outside it and was seen by Pakistanis as institutionally weak because the United States was never willing to become a full member. None of these arrangements addressed Pakistan's main concern, however—India.

At Pakistan's insistence, an additional agreement (the Agreement of Cooperation) on security was concluded with the

United States in March 1959, by which the United States committed itself to the "preservation of the independence and integrity of Pakistan" and agreed to take "appropriate action, including the use of armed forces, as may be mutually agreed upon . . . in order to assist the Government of Pakistan at its request." The Agreement of Cooperation also said nothing about India and was cast in the context of the Eisenhower Doctrine, which dealt with communist threats to the Middle East. Pakistan saw the agreement as representing a high level of United States commitment, however, and some United States officials apparently encouraged an interpretation that saw more in the agreement than was actually there. There was considerable self-deception on both sides—Pakistan believed that it had secured an ally in its rivalry with India, and the United States focused on Pakistan as an adherent to the anticommunist cause.

Tangible gains to Pakistan from the relationship were substantial. Between 1954 and 1965, the United States provided Pakistan with US$630 million in direct-grant assistance and more than US$670 million in concessional sales and defense-support assistance. The army received equipment for one additional armored division, four infantry divisions, and one armored brigade and received support elements for two corps. The air force received six squadrons of modern jet aircraft. The navy received twelve ships. The ports of Karachi (in West Pakistan) and Chittagong (in East Pakistan) were modernized. The program did not, however, provide for the wholesale modernization of the military, much less its expansion. Forces in Kashmir and East Pakistan were excluded, and there was a continuing tug-of-war between the United States and Pakistan as Pakistan sought to extend the scope of the program and wring more benefits out of it.

The impact on the military of this new relationship was intense. Pakistanis embraced the latest concepts in military organization and thinking with enthusiasm and adopted United States training and operational doctrine. The army and the air force were transformed into fairly modern, well-equipped fighting forces. In the course of the rearmament program, the military was substantially reorganized along United States lines, and hundreds of Pakistani officers were trained by United States officers, either in Pakistan or in schools in the United States. Although many British traditions remained, much of the tone of the army, especially the officer corps, was Americanized.

Pakistan's hopes for an equitable settlement of its disputes with India, especially over Kashmir, were probably small in any event, but by bringing the United States directly into the South Asian security equation, rapprochement with India became virtually impossible. More important, India responded to Pakistan's new alignment by turning to the Soviet Union for military and political support—and the Soviet leader at the time, Nikita S. Khrushchev, was only too happy to oblige. As a result, Pakistan not only incurred Soviet hostility but also ultimately triggered a Soviet military supply program in India that more than offset the United States assistance to Pakistan. Soviet displeasure was further heightened by Pakistan's decision to grant facilities at Peshawar for the United States to conduct U-2 aerial reconnaissance missions over the Soviet Union.

The Army Assumes Control

The developing relationship with the United States was only one of the dramatic experiences that the military underwent in the late 1950s. The political system had been performing very poorly, especially since the assassination of Prime Minister Liaquat Ali Khan in 1951 (see Constitutional and Political Inheritance, ch. 4). There was increasing public disillusionment with the system and little respect for political leaders, who were seen as incompetent and corrupt. In fact, decision-making power had been moving inexorably away from the leaders of the political parties and into the hands of the two national institutions that were seen as competent and honest—the bureaucracy and the army.

On October 7, 1958, President Iskander Mirza annulled the 1956 constitution by proclamation, dissolved the national and provincial assemblies, and banned political parties. Asserting that if Pakistan were to be saved, the army would have to assume political control. Mirza then declared martial law and appointed General Ayub Khan chief martial law administrator. Twenty days later, Ayub moved against Mirza, sending him into exile, and assumed the office of president himself. Thus began the second role of the military—self-appointed guardian of domestic affairs of state as well as defender against external enemies. The results were mixed, both for Pakistan and for its soldiers. The military continued to enjoy preferred access to resources in Pakistan, and an elaborate system of quasi-governmental bodies provided economic opportunities for military personnel, especially after retirement. The country as a whole welcomed army rule, which brought a period of stability and rapid economic growth and vigorously attacked the corruption that beset the country. The army ruled with a firm but light hand, retaining ultimate control but working largely through the bureaucracy.

Economic gains, however, were so badly distributed that they seemed hollow to many Pakistanis. The involvement of military personnel in governing detracted from their primary mission. Although the military remained popular, it became associated with the political divisions of the country and was no longer solely the symbol of national unity. Opposition began to develop, especially among intellectuals and politicians.

Ayub Khan lifted martial law in 1962, replacing it with an authoritarian constitution under which he was elected president (see Basic Democracies, ch. 1; Ayub Khan, 1958–69, ch. 4). While the new system had some constructive features, it failed to gain public support, and even though the army was no longer governing the country, Ayub Khan and his system were seen as unpopular manifestations of military rule.

Collapse of Pakistan's Security System

Pakistan's tie to the United States was a product of the post-World War II communist containment strategy and the fear of Soviet expansionism. By the end of the 1950s, a number of factors had changed—some to Pakistan's advantage, others not. The positive factor was the emergence of China as an independent international actor at odds with both the Soviet Union and India, thereby creating new policy options for Pakistan. Less favorable was a decline in international tensions that reduced the United States preoccupation with containment and, hence, Pakistan's value. At the same time, the Eisenhower administration was seeking to reclaim some of the ground it had lost with India, and this trend was strengthened as tensions grew between New Delhi and Beijing, Washington's principal bête-noire of the time.

Pakistan was able to profit from Sino-Indian hostility by securing China as an additional source of support, but ties to Beijing were anathema to Washington and caused serious problems in United States-Pakistan relations during the 1960s. Rapprochement between New Delhi and Washington also caused deep concern to Pakistanis. Pakistan was appalled when, at the time of the Sino-Indian War in 1962, the United States rushed to rearm India without meeting Pakistan's demands that assistance be coupled with effective pressure to force India to settle the Kashmir dispute. The United States reassured Pakistan that India was not arming against Pakistan, but Pakistan realized that the external equalizer it had brought into the subcontinent to make up its security deficit would now be devalued as the United States, at best, played an even-handed role or, at worst, shifted its principal attention to India.

The security situation deteriorated still further as India, which had hitherto spent relatively little on defense, engaged in a major buildup of forces that were primarily aimed at China but could as readily be turned against Pakistan. In addition, after 1964 India took a series of steps to incorporate Kashmir more closely into the Indian union, rendering less likely any negotiations on the matter with Pakistan. Under the circumstances, Pakistan decided that its chances of gaining Kashmir would only deteriorate; hence, it opted for early action.

The Indo-Pakistani War of 1965

In mid-1965, Pakistan sent guerrilla forces into the Indian-held territory of Kashmir in the hope of stirring up a rebellion that would either oust the Indians or at least force the issue back onto the international agenda. Pakistani forces did not find as much support among the Kashmiri population as they had hoped, but fighting spread by August, and a process of escalation culminated in a full-scale Indian offensive toward Lahore on September 6. Fighting, frequently very bitter, continued until a UN-sponsored cease-fire took hold on September 23. Both sides had tacitly agreed not to let the war spread to the East Wing of Pakistan.

The war was militarily inconclusive; each side held prisoners and some territory belonging to the other. Losses were relatively heavy—on the Pakistani side, twenty aircraft, 200 tanks, and 3,800 troops. Pakistan's army had been able to withstand Indian pressure, but a continuation of the fighting would only have led to further losses and ultimate defeat for Pakistan. Most Pakistanis, schooled in the belief of their own martial prowess, refused to accept the possibility of their country's military defeat by "Hindu India" and were, instead, quick to blame their failure to attain their military aims on what they considered to be the ineptitude of Ayub Khan and his government.

Pakistan was rudely shocked by the reaction of the United States to the war. Judging the matter to be largely Pakistan's fault, the United States not only refused to come to Pakistan's aid under the terms of the Agreement of Cooperation, but issued a statement declaring its neutrality while also cutting off military supplies. The Pakistanis were embittered by what they considered a friend's betrayal, and the experience taught them to avoid relying on any single source of support. For its part, the United States was disillusioned by a war in which both sides used United States-supplied equipment. The war brought other repercussions for the security relationship as well. The United States withdrew its military assistance advisory group in July 1967. In response to these events, Pakistan declined to renew the lease on the Peshawar military facility, which ended in 1969. Eventually, United States-Pakistan relations grew measurably weaker as the United States became more deeply involved in Vietnam and as its broader interest in the security of South Asia waned.

Iran, Indonesia, and especially China gave political support to Pakistan during the war, thus suggesting new directions in Pakistan that might translate into support for its security concerns. Most striking was the attitude of the Soviet Union. Its post-Khrushchev leadership, rather than rallying reflexively to India's side, adopted a neutral position and ultimately provided the good offices at Tashkent, which led to the January 1966 Tashkent Declaration that restored the status quo ante.

The aftermath of the 1965 war saw a dramatic shift in Pakistan's security environment. Instead of a single alignment with the United States against China and the Soviet Union, Pakistan found itself cut off from United States military support, on increasingly warm terms with China, and treated equitably by the Soviet Union. Unchanged was the enmity with which India and Pakistan regarded each other over Kashmir. The result was the elaboration of a new security approach, called by Ayub Khan the "triangular tightrope"—a tricky endeavor to maintain good ties with the United States while cultivating China and the Soviet Union. Support from other developing nations was also welcome. None of the new relationships carried the weight of previous ties with the United States, but, taken together, they at least provided Pakistan with a political counterbalance to India.

Pakistan needed other sources of military supply, most urgently because of its wartime losses and the United States embargo. After 1965 China became Pakistan's principal military supplier, providing matériel to all three services in substantial quantity and at attractive prices. Submarines and Mirage aircraft were also purchased from France. The Soviet Union sought to woo Pakistan with military equipment, but that program never really developed because of Moscow's concern not to jeopardize its more important relationship with India. The United States gradually relaxed its embargo; however, it was only in 1973 that substantial supplies again flowed to Pakistan.

The late 1960s were politically turbulent times for Pakistan; by 1969 conditions had deteriorated to the point where the army once again felt called on to intervene. On March 25, an ailing and discredited Ayub Khan transferred power to army commander in chief General Agha Mohammad Yahya Khan, who declared himself president as well as chief martial law administrator (CMLA) and announced that Pakistan would have national general elections—for the first time since independence—and a new constitution. The elections in December 1970 were fair but led to the breakup of Pakistan (see Yahya Khan and Bangladesh, ch. 1). In the process, the army and Pakistan's security situation deteriorated still further.

The largely Punjabi army was in a politically untenable position in East Pakistan, which had voted overwhelmingly for an autonomist party. Once it became clear that a compromise between the civilian leaders of West Pakistan and East Pakistan was unattainable, Yahya Khan was forced to choose between the two sides, and his actions were seen by the Bengalis of the East Wing as favoring the interests of West Pakistan, which were hardly distinguishable from those of the armed forces. Yahya decided to postpone indefinitely the convening of the new National Assembly, which would have been controlled by Bengalis. It was feared that a government dominated by East Pakistani interests would cut back sharply on military prerogatives and roll back the dominance of Punjab in national affairs. Within days, unrest spread throughout East Pakistan. Bengalis went on strike and stopped paying taxes. Bengali autonomists became separatists.

Army elements in East Pakistan were strengthened in the spring of 1971 and were used to suppress Bengali recalcitrance. The task was undertaken with ferocity; killing, rape, looting, and brutality were widespread and resulted in the flight of nearly 10 million refugees to India over six months. International outrage grew and forced the Richard M. Nixon administration in the United States to halt its attempts to reopen military supply lines to Pakistan.

The army was generally successful during the spring and summer of 1971 in restoring order in East Pakistan, but increasing Indian support of the antigovernment Bengali guerrillas known as the Mukti Bahini (Liberation Force) began to shift the balance. When Indian troops finally intervened directly in December, there was no hope of stopping them. Even though the garrison in East Pakistan had been reinforced, national strategy was still based on the assumption that Pakistan could not simultaneously defend both wings of the country against an Indian attack; hence, an attack in the east would be countered in the west. On December 3, Pakistani forces began hostilities in the west with attacks on Indian airfields. They had little success, and within twenty-four hours India had gained air superiority, launched attacks against West Pakistan, and blockaded the coast. Pakistani forces in East Pakistan surrendered to the Indian army on December 16, and India offered a cease-fire. In the face of superior force on all fronts, Pakistan had little choice but to accept the breakup of the country.

The armed forces were shattered and their equipment destroyed; 9,000 troops were lost, and 90,000 prisoners of war were in the hands of Indians and Bengalis in Bangladesh (the former East Pakistan). Yahya Khan resigned in disgrace, and the winner of the elections in West Pakistan, Zulfiqar Ali Bhutto, succeeded him as CMLA and president. Pakistan, a country originally created in the name of religion, lost its raison d'être as the homeland of Muslims in the subcontinent and was much reduced in size. Although the politicians were ultimately responsible for the events of 1971, the army and its leaders were the obvious villains.

The security situation of the nation also changed. Any illusions of parity vis-à-vis India were demolished. Although both China and the United States had tilted toward Pakistan politically, it was abundantly clear that neither of those superpowers was in a position to offset Indian primacy in the region, especially in view of the friendship treaty that India had signed with the Soviet Union in August 1971, just before the outbreak of hostilities. The Soviet Union, forced to choose sides, opted for India, and the rapprochement that had taken place between Pakistan and the Soviet Union evaporated. Pakistan stood largely alone and at the mercy of India. The 1972 bilateral

Simla Agreement restored most of the status quo that existed before the 1971 war in the relations between the two nations. The agreement states that "the two countries are resolved to settle their differences by peaceful means through bilateral negotiations or by any other peaceful means mutually agreed upon between them." Although India maintained the more narrow interpretation that disputes be settled bilaterally, Pakistan in subsequent years favored a looser interpretation—one that did not exclude a multilateral settlement of the Kashmir dispute.

Yet the loss of East Pakistan also had positive implications for Pakistan's security. The loss of the East Pakistani population as a recruitment pool was of only minor significance. By shedding its most dissident and poorest province, Pakistan emerged stronger and was able to focus its energies more effectively. A major strategic problem—the geographic division of the country—was eliminated. The loss of East Pakistan also removed the need for a Pakistani role in Southeast Asia. Pakistan withdrew from SEATO, and Bhutto refocused national attention toward Muslim West Asia. He apparently tried to develop ways of putting the Kashmir issue to rest so that Pakistan could greatly reduce its preoccupation with South Asia. No longer closely tied to the United States, Bhutto sought a larger role for Pakistan among the nonaligned countries and, especially, within the Islamic world. A brilliant diplomat, he was able in a very few years to restore Pakistan's prestige, stake out a leading role for Pakistan among Muslim nations, court the superpowers, and even establish cordial relations with Bangladesh.

These triumphs were not shared with the military, as Bhutto moved to create a "professional but docile" military. Senior officers were dismissed, and their replacements were chosen by Bhutto. The military establishment was reorganized so that it would be under more effective civilian control. Bhutto's 1973 constitution narrowly defined the role of the military as defending Pakistan against external aggression and "subject to law" acting in aid-to-the-civil power when called on so to do. Any attempt to abrogate the constitution was deemed high treason (see Zulfiqar Ali Bhutto and a New Constitutional System, ch. 1).

In 1972 Bhutto established the Federal Security Force of some 18,000 men to provide assistance to the civil administration and police and to do civic-action work. Not under military control, the Federal Security Force was, in effect, Bhutto's private political army. The military, beaten and demoralized, had no choice but to accept this further setback, even as it harbored deep concerns over the impact Bhutto was having on the integrity of the army and its ability to defend Pakistan.

In 1973 Bhutto began to focus on rebuilding the tamed military because Pakistan continued to face serious security threats from abroad, highlighted by the Indian nuclear test in 1974, and at home—a major insurgency from 1973 to 1977 in Balochistan, which ultimately required the involvement of 80,000 army troops. New military production facilities and a navy air wing were established. Bhutto's diplomacy resulted in a partial lifting of the United States embargo on military sales to Pakistan in 1973 and a complete removal of the embargo in 1977. He also used diplomacy to tap into the burgeoning oil revenues of the Middle East; still, Pakistan could not afford to buy much, and its inventories of weapons were increasingly made up of outdated and ill-matched equipment from a variety of sources. Nonetheless, the army's self-confidence again began to grow. Expenditures on defense by 1974 had reattained the 1969 level—even though the gross national product (GNP—see Glossary) was little more than half of the amount that had been produced before Bangladesh became independent. The defense budget continued to increase over the next several years, supporting a somewhat expanded strength—428,000 personnel in 1976. Pakistan's nuclear program was also established by Bhutto.

Bhutto's domestic position, however, eroded rapidly in the mid-1970s, and, as his charisma waned, he turned to the army to deal with domestic unrest. The elections of March 1977—widely thought to be rigged—resulted in mass demonstrations demanding Bhutto's resignation. General Mohammad Zia ul-Haq, chief of the army staff—a new title for service chiefs replacing the former title of commander in chief—saw that the army was unwilling to engage in the violence that would be necessary to put down the unrest. In a stunning move, Zia arrested Bhutto and other political leaders on July 5, 1977, and declared Pakistan's third period of martial law.

The Military Reasserts Itself

General Zia asserted that this military intervention in politics would be brief and that there would be new elections within ninety days, but he had the longest tenure of any Pakistani ruler. Although he came to power more as a spokesman of military interests—a first among equals—and was thought to be a political naif, he was highly skilled in gathering power into his own hands.

On assuming power, Zia named himself chief martial law administrator and suspended parts of the 1973 constitution. (Zia assumed the presidency as well in September 1978.) Because it appeared that Bhutto, if freed and available as a candidate, might easily win the elections, Zia postponed them and undertook a campaign to discredit his predecessor politically. Zia's initial assumption of power was peaceful; even his subsequent decision to allow Bhutto to be hanged, after Bhutto's conviction as an accomplice to murder a political opponent, did not bring disturbances severe enough to threaten his regime. There was, however, continued opposition to military rule, and Zia was able to maintain himself in power only through a combination of political luck, skill, and authoritarianism.

Although the military regime was often repressive, state violence was downplayed, and some observers believe that human rights conditions were better than during the Bhutto years. Zia also emphasized the corruption in political life and the need for reform. Ethnic resistance in Balochistan and the North-West Frontier Province was dealt with adroitly; only the ethnic Sindhis remained profoundly alienated (see Zia ul-Haq and Military Domination, 1977–88, ch. 1). Zia also proved politically skillful in employing a strategy of continually holding out the promise of free elections when circumstances permitted, making political concessions that would strengthen rather than undermine his position and, especially after 1979, co-opting influential political groups among orthodox Muslims.

The first years of Zia's tenure marked another low point in the security situation. The Iranian Revolution of 1979 overthrew the Shah, one of Pakistan's staunchest friends, and the missionary zeal of its new Islamist regime did not bode well for Pakistan-Iran relations. The Saur Revolution (April Revolution) in Afghanistan in 1978 ousted a government that had become conciliatory in its relations with Pakistan, replacing it with a group that also preached radical change—this time, Marxist. When the Soviet army invaded Afghanistan in December 1979, Pakistan found itself in a security nightmare—for the first time, the Soviet Union posed a potentially immediate threat.

Relations with the United States were also at a low point. The administration of President Jimmy Carter had adopted an extremely hard line on Pakistan's nuclear program and suspended all military and economic assistance in April 1979. In March 1979, after the Iranian Revolution, Pakistan withdrew from a moribund CENTO. Tensions with the United States peaked when a Pakistani mob burned the United States embassy in Islamabad in November 1979, killing two Americans and two Pakistani employees, in response to a British radio broadcast of Ayatollah Ruhollah Khomeini's speech, in which he falsely accused the United States of invading the Grand Mosque in Mecca. Although China remained a good friend, political scientist Robert G. Wirsing's assessment proved accurate: "Never before had Pakistan been quite so isolated and quite so threatened at the same time."

Pakistan Becomes a Frontline State

The Soviet invasion of Afghanistan made Pakistan a country of paramount geostrategic importance. In a matter of days, the United States declared Pakistan a "frontline state" against Soviet aggression and offered to reopen aid and military assistance deliveries. For the remainder of Zia's tenure, the United States generally ignored Pakistan's developing nuclear program. Other donors also rallied to Pakistan as it stood firm against Soviet blustering, hospitably received over 3 million Afghan refugees who poured across the borders, provided a conduit for weapons and other support, and gave a safe haven to the Afghan *mujahidin* (see Glossary). Pakistan's top national security agency, the army's Directorate for Inter-Services Intelligence, monitored the activities of and provided advice and support to the *mujahidin,* and commandos from the army's Special Services Group helped guide the operations inside Afghanistan. In the Muslim world, Pakistan increasingly assumed a leading role. As a long-term goal, Zia envisioned the emergence of an Islamic government in Kabul that would provide Pakistan with geostrategic depth, facilitate access to Muslim West Asia, and forswear a revision of the contentious Pakistan-Afghanistan boundary.

Pakistan paid a price for its activities. The refugee burden, even if offset in part by foreign assistance, created dangerous pressures within Pakistani society. Afghan and Soviet forces conducted raids against *mujahidin* bases inside Pakistan, and a campaign of terror bombings and sabotage in Pakistan's cities, guided by Afghan intelligence agents, caused hundreds of casualties. In 1987 some 90 percent of the 777 terrorist incidents recorded worldwide took place in Pakistan. The actual danger to Pakistan, however, was probably never very great. There is no concrete evidence to support the revitalized "Great Game" argument that the Soviet invasion was a modern manifestation of Russia's historical drive to garner access to a warm-water port and that it was but a first step on a road through Pakistan to the Arabian Sea. Nor was it likely that the Soviet Union would have conducted major military operations against Pakistan as long as Islamabad did not flaunt its support for the *mujahidin.*

The Soviet invasion enabled Pakistan's army to present itself as the defender of the nation in times of trouble, making criticism of military rule almost unpatriotic. Zia used the situation to strengthen his grip on internal affairs by appealing to national unity and pointing to Pakistan's growing international stature. In addition, the substantial amounts of aid money coming from various sources boosted the economy and, in the short run at least, more than offset the costs of the refugees and rearming the military. Overall, the economy grew rapidly in the Zia years, in large part because of remittances from many Pakistanis who worked abroad (see Impact of Migration to the Persian Gulf Countries, ch. 2; Labor, ch. 3).

Zia's ability to obtain high levels of support and modern weaponry strengthened his position within the military establishment and enabled Pakistan once again to build up a credible military capability. Under the United States assistance program, Pakistan bought F–16 aircraft; upgraded M–48 tanks, Harpoon naval missiles, helicopters, and artillery; and received second-hand frigates on loan. In the four years after the invasion, Pakistan's armed forces grew by nearly 12 percent, from 428,000 to 478,000 persons. A substantial amount of the costs of modernization and expansion were covered by United States aid and financial contributions from Saudi Arabia and Persian Gulf countries.

Zia was extremely skillful in protecting his base in the military. To ensure control, he was concurrently chief of the army staff, chief martial law administrator, and president, and he carefully juggled senior military appointments. The satisfaction of the military was also enhanced by arrangements under which Pakistani service personnel were seconded to the armed forces of Persian Gulf countries, where emoluments were much more generous than in Pakistan. Retiring officers received generous benefits, sometimes including land allocations, and often found lucrative positions in government service or in parastatal economic enterprises. The assignment of serving officers to approximately 10 percent of the senior posts in the civilian administration also provided opportunities for economic gain, sometimes in ways that were ultimately harmful to the army's image of itself. For example, some military personnel reportedly participated in the rapidly growing narcotics business.

Zia had learned well the lesson of 1965 and was careful not to allow the nation to return to the status of a client state of the United States. Even as Pakistan faced the Soviet Union in Afghanistan, it kept that threat in perspective. Immediately after the Soviet invasion of Afghanistan in December 1979, Zia declined the Carter administration's assistance package offer of US$400 million as "peanuts." It was not until 1981 that Pakistan concluded an assistance agreement with the United States, which provided for US$3.2 billion over six years, divided equally between economic and military aid. This agreement was extended in 1986 to provide an additional US$4.0 billion over the next six years. Zia was careful to avoid the trappings of a formal alliance, preferring continued involvement in the Nonaligned Movement—which Pakistan joined in 1979—and with the Islamic nations of the Middle East through his leading role in the Organization of the Islamic Conference (see Pakistan and the World During the Zia Regime, ch. 1).

Credit for the Soviet defeat in Afghanistan lay mainly with the *mujahidin* and their Pakistani mentors, but would hardly have come about had Soviet leader Mikhail S. Gorbachev not decided to cut back drastically on Soviet foreign entanglements. After tedious negotiations, an agreement was reached in April 1988, providing for the withdrawal of Soviet troops by February 15, 1989.

Zia's policies inevitably led to a worsening of relations with India, which was disturbed by the reentry of the United States into the South Asian security equation and by what India saw as the impetus to a new arms race. India responded with large-scale arms purchases of its own, primarily from the Soviet Union, which more than matched anything that the United States provided to Pakistan. Zia took considerable pains to reduce tensions and launched several peace initiatives, which New Delhi, however, failed to accept. Whether Zia saw his own efforts merely as diplomatic maneuvers was unclear, but they reflected a growing realization in Pakistan that unconstrained enmity with India was simply too dangerous and beyond Pakistan's means.

There were periods of considerable tension between Pakistan and India. In November 1986, India launched its largest maneuver ever, Operation Brass Tacks, menacingly close to the Pakistan border. The Pakistani army responded with threatening countermovements, and in early 1987 there was serious concern that war might break out. The India-Pakistan hot line was brought into use, and Zia skillfully seized the initiative by traveling to India to view a cricket game, using the opportunity to meet with Indian leaders to defuse the situation.

Among the major disputes between the two countries, only that over the Siachen Glacier, which is located in a remote area of northern Kashmir where boundaries are ill defined, has led to fighting in recent years. The two armies had been in desultory but very costly (primarily because of exposure to the elements) high-altitude combat there since 1984, when Indian forces moved into previously unoccupied territory at the extreme northern end of the Kashmir Line of Control.

Aside from Afghanistan, the most problematic element in Pakistan's security policy was the nuclear question. Zia inherited an ambitious program from Bhutto and continued to develop it, out of the realization that, despite Pakistan's newly acquired weaponry, it could never match India's conventional power and that India either had, or shortly could develop, its own nuclear weapons. Even after the invasion of Afghanistan, Pakistan almost exhausted United States tolerance, including bungled attempts to illegally acquire United States nuclear-relevant technology and a virtual public admission in 1987 by the head of Pakistan's nuclear program that the country had developed a weapon. As long as Pakistan remained vital to United States interests in Afghanistan, however, no action was taken to cut off United States support. Pakistani attempts to handle the problem bilaterally with India led nowhere, but a significant step was taken with a nonformalized 1985 agreement that neither India nor Pakistan would attack the other's nuclear facilities.

Zia showed a remarkable ability to keep himself in power, to promote Pakistan's international position, and to bring a modest degree of economic prosperity to Pakistan. His problem was how to devolve power. Beginning in 1985, a process of demilitarization of the regime was launched, and Zia was elected civilian president of Pakistan through some highly dubious maneuvering (see Zia ul-Haq, 1978–88, ch. 4). In late 1985, he ended martial law and revised the 1973 constitution in ways that legitimized all actions taken by the martial law government since 1977 and strengthened his position as president. Mohammad Khan Junejo, whom Zia appointed prime minister in March 1985, managed to develop some degree of autonomy from Zia and persuaded him to allow political parties to organize; Junejo also watered down some of Zia's constitutional proposals, notably blocking the creation of the National Security Council, which would have institutionalized the role of the military.

The experiment in controlled democracy floundered in May 1988, when Zia abruptly dismissed the Junejo government for reasons that were not altogether clear but may have involved Junejo's attempt to gain a voice in security matters. Zia promised new elections, but most observers assumed that he would once again postpone them rather than take the risk that Benazir Bhutto, Zulfiqar's daughter, who had returned from exile abroad to a tumultuous welcome in Pakistan in 1986, would come to power. Benazir's program included revenge for her father's death and punishment of Zia for staging the 1977 coup, which, under the 1973 constitution, rendered him liable to the death sentence. The crisis facing Pakistan resolved itself suddenly, however, when Zia was killed in a mysterious airplane crash in August 1988. Ghulam Ishaq Khan, a senior bureaucrat who was president of the Senate, succeeded to the presidency, and after consultations with the new chief of the army staff, General Mirza Aslam Beg, rather surprisingly decided to let the elections proceed as scheduled.

The Armed Forces in a New World Order

The Zia era ended as it had begun, with a Bhutto in power, for Benazir's party emerged with a narrow victory. Her position was much different from that of her father. She became prime minister under a constitution that left great power in the hands of the president, her parliamentary majority was narrow, and the army was strong, self-confident, and unwilling to renounce its political role. As the price of power, Benazir had to negotiate an arrangement with President Ishaq Khan and General Beg by which she reportedly promised to keep Zia's constitutional changes and to limit her involvement in military affairs,

Two F-16 fighters on patrol
Artillery crew on duty in Siachen Glacier, close to India-Pakistan border
Courtesy Embassy of Pakistan, Washington

including management of the fighting in Afghanistan and nuclear weapons policy.

Several times Benazir ineffectually challenged the armed forces and the president on military matters. She was never able to find a comfortable relationship with these two other major players of the triangle of political power in Pakistan. She showed interest in improving relations with India but had little room to take concrete steps. She skillfully cultivated her good ties to Washington, but overall her performance as prime minister was disappointing, and when the president—with the obvious backing of the army—dismissed her in August 1990 and called for new elections, there was little opposition.

The elections brought to power the Islamic Democratic Alliance (Islami Jamhoori Ittehad—IJI), a coalition that enjoyed the implicit support of both the president and the armed forces. Punjab's chief minister, Mian Nawaz Sharif, a businessman and protégé of Zia, became prime minister. Although the dismissal of Benazir had been against the spirit, if not the letter, of the constitution, the new power arrangement seemed to offer Pakistan favorable prospects for stable representative rule because the three power centers were all in apparent alignment, and Nawaz Sharif represented the interests of the Punjabi majority. The arrangement worked adequately for some time, and when General Beg's time for retirement as chief of the army staff came, he did not attempt to force an extension of his tour of duty.

Beg's replacement, General Asif Nawaz Janjua, was a much lower-profile leader and sought to lead the army away from corruption and toward a renewed emphasis on professionalism and a sensible adaptation to the post-Cold War realities of Pakistan's strategic position. The army, however, was drawn into politics in May 1992 when the law-and-order situation in Sindh deteriorated so badly that the provincial government invited the army to restore public order under Article 147 of the constitution. Although the army could not solve Sindh's many problems, it made significant progress in combatting the cycle of terror, banditry, and kidnapping that had plagued the province. The army stopped short of imposing martial law, but it intervened in the politics of the province and, in the process, moved against political allies of Nawaz Sharif, the IJI coalition prime minister, who was already at odds with the president.

General Janjua died suddenly in January 1993, and President Ishaq Khan used his prerogative to reach well down the list of lieutenant generals to appoint Abdul Waheed, a highly regarded officer without apparent political aspirations. Waheed seemed to fit Pakistani political scientist Mohammad Waseem's description as "the transition from a group of conservative generals led by Zia who were inspired by Islamic ideals to a relatively liberal and modernist generation of military officers who have positive attitudes toward Western-style democracy."

Waheed was quickly called upon to demonstrate his commitment to the democratic process. When a power struggle between the president and the prime minister in April 1993 resulted in Prime Minister Nawaz Sharif's ouster, the military resisted the temptation to take charge during the ensuing period of political turmoil. In July Waheed brokered a settlement in which both the prime minister and the president resigned, a neutral caretaker government was appointed, and new elections were scheduled for October (see "The Silent Revolution": A Year of Political Struggle, ch. 4).

There remained different points of view among officers, almost all of whom had little respect for politicians and feared that an incompetent civilian leader might irreparably damage their core values—the integrity of the military and the security of Pakistan. Some officers were politically ambitious and had found their period of power under Zia rewarding—financially and otherwise. Many, however, believed that any political activity, whether in the context of martial law or in the context of helping deal with crises caused by politicians' ineptitude, undermined discipline and morale and detracted from the ability of the armed forces to perform military missions. Retired General Shaukat Riza, describing an earlier period of martial law, observed: "After a short period of hot, righteous action, military men succumb to setting their mark on whatever is served up to them. Martial Law is disarmed, leaving in its wake a debris of shattered dreams and wasting social order."

On balance, the army preferred to avoid direct involvement unless the political order threatened to collapse completely. The crucial question for Pakistan's political future was in the shaping of the middle ground. Should the armed forces simply be recognized as having a voice in Pakistan's politics, or should their role be formally institutionalized? Zia's attempts to do the latter through creation of a National Security Council had been successfully resisted by Junejo, but the question remained central to Pakistan's security as well as to its politics.

The external relations of the military deteriorated sharply in the post-Zia period because of the collapse of Pakistan's relationship with the United States. President George Bush determined in October 1990 that he could no longer certify that Pakistan did not possess nuclear weapons and, as required by the Pressler Amendment to the Foreign Assistance Act, terminated all United States assistance to Pakistan that was not already in the pipeline. Pakistan handled the cutoff with little public rancor and committed itself to freezing the nuclear program in an attempt to placate the United States. Washington permitted such commercial purchases as spare parts for aircraft and the continued joint naval and special forces exercises, but such key items as fighter aircraft on order were kept in abeyance. Further, the United States moved to reclaim nine ships that were on loan—about half of Pakistan's surface fleet.

The impact on Pakistan's military readiness by the United States decision to halt assistance has been described by observers as near catastrophic, but even more important than the money and equipment involved was the strategic signal sent by the aid cutoff. As long as Pakistan was in the front line of opposition to the Soviet invasion of Afghanistan, the United States found ways of continuing its aid despite Pakistan's nuclear program. Once the Soviet forces left Afghanistan and the Soviet Union itself ceased to exist, Pakistan's importance dwindled. Whatever limited successes Pakistan may have had in salvaging parts of the relationship with the United States, it was clear that the end of the Cold War marked the end of Pakistan's strategic role.

The loss of United States support came at a difficult time. Unrest in Indian Kashmir had developed rapidly after 1989, and Pakistan inevitably supplied moral and covert matériel support, thus raising the specter of a new conflict with India. There were serious concerns in early 1990 that a war might break out. At United States prompting, both sides took effective steps to reduce the danger. Neither country wanted a conflict, but Pakistan remained in a quandary because it could not ignore events in Kashmir although it did not have substantial international support for its position. The United States and China made clear their unwillingness to provide political or matériel support to Pakistan, thus increasing still further the latter's sense of isolation.

The Soviet withdrawal from Afghanistan removed a potential threat to Pakistan, and the substantial retreat of Russia from the security affairs of the subcontinent offset somewhat the withdrawal of the United States. For the first time since 1947, Pakistan was not concerned about a two-front threat. Further, the emergence of five independent Muslim republics in Central Asia raised hopes that they might become allies and offer Pakistan both the political support and the strategic depth it lacked. As long as Afghanistan was in chaos, Pakistan would lack direct access to the new republics. However, it was still far from certain in the early 1990s whether or not the republics would find Pakistan a desirable political partner.

Approaching the next century, Pakistan faces yet another reconfiguration of the forces that determine its security environment. As Russia, China, and the United States stand back from South Asia, there are fewer constraints on India. Yet other sweeping changes are under way in the international environment. Pakistan remains engaged in its search for outside help to ensure its security. The end of the Cold War only changed the parameters of the problem.

The Armed Services

Constitutional Basis and Missions

Article 243 of the 1973 constitution states that the federal government controls the armed forces and gives the president power to raise and maintain active and reserve forces, grant commissions, and appoint the chiefs of staff of the three services (see President, ch. 4). Under Article 242, the president is commander in chief of the armed forces. The original intent was that the president act according to the guidance of the prime minister. However, the Eighth Amendment to the nominally "revived" but fundamentally altered 1973 constitution, promulgated in 1985 by President Zia, specifies in Article 90 that national executive power is vested in the president.

Article 245 prescribes the functions of the armed forces as defense of the nation against external aggression or threat of war and, subject to law, aid-to-the-civil power when called upon. This article is intended to keep the military from acting independently of the elected political leadership in domestic affairs. It was notably unsuccessful in protecting Zulfiqar Ali Bhutto from Zia's demand for "accountability," culminating in Bhutto's trial, conviction, and eventual execution on a charge of conspiring to murder one of his political opponents. Article 244 prescribes the oath taken by the armed forces, including the pledge "not to engage myself in any political activities whatsoever." This requirement is not, however, meant to restrict members of the armed forces from voting.

Article 39 enjoins the state to enable people from all parts of Pakistan to join the armed forces. It does not, however, require proportional representation of provinces, and only modest progress has been made in making the military more geographically representative.

In addition to the constitutionally prescribed missions of defending the country (including protecting the borders and coastline) and continuing the traditional aid-to-the-civil power, the army has an unstated, self-appointed mission of guarding the domestic order—"guardian of the family silver," as Pakistani journalist Mushahid Hussain puts it. It is this concept of its mission that has led the military to assume power on three separate occasions.

The military engages in a broad range of public service and economic activities and plays a leading role in dealing with natural disasters. The armed services do not, however, have a record of participating in foreign disaster relief. The military has engaged in civic-action work in strategically sensitive areas, especially Balochistan, but does not see itself as having a generalized role in civic action and economic development. General Waheed even resisted a military role in antinarcotics work, probably fearing its temptation as well as its distraction from the military's primary role as the defender of the country.

Defense Strategy

Pakistan remains, despite its substantial military force, a nation with a gaping security deficit. India has forces sometimes almost three times as large as Pakistan's, and this disparity is only partially offset by India's need to defend its border with China. Senior Pakistani officers are well aware of the fact that their forces are not equal to India's, and few would willingly provoke a test of strength. Further, although Pakistan had built up its fuel and ammunition reserves to forty-five days' supplies by 1992, past experience has taught the nation not to count on replenishment. War avoidance has been the primary goal of Pakistani security policy, especially since the Zia years. At the same time, the military accepts the fact that war is possible and is determined to acquit itself well.

Pakistan, like virtually every other nation, proclaims that its forces and strategy are defensive. Faced with a much superior enemy, uncertain sources of supply, and little strategic depth, Pakistan cannot expect to absorb an initial attack and to successfully fight a protracted defensive war. Thus, in terms of conventional strategy, Pakistan has emphasized a doctrine of "offensive defense," which provides for quick preemptive strikes once a war begins in order to disrupt an enemy advance and inflict high costs. In addition, such actions are designed to gain salients in enemy territory, which can be used as trade-offs in peace negotiations. Navy and air force roles would be mainly defensive. The large-scale exercise Zarb-e-Momin (Sword of the Faithful), which took place in late 1989, was held far enough away from the border not to frighten India, and, indeed, foreign observers were invited. Its scenario and the publicity that attended it were, however, meant to illustrate the offensive-defense doctrine and to make sure that India understood it.

Ministry of Defence

The minister of defense is a civilian member of the cabinet, chairs the Defence Council, and is in turn a member of the higher-level Cabinet Defence Committee. The Ministry of Defence has a permanent staff of civil servants headed by the defense secretary general. Of particular importance to the Ministry of Defence is the adviser for military finance, who heads the Military Finance Division in the Ministry of Finance but is attached to the Ministry of Defence. The adviser functions as the principal financial officer of the defense ministry and the subordinate services.

The Joint Chiefs of Staff Committee deals with all problems bearing on the military aspects of state security and is charged with integrating and coordinating the three services. In peacetime, its principal function is planning; in time of war, its chairman is the principal staff officer to the president in the supervision and conduct of the war. The secretariat of the committee serves as the principal link between the service headquarters and the Ministry of Defence in addition to coordinating matters between the services. The three branches within the Joint Chiefs of Staff Committee deal with planning, training, and logistics. Affiliated with the committee are the offices of the engineer in chief, the director general of medical service, the director of inter-services intelligence, and the director of inter-services public relations. The Joint Chiefs of Staff Committee supervises the National Defence College, the

Joint Services Staff College, and the Inter-Service Selection Board.

The Directorate for Inter-Services Intelligence is of particular importance at the joint services level. The directorate's importance derives from two sources. First, it is the agency charged with managing covert operations outside of Pakistan—whether in Afghanistan, Kashmir, or farther afield. Second, in the past it was deeply involved in domestic politics and kept track of the incumbent regime's opponents. In addition, when the regime was unpopular with the military and the president (as was Benazir Bhutto's first government), the agency helped topple it by working with opposition political parties.

Army and Paramilitary Forces

The key holder of power in the armed forces and, along with the president and the prime minister, one of the triumvirate that runs the country is the chief of the army staff (COAS)—formerly called the commander in chief. In 1994 this post was held by General Abdul Waheed. The COAS operates from army headquarters in Rawalpindi, near Islamabad. From this position, both Ayub Khan and Zia seized power. Other senior staff positions, at the lieutenant general level, include a chief of general staff, who supervises army intelligence and operations; the master general of ordnance; the quartermaster general; the adjutant general; the inspector general for evaluation and training; and the military secretary. The headquarters function also includes the chief of the Corps of Engineers, the judge advocate general, and the comptroller of civilian personnel, all of whom report to the vice chief of the army staff.

The army is organized into nine corps: First Corps at Mangla; Second Corps at Multan; Fourth Corps at Lahore; Fifth Corps at Karachi; Tenth Corps at Rawalpindi; Eleventh Corps at Peshawar; Twelfth Corps at Quetta; Thirtieth Corps at Gujranwala; and Thirty-first Corps at Bahawalpur. There is also the Northern Area Command, headquartered at Gilgit, directly responsible to army general headquarters.

Active army strength in 1994 was 520,000. In addition, there were 300,000 reserve personnel. Reserve status lasts for eight years after leaving active service or until age forty-five for enlisted men and age fifty for officers.

In 1994 major weapons included nearly 2,000 tanks (mainly Chinese but also 120 M–47s and 280 M–48A5s of United States origin); 820 M–113 armored personnel carriers; 1,566 towed artillery pieces; 240 self-propelled artillery pieces; forty-five multiple rocket launchers; 725 mortars; 800 Cobra, TOW, and Green Arrow antitank guided weapons; eighteen Hatf surface-to-surface missiles; 2,000 air defense guns; and 350 Stinger and Redeye missiles and 500 Anza surface-to-air missiles. The army's combat aircraft inventory consisted of twenty AH–1F airplanes equipped with TOW missiles (see table 14, Appendix).

Paramilitary organizations, which are mainly of symbolic importance, include the 185,000-member National Guard, comprising the Janbaz Force—locally recruited militia mainly charged with air defense—and two programs similar to the United States Reserve Officers Training Corps, the National Cadet Corps and the Women Guard. The Women Guard, unlike the National Cadet Corps, includes individuals trained in nursing, welfare, and clerical work. There are also some women in the Janbaz Force, and a very small number of women are recruited into the regular service in limited numbers to perform medical and educational work.

Paramilitary internal security forces are organized on the provincial level but are subordinate to the Ministry of Interior and are commanded by seconded army generals. These forces are in effect an extension of the army for internal security duties. The Pakistan Rangers, headquartered in Lahore, deal with unrest in Punjab, while the Mehran Force performs similar functions in Sindh. In 1994 their strengths were 25,000 and 24,000, respectively, divided into "wings" of approximately 800 men each. The Frontier Corps, with a strength of 65,000, is based in Peshawar and Quetta with responsibility for the North-West Frontier Province and Balochistan. The corps is responsible to both the Ministry of States and Frontier Regions and to army headquarters. The corps is divided into twenty-seven local units—fourteen in the North-West Frontier Province and thirteen in Balochistan—and includes the Chitral Scouts, the Khyber Rifles, the Kurram Militia, the Tochi Scouts, the South Waziristan Scouts, the Zhob Militia, and the Gilgit Scouts. There is also a Coast Guard, subordinate to the Ministry of Interior and staffed by army personnel.

In times of natural disaster, such as the great floods of 1992, army engineers, medical and logistics personnel, and the armed forces play a major role in bringing relief and supplies. The army also engages in extensive economic activities. Most of these enterprises, such as stud and dairy farms, are for the army's own use, but others perform functions beneficial to the local civilian economy. Army factories produce such goods as sugar, fertilizer, and brass castings and sell them to civilian consumers.

Several army organizations perform functions that are important to the civilian sector across the country. For example, the National Logistics Cell is responsible for trucking food and other goods across the country; the Frontier Works Organization built the Karakoram Highway to China; and the Special Communication Organization maintains communications networks in remote parts of Pakistan.

Navy

In 1994 the navy had some 22,000 personnel. The force includes a small Naval Air Arm and the approximately 2,000-member paramilitary Maritime Security Agency, charged primarily with protecting Pakistan's exclusive economic zone. The naval reserve consists of about 5,000 personnel.

In 1994 the navy had four commands: COMPAK—the fleet; COMLOG—logistics; COMFORNAV—naval installations in the north of Pakistan; and COMKAR—naval headquarters and the only major base at Karachi. There are long-range plans to build a new naval base at Ormara, 240 kilometers west of Karachi, and to improve harbors at Gwadar and Pasni to help alleviate overdependence on Karachi.

The navy's principal combatants in 1994 were six submarines of French origin equipped with United States Harpoon missiles; negotiations with the French for three additional submarines have been reported. The navy had three active old destroyers (one of British and two of United States origin), four United States-made guided missile frigates, six other frigates (two from Britain and four from the United States), and two United States-made and one French-made mine warfare craft. One destroyer and four frigates carried Harpoon missiles; the navy had acquired an unknown number of Mistral close-in surface-to-air missiles from France. There were eight missile craft, and thirteen coastal combatant and patrol craft, all of Chinese origin. The Naval Air Arm had four combat aircraft flown by air force personnel and armed with Exocet missiles and sixteen armed helicopters. The delivery of three P–3C Orion long-range reconnaissance aircraft from the United States had been suspended since 1990 (see table 15, Appendix).

In 1991 a naval special warfare marine commando unit, with a strength of between 150 and 200 men, was established. Its functions, in addition to hull inspection and special operations, included operating three midget submarines.

Although the navy clearly needs to grow, its immediate future is threatened by a reduction in equipment brought about by the Pressler Amendment imposed in 1990 (see The Armed Forces in a New World Order, this ch.). The navy had to return four Brooke (Badr)-class and four Garcia (Saif)-class frigates to the United States at the end of their five-year lease. In addition, one British-made destroyer, the *Babur*, was retired in 1994. At the same time, all three United States destroyers became fully operational, and an additional six Amazon-class frigates purchased from Britain were to be delivered in late 1994.

Air Force

In 1994 the air force had 45,000 active personnel and 8,000 reserve personnel. Headquartered in Rawalpindi, it comprises directorates for operations, maintenance, administration, and electronics. There are three air defense districts—north, central, and south.

In 1994 the air force was organized into eighteen combat squadrons, with a total of 430 combat aircraft. The mainstay of the air force was the F–16 fighter. Of the forty aircraft originally acquired, thirty-four were in service, divided among three squadrons. Some were reportedly grounded because of a lack of spare parts resulting from the 1990 United States suspension of military transfers to Pakistan (see The United States and the West, ch. 4). Pakistan had an additional seventy-one F–16s on order, but delivery has been suspended since 1990. Other interceptors included 100 Chinese J–6s (which were scheduled to be phased out) and eighty J–7s, organized into four squadrons and two squadrons, respectively. Air-to-air missiles included the Sparrow, Sidewinder, and Magic (see table 16, Appendix).

To fulfill its ground-attack role, the air force had three squadrons of Chinese Q–5s (a total of fifty aircraft) as well as one squadron of eighteen Mirage IIIs (EP and DP) and three squadrons (fifty-eight aircraft) of Mirage 5s, one squadron of which was equipped with Exocet missiles and was deployed in an antiship role. The Mirage 5s are scheduled to be upgraded with French assistance.

In 1994 Pakistan also took out of storage thirty of forty-eight Mirage III–Os that it had originally acquired from Australia. They were grouped into a fighter squadron.

The backbone of the transport fleet was formed by twelve C–130 Hercules, which had recently been upgraded; plans to acquire more were stymied by the dispute with the United States over Pakistan's nuclear program. There were also smaller transport aircraft and a variety of reconnaissance and training aircraft.

Personnel and Training

The manpower base of Pakistan, with its population of more than 120 million, is more than adequate to maintain force levels that the country can afford. In 1994 there were an estimated 6.4 million men and 5.7 million women between the ages of eighteen and twenty-two and another 10 million men and 9 million women between the ages of twenty-three and thirty-two. About two-thirds of the individuals in these groups were estimated to be physically fit for service. Although there is provision for conscription, it has not proven necessary because there are more than enough volunteers for a profession that is both honored and, by Pakistani standards, financially rewarding.

Although recruitment is nationwide and the army attempts to maintain an ethnic balance, most recruits, as in British times, come from a few districts in northern Punjab Province and the adjacent North-West Frontier Province. Most enlisted personnel come from rural families, and although they must have passed the sixth-grade level in school, many have only rudimentary literacy skills and very limited awareness of the modern-day skills needed in a contemporary army (see Education, ch. 2). Recruits are processed gradually through a paternalistically run regimental training center, perhaps learning to wear boots for the first time, taught the official language, Urdu, if necessary, and given a period of elementary education before their military training actually starts. In the thirty-six-week training period, they develop an attachment to the regiment they will remain with through much of their careers and begin to develop a sense of being a Pakistani rather than primarily a member of a tribe or a village. Stephen P. Cohen, a political scientist specializing in military affairs, has noted that the army "encourages the *jawan* (basic private) to regard his regiment and his unit as his home or substitute village; and it invests a great deal of time and effort into . . . 'man management,' hoping to compensate in part for generally inferior military technology by very highly disciplined and motivated soldiers." Enlisted men usually serve for fifteen years, during which they participate in regular training cycles and have the opportunity to take academic courses to help them advance.

About 320 men enter the army annually through the Pakistan Military Academy at Kakul (in Abbotabad) in the North-West Frontier Province; a small number—especially physicians and technical specialists—are directly recruited, and these persons are part of the heart of the officer corps. They, too, are overwhelmingly from Punjab and the North-West Frontier Province and of middle-class, rural backgrounds. The product of a highly competitive selection process, members of the officer corps have completed ten years of education and spend two years at the Pakistan Military Academy, with their time divided about equally between military training and academic work to bring them up to a baccalaureate education level, which includes English-language skills. There are similar programs for the navy at Rahbar (in Karachi) and for the air force at Sarghoda.

The army has twelve other training establishments, including schools concentrating on specific skills such as artillery, intelligence, or mountain warfare. Plans are being drawn up for the National University of Science and Technology, which would subsume the existing colleges of engineering, signals, and electrical engineering. At the apex of the army training system is the Command and Staff College at Quetta, one of the few institutions inherited from the colonial period. The college offers a ten-month course in tactics, staff duties, administration, and command functions through the division level. Students from foreign countries, including the United States, have attended the school but reportedly have been critical of its narrow focus and failure to encourage speculative thinking or to give adequate attention to less glamorous subjects, such as logistics. The air force has an advanced technical training facility at Korangi Creek near Karachi for courses in aeronautical engineering, and the navy's technical training is carried out at Karsaz Naval Station in Karachi.

The senior training institution for all service branches is the National Defence College at Rawalpindi, which was established in 1978 to provide training in higher military strategy for senior officers. It also offers courses that allow civilians to explore the broader aspects of national security. In a program begun in the 1980s to upgrade the intellectual standards of the officer corps and increase awareness of the wider world, a small group of officers has been detailed to academic training, achieving master's degrees and even doctorates at universities in Pakistan and abroad.

Pakistani officers were sent abroad during the 1950s and into the 1960s for training in Britain and other Commonwealth countries, and especially to the United States, where trainees numbering well in the hundreds attended a full range of institutions ranging from armored and infantry schools to the higher command and staff institutions. After 1961 this training was coordinated under the International Military Education and Training (IMET) program, but numbers varied along with vicissitudes in the United States-Pakistan military relationship. Of some 200 officers sent abroad annually in the 1980s, over two-thirds went to the United States, but the cessation of United States aid in 1990 halted the IMET program. In 1994 virtually all foreign training was in Commonwealth countries.

Pay scales and benefits for enlisted personnel are attractive by Pakistani standards. Officer pay is substantially higher, but with inflation and a generally expanding economy, officers find it harder to make do and feel that they are falling well behind their civilian counterparts in the civil service, where salaries are somewhat higher and the opportunities for gain considerably greater.

Officers retire between the ages of fifty-two and sixty, depending on their rank. The retirement age for enlisted personnel varies similarly according to grade. Retirement pay is modest, especially for enlisted men, but the armed services find ways to make the retiree's lot easier. Especially during periods of martial law, retired senior officers have found second, financially rewarding careers in government-controlled organizations. Land grants to retired officers have been common, and scholarships and medical care are available on a relatively generous basis. In the event of an officer's death on active duty, certain provisions, including grants of free housing, are often extended to his family.

The Fauji Foundation is a semiautonomous organization run for the benefit of active and, especially, retired military personnel and their families. It engages in a variety of lucrative businesses throughout Pakistan and annually produces a surplus of US$30 million for its beneficiaries. The Baharia Foundation provides a similar service to navy families, as does the Shaheen Foundation to those of the air force.

Uniforms, Ranks, and Insignia

Pakistani military uniforms closely resemble those of the British armed services. The principal colors are greenish brown for the army, navy blue for the navy, and light blue for the air force. Brown and black camouflage fatigues are commonly worn by army troop units. Rank insignia also are similar to those used by the British (see fig. 11; fig. 12).

The rank structure is also patterned on the British model. Following the British Indian tradition, there are three junior commissioned officer (JCO) grades between enlisted and officer rank for those who rise by promotion from among enlisted recruits. The junior commissioned officer is a continuation of the former viceroy's commissioned officer rank. During the early days of the army, there was a large cultural gap between officers and enlisted personnel. In the early 1990s, JCOs had wide responsibilities in the day-to-day supervision of lower grades, but they were a group that may have outlived its usefulness because officers have become "more Pakistani" and less dependent on British models and because the education level of enlisted men has risen. Promotion to JCO rank, however, remains a powerful incentive for enlisted personnel; thus, if JCO ranks are ever phased out, it will likely be a slow process.

Military Production

Pakistan began with virtually no military production capability, and, because of its limited economic means and lack of foreign markets, there is little prospect of the country's ever developing industrial facilities that could cover its equipment needs. However, it has taken a series of partial steps in some of the most crucial fields and aspired to become self-sufficient, at least in such basic areas as aircraft overhaul and modernization and tank and helicopter sales. Symbolic of Pakistan's determination to move to a degree of self-sufficiency was the creation of the Ministry of Defence Production in September 1991.

The Ministry of Defence Production has been responsible for promoting and coordinating a patchwork of military production facilities that have developed since independence. The oldest of these facilities is the Pakistan Ordnance Factory at Wah Cantonment, near Rawalpindi, established in 1951, to produce small arms, ammunition, and explosives. During the

PAKISTANI RANK	2D LIEUTENANT	LIEUTENANT	CAPTAIN	MAJOR	LIEUTENANT COLONEL	COLONEL	BRIGADIER	MAJOR GENERAL	LIEUTENANT GENERAL	GENERAL	FIELD MARSHAL
ARMY											
U.S. RANK TITLE	2D LIEUTENANT	1ST LIEUTENANT	CAPTAIN	MAJOR	LIEUTENANT COLONEL	COLONEL	BRIGADIER GENERAL	MAJOR GENERAL	LIEUTENANT GENERAL	GENERAL	GENERAL OF THE ARMY
PAKISTANI RANK	PILOT OFFICER	FLYING OFFICER	FLIGHT LIEUTENANT	SQUADRON LEADER	WING COMMANDER	GROUP CAPTAIN	AIR COMMODORE	AIR VICE MARSHAL	AIR MARSHAL	AIR CHIEF MARSHAL	MARSHAL OF THE AIR FORCE
AIR FORCE	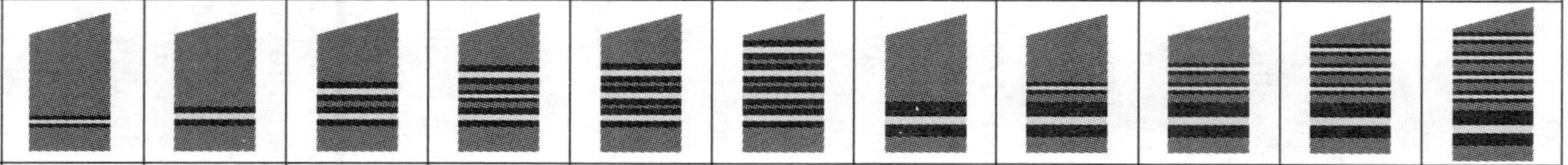										
U.S. RANK TITLE	2D LIEUTENANT	1ST LIEUTENANT	CAPTAIN	MAJOR	LIEUTENANT COLONEL	COLONEL	BRIGADIER GENERAL	MAJOR GENERAL	LIEUTENANT GENERAL	GENERAL	GENERAL OF THE AIR FORCE
PAKISTANI RANK	ACTING SUB-LIEUTENANT	MIDSHIPMAN	LIEUTENANT	LIEUTENANT COMMANDER	COMMANDER	CAPTAIN	COMMODORE	REAR ADMIRAL	VICE ADMIRAL	ADMIRAL	ADMIRAL OF THE FLEET
NAVY											
U.S. RANK TITLE	ENSIGN	LIEUTENANT JUNIOR GRADE	LIEUTENANT	LIEUTENANT COMMANDER	COMMANDER	CAPTAIN	REAR ADMIRAL LOWER HALF	REAR ADMIRAL UPPER HALF	VICE ADMIRAL	ADMIRAL	FLEET ADMIRAL

Figure 11. Officer Ranks and Insignia, 1994

PAKISTANI RANK	JAWAN	SEPOY	LANCE NAIK	NAIK	HAVILDAR	COMPANY QUARTERMASTER HAVILDAR	COMPANY HAVILDAR MAJOR	WARRANT OFFICER CLASS II	WARRANT OFFICER CLASS I	JAMADAR	SUBEDAR	SUBEDAR MAJOR
ARMY	NO INSIGNIA	NO INSIGNIA										
U.S. RANK TITLE	BASIC PRIVATE	PRIVATE	PRIVATE 1ST CLASS	CORPORAL/ SPECIALIST	SERGEANT	STAFF SERGEANT	SERGEANT 1ST CLASS	MASTER SERGEANT/ FIRST SERGEANT	SERGEANT MAJOR/ COMMAND SERGEANT MAJOR	NO RANK	NO RANK	NO RANK

PAKISTANI RANK	AIRCRAFTS-MAN	LEADING AIRCRAFTSMAN / SENIOR AIRCRAFTSMAN		JUNIOR TECHNICIAN	CORPORAL TECHNICIAN	NO RANK	SENIOR TECHNICIAN	CHIEF TECHNICIAN	WARRANT OFFICER	MASTER WARRANT OFFICER
AIR FORCE	NO INSIGNIA									
U.S. RANK TITLE	AIRMAN BASIC	AIRMAN		AIRMAN 1ST CLASS	SENIOR AIRMAN/ SERGEANT	STAFF SERGEANT	TECHNICAL SERGEANT	MASTER SERGEANT	SENIOR MASTER SERGEANT	CHIEF MASTER SERGEANT

PAKISTANI RANK	NO RANK	ORDINARY SEAMAN	ABLE SEAMAN	LEADING SEAMAN	NO RANK	PETTY OFFICER	CHIEF PETTY OFFICER	NO RANK	NO RANK
NAVY		NO INSIGNIA	NO INSIGNIA						
U.S. RANK TITLE	SEAMAN RECRUIT	SEAMAN APPRENTICE	SEAMAN	PETTY OFFICER 3D CLASS	PETTY OFFICER 2D CLASS	PETTY OFFICER 1ST CLASS	CHIEF PETTY OFFICER	SENIOR CHIEF PETTY OFFICER	MASTER CHIEF PETTY OFFICER

Figure 12. Enlisted Ranks and Insignia, 1994

period of reliance on United States supply, there was little attention given to domestic production, but after the assistance cutoffs in 1965 and 1971, Pakistan—with China's help—set about expanding its facilities, including the modernization of Wah. The Heavy Industries facility at Taxila was established in 1971 as an equipment rebuilding facility, followed in 1973 by the Pakistan Aeronautical Complex at Kamra, north of Islamabad. The air force assembled Chinese F–6s and French Mirages; produced the Mushshak trainer, which was based on the Swedish SAAB Safari/Supporter; maintained radar and avionics equipment; and in the mid-1990s was in the process of developing the Karakorum jet trainer in a joint project with China.

The ministry also includes seven other specialized organizations devoted to research and development, production, and administration. Total personnel strength in 1993 was more than 50,000, including 2,600 professionals. The government estimated annual production in the early 1990s at US$500 million including about US$30 million in exports. For example, Mushshaks were provided to Iran as light trainers and observation aircraft. Exports ranked high among the ministry's goals.

The navy is supported mainly by a facility at the Karachi Shipyard, which has limited production capacity and in 1994 had to its credit only an 831-ton tanker and a prototype 200-ton coastal patrol vessel. In 1987 development of a submarine repair and rebuild facility at Port Qasim was begun.

Pakistan's nuclear program is shrouded in secrecy, but there is little doubt that nuclear weapons have been produced or at least have reached the developmental stage of a final "turn of a screw"; and, although the program is believed to have been technically arrested in 1992, the capability to produce weapons exists. Estimates put the inventory at between seven and fifteen weapons, at least some of which are deliverable by airdrop from C–130 or F–16 aircraft. Although F–16s supplied by the United States had the electronic wiring removed (necessary for launching nuclear weapons), some United States observers reported that Pakistanis could easily overcome this technological obstacle.

In the early 1990s, Pakistan was also engaged in a missile development program, for which it had received substantial Chinese assistance. The Hatf–1 surface-to-surface missile, which can carry a payload of up to 500 kilograms as far as eighty kilometers, was introduced in 1992; the Hatf–2, which could be in service by 1995, also carries a 500-kilogram payload but has a 300-kilometer range. In 1994 there were unconfirmed reports of a longer range Hatf–3 missile under development.

Budget

Faced with the problem of defense against a much larger enemy from a relatively weak resource base, the military must lay claim to a disproportionate share of the nation's resources even to maintain a minimally effective defensive capability. The military was fortunate in that successive governments—with the exception of the early Bhutto years—believed it necessary to support the armed services as much as possible. This attitude also persisted among the public at large, who accepted the danger from India as real and present.

From 1958 until 1973, the published defense budget accounted for between 50 and 60 percent of total government expenditures. After that time, the proportions were much lower, falling to 40 and even 30 percent levels and ranging between 5 and 7 percent of GNP. At the same time, however, because of an expanding economy, actual expenditures—even allowing for inflation—showed considerable increases. The defense budget for fiscal year (FY—see Glossary) 1993 was set at Rs94 billion (for value of the rupee—see Glossary), or US$3.3 billion, which represented 27 percent of government spending and almost 9 percent of the gross domestic product (GDP—see Glossary). The published budget understated expenditures by excluding procurement and defense-related research and development as well as funds spent on such activities as intelligence and the nuclear program.

Military Justice

The military justice system rests on three similar service laws: the Pakistan Army Act (1952), the Pakistan Air Force Act (1953), and the Pakistan Navy Ordinance (1961). The acts are administered by the individual services under the central supervision of the Ministry of Defence.

The army has a four-tier system; the air force and navy, three-tier systems. The top two levels of all three systems are the general courts-martial and district courts-martial; the third level comprises the field general courts-martial in the army and air force and the equivalent summary general courts-martial in the navy. The army also has a further level, the summary courts-martial.

The differences in court levels reflect whether their competence extends to officers or only to enlisted men and the severity of the punishment that may be imposed. Sentences of military courts must be approved by the convening authority, that is, the commanding general of the organization concerned. Every decision of a court-martial higher than summary court-martial level must be concurred in by a majority of the members of the court; where a vote is split evenly, the law provides that the "decision shall be in favor of the accused." There is a right of appeal within the military court system, but no civilian court has the right to question the judgment of a military court. In cases where a military person is alleged to have committed a crime against a civilian, the central government determines whether military or civilian courts have jurisdiction. Double jeopardy is prohibited. Former servicemen in civilian life who are accused of felonies committed while on active duty are liable for prosecution under the jurisdiction of military courts. These courts are empowered to mete out a wide range of punishments—including death. All sentences of imprisonment are served in military prisons or detention barracks.

In contrast to the civilian court system, the introduction of Islamic law (sharia—see Glossary) has had little effect on the military justice system. The Federal Shariat Court has, however, ordered the military to make more liberal provisions to appeal, to confront witnesses, and to show just cause (see Judiciary, ch. 4). It was not clear in early 1994 what practical effect these directives have had.

Foreign Security Relationships

Pakistan must look abroad for both material assistance and political support. Its principal tie has been with the United States. When relations were good, this connection meant access to funds, sophisticated weaponry, training, and an enhanced sense of professionalism. When relations were bad, it meant bitter disillusionment and the severing of support at critical junctures. These wide swings of fortune are something to which Pakistanis have become accustomed, and they recognize that, whatever the provocation, the tie to the United States has too much potential benefit to be discarded lightly.

Relations with China in the early 1990s were less emotionally intense and much more stable. China has been a steady source of military equipment and has cooperated with Pakistan in setting up weapons production and modernization facilities. Within months of the 1965 and 1971 wars, China began to resupply the depleted Pakistani forces. Between 1965 and 1982, China was Pakistan's main military supplier, and matériel has continued to be transferred. In 1989 Pakistan and China discussed the transfer of a nuclear submarine, and China was helpful in developing Pakistan's missile and, allegedly, nuclear weapons programs. But Chinese weaponry was inferior to that supplied by the West and also to what India received from the former Soviet Union and hoped to continue to receive from Russia. The Pakistanis dispatched a military mission to Moscow in October 1992, probably to explore the possibilities of acquiring surplus Russian and East European equipment at low prices.

The Pakistani military's close ties to the nations of the Middle East are based on a combination of geography and shared religion. The closest ties are with Saudi Arabia—a sporadically generous patron; much of the equipment bought from the United States during the 1980s, for example, was paid for by the Saudis. The smaller Persian Gulf states also have been sources of important financial support. The flow of benefits has been reciprocated. Beginning in the 1960s, Pakistanis have been detailed as instructors and trainers in Saudi Arabia, Jordan, Syria, Libya, Kuwait, and the United Arab Emirates. Pakistani pilots, sailors, and technicians have played key roles in some Persian Gulf military forces, and Arabs have been trained both in their home countries and in military training establishments in Pakistan. After unrest in Saudi Arabia in 1979, Pakistan assigned two combat divisions there as a low-profile security force. This unofficial arrangement ended in 1987, however, reportedly when Pakistan refused the Saudi demand to withdraw all Shia (see Glossary) troops. Some 500 advisers, however, remained behind. These exchanges had built up close contacts between the forces of Pakistan and the Arab host countries and were profitable to Pakistan and to the individual Pakistanis assigned abroad, who were paid at much higher local pay scales.

Pakistan has a particular interest in cooperating with neighboring Iran, with which it had occasionally difficult relations after the Iranian Revolution of 1979. In more recent years, however, delegations have been exchanged, and Pakistan has sold military equipment to Iran. Pakistan also has military ties with Turkey and would like to use these, as well as its Iranian connections, as a bridge to the new Muslim states of Central Asia. When the situation in Afghanistan again becomes normal, Pakistan will no doubt attempt to capitalize on the support it gave the *mujahidin* by forging close military links to its second-most-important neighbor to the west.

Pakistan has sent troops abroad as part of United Nations (UN) peacekeeping efforts. The first such troops served in West Irian (as Indonesia's Irian Jaya Province was then called) in the 1962–63 period. In early 1994, Pakistan contributed two infantry battalions to the United Nations Protection Force in Bosnia and Herzegovina (UNPROFOR BH) and two infantry brigades to the United Nations Operation in Somalia (UNOSOM). Pakistan's contribution of 7,150 troops to UNOSOM was the largest single national contingent in any UN peacekeeping force as of early 1994. At the time, Pakistan also had participating observers in a number of other UN missions in Croatia, the Iraq-Kuwait demilitarized border zones, Liberia, Mozambique, and Western Sahara. Pakistan also dispatched an armored brigade to Saudi Arabia during the 1991 Persian Gulf War. However, it was assigned well away from the front—ostensibly to defend the holy cities of Mecca and Medina—thus reducing the possibility that any Pakistani troops might have somehow become involved in actual combat with Iraqi troops. Such an eventuality could have proven explosive in Pakistan and could have caused uncontrollable unrest. Pakistani sentiment in favor of Iraq was widespread, and even the COAS, General Beg, spoke out in support of Saddam Husayn.

The Role of Islam

Zulfiqar Ali Bhutto introduced certain Islamic practices, notably prohibition of alcoholic beverages, into the army, and Zia encouraged still more, including the assignment of mullahs (see Glossary) as chaplains, some of whom reportedly go into combat with the troops. Modest mosques have been built in military training areas, Islamic texts are being introduced into training courses, mid-grade officers must take courses and examinations on Islam, and there are serious attempts under way to define an Islamic military doctrine, as distinct from the Western doctrines that the Pakistanis have been following.

In the early 1990s, Islamic military doctrine had not replaced more traditional military doctrines, and it probably never will. Stephen P. Cohen has, however, highlighted several interesting points that have emerged. For instance, Islam has traditionally been identified with the concept of jihad, a righteous religious "striving" against unbelievers, and Islamic governments have been assiduous in describing whatever wars they fight—even against other Muslims—as jihad. Recent thinking, however, has emphasized that jihad is not a perpetual invitation to wage war against nonbelievers and, indeed, that it need not necessarily entail violence. More specifically, Pakistani writers have rejected as un-Islamic the idea of total war that emerged in Europe in the nineteenth and twentieth centuries. They emphasize the Quranic injunctions to conciliation and persuasion and see force only as a last resort.

Further, these Pakistani theorists see the function of force less as a capability for combat than as something that strikes terror into the hearts of enemies and thus can actually prevent war. There is an obvious parallel here to the idea that the most terrifying of all weapons, nuclear ordnance, can act as a deterrent to war. Many Western military writers have portrayed the era of United States-Soviet mutual deterrence in these terms, and some have even applied this view as a rationale for Pakistani and Indian nuclear capabilities. Pakistani writers find this approach a convenient justification for their nuclear programs, and, indeed, most of the "Islamic" thinking on war still looks more like retroactive rationalizations for strategies already adopted rather than guideposts to new departures. Furthermore, Pakistanis are well aware that air combat tactics or at-sea replenishment techniques are not determined by religion, and the armed forces will continue to look for secular guidance.

At the personnel level, the generation of cosmopolitan officers who were trained in British and United States traditions and consider religion a purely personal matter is passing from the scene. The new generation of officers is less exposed to foreign influences and is, increasingly, a product of a society that has been much more influenced by "orthodox" Islam, in which the primacy of Islam is continually emphasized and accepted.

Relatively few Pakistanis have turned to Islamic fundamentalism, and, because of the demands of their profession, Pakistani officers and soldiers seem likely to keep at least one foot in the modernist camp. Senior generals are reportedly concerned about religion looming too large in military affairs, but unless there are major changes in society and politics, the armed forces may increasingly see itself as an Islamic as well as a nationalist force.

Internal Security

Role and Structure of the Security Forces

Before independence, the security forces of British India were primarily concerned with the maintenance of law and order but were also called on to perform duties in support of the political interests of the government. The duties of the police officer in a formal sense were those of police the world over: executing orders and warrants; collecting and communicating upward intelligence concerning public order; preventing crime; and detecting, apprehending, and arresting criminals. These duties were specified in Article 23 of the Indian Police Act of 1861, which (together with revisions dating from 1888 and the Police Rules of 1934), is still the basic document for police activity in Pakistan.

The overall organization of the police forces remained much the same after partition. Except for centrally administered territories and tribal territories in the north and northwest, basic law and order responsibilities have been carried out by the four provincial governments. The central government has controlled a series of specialized police agencies, including the Federal Investigative Agency, railroad and airport police forces, an anticorruption task force, and various paramilitary organizations such as the Rangers, constabulary forces, and the Frontier Corps. Zulfiqar Ali Bhutto established the Federal Security Force and gave it wide-ranging powers, but the force was abolished when the military regime of Zia ul-Haq seized power in 1977.

Under the constitution, criminal law and procedure are listed as subjects that are the concurrent responsibility of the central and provincial governments. The federal government, however, has extensive power to assert its primacy, especially in any matter relating to national security. The police forces of the four provinces are independent, and there is no nationwide integration; nevertheless, the federal minister of interior provides overall supervision.

Senior positions in the police are filled from the Police Service of Pakistan (PSP). The Police Service of Pakistan is not an operational body; rather, it is a career service similar to the Civil Service of Pakistan, from which officers are assigned to the provincial services or, on rotation, to central government agencies where their skills are needed. Recruitment to the PSP is through an annual national examination that is common for several centrally recruited services, including the civil service and the foreign and the customs services. Because the PSP is a relatively well-paid and powerful service, it attracts students who rank highest in the selection process. Successful candidates receive two years of training at the Police Training College in Sihala, near Islamabad, and are then assigned to duty with one of the provincial forces.

The PSP is overwhelmingly male in composition, but the October 1993 return of Benazir Bhutto to power may result in some bold changes. In January 1994, Benazir announced the opening of Pakistan's first all-female police station. About fifty female officers of the Rawalpindi police station will supplement Punjab's provincial police force of 85,000 men. As part of her campaign for equal rights for women, Benazir also promised to place women in 10 percent of top police posts, to appoint women to the Supreme Court, and to establish special courts for cases against women.

The senior officer ranks in the police service are the inspector general, who heads a provincial police force, and a deputy inspector general, who directs the work of a division or "range," which coordinates police work within various parts of a province. There are also assistant inspectors general in each province. The principal focus of police activity is at the district level, which is headed by a superintendent, and the subdistrict level, usually under the direction of an assistant or deputy superintendent. The latter is not necessarily drawn from the Police Service of Pakistan. At each level, police officials report to the political or civil service heads of the respective administrative level; the inspectors general, however, have direct links to the federal Ministry of Interior. Larger municipalities have their own police forces, but these are responsible to the provincial structure of police authority.

The great majority of police personnel are assigned to subdistricts and police stations and are not at the officer level. Their ranks are inspector, sergeant, subinspector, assistant subinspector, head constable, and constable. As one descends the rank hierarchy, education levels, skills, and motivation decrease precipitously—even dramatically at the lower levels. Although constables are supposed to have a modest amount of education, their wages are comparable to those of an unskilled laborer (about US$40 per month), and a head constable—the height of aspiration for many policemen—is paid only at the level of a semiskilled worker.

Police in Pakistan are generally unarmed. For crowd control, police are trained to use a *lathi*, a five-foot wooden staff that may be weighted. *Lathi* are used either to hold crowds back or as clubs. Tear gas and firearms are available, and police formations hunting down armed bands of robbers, or *dacoits*, have adequate firepower available.

Character of the Security Forces

Independence had little impact on the police forces, which, like the military, simply switched their allegiance from the British to a new, indigenous regime. The great mass of police work remained the same, and the political role of the police in supporting the British soon found a parallel in independent Pakistan, as the regime was itself beset by political disturbances and extended the definition of crime to include such antistate activities as terrorism and subversion. Even though the forces of law and order had become the instruments of an indigenous government, any significant advantages that had accrued from the changeover have largely been dissipated.

Public attitudes toward the police, historically regarded with distrust and fear, have not changed; indeed, the police are held in low esteem. In British times, the Indian Police Service—the predecessor of the PSP—was nearly incorruptible and was fairly immune from political pressure that did not emanate from London. Since independence, however, politicization of the police has become increasingly pervasive. Corruption in the lower ranks has proliferated and permeated the PSP; in the frequent periods when Pakistan was under oppressive rule, the police were as repressive as they were in British times.

Police tactics in British India were never gentle, but in contemporary Pakistan, according to the *Herald*, a magazine published in Karachi, "The police have institutionalized torture to a point where it is viewed as the primary method of crime detention. Police torture has become so commonplace that it has slowly lost the capacity to shock and disgust." These charges were echoed by Amnesty International's especially bleak appraisal of Pakistan's human rights situation in its June 1992 "International News Release" report. The report, reflecting the law-and-order breakdown in Sindh and the government's reaction to it, stated that government opponents often are harassed, placed under arrest, and detained for unspecified periods of time. Scores of prisoners of conscience have been held for their political activities or religious beliefs. The practice of repeatedly bringing false charges against members of the political opposition is a widely used tactic in Pakistani politics and has been used to arrest thousands of opposition party activists. According to the United States Department of State's *Country Reports on Human Rights Practices for 1993*, there were no significant efforts in 1992 or 1993 to reform either the police or the judicial system, and authorities continued to be lax in their prosecution of abuses in these areas. Pakistani and international human rights organizations have demanded that steps be taken to reverse the trend by bringing torturers to justice and by taking such procedural steps as reducing the time prisoners spend in places of first arrest, where most torture takes place.

Torture is a particularly acute problem in cases in which the suspect is thought to have committed a political crime, but it is not uncommon in serious criminal cases. General police brutality in handling all suspects is routine. Police frequently act without warrants or other proper authorization, and individuals disappear into the criminal justice process for weeks before they can be found and, through writs of habeas corpus, be brought into regular judicial channels. Rape of prisoners, both male and female, is common. Prisoners often die in detention but are reported as killed in the course of armed encounters. Police also are alleged to extort money from families of prisoners under threat of ill treatment. The performance of the police and their failure to act against political groups that run their own torture machinery are especially bad in Sindh, but there is no Pakistani who looks on an encounter with the police with equanimity.

Amnesty International and other human rights groups welcomed the establishment in 1993 of a Human Rights Commission by the interim government of Moeen Qureshi and recommended to his successor, Benazir Bhutto, that the new government investigate past torture cases and enforce safeguards against the use of torture. Despite continued trouble in Sindh, observers have discerned what appears to be a genuine interest by the current government in addressing some of the more egregious human rights problems endemic in Pakistan today.

Crime

Part of the responsibility for the deterioration of police performance has been a widespread increase in the amount of crime. New kinds of crime have developed—especially those related to illegal drugs—and criminals have substantially greater firepower (see Narcotics, this ch.). Since the war in Afghanistan, Pakistan has been awash in guns. Kalashnikov automatic weapons have become ubiquitous and may be rented in Karachi on an hourly basis. In Karachi criminal violence, especially kidnapping for ransom and, in effect, open warfare among political groups, rendered the city so dangerous that in May 1992 the military had to be called in to launch Operation Cleanup to apprehend criminals and terrorists and to seize unauthorized weapons. Criminality extends into all levels of society. Known criminals have ties to political figures and are able to frustrate legitimate attempts to enforce law and order. In early 1994, the army was still actively involved in law enforcement in Sindh.

Crime statistics are reported but cannot be considered reliable. Throughout the 1980s, there appeared to be an incremental increase in the number of crimes reported each year. According to the *Pakistan Statistical Yearbook, 1991,* from 8,000 to 20,000 murders or attempted murders, 3,500 to 6,000 kidnappings or abductions, 100 to 600 robberies, and 120,000 to 250,000 other crimes were reported annually between 1981 and 1990.

Narcotics

Narcotics have become a multiple challenge to law enforcement authorities. In the late 1980s, Pakistan and Afghanistan exported nearly half the world's heroin, and, although their relative share declined somewhat thereafter, they remain among the world's major producers. Pakistan, especially under United States prodding, has attempted to cut back the cultivation of poppies, but the government's influence has not extended effectively into tribal areas. In addition, various political and economic forces have been brought to bear to keep narcotics police from pursuing their work too assiduously. In 1991 the Pakistan Narcotics Control Board—an organization that was supposed to have close ties to the United States Drug Enforcement Administration—was so riddled with corruption that its new director had to fire a majority of the staff. The vast profits generated by the narcotics industry not only had corrupted the enforcement authorities, including, it was rumored, some military units, but also had funded many other related crimes.

Courts and Criminal Procedure

Pakistan has an extensive penal code of some 511 articles, based on the Indian Penal Code of 1860, extensively amended during both the preindependence and the postindependence eras, and an equally extensive Code of Criminal Procedure. Numerous other laws relating to criminal behavior have also been enacted. Much of Pakistan's code deals with crimes against persons and property—including the crime of *dacoity* (robbery by armed gangs) and the misappropriation of property.

Pakistani courts can, and do, impose the death sentence, as well as imprisonment, forfeiture of property, and fines. Imprisonment is either "rigorous"—the equivalent of hard labor for up to fourteen years—or "simple"—confinement without hard labor. Another form is "banishment," which involves serving in a maximum security prison for periods of seven years to life. In February 1979, Zia ul-Haq issued new laws that punished rape, adultery, and the "carnal knowledge of a virgin" by stoning; first-time theft by amputation of the right hand; and consumption of alcohol by eighty lashes. Stoning and amputation, it should be noted, had not been carried out as of early 1994—at least not outside of the tribal area where tribal custom, rather than the Pakistani penal code, is the law of the land.

Article 45 of the constitution bestows on the president the right to grant a pardon or to remit, suspend, or commute any sentence passed by any court. There are also legal provisions for parole.

In principle, articles 9 through 13 of the constitution and provisions of the codes guarantee most of the same protections that are found in British and United States law. These rights include, for example, the right to bail and to counsel, the right of habeas corpus, the right of cross-examination, the right of representation, the right of being informed of charges, the right of appeal, and the right of the prevention of double jeopardy.

The code contains copious provisions for punishment of crimes against the state or against public tranquillity. These crimes extend to conspiracy against the government, incitement of hatred, contempt or disaffection toward a lawfully constituted authority, unlawful assembly, and public disturbances. Punishments range from terms of imprisonment to life in prison or death.

In most instances, a person apprehended appears before a magistrate or assistant commissioner, who decides on bail; the magistrate may also try less serious cases. Serious cases are tried before the sessions courts, which can award punishments up to death. The provincial high court hears appeals and automatically reviews any conviction involving the death penalty. The highest level of appeal for criminal cases is the federal Supreme Court.

Under the Suppression of Terrorist Activities (Special Courts) Act of 1975, the government established special courts to try cases involving crimes of a "terrorist" nature (for example, murder and sabotage). In 1987 another ordinance was passed establishing Speedy Trial Courts, which were empowered to hand down a death penalty after a three-day trial in which almost no adjournments were permitted. The jurisdictional authority of both kinds of courts was amended in 1988, but they have continued to operate. In 1991 the Speedy Trial Courts were given new jurisdictional authority to try particularly heinous crimes under the constitution's Twelfth Amendment. These courts handle cases that attract widespread public attention, especially those dealing with murder and drug offenses and in which the government believes that justice must be meted out rapidly. Only one appeal is permitted. In 1990 special "accountability" courts were set up to try individuals from Benazir's first administration who were charged with corruption. In late 1993, Benazir announced that her government would stop referring new cases to the special courts and would allow the constitutional authority for these courts to lapse in 1994.

The court system and the provisions of criminal law do not extend into the tribal areas along the Afghan border. These areas are administrated by political agents who work with tribal leaders to maintain law and order according to tribal standards.

Prisons

Under the 1962 West Pakistan Jail Warden Service Rules, prisons are managed by a career prison service, which sets qualifications for wardens, but these guidelines are reportedly not well observed. The service is organized by province under an inspector general of prisons. At division level, the senior official is the director of prisons, and there are jail superintendents at district and municipal levels. Simple lockups are maintained in some villages. There are some female wardens to handle female prisoners, but more are needed.

Prisons are not salubrious places. The common criminal from a poor background is assigned to Class C confinement, with virtually no amenities. Abuse is common. Prisoners of higher social status are assigned to Class B prisons, where conditions are better, and they can purchase better food and some amenities. Class A prisons are for "prominent" offenders. Conjugal visits are not the rule but are allowed in some cases.

Juveniles are handled separately in both the court system and in confinement. The criminal code prescribes special courts for offenders under age fifteen unless they are charged with a particularly serious offense and a high court orders that they be tried before a regular sessions court. There are juvenile wards in regular jails for offenders up to age twenty-one. In addition, a few reform institutions for boys between eleven and twenty years of age attempt to rehabilitate young offenders.

Islamic Provisions

The process of Islamization that has taken place in Pakistan, especially in the Zia years, has raised considerable concern about criminal law. In February 1979, President Zia promulgated a new legal code for Pakistan based on Islamic law and established the Federal Shariat Court to hear appeals arising from the new code. The Federal Shariat Court also has other extensive powers (see Role of Islam, ch. 4). It lies within the discretion of the court of first instance to decide whether to try a case under civil or sharia law. If the latter, then the appeals process goes to the Federal Shariat Court, rather than to the high courts.

Sharia law was not intended to replace the criminal code but to bring specific parts of it into accordance with the Quran and the sharia. Its most notable provisions are contained in the *hudood* (sing., *hadd*) ordinances promulgated in 1979. The first ordinance deals with offenses against property, the second with *zina* (adultery) and *zina-bil-jabr* (rape), the third with *qazf* (false accusation of *zina*), and the fourth with prohibition of alcoholic beverages. Under the ordinances, there are two levels of cases: *hudood* cases, which have particularly strict Islamic evidentiary requirements and call for specific "Islamic" punishments; and *tazir* cases, where the evidence requirements are less strict and the punishments less draconian.

A later decision by the Federal Shariat Court has made defiling the name of the Prophet Muhammad punishable by a mandatory death penalty. This decision has raised concerns in Pakistan's small Christian community and especially among the badly persecuted Ahmadiyya religious minority. Orthodox Pakistani Muslims consider Ahmadiyyas heretical, and the group has been prohibited from asserting any claim to being Muslim—even the use of everyday Islamic greetings (see Non-Muslim Minorities, ch. 2).

As a *hadd* crime, rape is punishable by hanging; adultery and fornication, as well as *qazf*, by stoning to death. Crimes against property of substantial value call for amputation of hands or feet. Public drunkenness and, in the case of Muslims, any consumption of alcohol, are punishable by flogging.

For the most part, Islamic punishments have not been carried out, the sole exception being flogging, which has been imposed primarily for *tazir* crimes, as well as for narcotics-related crimes. In addition, alleged political crimes also resulted in flogging during the last period of martial law (1977–85). *Hudood* sentences of amputation have been passed but either have been reversed on appeal or have not been carried out. Occasional stonings for adultery have always taken place in tribal and other rural areas, but no sentence of stoning under the 1979 *hudood* laws has been carried out.

The Federal Shariat Court has been involved mainly with noncriminal matters, aside from the review of *hudood* convictions, which in most cases the Federal Shariat Court has reversed. In other matters, such as provision of equal treatment under the law and requirement for a standard of evidence, its application of Islamic principles has even served as a liberalizing factor, including in the military justice system. Overall, as of early 1994 Islamic legal intrusions have had only a limited effect on criminal law, although the potential for growth is there, especially under the more activist leadership that the Federal Shariat Court has shown since 1990.

Among the more notable peculiarities of the new enactments is the issue of rape. On the one hand, the crime is rarely proven because four adult Muslim males of good reputation must appear as witness to the act. If the charge fails, then the woman who has brought it can be punished for false accusation or, more commonly, for adultery herself because through her charge she has admitted an illicit sexual act. In 1991 two-thirds (some 2,000) of the women imprisoned in Pakistan were being held on such charges. This treatment, of course, has a very chilling effect on women who are raped.

Laws passed in the 1980s give the victim of a murder or other violence, or the victim's heirs, the right to inflict an equivalent harm. At the same time, however, there is a legal alternative in payment of blood money, which enables wealthy Pakistanis to avoid punishment by paying money. Under the law, only half of the amount must be paid if the victim is female.

In 1984 parts of the Indian Evidence Act of 1872 were changed with much fanfare to meet Islamic criteria, but there was little real change. Demands by Islamic enthusiasts that the testimony of two women be considered the equivalent of that of one man were met only symbolically. The *hudood* ordinances, however, do contain evidential provisions that discriminate sharply against women.

In May 1991, the National Assembly passed the Shariat Bill, intended to bring the entire justice system into accord with Islamic norms. These norms had not yet been established, and, as of early 1994, no serious attempt had been made to draft and pass the laws and constitutional amendments that would be required. Many observers believed that the act was meant as an empty sop to Islamist extremists, but it seemed likely that there would be constant pressure to implement the act more fully.

Emergency Provisions

The British colonial constitutional provisions and penal codes gave the authorities ample scope for overriding regular legal procedures in the case of persons suspected of political agitation or threats to the public order. These provisions and codes were perpetuated and strengthened in Pakistan. The Security of Pakistan Act empowers authorities to move against any person "acting in a manner prejudicial to the defence, external affairs and security of Pakistan or the maintenance of public order." Under the act, persons may be detained, their business activities, employment, or movements may be restricted, and they may be required to report regularly to a magistrate.

Article 144 of the Code of Criminal Procedure allows the government to act preventively if it perceives the danger of public disorder. A magistrate may prohibit meetings of five or more persons, forbid the carrying of firearms, and impose "preventive detention" on anybody thought likely to disturb public order. Although a detainee is entitled to be informed of the reason for his detention and to a fair review of the case, these restrictions are in practice easy to circumvent, and the constitution specifically denies such detainees procedural guarantees. The government, especially in periods of martial law, has used Section 144 frequently when feeling its position could be threatened by demonstrations and public opposition to its policies; Section 144's provisions have also been used, however, to contain disorder that is not political.

In 1991 Pakistan adopted the Terrorist Affected Areas (Special Courts) Ordinance, which extends the authority of Speedy Trial Courts and gives the police expanded powers to use weapons. The Maintenance of Public Order Act allows detention without trial for three months, extendable to twelve months in some cases. This act has been used to silence political opponents of the government.

Although persons accused of crimes are entitled to bail, there have been a number of restrictions placed on this right in cases involving alleged threats to national security. In late 1992, the law requiring automatic bail for anyone in jail for two years who had not yet been convicted was rescinded, and the high courts were prohibited from hearing bail applications from persons facing trial in the special courts set up in 1975 to try terrorists. A Pakistani jurist commented: "The government can now arrest anyone, call him a terrorist, and keep him in prison indefinitely."

Subversion and Civil Unrest

Internal threats to Pakistan come from several sources. The greatest danger to the democratic constitutional structure is posed by the recurrent intervention in the government of the Pakistani military and, since the Zia years, by the president who, under the controversial Eighth Amendment to the constitution, is empowered to arbitrarily dismiss the prime minister and National Assembly as well as the provisional governors. It could be argued that the military has only intervened when the political situation has deteriorated hopelessly and that the threat is in fact from much more deep-seated problems.

Another danger is the problem of ethnic unrest. Punjab, with almost 60 percent of the population, dominates almost all aspects of national life. This fact is resented by smaller ethnic groups, all of whom have at one time been actively dissident.

For the most part, with the exception of Sindh, the situation was quiet in the early 1990s. Sparsely settled Balochistan required an extensive pacification campaign by the army from 1973 to 1977 as Baloch fought an insurgency fueled by economic grievances and a desire for regional autonomy. Of special concern to Baloch dissidents was the influx of Punjabi settlers into their resource-rich but sparsely populated lands. Soviet assistance to Baloch dissidents was alleged. During the government of Zulfiqar Ali Bhutto, hostilities in Balochistan were protracted, but the succeeding regime of Zia ul-Haq relied successfully on an economic rather than military approach in Balochistan, and was, in large part, able to diffuse the situation. The potential for unrest remains, however, because Baloch feel threatened by the growing numbers of non-Baloch moving into the province. The North-West Frontier Province has long been restive and subject to Kabul's blandishments on the basis of shared Pakhtun identity, but Afghanistan no longer offers a feasible alternative, and the Afghan Pakhtun tribal groups have benefitted from Pakistan's modest prosperity. Some Kashmiris in Pakistani-held Azad (Free) Kashmir probably envision a future independent of Pakistan, but their attentions have been absorbed by the problems of Indian-held Kashmir.

In the early 1990s, the principal challenge came from Sindh, Pakistan's second most populous province, where the indigenous population was under increasing pressure from non-Sindhis who had migrated there. Based on their ethnic identity, Sindhis have formed several political movements, notably the Jaye Sindh, which the government perceived as threatening to Pakistan's unity. Islamabad also claimed that these groups were receiving help from India in their quest to establish a "Sindhudesh," or independent homeland for Sindhis. The *muhajir* (immigrants from India and their descendants) minority in Sindh, which dominates Karachi, has been in sharp conflict with the Sindhis and other ethnic groups. Further, large numbers of kidnapping and bombings in Sindh—the virtual breakdown of law and order—necessitated the imposition of army rule in 1992 (see Prospects for Social Cohesion, ch. 2).

An additional source of unrest has been the rampant gun culture and spread of narcotics-based corruption, particularly since the war in Afghanistan. Pakistanis have always been well armed, but the availability of cheap, modern weapons has meant that criminals and private citizens have significant firepower at their disposal. Because most violence is criminal or anomic, it does not pose a direct threat to the state, but should the crisis of governability in Sindh spread more broadly, it could place unbearable stress on the nation.

In the early 1990s, foreign-sponsored subversion in Pakistan appeared to be insignificant. The Afghans were too preoccupied with their own concerns to agitate along the frontier, and the Soviet Union, which had long had adversarial relations with Pakistan, had fragmented into a number of self-absorbed states occupied by the struggle for survival in a new postcommunist world. India had ties to dissident groups in Sindh and perhaps elsewhere; these, however, were probably maintained in order to remind Pakistan that its involvement with Punjabi Sikh and Kashmiri Muslim insurgents in India was not cost-free. In its more youthfully exuberant days, the Islamic regime in Iran was involved in subversive support of Shia elements in Pakistan, but such activity was no longer a significant factor.

During the Zia period, a group called Al-Zulfiqar, operating from Damascus and Kabul and seeking to destabilize the government through terrorist actions, hijacked an aircraft in 1981. Murtaza Bhutto, a son of Zulfiqar Ali Bhutto, was involved, and Al-Zulfiqar claimed to have some relationship to the Pakistan People's Party (PPP), which was totally denied by the PPP. Although authorities have reported continued activity by Al-Zulfiqar, its existence is shadowy at best, and with the return of democratic rule, its activities have been insignificant. There are no other known, organized subversive groups that threaten the government in any serious way.

Pakistan's attitude toward terrorism is somewhat more ambivalent than that of most other countries. On the one hand, Al-Zulfiqar demonstrated to Pakistan the importance of international cooperation in combatting international terrorism as manifested in airplane hijackings and bombings. On the other hand, however, Pakistan has had no qualms about supporting insurgents in India, some of whom are engaged in activities that can only be described as terrorist.

In January 1993, the United States warned Pakistan that it was under "active continuing review" for possible inclusion on the Department of State list of terrorist countries for its alleged support of terrorist activities in India. By July, however, the

United States had withdrawn its threat, having determined that Pakistan had implemented "a policy for ending official support for terrorism in India."

As Pakistan approached the end of its first half-century of existence, its security problems had changed, yet were in many ways the same. The global setting had altered radically, but the enmity with India remained a constant, although it had gained in predictability and, probably, stability. Subversion was still a potential rather than an active threat. Problems of law and order were more acute, but the means of dealing with them had not changed greatly. Rather, Pakistan's security problems were rooted in its own polity and society. Repeated political collapse, corruption, inability to define its ethnic and religious identities, and failure to meet the needs of the people—these are challenges that could eviscerate a state even with the most capable military machine and efficient security apparatus. Pakistan, as it considers its continuing security dilemma and the international image it wishes to project, must energetically confront and deal with these harsh realities.

* * *

The government of Pakistan goes to considerable lengths to protect dissemination of information about its armed forces, making research on the military difficult. One of the few officially sanctioned publications is *Defenders of Pakistan* by Brian Tetley, essentially a coffee-table book but with useful information on the role, functions, and organization of the armed forces. For early history, Fazl Muqeem Khan's *The Story of the Pakistan Army* remains an indispensable source. Research by United States and Pakistani scholars during the 1980s has considerably enriched the understanding of the military. The historical picture is amplified by the two volumes of Shaukat Riza's *The Pakistan Army* and Pervaiz Iqbal Cheema's *Pakistan's Defence Policy, 1947–58.* Hasan-Askari Rizvi has contributed two excellent studies—*The Military and Politics in Pakistan* and *Pakistan and the Geostrategic Environment,* both of which cover the modern period, as does Robert G. Wirsing's *Pakistan's Security under Zia, 1977–1988.* Foremost in the analytical field is Stephen P. Cohen's *The Pakistan Army.* The most current information is available from the annual International Institute for Strategic Studies' *The Military Balance* and *Jane's Defence Weekly,* as well as several publications authored by Richard P. Cronin and Barbara Leitch LePoer of the Congressional Research Service of the Library of Congress. Of these, *South Asia: U.S. Interests and Policy Issues* is particularly useful. (For further information and complete citations, see Bibliography.)

Appendix

Table

Table 1. Metric Conversion Coefficients and Factors

When you know	Multiply by	To find
Millimeters	0.04	inches
Centimeters	0.39	inches
Meters	3.3	feet
Kilometers	0.62	miles
Hectares	2.47	acres
Square kilometers	0.39	square miles
Cubic meters	35.3	cubic feet
Liters	0.26	gallons
Kilograms	2.2	pounds
Metric tons	0.98	long tons
	1.1	short tons
	2,204.0	pounds
Degrees Celsius (Centigrade)	1.8 and add 32	degrees Fahrenheit

Table 2. Population Growth, Selected Years, 1951–93

Year	Population[1] (in millions)	Average Annual Growth Rate
1951	33.7	n.a.[2]
1961	42.9	2.3
1971	65.2	3.7
1981	84.2	3.1
1987	100.7	3.1
1992	118.0	3.1
1993	123.4	3.1

[1] Estimated.
[2] n.a.—not available.

Source: Based on information from Pakistan, Planning Commission, *Seventh Five-Year Plan, 1988–93; and Perspective Plan, 1988–2003,* Islamabad, 1988; and World Bank, *World Development Report, 1992,* New York, 1992, 268.

Table 3. Gross Domestic Product by Sector, Selected Fiscal Years, 1982–93
(in percentages at current factor cost)

Sector	1982	1987	1992[1]	1993[1]
Agriculture, forestry, and fishing	31.6	26.3	25.6	25.0
Mining and quarrying	0.4	0.7	0.7	0.7
Manufacturing	15.1	16.7	17.5	17.3
Utilities	2.2	2.3	3.3	3.7
Construction	4.5	4.4	4.2	4.2
Wholesale and retail trade	15.1	15.7	17.0	16.1
Transportation and communications	9.4	8.7	8.4	10.3
Banking and insurance	2.5	3.2	3.1	2.9
Ownership of dwellings	4.5	4.9	4.4	4.4
Public administration and defense	7.3	9.9	8.4	7.8
Other services	7.3	7.4	7.5	7.6
TOTAL[2]	100.0	100.0	100.0	100.0

[1] Provisional.
[2] Figures may not add to totals because of rounding.

Source: Based on information from Economist Intelligence Unit, *Country Profile: Pakistan, Afghanistan, 1993–94*, London, 1993, 21; and Pakistan, Federal Bureau of Statistics, Statistics Division, *Pakistan Statistical Yearbook, 1991*, Karachi, 1991, 473–74.

Table 4. Government Budget, Fiscal Years 1990–93[1]
(in billions of rupees)[2]

	1990	1991	1992[3]	1993[4]
Revenues				
Tax revenues				
Income and corporation taxes	14.3	19.1	25.9	31.3
Property taxes	1.4	1.7	2.1	3.9
Excise duties	23.3	25.0	32.3	44.3
Sales taxes	15.6	16.9	21.5	26.9
Taxes on international trade	50.7	50.5	62.5	71.4
Other	14.1	16.4	22.8	26.0
Total tax revenues	119.4	129.6	167.2	203.8
Nontax revenues	39.4	34.2	55.5	58.0
Total revenues	158.8	163.9	222.6	261.9
(of which, provincial revenues)	6.6	7.1	15.7	18.9
Expenditures				
Current expenditures				
Defense	58.7	64.6	75.8	82.2
Interest on debt	46.7	50.0	63.6	75.5
Subsidies	9.0	10.7	10.1	7.3
Other	51.1	70.3	82.9	92.3
Total current expenditures	165.6	195.7	232.4	257.3
Development expenditures	56.1	65.3	83.2	72.3
Total expenditures	221.6	261.0	315.6	329.7
Income from autonomous agencies	6.8	7.9	14.3	3.2
Budget deficit	56.1	89.2	78.7	64.6
Deficit financed by				
External (net)	22.9	22.1	21.8	17.1
Domestic nonbank	29.6	23.7	-0.6	26.2
Domestic banks	3.5	43.4	57.5	21.3

[1] Includes federal aid to provincial governments. Figures may not add to totals because of rounding.
[2] For value of the rupee—see Glossary.
[3] Provisional.
[4] Proposed.

Source: Based on information from Pakistan, Ministry of Finance, *Economic Survey: Statistical Supplement, 1991–92,* Islamabad, 1992, 162–64.

Table 5. Balance of Trade, Selected Fiscal Years, 1980–92 (in billions of rupees) [1]

Year	Exports	Imports	Balance
1980	23.4	46.9	-23.5
1985	38.0	89.8	-51.8
1990	106.5	148.9	-42.4
1991	138.3	171.1	-32.8
1992[2]	171.7	229.9	-58.2

[1] For value of the rupee—see Glossary.
[2] Provisional.

Source: Based on information from Pakistan, Ministry of Finance, *Economic Survey: Statistical Supplement, 1991–92,* Islamabad, 1992, 190.

Table 6. Composition of Imports, Fiscal Years 1989–92 (in millions of rupees) [1]

Commodity	1989	1990	1991	1992[2]
Chemicals	13,046	15,259	15,448	21,997
Drugs and medicines	3,318	3,723	4,408	5,184
Dyes and colors	1,419	1,868	2,136	2,945
Chemical fertilizers	3,534	4,437	5,911	6,367
Electrical goods	4,962	4,259	4,929	7,469
Nonelectrical machinery	26,597	25,438	30,195	54,527
Transportation equipment	8,403	10,119	11,443	20,638
Paper products	2,734	2,876	3,216	4,027
Iron and steel	7,131	6,993	7,100	10,236
Nonferrous metals	2,018	2,594	2,110	2,784
Oil and oil products	18,509	24,937	37,823	34,406
Edible oils	8,576	8,262	9,020	10,025
Grains, pulses, and flour	8,598	9,241	3,855	9,979
Other	26,996	28,847	38,449	39,305
TOTAL	135,841	148,853	176,043	229,889

[1] For value of the rupee—see Glossary.
[2] Provisional.

Source: Based on information from Pakistan, Ministry of Finance, *Economic Survey: Statistical Supplement, 1991–92,* Islamabad, 1992, 203.

Table 7. Composition of Exports, Fiscal Years 1989–92 (in millions of rupees)[1]

Commodity	1989	1990	1991	1992[2]
Fish products	2,096	2,024	2,575	2,852
Rice	5,967	5,144	7,848	10,340
Raw cotton	18,032	9,550	9,553	12,944
Cotton waste	240	597	1,255	1,482
Cotton yarn	11,645	17,917	26,675	29,170
Cotton cloth	8,947	12,000	15,199	20,372
Leather	4,702	6,002	6,184	5,991
Oil and oil products	352	235	2,228	2,048
Synthetic textiles	2,240	4,556	7,807	10,430
Footwear	365	504	724	997
Ready-made garments	9,692	14,341	18,666	25,823
Surgical instruments	1,221	1,502	1,901	2,253
Carpets	4,451	4,923	5,003	5,709
Sporting goods	1,369	2,311	3,099	3,515
Other	18,864	24,863	30,792	37,829
TOTAL	90,183	106,469	139,509	171,755

[1] For value of the rupee—see Glossary.
[2] Provisional.

Source: Based on information from Pakistan, Ministry of Finance, *Economic Survey: Statistical Supplement, 1991–92,* Islamabad, 1992, 194–97.

Table 8. Balance of Payments, Fiscal Years 1988–92 (in millions of United States dollars at current prices)

	1988	1989	1990	1991	1992[1]
Exports	4,362	4,634	4,926	5,902	6,884
Imports	-6,919	-7,207	-7,411	-8,385	-9,095
Invisibles (net)	875	639	594	312	-325
Current account balance	-1,682	-1,934	-1,891	-2,171	-2,536
Private capital (net)	330	328	473	506	1,730
Public capital (net)	1,242	1,659	1,840	1,737	929
Capital account balance	1,572	1,987	2,313	2,243	2,659
Errors and omissions (net)	-30	-42	-45	-66	74
Change in reserves (minus sign indicates increase)	140	-11	-377	-6	-197

[1] Provisional.

Source: Based on information from Pakistan, Ministry of Finance, *Economic Survey: Statistical Supplement, 1991–92,* Islamabad, 1992, 189.

Table 9. Estimated Labor Force by Sector, Fiscal Years 1981, 1991, and 1992
(in thousands)

Sector	1981	1991	1992
Agriculture	13,010	16,260	16,670
Mining and manufacturing	3,480	4,080	4,210
Construction	1,200	2,030	2,090
Electric power and gas	230	190	190
Transportation and communications	1,150	1,550	1,600
Trade	2,840	3,790	3,900
Other services	2,790	3,880	4,010
Other	950	1,030	1,150
TOTAL	25,650	32,810	33,820

Source: Based on information from Pakistan, Ministry of Finance, *Economic Survey: Statistical Supplement, 1991–92,* Islamabad, 1992, 30.

Table 10. Area of Major Crops, Selected Fiscal Years, 1961–92
(in thousands of hectares)

Crop	1961	1981	1991	1992[1]
Wheat	4,639	6,984	7,911	7,823
Rice	1,181	1,933	2,113	2,097
Corn	480	769	845	847
Chickpeas	1,106	843	1,092	1,021
Sugarcane	388	825	884	880
Cotton	1,293	2,108	2,662	2,836

[1] Provisional.

Source: Based on information from Pakistan, Ministry of Finance, *Economic Survey: Statistical Supplement, 1991–92,* Islamabad, 1992, 63.

Table 11. Production of Major Crops, Selected Fiscal Years, 1961–92
(in thousands of tons)

Crop	1961	1981	1991	1992[1]
Wheat	3,814	11,475	14,565	14,694
Rice	1,030	3,123	3,261	3,243
Corn	439	970	1,185	1,204
Chickpeas	610	337	531	499
Sugarcane	11,641	32,359	35,989	35,658
Cotton	301	715	1,637	2,181

[1] Provisional.

Source: Based on information from Pakistan, Ministry of Finance, *Economic Survey: Statistical Supplement, 1991–92,* Islamabad, 1992, 64.

Table 12. Average Growth Rate of Selected Industrial Products, Fiscal Years 1988–92
(in percentage change from previous year)

Product	1988	1989	1990	1991	1992[1]
Cotton yarn	16.83	10.64	20.28	14.22	11.30
Cotton cloth	18.30	-4.18	9.26	-0.65	5.60
Jute goods	-1.85	-6.82	-7.80	3.24	3.64
Vegetable ghee	14.45	28.55	7.37	3.85	10.71
Cigarettes	1.92	-22.43	2.26	-0.70	-4.98
Fertilizers	-2.42	2.52	3.72	-2.70	-5.28
Cement	8.67	0.75	5.09	4.63	6.90
Soda ash	2.92	7.61	3.60	5.55	24.02
Caustic soda	11.66	8.48	11.28	6.08	4.33

[1] Provisional.

Source: Based on information from Pakistan, Ministry of Finance, *Economic Survey: Statistical Supplement, 1991–92,* Islamabad, 1992, 107.

Table 13. Heads of State and Heads of Government, 1947–94

Leader	Position	Term of Office[1]
Mohammad Ali Jinnah	Governor General	August 1947–September 1948
Liaquat Ali Khan	Prime Minister	August 1947–October 1951
Khwaja Nazimuddin	Governor General	September 1948–October 1951
Ghulam Mohammad	Governor General	October 1951–August 1955
Khwaja Nazimuddin	Prime Minister	October 1951–April 1953
Mohammad Ali Bogra	Prime Minister	April 1953–August 1955
Iskander Mirza	Governor General/President	August 1955–October 1958
Chaudhuri Mohammad Ali	Prime Minister	August 1955–September 1956
H.S. Suhrawardy	Prime Minister	September 1956–October 1957
I.I. Chundrigar	Prime Minister	October–December 1957
Firoz Khan Noon	Prime Minister	December 1957–October 1958
Mohammad Ayub Khan	CMLA/President[2]	October 1958–March 1969
Agha Mohammad Yahya Khan	CMLA/President	March 1969–December 1971
Zulfiqar Ali Bhutto	CMLA/President/Prime Minister	December 1971–July 1977
Fazal Elahi Chaudhry	President	August 1973–September 1978
Mohammad Zia ul-Haq ...	CMLA/President	July 1977–August 1988
Mohammad Khan Junejo ..	Prime Minister	March 1985–May 1988
Ghulam Ishaq Khan	President	August 1988–July 1993
Benazir Bhutto	Prime Minister	December 1988–August 1990
Ghulam Mustapha Jatoi	Prime Minister (caretaker)	August–November 1990
Mian Nawaz Sharif	Prime Minister	November 1990–April 1993
Balakh Sher Mazari	Prime Minister (caretaker)	April–May 1993
Mian Nawaz Sharif	Prime Minister	May–July 1993
Wassim Sajjad	President (caretaker)	July–November 1993
Moeen Qureshi	Prime Minister (caretaker)	July–October 1993
Benazir Bhutto	Prime Minister	October 1993–
Farooq Leghari	President	November 1993–

[1] When a head of state or head of government held more than one position, not all offices were for exactly the same term. Dates shown are for the longest period a leader was in power. The title of the head of state was changed from governor general to president under the 1956 constitution.

[2] CMLA—chief martial law administrator.

Table 14. Order of Battle and Major Equipment of Ground Forces, 1994

		Organization or Equipment
Personnel	520,000	
Military units ..	9	Corps headquarters
	1	Area command (division)
	2	Armored divisions
	19	Infantry divisions
	7	Independent armored brigades
	9	Independent infantry brigades
	9	Corps artillery brigades (2 more forming)
	1	Air defense command (3 air defense groups; 8 brigades)
	7	Engineering brigades
	3	Armed reconnaissance regiments
	1	Special forces group (3 battalions)
	7	Aircraft squadrons
	8	Helicopter squadrons
	1	Independent observation flight
Equipment	1,950+	Tanks
	820	Armored personnel carriers
	1,566	Towed artillery
	240	Self-propelled artillery
	45	Multiple rocket launchers
	725	Mortars
	18	Surface-to-surface missiles
	800	Antitank guided weapons
	850	Surface-to-air missiles

Source: Based on information from *The Military Balance, 1994–1995*, London, 1994, 159–61.

Table 15. Order of Battle and Major Equipment of Naval Forces, 1994

		Organization or Equipment
Personnel	22,000[1]	
Military units ...	4	Commands, including 1 fleet headquarters
Equipment	6	Submarines
	3	Destroyers
	10	Frigates
	13	Patrol and coastal combatant craft
	4	Inshore craft
	3	Mine warfare craft
	3	Support and miscellaneous
	4	SA–316B (antisubmarine warfare) helicopters
	6	Sea King Mk 45 (antisubmarine warfare) helicopters
	6	Lynx HAS MK–3 (antisubmarine warfare) helicopters
	4	Atlantic aircraft (operated by air force)

[1] Includes Naval Air Arm and Maritime Security Agency.

Source: Based on information from *The Military Balance, 1994–1995*, London, 1994, 159–61.

Table 16. Order of Battle and Major Equipment of Air Force, 1994

		Organization or Equipment
Personnel	45,000	
Military units	7	Fighter/ground attack squadrons
	10	Fighter squadrons
	1	Reconnaissance squadron
	12	Transport squadrons
	1	Helicopter search-and-rescue squadron
	1	Helicopter transport squadron
	7	Air defense surface-to-air batteries
	1	Antisubmarine warfare/maritime reconnaissance squadron
Equipment		
Fighter/ground attack aircraft	100	J–6/JJ–6
	34	F–16
	80	J–7
	50	Q–5
	30	Mirage III–O
	15	Mirage III–EP

Table 16. Order of Battle and Major Equipment of Air Force, 1994

		Organization or Equipment
	3	Mirage III–DP
	58	Mirage–5
Transports	12	C–130
	1	L–12
	3	Boeing 707
	3	Falcon 20
	2	F–27–200
	2	Beech
Search and rescue	6	SA–319
Reconnaissance	12	Combat-capable Mirage III–RP
Helicopters (transport) ...	12	SA–316
	4	SA–321
	12	SA–315 B Lama
Training	12	CJ–6
	30	JJ–5
	24	Mashshaq
	6	MiG–15UTI
	10	T–33A
	44	T–37BC

Source: Based on information from *The Military Balance, 1994–1995*, London, 1994, 159–61.

Bibliography

Chapter 1

Abbott, Freeland. *Islam and Pakistan.* Ithaca: Cornell University Press, 1968.

Abbott, Freeland. "Pakistan and the Secular State." Pages 352–70 in Donald E. Smith, ed., *South Asian Politics and Religion.* Princeton: Princeton University Press, 1966.

Adams, Charles J. "The Ideology of Mawlana Maududi." Pages 371–97 in Donald E. Smith, ed., *South Asian Politics and Religion.* Princeton: Princeton University Press, 1966.

Afzal, M. Rafique. *Political Parties in Pakistan, 1947–1958.* Islamabad: National Commission on Historical and Cultural Research, 1976.

Ahmad, Aziz. *An Intellectual History of Islam in India.* Chicago: Aldine, 1969.

Ahmad, Aziz. *Islamic Modernism in India and Pakistan, 1857–1964.* New York: Oxford University Press, 1964.

Ahmad, Manzooruddin, ed. *Contemporary Pakistan: Politics, Economy, and Society.* Durham, North Carolina: Carolina Academic Press, 1980.

Ahmad, Mumtaz. "Pakistan." Pages 229–46 in Shireen T. Hunter, ed., *The Politics of Islamic Revivalism.* Bloomington: Indiana University Press, 1988.

Ahmad, Mushtaq. *Government and Politics in Pakistan.* New York: Praeger, 1963.

Ahmed, Akbar S. "A Third Encounter of a Close Kind," *History Today* [London], 39, November 1989, 49.

Ali, Tariq. *Can Pakistan Survive?* New York: Penguin, 1983.

Ali, Tariq. *Military Rule or People's Power?* London: Cape, 1970.

Asghar Khan, Muhammad. *Generals in Politics: Pakistan, 1958–1982.* New Delhi: Vikas, 1983.

Ayub Khan, Mohammad. *Friends Not Masters: A Political Autobiography.* New York: Oxford University Press, 1967.

Aziz, K.K. *The Making of Pakistan: A Study in Nationalism.* London: Chatto and Windus, 1967.

Aziz, K.K. *Party Politics in Pakistan, 1947–1958.* Islamabad: National Commission on Historical and Cultural Research, 1976.

Bahadur, Lal. *The Muslim League: Its History, Activities, and Achievements.* Lahore: Book Traders, 1979.

Basham, A.L. *The Wonder That Was India.* New York: Grove Press, 1954.

Baxter, Craig. *Bangladesh: A New Nation in an Old Setting.* Boulder, Colorado: Westview Press, 1984.

Baxter, Craig. "India and Pakistan." Pages 267–96 in Gregory Henderson, Richard Ned Lebow, and John G. Stoessinger, eds., *Divided Nations in a Divided World.* New York: McKay, 1974.

Baxter, Craig. "Pakistan and Bangladesh." Pages 209–62 in Frederick L. Shiels, ed., *Ethnic Separatism and World Politics.* Lanham, Maryland: University Press of America, 1984.

Baxter, Craig. "Pakistan Votes—1970," *Asian Survey,* 11, No. 3, March 1971.

Baxter, Craig. "The United States and Pakistan: The Zia Era and the Afghan Connection." Pages 479–506 in Daniel Pipes and Adam Garfinkle, eds., *Friendly Tyrants: An American Dilemma.* New York: St. Martin's Press, 1991.

Baxter, Craig. *Zia's Pakistan: Politics and Stability in a Frontline State.* Boulder, Colorado: Westview Press, 1985.

Baxter, Craig, and Syed Razi Wasti, eds. *Pakistan Authoritarianism in the 1980s.* Lahore: Vanguard, 1991.

Bhattacharya, Sachchidananda. *A Dictionary of Indian History.* Calcutta: Calcutta University, 1967.

Bhutto, Zulfikar Ali. *The Great Tragedy.* Karachi: Pakistan People's Party, 1971.

Bhutto, Zulfikar Ali. *The Myth of Independence.* Karachi: Oxford University Press, 1969.

Binder, Leonard. *Religion and Politics in Pakistan.* Berkeley: University of California Press, 1963.

Bokhari, Imtiaz H., and Thomas Perry Thornton. *The 1972 Simla Agreement: An Asymmetrical Negotiation.* Washington: Foreign Policy Institute, Johns Hopkins University, 1988.

Braibanti, Ralph J.D. *Evolution of Pakistan's Administrative System: The Collected Papers of Ralph Braibanti.* Ed., Jameelur Rehman

Khan. Islamabad: Pakistan Public Administration Research Centre, 1987.

Brice, William C., ed. *An Historical Atlas of Islam.* Leiden: Brill, 1981.

Burke, S.M. *Mainsprings of Indian and Pakistani Foreign Policies.* Minneapolis: University of Minnesota Press, 1974.

Burke, S.M. *Pakistan's Foreign Policy: An Historical Analysis.* London: Oxford University Press, 1973.

Burki, Shahid Javed. *Historical Dictionary of Pakistan.* Metuchen, New Jersey: Scarecrow Press, 1991.

Burki, Shahid Javed. *Pakistan: A Nation in the Making.* Boulder, Colorado: Westview Press, 1986.

Burki, Shahid Javed. *Pakistan under Bhutto, 1971–1977.* (2d ed.) London: Macmillan, 1988.

Burki, Shahid Javed, and Craig Baxter. *Pakistan under the Military: Eleven Years of Zia ul-Haq.* Boulder, Colorado: Westview Press, 1991.

Callard, Keith. *Pakistan: A Political Study.* London: Allen and Unwin, 1957.

Callard, Keith. *Pakistan's Foreign Policy: An Interpretation.* New York: Institute of Pacific Relations, 1959.

Callard, Keith. *Political Forces in Pakistan, 1947–1959.* New York: Institute of Pacific Relations, 1959.

Case, Margaret H. *South Asia History, 1750–1950: A Guide to Periodicals, Dissertations, and Newspapers.* Princeton: Princeton University Press, 1968.

Chopra, Pran, ed. *Contemporary Pakistan: New Aims and Images.* New Delhi: Vikas, 1983.

Choudhury, G.W. *Constitutional Development in Pakistan.* (2d ed.) Vancouver: Publications Centre, University of British Columbia, 1969.

Choudhury, G.W. *The Last Days of United Pakistan.* Bloomington: Indiana University Press, 1975.

Cohen, Stephen P. *The Pakistan Army.* Berkeley: University of California Press, 1984.

Coupland, Reginald. *The Future of India.* London: Oxford University Press, 1944.

Coupland, Reginald. *Indian Politics, 1936–1942.* London: Oxford University Press, 1943.

Coupland, Reginald. *The Indian Problem, 1833–1935.* London: Oxford University Press, 1942.

Davies, C. Collin. *An Historical Atlas of the Indian Peninsula.* London: Oxford University Press, 1959.

Embree, Ainslie, ed. *Pakistan's Western Borderlands.* Durham, North Carolina: Carolina Academic Press, 1978.

Faruki, Kamal A. "Pakistan: Islamic Government and Society." Pages 53–78 in John L. Esposito, ed., *Islam in Asia.* New York: Oxford University Press, 1987.

Feldman, Herbert. *The End and the Beginning: Pakistan, 1969–1972.* London: Oxford University Press, 1972.

Feldman, Herbert. *From Crisis to Crisis: Pakistan, 1962–1969.* London: Oxford University Press, 1972.

Feldman, Herbert. *Revolution in Pakistan: A Study of the Martial Law Administration.* Karachi: Oxford University Press, 1967.

Gascoigne, Bamber. *The Great Moghuls.* London: Jonathan Cape, 1971.

Gilmartin, David. *Empire and Islam: Punjab and the Making of Pakistan.* Berkeley: University of California Press, 1988.

Gupta, Sisir. *Kashmir: A Study in India-Pakistan Relations.* Bombay: Asia Publishing House, 1966.

Hamid, Abdul. *Muslim Separatism in India.* Karachi: Oxford University Press, 1971.

Haq, M.U. *Muslim Politics in Modern India.* Meerut, India: Meenakshi, 1970.

Hardy, Peter. *The Muslims of British India.* Cambridge: Cambridge University Press, 1972.

Hardy, Peter. *Partners in Freedom and True Muslims: The Political Thought of Some Muslim Scholars in British India, 1912–1947.* Lund, Sweden: Studentlitteratur, 1971.

Harrison, Selig S. *In Afghanistan's Shadow: Baluch Nationalism and Soviet Temptations.* New York: Carnegie Endowment for International Peace, 1981.

Hasan, K. Sarwar. *The Transfer of Power.* Karachi: Pakistan Institute of International Affairs, 1966.

Hayes, Louis D. *Politics in Pakistan: The Struggle for Legitimacy.* Boulder, Colorado: Westview Press, 1984.

Heeger, Gerald. "After the 'Tilt': The Making of U.S. Foreign Policy Toward Pakistan, 1972–1974." Pages 125–42 in Lloyd I. Rudolph and Susanne Hoeber Rudolph, eds., *The Regional*

Imperative: U.S. Foreign Policy Towards South Asian States. New Delhi: Concept, 1980.

Heitzman, James, and Robert L. Worden, eds. *Bangladesh: A Country Study.* Washington: GPO, 1989.

Hodson, H.V. *The Great Divide: Britain, India, Pakistan.* London: Hutchinson, 1969.

Hutchins, Francis G. *The Illusion of Permanence: British Imperialism in India.* Princeton: Princeton University Press, 1967.

Ikram, S.M. *Modern Muslim India and the Birth of Pakistan.* Lahore: Ashraf, 1965.

Ikram, S.M., and Percival Spear, eds. *The Cultural Heritage of Pakistan.* Karachi: Oxford University Press, 1955.

Jahan, Rounaq. "India, Pakistan, and Bangladesh." Pages 299–339 in Gregory Henderson, Richard Ned Lebow, and John G. Stoessinger, eds., *Divided Nations in a Divided World.* New York: McKay, 1974.

Jahan, Rounaq. *Pakistan: Failure in National Integration.* New York: Columbia University Press, 1972.

Jalal, Ayesha. *The Sole Spokesman: Jinnah, the Muslim League and the Demand for Pakistan.* Cambridge: Cambridge University Press, 1985.

Jalal, Ayesha. *The State of Martial Rule: The Origins of Pakistan's Political Economy of Defence.* Lahore: Vanguard, 1991.

James, Morrice, with Peter Lyon. *Pakistan Chronicle.* New York: St. Martin's Press, 1993.

Keith, Arthur B. *A Constitutional History of India.* Allahabad, India: Central Book Depot, 1937.

Khaliquzzaman, Choudhry. *Pathway to Pakistan.* Karachi: Longman, 1961.

Korbel, Josef. *Danger in Kashmir.* (Rev. ed.) Princeton: Princeton University Press, 1966.

Korson, J. Henry, ed. *Contemporary Problems of Pakistan.* Leiden: Brill, 1974.

Lamb, Alastair. *Kashmir: A Disputed Legacy, 1846–1990.* Karachi: Oxford University Press, 1992.

Latif, Syed Muhammad. *Lahore: Its History, Architectural Remains, and Antiquities.* Lahore: New Imperial Press, 1892. Reprint. Lahore: Syed Muhammad Minhajuddin, 1957. (First Pakistani edition, Lahore: Sandhu Printers, 1981.)

Lelyveld, David. *Aligarh's First Generation: Muslim Solidarity in British India.* Princeton: Princeton University Press, 1978.

Low, David A. *The Political Inheritance of Pakistan.* New York: St. Martin's Press, 1991.

Low, David A . *Soundings in Modern South Asian History.* Berkeley: University of California Press, 1968.

Low, David A., ed. *Congress and the Raj.* London: Arnold-Heinemann, 1977.

Lumby, E.W.R. *The Transfer of Power in India.* London: George Allen and Unwin, 1954.

Majumdar, R.C. *History of the Freedom Movement in India,* 3. Calcutta: Firma Mukhopadhyay, 1962–63.

Malik, Hafeez. *Moslem Nationalism in India and Pakistan.* Washington: Public Affairs Press, 1963.

Malik, Hafeez, ed. *Iqbal: Poet-Philosopher of Pakistan.* New York: Columbia University Press, 1971.

Mansergh, N., and E.W.R. Lumby, eds. *The Transfer of Power, 1942–47.* (5 vols.) London: Her Majesty's Stationery Office, 1970–71.

Mason, Philip. *A Matter of Honour: An Account of the Indian Army, Its Officers and Men.* London: Cape, 1974.

Mehra, Parshotam. *A Dictionary of Modern Indian History, 1707–1947.* Delhi: Oxford University Press, 1985.

Merriam, Allen Hayes. *Gandhi vs. Jinnah: The Debate over the Partition of India.* Calcutta: Minerva, 1980.

Metcalf, Barbara Daly. *Islamic Revival in British India: Deoband, 1860–1900.* Princeton: Princeton University Press, 1982.

Metcalf, Thomas R. *The Aftermath of Revolt: India, 1857–1870.* Princeton: Princeton University Press, 1964.

Michel, Aloys A. *The Indus River: A Study of the Effects of Partition.* New Haven: Yale University Press, 1967.

Minault, Gail. *The Khilafat Movement.* New York: Columbia University Press, 1982.

Moon, Penderel. *Divide and Quit.* London: Chatto and Windus, 1962.

Moore, R.J. *The Crisis of Indian Unity, 1917–1940.* Oxford: Clarendon Press, 1974.

Muhammad Ali, Chaudhri. *The Emergence of Pakistan.* New York: Columbia University Press, 1967.

Mujahid, Sharif al-. *Quaid-i-Azam Jinnah: Studies in Interpretation.* Karachi: Quaid-i-Azam Academy, 1981.

Munir, Muhammad. *From Jinnah to Zia.* Lahore: Vanguard, 1980.

Muqeem Khan, Fazal. *Pakistan's Crisis in Leadership.* Islamabad: National Book Foundation, 1973.

Noman, Omar. *Pakistan: Political and Economic History since 1947.* London: Kegan Paul, 1988.

Oldenburg, Philip. "The Breakup of Pakistan." Pages 143–69 in Lloyd I. Rudolph and Susanne Hoeber Rudolph, eds., *The Regional Imperative: U.S. Foreign Policy Towards South Asian States.* New Delhi: Concept, 1980.

Page, David. *Prelude to Partition: The Indian Muslims and the Imperial System of Control, 1920–1932.* Delhi: Oxford University Press, 1982.

Philips, C.H., and Mary Doreen Wainwright, eds. *The Partition of India: Policies and Perspectives, 1935–1947.* London: Allen and Unwin, 1970.

Possehl, Gregory, ed. *Ancient Cities of the Indus.* New Delhi: Vikas, 1979.

Qureshi, Ishtiaq Husain. *The Struggle for Pakistan.* Karachi: University of Karachi Press, 1965.

Rajput, A.B. *Muslim League: Today and Yesterday.* Lahore: Ashraf, 1948.

Rajput, A.B. *Religion, Politics, and Society.* New York: Oxford University Press, 1987.

Richards, John F. *The Mughal Empire.* New York: Cambridge University Press, 1993.

Rizvi, Hasan-Askari. *Internal Strife and External Intervention: India's Role in the Civil War in East Pakistan [Bangladesh].* Lahore: Progressive, 1981.

Rizvi, Hasan-Askari. *The Military and Politics in Pakistan, 1947–86.* (3d ed.) Lahore: Progressive, 1986.

Sayeed, Khalid B. "The Historical Origins of Some of Pakistan's Persistent Political Problems." Pages 27–44 in A. Jayaratnam Wilson and Dennis Dalton, eds., *The States of South Asia: Problems of National Integration.* New Delhi: Vikas, 1982.

Sayeed, Khalid B. *Pakistan: The Formative Phase.* Karachi: Pakistan Publications, 1960.

Sayeed, Khalid B. *The Political System of Pakistan.* Boston: Houghton Mifflin, 1967.

Sayeed, Khalid B. *Politics in Pakistan: The Nature and Direction of Change.* New York: Praeger, 1980.

Schwartzberg, Joseph E., ed. *A Historical Atlas of South Asia.* New York: Oxford University Press, 1992.

Shaikh, Farzana. *Community and Consensus in Islam: Muslim Representation in Colonial India, 1860–1947.* Cambridge: Cambridge University Press, 1989.

Shakir, Moin. *Khilafat to Partition.* New Delhi: Kalamkar Prakashan, 1970.

Sisson, Richard, and Leo E. Rose. *War and Secession: Pakistan, India, and the Creation of Bangladesh.* Berkeley: University of California Press, 1990.

Smith, Vincent Arthur. *The Oxford History of India.* (3d. ed.) Ed., Percival Spear. Oxford: Clarendon Press, 1968.

Smith, Wilfred Cantwell. *Islam in Modern History.* New York: Mentor Books, 1959.

Smith, Wilfred Cantwell. *Modern Islam in India.* Lahore: Ashraf, 1963.

Smith, Wilfred Cantwell. *Pakistan as an Islamic State.* Lahore: Ashraf, 1951.

Spear, Percival. *A History of India,* 1. Harmondsworth, United Kingdom: Penguin, 1965.

Spear, Percival. *Twilight of the Mughals.* Cambridge: Cambridge University Press, 1951.

Syed, Anwar H. *The Discourse and Politics of Zulfikar Ali Bhutto.* New York: St. Martin's Press, 1992.

Symonds, Richard. *The Making of Pakistan.* London: Faber, 1951.

Tahir-Kheli, Shirin. *The United States and Pakistan: The Evolution of an Influence Relationship.* New York: Praeger, 1982.

Talbot, Ian. *Provincial Politics and the Pakistan Movement.* Karachi: Oxford University Press, 1988.

Tarn, W.W. *The Greeks in Bactria and India.* Cambridge: Cambridge University Press, 1951.

Thapar, Romila. *A History of India,* 2. Harmondsworth, United Kingdom: Penguin Books, 1966.

Vertzberger, Yaacov. *The Enduring Entente: Sino-Pakistan Relations, 1960–80.* New York: Praeger, 1983.

Von Vorys, Karl. *Political Development in Pakistan*. Princeton: Princeton University Press, 1965.

Waseem, Mohammad. *Pakistan under Martial Law, 1977–1985*. Lahore: Vanguard, 1987.

Weinbaum, Marvin. "The March 1977 Elections: Where Everyone Lost," *Asian Survey*, 17, July 1977, 7.

Wheeler, Richard S. *The Politics of Pakistan: A Constitutional Quest*. Ithaca, New York: Cornell University Press, 1970.

Wheeler, Robert Eric Mortimer. *Early India and Pakistan: To Ashoka*. (Rev. ed.) New York: Praeger, 1968.

Wheeler, Robert Eric Mortimer. *Five Thousand Years of Pakistan*. London: Johnson, 1950.

Wilcox, Wayne Ayres. *Pakistan: The Consolidation of a Nation*. New York: Columbia University Press, 1963.

Wirsing, Robert G. *Pakistan's Security under Zia, 1977–1988: The Policy Imperatives of a Peripheral Asian State*. New York: St. Martin's Press, 1991.

Wolpert, Stanley. *Jinnah of Pakistan*. New York: Oxford University Press, 1984.

Wolpert, Stanley. *A New History of India*. (4th ed.) New York: Oxford University Press, 1992.

Wolpert, Stanley. *Zulfi Bhutto of Pakistan: His Life and Times*. New York: Oxford University Press, 1993.

Wriggins, W. Howard, ed. *Pakistan in Transition*. Islamabad: University of Islamabad Press, 1975.

Ziring, Lawrence. *The Ayub Khan Era: Politics in Pakistan, 1958–1969*. Syracuse, New York: Syracuse University Press, 1971.

Ziring, Lawrence. *Pakistan: The Enigma of Political Development*. Boulder, Colorado: Westview Press, 1980.

Ziring, Lawrence, Ralph Braibanti, and W. Howard Wriggins, eds. *Pakistan: The Long View*. Durham, North Carolina: Duke University Press, 1977.

Chapter 2

Abbasi, Nasreen, and Mohammad Irfan. "Socioeconomic Effects of International Migration on Pakistani Families Left Behind." Pages 177–93 in Fred Arnold and Nasra Shah, eds., *Asian Labor Migration: Pipeline to the Middle East*. Boulder, Colorado: Westview Press, 1986.

Ahmed, Akbar S. *Discovering Islam: Making Sense of Muslim History and Society.* London: Routledge and Kegan Paul, 1988.

Ahmed, Akbar S. *Millennium and Charisma among Pathans.* London: Routledge and Kegan Paul, 1976.

Ahmed, Akbar S. *Pakistan Society: Ethnicity and Religious Identity.* Karachi: Oxford University Press, 1986.

"AIDS Cases Said Increasing," *Nawa-i-Waqt* [Lahore], April 14, 1991. Joint Publications Research Service, *Epidemiology.* (JPRS-TEP-91-018.) August 27, 1991, 28–29.

Ali, Imran. *The Punjab under Imperialism, 1885–1947.* New York: Columbia University Press, 1988.

Banuazizi, Ali, and Myron Weiner, eds. *The State, Religion, and Ethnic Politics: Afghanistan, Iran, and Pakistan.* Syracuse, New York: Syracuse University Press, 1986.

Barth, Frederick, ed. *Ethnic Groups and Boundaries: The Social Organization of Culture Difference.* London: Allen and Unwin, 1970.

Baxter, Craig, Yogendra K. Malik, Charles H. Kennedy, and Robert C. Oberst. *Government and Politics in South Asia.* (2d. ed.) Boulder, Colorado: Westview Press, 1993.

Burki, Shahid Javed. *Pakistan: A Nation in the Making.* Boulder, Colorado: Westview Press, 1986.

Burki, Shahid Javed. "Pakistan under Zia, 1977–1988," *Asian Survey,* 28, No. 10, October 1988, 1082–1100.

Burki, Shahid Javed, and Robert LaPorte, Jr., eds. *Pakistan's Development Priorities: Choices for the Future.* Karachi: Oxford University Press, 1984.

Carroll, Lucy. "Nizam-i-Islam: Processes and Conflicts in Pakistan's Programme of Islamisation, with Special Reference to the Position of Women," *Journal of Commonwealth and Comparative Politics,* 20, 1982, 57–95.

Clark, Grace. "Pakistan's Zakat and 'Ushr as a Welfare System." Pages 79–95 in Anita M. Weiss, ed., *Islamic Reassertion in Pakistan: The Application of Islamic Laws in a Modern State.* Syracuse, New York: Syracuse University Press, 1986.

Donnan, Hastings, and Pnina Werbner, eds. *Economy and Culture in Pakistan: Migrants and Cities in a Muslim Society.* Basingstoke, United Kingdom: Macmillan, 1991.

Duncan, Ann. *Women in Pakistan: An Economic and Social Strategy.* Washington: World Bank, 1989.

Dutt, Ashok K., and M.M. Geib. *Atlas of South Asia.* Boulder, Colorado: Westview Press, 1987.

Esposito, John L. *Islam: The Straight Path.* New York: Oxford University Press, 1988.

Esposito, John L. *Islam and Politics.* (3d ed.) Syracuse, New York: Syracuse University Press, 1991.

Farmer, B.H. *An Introduction to South Asia.* London: Methuen, 1983.

Gellner, Ernest. *Muslim Society.* Cambridge: Cambridge University Press, 1983.

"Government AIDS Policy," *Pakistan Times* [Islamabad], April 12, 1991. Joint Publications Research Service, *Epidemiology.* (JPRS-REP–91–010.) May 16, 1991, 26–27.

Hafeez, Sabeeha. *The Changing Pakistan Society.* Karachi: Royal Book Company, 1991.

Johnson, Basil Leonard Clyde. *Development in South Asia.* Harmondsworth, United Kingdom: Penguin Books, 1983.

Kureshy, K.U. *A Geography of Pakistan.* Karachi: Oxford University Press, 1978.

Lamb, Christina. *Waiting for Allah: Pakistan's Struggle for Democracy.* New York: Viking, 1991.

Moorhouse, Geoffrey. *To the Frontier.* New York: Holt, Rinehart, and Winston, 1985.

Mumtaz, Khawar, and Farida Shaheed. *Women of Pakistan: Two Steps Forward, One Step Back?* London: Zed Press; and Karachi: Vanguard, 1987.

Naim, C.M., ed. *Iqbal, Jinnah, and Pakistan: The Vision and the Reality.* Syracuse, New York: Maxwell School at Syracuse University, 1979.

Nasr, Seyyed Vali Reza. "Students, Islam, and Politics: Islami Jami'at-i Tulaba in Pakistan," *Middle East Journal,* 46, No. 1, Winter 1992, 59–76.

Noman, Omar. *Pakistan: Political and Economic History since 1947.* London: Kegan Paul, 1990.

Pakistan. *National Conservation Strategy Report.* Islamabad: 1992.

Pakistan. Federal Bureau of Statistics. Statistics Division. *Pakistan Statistical Yearbook, 1991.* Karachi: 1991.

Pakistan. Federal Bureau of Statistics. Statistics Division. *Population Census of Pakistan, 1951.* Islamabad: Population Census Organization, 1951.

Pakistan. Federal Bureau of Statistics. Statistics Division. *Population Census of Pakistan, 1961.* Islamabad: Population Census Organization, 1961.

Pakistan. Federal Bureau of Statistics. Statistics Division. *Population Census of Pakistan, 1972.* Islamabad: Population Census Organization, 1972.

Pakistan. Federal Bureau of Statistics. Statistics Division. *Population Census of Pakistan, 1981.* Islamabad: Population Census Organization, 1981.

Pakistan. Federal Bureau of Statistics. Women's Division. *Women in Pakistan: A Statistical Profile.* Islamabad: 1985.

Pakistan. Ministry of Education. *Pakistan Culture.* Islamabad: National Book Foundation, 1986.

Pakistan. Planning Commission. "Eighth Five-Year Plan (1993–98) Approach Paper." Islamabad: 1992.

Pakistan. Planning Commission. *The Fifth Five-Year Plan, 1978–1983.* Karachi: Manager of Publications, 1978.

Pakistan. Planning Commission. *Seventh Five-Year Plan, 1988–93; and Perspective Plan, 1988–2003.* Islamabad: Printing Corporation of Pakistan Press, 1988.

Pakistan. Planning Commission. *The Sixth Five-Year Plan, 1983–1988.* Karachi: Manager of Publications, 1983.

Pakistan Commission on the Status of Women. *Report of the Commission on the Status of Women in Pakistan.* Islamabad: 1986.

PC Globe 5.0: The New World Order, 1992. (Computer program based on World Bank statistics, 1991.) Broderbund. Tempe, Arizona: 1992.

Quddus, Naseem Jaffer. *Problems of Education in Pakistan.* Karachi: Royal Book Company, 1990.

Qureshi, Ishtiaq Husain. *Education in Pakistan: An Inquiry into Objectives and Achievements.* Karachi: Ma'aref, 1975.

Reeves, Richard. *Passage to Peshawar.* New York: Simon and Schuster, 1984.

Sathar, Zeba, et al. "Women's Status and Fertility Change in Pakistan," *Population and Development Review,* 14, No. 3, September 1988, 415–32.

Schackle, Christopher. "Punjabi in Lahore," *Modern Asian Studies,* 4, No. 3, 1970, 239–67.

Shah, Nasra M., ed. *Pakistani Women: A Socioeconomic and Demographic Profile.* Islamabad: Pakistan Institute of Development Economics; and Hawaii: East-West Population Institute, 1986.

Shaheed, Farida. "Diversification of Women's Training and Employment in Pakistan." (Unpublished report.) Islamabad: 1987.

Shaheed, Farida, and Khawar Mumtaz. *Women's Economic Participation in Pakistan.* Islamabad: UNICEF Pakistan, 1992.

Siddiqi, A.H. *Baluchistan: Its Society, Resources, and Development.* Lanham, Maryland: University Press of America, 1991.

Sidhwa, Bapsi. *The Bride.* London: Jonathan Cape, 1983.

Sweetser, Anne T. "Healing Power and Medical Practice in Pakistani Society." Pages 95–108 in Charles Kennedy, ed., *Pakistan, 1992.* Boulder, Colorado: Westview Press, 1993.

Tandon, Prakash. *Punjabi Century.* Berkeley: University of California Press, 1968.

United Nations Development Programme. *Human Development Report, 1991.* New York: Oxford University Press, 1991.

United Nations Educational, Scientific, and Cultural Organization. *Human Development Report, 1992.* New York: Oxford University Press, 1992.

United Nations Educational, Scientific, and Cultural Organization. *Statistical Yearbook, 1989.* New York: 1989.

United Nations High Commissioner for Refugees. *UNHCR Activities Financed by Voluntary Funds: Report for 1990–91 and Proposed Programs and Budget for 1992.* (SW Asia, North Africa, and the Middle East. UN doc. A/AC. 96/774 part V.) Geneva: August 28, 1991.

United States. Department of State. Bureau of International Narcotics Matters. *International Narcotics Control Strategy Report.* Washington: March 1991.

United States. Embassy in Islamabad. *Health and Medical Information.* Washington: Department of State, January 1992.

Weiner, Myron, and Ali Banuazizi, eds. *The State and the Restructuring of Society in Afghanistan, Iran, and Pakistan.* Syracuse, New York: Syracuse University Press, 1993.

Weiss, Anita M. *Culture, Class, and Development in Pakistan: The Emergence of an Industrial Bourgeoisie in Punjab.* Boulder, Colorado: Westview Press, 1991.

Weiss, Anita M. *Walls Within Walls: Life Histories of Working Women in the Old City of Lahore.* Boulder, Colorado: Westview Press, 1992.

Weiss, Anita M., ed. *Islamic Reassertion in Pakistan: The Application of Islamic Laws in a Modern State.* Syracuse, New York: Syracuse University Press, 1986.

Women's Action Forum. "Law of Evidence: WAF (National) Position Paper." (Lahore Chapter.) Lahore: 1983.

World Bank. *Islamic Republic of Pakistan. Health Sector Study: Key Concerns and Solutions.* Washington: June 25, 1993.

World Bank. *Pakistan: Family Health Project.* Washington: January 25, 1993.

World Bank. *World Development Report, 1988.* New York: Oxford University Press, 1988.

World Bank. *World Development Report, 1991.* New York: Oxford University Press, 1991.

World Bank. *World Development Report, 1992.* New York: Oxford University Press, 1992.

World Bank. *World Development Report, 1994.* New York: Oxford University Press, 1994.

World Health Organization. *Evaluation of the Strategy for Health for All by the Year 2000, 7th Report.* Geneva: Global Review, 1987.

World Health Organization. *World Health Organization: Annual Statistics, 1990.* Geneva: 1990.

Zia, Shehla, Hina Jilani, and Asma Jahangir. *Muslim Family Laws and the Implementation in Pakistan.* Islamabad: Women's Division, Government of Pakistan, 1982.

Zia ul-Haq, Mohammad. *Introduction of Islamic Laws: Address to the Nation.* Islamabad: February 10, 1979.

(Various issues of the following periodicals were also used in the preparation of this chapter: *Herald* [Karachi]; and *Newsline* [Karachi]).

Chapter 3

Adams, John, and Iqbal Sabiha. *Exports, Politics, and Economic Development: Pakistan, 1970–82.* Boulder, Colorado: Westview Press, 1983.

Addleton, Jonathan S. *Undermining the Centre: The Gulf Migration and Pakistan.* Karachi: Oxford University Press, 1992.

Ahmad, Masood, and Gary P. Kutcher. *Irrigation Planning with Environmental Considerations: A Case Study of Pakistan's Indus Basin.* (World Bank Technical Paper, No. 166.) Washington: World Bank, 1992.

Ahmed, Viqar, and Rashid Amjad. *The Management of Pakistan's Economy, 1947–1982.* Karachi: Oxford University Press, 1984.

Azam, K.M. *Economics and Politics of Development: An Islamic Perspective.* Karachi: Royal Book Company, 1988.

Bhatia, B.M. *Pakistan's Economic Development, 1948–78: The Failure of a Strategy.* New Delhi: Vikas, 1979.

Bhatia, B.M. *Pakistan's Economic Development, 1948–88: Freedom to Bondage.* Delhi: Konark, 1989.

Burki, Shahid Javed. "Economic Policy after Zia ul-Haq." Pages 43–55 in Charles H. Kennedy, ed., *Pakistan: 1992.* Boulder, Colorado: Westview Press, 1993.

Burki, Shahid Javed. *Pakistan: The Continuing Search for Nationhood.* Boulder, Colorado: Westview Press, 1991.

Burki, Shahid Javed. *Pakistan: A Nation in the Making.* Boulder, Colorado: Westview Press, 1986.

Burki, Shahid Javed. "Pakistan's Development: An Overview," *World Development,* 9, No. 3, March 1981, 310–14.

Burki, Shahid Javed. "Pakistan's Economy in the Year 2000: Two Possible Scenarios." Pages 1–15 in Henry J. Korson, ed., *Contemporary Problems of Pakistan.* Boulder, Colorado: Westview Press, 1993.

Burki, Shahid Javed. *Pakistan under Bhutto, 1971–1977.* (2d ed.) London: Macmillan, 1988.

Burki, Shahid Javed, and Craig Baxter. *Pakistan under the Military: Eleven Years of Zia ul-Haq.* Boulder, Colorado: Westview Press, 1991.

Cameron, John, and Mohammad Irfan. *Enabling People to Help Themselves: An Employment and Human Resources Strategy for Pakistan in the 1990s.* Geneva: International Labour Organisation, World Employment Programme, 1991.

Ebinger, Charles K. *Pakistan: Energy Planning in a Strategic Vortex.* Bloomington: Indiana University Press, 1981.

Economist Intelligence Unit. *Country Profile: Pakistan, Afghanistan, 1991–92.* London: 1991.

Economist Intelligence Unit. *Country Profile: Pakistan, Afghanistan, 1992–93.* London: 1992.

Economic Intelligence Unit. *Country Profile: Pakistan, Afghanistan, 1993–94.* London: 1993.

Gustafson, W. Eric. "Economic Reforms under the Bhutto Regime," *Journal of Asian and African Studies* [Leiden], 8, Nos. 3–4, October 1973, 241–58.

Institute of Policy Studies. *Development Strategy for the Sixth Plan, 1983–88.* Islamabad: 1983.

Iqbal, Munawar, ed. *Pakistan: State of the Economy in a Long-run Perspective.* Islamabad: Institute of Policy Studies, 1989.

Jafarey, Saqib. "Emigration and Development in Pakistan," *South Asia Bulletin,* 2, Fall 1982, 1–11.

James, William, and Subroto Roy, eds. *Foundations of Pakistan's Political Economy: Towards an Agenda for the 1990s.* Newbury Park, California: Sage, 1992.

Johnson, B.L.C. *Development in South Asia.* Harmondsworth, United Kingdom: Penguin Books, 1983.

Kennedy, Charles H., ed. *Pakistan: 1992.* Boulder, Colorado: Westview Press, 1993.

Khan, Mahmood Hasan. *Underdevelopment and Agrarian Structure in Pakistan.* Boulder, Colorado: Westview Press, 1981.

Khan, Shahrukh Rufi. *Profit and Loss Sharing: An Islamic Experiment in Finance and Banking.* Karachi: Oxford University Press, 1987.

Khan, Tufail Ahmad. *Glimpses of Pakistan Economy, 1980–88.* Karachi: Business Research and Service Institute, 1989.

Korson, J. Henry, ed. *Contemporary Problems of Pakistan.* Boulder, Colorado: Westview Press, 1993.

Michel, Aloys A. *The Indus Rivers.* New Haven: Yale University Press, 1987.

Mustafa, Syed Mahdi. *Focus on the Pakistani Economy.* Karachi: Royal Book Company, 1989.

Nabi, Ijaz. *The Quality of Life in Pakistan.* Lahore: Vanguard, 1986.

Nabi, Ijaz, Naved Hamid, and Shahid Zahid. *The Agrarian Economy of Pakistan.* Karachi: Oxford University Press, 1986.

Naqvi, Syed Nawab Haider, and Khwaja Sarmad. *Pakistan's Economy Through the Seventies.* Islamabad: Pakistan Institute of Development Economics, 1984.

Naqvi, Syed Nawab Haider, et al. *Structural Change in Pakistan's Agriculture.* Islamabad: Pakistan Institute of Development Economics, 1989.

Naseem, S. M. *Underdevelopment, Poverty, and Inequality in Pakistan.* Karachi: Vanguard, 1981.

National Bank of Pakistan. Economic Research Wing. *Pakistan's Economy: Key Indicators.* Karachi: 1993.

Nayak, Pandav. *Pakistan: Political Economy of a Developing State.* New Delhi: Patriot, 1988.

Noman, Omar. *Pakistan: A Political and Economic History since 1947.* London: Kegan Paul, 1990.

Pakistan. Federal Bureau of Statistics. Statistics Division. *Pakistan Statistical Yearbook, 1991.* Karachi: 1991.

Pakistan. Ministry of Finance. *Demands for Grants and Appropriations: The Budget, 1992–93.* Islamabad: 1992.

Pakistan. Ministry of Finance. *Economic Survey, 1990–91.* Islamabad: 1991.

Pakistan. Ministry of Finance. *Economic Survey, 1991–92.* Islamabad: 1992.

Pakistan. Ministry of Finance. *Economic Survey: Statistical Supplement, 1991–92.* Islamabad: 1992.

Pakistan. Ministry of Finance. *Estimates of Foreign Assistance, 1992–93.* Islamabad: 1992.

Pakistan. Ministry of Finance. *Explanatory Memorandum on the Budget, 1992–93.* Islamabad: 1992.

Pakistan. Ministry of Finance. *Federal Budget in Brief, 1992–93.* Islamabad: 1992.

Pakistan. Planning Commission. *Seventh Five Year Plan, 1988–93; and Perspective Plan, 1988–2003.* Islamabad: Printing Corporation of Pakistan Press, 1988.

Pakistan Year Book, 1991–92. (19th ed.) Ed., Rafique Akhtar. Karachi: East and West, 1991.

Pakistan Year Book, 1992–93. (20th ed.) Ed., Rafique Akhtar. Karachi: East and West, 1992.

Papanek, Gustav F. *Pakistan's Economic Development: Social Goals and Private Incentives.* Cambridge: Harvard University Press, 1967.

Park, Keith K.H., and Antoine W. van Agtmael, eds. *The World's Emerging Stock Markets.* Chicago: Probus, 1993.

Qasir, Nadeem. *Pakistan Studies: An Investigation into the Political Economy, 1948–1988.* Karachi: Oxford University Press: 1991.

Qureshi, Saleem. "Islam and Development: The Zia Regime in Pakistan," *World Development,* 8, Nos. 7–8, September 1980, 563–76.

Rosen, George. *Western Economists and Eastern Societies: Aspects of Change in South Asia, 1950–1970.* Baltimore: Johns Hopkins University Press, 1985.

Shah, Nasra M., ed. *Pakistani Women: A Socioeconomic and Demographic Profile.* Islamabad: Pakistan Institute of Development Economics; and Hawaii: East-West Population Institute, 1986.

Stanford, Richard A., ed. *Rural Development in Pakistan.* Durham, North Carolina: Carolina Academic Press, 1980.

State Bank of Pakistan. *Annual Report, 1991–92.* Karachi: 1992.

Tsakok, Isabelle. "The Export of Manpower from Pakistan to the Middle East, 1975–1981," *World Development,* 10, No. 4, April 1982, 319–26.

United Nations Industrial Development Organization. *Pakistan: Towards Industrial Liberalization and Revitalization.* Oxford: Blackwell for UNIDO, 1990.

United States. Department of Commerce. International Trade Administration. *Foreign Economic Trends and Their Implications for the United States: Pakistan.* (FET 92–09.) Washington: April 1992.

Weiss, Anita M. *Culture, Class, and Development in Pakistan: The Emergence of an Industrial Bourgeoisie in Punjab.* Boulder, Colorado: Westview Press, 1991.

World Radio TV Handbook, 1994. Ed., Andrew G. Sennitt. Amsterdam: Billboard Books, 1994.

(Various issues of the following publications were also used in the preparation of this chapter: *Asian Wall Street Journal* [Hong Kong]; *Economic Outlook* [Karachi]; *Economic Review* [Karachi]; *Economist* [London]; Economist Intelligence Unit, *Country Report: Pakistan, Afghanistan* [London]; *Far Eastern Economic Review* [Hong Kong]; *Financial Times* [London]; *International Financial Statistics*; *National Bank of Pakistan Monthly Economic Letter* [Karachi]; and *Pakistan and Gulf Economist* [Karachi].)

Chapter 4

Ahmad, Munir. *The Civil Servant in Pakistan.* Karachi: Oxford University Press, 1964.

Ahmad, Mushtaq. "A Challenging Assignment," *Dawn* [Karachi], November 12, 1990, 7.

Ahmad, Mushtaq. *Government and Politics in Pakistan.* New York: Praeger, 1963.

Ahmed, Jamil-ud-din, ed. *Some Recent Speeches and Writings of Mr. Jinnah.* (2 vols.) Lahore: Ashraf, 1952.

Ali, Chaudhri Muhammad. *Emergence of Pakistan.* New York: Columbia University Press, 1967.

Ali, Salamat. "City under Siege," *Far Eastern Economic Review* [Hong Kong], December 3, 1992, 17–18.

Amin, Tahir. "Pakistan in 1993: Some Dramatic Changes," *Asian Survey,* 34, No. 2, February 1994, 191–99.

Ayub Khan, Mohammad. *Friends Not Masters: A Political Autobiography.* New York: Oxford University Press, 1967.

Azfar, Kamal. "Constitutional Dilemmas in Pakistan." Pages 49–85 in Shahid Javed Burki and Craig Baxter, *Pakistan under the Military: Eleven Years of Zia ul-Haq.* Boulder, Colorado: Westview Press, 1991.

Aziz, K.K. *The Making of Pakistan: A Study in Nationalism.* London: Chatto and Windus, 1967.

Baxter, Craig. "Pakistan Becomes Prominent in the International Arena." Pages 137–53 in Shahid Javed Burki and Craig Baxter, *Pakistan under the Military: Eleven Years of Zia ul-Haq.* Boulder, Colorado: Westview Press, 1991.

Baxter, Craig, Yogendra K. Malik, Charles H. Kennedy, and Robert C. Oberst. *Government and Politics in South Asia.* (2d ed.) Boulder, Colorado: Westview Press, 1993.

Becker, Mary L. "The All-India Muslim League: 1906–1947." (Ph.D. dissertation.) Cambridge: Radcliffe College, 1957.

Bhutto, Benazir. *Daughter of Destiny.* New York: Simon and Schuster, 1989.

Binder, Leonard. "Islam, Ethnicity, and the State in Pakistan: An Overview." Pages 259–66 in Ali Banuazizi and Myron Weiner, eds., *The State, Religion, and Ethnic Politics: Afghanistan, Iran, and Pakistan.* Syracuse, New York: Syracuse University Press, 1986.

Binder, Leonard. *Religion and Politics in Pakistan.* Berkeley: University of California Press, 1961.

Bolitho, Hector. *Jinnah: The Creator of Pakistan.* London: Murray, 1954.

Braibanti, Ralph. "Public Bureaucracy and Judiciary in Pakistan." Pages 360–440 in Joseph LaPalombara, ed., *Bureaucracy and Political Development.* Princeton: Princeton University Press, 1963.

Burke, S.M., and Lawrence Ziring. *Pakistan's Foreign Policy: An Historical Analysis.* (2d ed.) Karachi: Oxford University Press, 1990.

Burki, Shahid Javed. *Historical Dictionary of Pakistan.* Metuchen, New Jersey: Scarecrow Press, 1991.

Burki, Shahid Javed. "Pakistan." Pages 201–16 in Francis Robinson, ed., *The Cambridge Encyclopedia of India, Pakistan, Bangladesh, Sri Lanka, Nepal, Bhutan, and the Maldives.* Cambridge: Cambridge University Press, 1989.

Burki, Shahid Javed. *Pakistan: The Continuing Search for Nationhood.* Boulder, Colorado: Westview Press, 1991.

Burki, Shahid Javed. *Pakistan: A Nation in the Making.* Boulder, Colorado: Westview Press, 1986.

Burki, Shahid Javed, and Craig Baxter. *Pakistan under the Military: Eleven Years of Zia ul-Haq.* Boulder, Colorado: Westview Press, 1991.

Bussey, John. "Pakistan Reform Clouded by Civil Strife," *Asian Wall Street Journal* [Hong Kong], August 1, 1991, 1.

Callard, Keith. *Political Forces in Pakistan, 1947–1959.* New York: Institute of Pacific Relations, 1959.

Canfield, Robert L. "Restructuring in Greater Central Asia: Changing Political Configurations," *Asian Survey,* 32, No. 10, October 1992, 875–87.

Choudhury, G.W. *Constitutional Development in Pakistan.* (2d ed.) Vancouver: Publications Centre, University of British Columbia,1969.

Choudhury, G.W. *Democracy in Pakistan.* Dacca: Green Book House, 1963.

Choudhury, G.W. *Documents and Speeches on the Constitution of Pakistan.* Dacca: Green Book House, 1967.

Choudhury, G.W. *The Last Days of United Pakistan.* Bloomington: Indiana University Press, 1975.

Cohen, Stephen P. *The Pakistan Army.* Berkeley: University of California Press, 1984.

Coll, Steve. "In Bombings, Two Indias Meet," *Washington Post,* March 14, 1993, A1, A22.

Coll, Steve. "Pakistan's Road to Prosperity?" *Washington Post,* July 4, 1992, A15.

Desmond, Edward W. "The Undoing of Benazir," *Time,* January 29, 1990, 56.

Economist Intelligence Unit. *Country Report: Pakistan, Afghanistan* [London], Nos. 1–3, 1992.

Economist Intelligence Unit. *Country Report: Pakistan, Afghanistan* [London], No. 4, 1993.

Epstein, Leon D. "Parliamentary Government." Pages 419–25 in David L. Sills, ed., *International Encyclopedia of the Social Sciences,* 11. New York: Macmillan, 1968.

Feldman, Herbert. *A Constitution for Pakistan.* Karachi: Oxford University Press, 1955.

Gledhill, A. *Pakistan: The Development of Its Laws and Constitution.* London: Stevens, 1957.

Hussain, Asaf. *Elite Politics in an Ideological State.* Folkestone, United Kingdom: Dawson, 1979.

Hyman, Anthony. *Pakistan: Toward a Modern Muslim State.* (Conflict Studies Series, No. 227.) London: Research Institute for the Study of Conflict and Terrorism, 1990.

Iqbal, Sir Muhammed. *The Reconstruction of Religious Thought in Islam.* London: Oxford University Press, 1934.

Jalal, Ayesha. *The Sole Spokesman: Jinnah, the Muslim League, and the Demand for Pakistan.* New York: Cambridge University Press, 1985.

Jennings, Sir Ivor. *Constitutional Problems in Pakistan.* Cambridge University Press, 1957.

Jillani, Anees. "Judicial Activism and Islamization after Zia: Toward the Prohibition of Riba." Pages 57–73 in Charles H. Kennedy, ed., *Pakistan: 1992.* Boulder, Colorado: Westview Press, 1993.

Jillani Anees. "Pakistan and CENTO: An Historical Analysis," *Journal of South Asian and Middle Eastern Studies,* 15, No. 1, Fall 1991, 40–53.

Kennedy, Charles H., ed. *Pakistan: 1992.* Boulder, Colorado: Westview Press, 1993.

Khan, Ata. "Chronology of Events: September 1988–April 1992." Pages 167–83 in Charles H. Kennedy, ed., *Pakistan: 1992.* Boulder, Colorado: Westview Press, 1993.

Khan, Fazal Muqeem. *The Story of the Pakistan Army.* Karachi: Oxford University Press, 1963.

Khan, Mohammad Asghar, ed. *Islam, Politics, and the State.* London: Zed Books, 1985.

Khan, Rais A. "Pakistan in 1991: Light and Shadows," *Asian Survey,* 32, No. 2, February 1992, 197–206.

Khan, Rais A. "Pakistan in 1992: Waiting for Change," *Asian Survey,* 33, No. 2, February 1993, 129–40.

LaPorte, Robert, Jr. *Power and Privilege: Influence and Decision-Making in Pakistan.* Berkeley: University of California Press, 1975.

Mahmood, Safdar. *Constitutional Foundations of Pakistan.* (2d ed.) Lahore: Jang, 1990.

Malik, Hafeez. *Moslem Nationalism in India and Pakistan.* Washington: Public Affairs Press, 1963.

Malik, Hafeez. "Nationalism and the Quest for Ideology in Pakistan." Pages 271–300 in Lawrence Ziring, Ralph Braibanti, and W. Howard Wriggins, eds., *Pakistan: The Long View.* Durham, North Carolina: Duke University Press, 1977.

Moore, Molly. "Pakistan's Fragile Democracy under Strain," *Washington Post,* January 10, 1993, A23.

Moore, Molly, and John Ward Anderson. "Islamic Law—and Zeal—Rise to Challenge Secular Politics in Pakistan," *Washington Post,* October 21, 1992, A29, A33.

Munir, Muhammad. *From Jinnah to Zia.* Lahore: Vanguard, 1979.

Nasr, Seyyed Vali Reza. "Democracy and the Crisis of Governability in Pakistan," *Asian Survey,* 32, No. 6, June 1992, 521–37.

Nasr, Seyyed Vali Reza. "Students, Islam, and Politics: Islami Jami'at-i Tulaba in Pakistan," *Middle East Journal,* 46, No. 1, Winter 1992, 59–76.

Pakistan. Ministry of Information and Broadcasting. *Nawaz Sharif: Nation's Choice for a Leap Forward.* Islamabad: 1990.

Pakistan. Ministry of Information and Broadcasting. *Pakistan, 1991: An Official Handbook.* Islamabad: 1991.

Pakistan. Ministry of Justice and Parliamentary Affairs. *The Constitution of the Islamic Republic of Pakistan (as Modified up to 19th March 1985)*. Islamabad: Federal Judicial Academy, 1985.

Palmer, Norman D. "Pakistan: The Long Search for Foreign Policy." Pages 403–29 in Lawrence Ziring, Ralph Braibanti, and W. Howard Wriggins, eds., *Pakistan: The Long View.* Durham, North Carolina: Duke University Press, 1977.

Qureshi, Ishtiaq Husain. *Pakistan: An Islamic Democracy.* Lahore: Institute of Islamic Culture, 1956.

Rajput, A.B. *Muslim League: Yesterday and Today.* Lahore: Ashraf, 1948.

Richter, William L. "The 1990 General Elections in Pakistan." Pages 19–41 in Charles H. Kennedy, ed., *Pakistan: 1992.* Boulder, Colorado: Westview Press, 1993.

Rose, Leo. "Pakistan and the World." Pages 249–55 in Francis Robinson, ed., *The Cambridge Encyclopedia of India, Pakistan, Bangladesh, Sri Lanka, Nepal, Bhutan, and the Maldives.* Cambridge: Cambridge University Press, 1989.

Rosett, Claudia. "Pakistan's Free Marketeer," *Asian Wall Street Journal* [Hong Kong], July 12–13, 1991, 6.

Sayeed, Khalid B. *Pakistan: The Formative Phase.* (2d ed.) London: Oxford University Press, 1968.

Sayeed, Khalid B. "Political Leadership and Institution-building under Jinnah, Ayub, and Bhutto." Pages 241–70 in Lawrence Ziring, Ralph Braibanti, and W. Howard Wriggins, eds., *Pakistan: The Long View.* Durham, North Carolina: Duke University Press, 1977.

Sayeed, Khalid B. *The Political System of Pakistan.* Boston: Houghton Mifflin, 1967.

Sayeed, Khalid B. *Politics in Pakistan: The Nature and Direction of Change.* New York: Praeger, 1980.

Sehbai, Shaheen. "Emergency Lifted: Major Concessions to Industry," *Dawn* [Karachi], November 8, 1990, 1.

Sharif, Mian Mohammad Nawaz. "Address by His Excellency Mr. Mohammad Nawaz Sharif, Prime Minister of the Islamic Republic of Pakistan at the Tenth Conference of heads of State of Government of Non-Aligned Countries, Jakarta, September 1, 1992." Washington: Embassy of Pakistan, 1992.

Sharif, Mian Mohammad Nawaz. "Text of the Inaugural Address of the Prime Minister of Pakistan at the Extraordinary Session of the ECO Council of Ministers at Islamabad on 28th November 1992. Washington: Embassy of Pakistan, 1992.

Sherwani, Latif Ahmed. *Pakistan, China, and America.* Karachi: Council for Pakistan Studies, 1980.

Smith, W.C. *Modern Islam in India.* London: Gollancz, 1946.

Syed, Anwar H. *Pakistan: Islam, Politics, and National Solidarity.* New York: Praeger, 1982.

Syed, Anwar H. "Political Parties and the Nationality Question in Pakistan," *Journal of South Asian and Middle Eastern Studies,* 12, No. 1, Fall 1988, 42–75.

Symonds, Richard. *The Making of Pakistan.* (2d ed.) London: Faber, 1950.

United Nations. *Membership of Principal United Nations Organs in 1993.* (ORG/1155/Rev. 1.) New York: January 4, 1993.

United Nations. Department of Public Information. *States Members of the United Nations.* New York: 1990.

United Nations. Food and Agriculture Organization. *FAO Annual Review.* Rome: 1991.

United Nations Development Programme. *1992 UNDP Annual Report.* New York: 1992.

United Nations Population Fund. "Dr. Nafis Sadik Appointed UNFPA Executive Director." (Press Release.) New York: April 20, 1987.

Waseem, Mohammad. "Pakistan's Lingering Crisis of Dyarchy," *Asian Survey,* 32, No. 7, July 1992, 617–34.

Wilcox, Wayne Ayres. *Pakistan: The Consolidation of a Nation.* New York: Columbia University Press, 1963.

Wolpert, Stanley. *Jinnah of Pakistan.* New York: Oxford University Press, 1984.

Wriggins, W. Howard. "The Balancing Process in Pakistan's Foreign Policy." Pages 301–39 in Lawrence Ziring, Ralph Braibanti, and W. Howard Wriggins, eds., *Pakistan: The Long View.* Durham, North Carolina: Duke University Press, 1977.

Zakaria, Nasim. *Parliamentary Government in Pakistan.* Lahore: New Publishers, 1958.

Ziring, Lawrence. "Benazir Bhutto: A Political Portrait," *Asian Affairs,* 18, No. 3, Fall 1991, 178–89.

Ziring, Lawrence. "Dilemma and Challenge in Nawaz Sharif's Pakistan." Pages 1–18 in Charles H. Kennedy, ed., *Pakistan: 1992.* Boulder, Colorado: Westview Press, 1993.

Ziring, Lawrence. *Pakistan: The Enigma of Political Development.* Folkestone, United Kingdom: Dawson, 1980.

Ziring, Lawrence. "The Second Stage in Pakistani Politics: The 1993 Elections," *Asian Survey,* 33, No. 12, December 1993, 1175–85.

Ziring, Lawrence, Ralph Braibanti, and W. Howard Wriggins, eds., *Pakistan: The Long View.* Durham, North Carolina: Duke University Press, 1977.

(Various issues of the following publications were also used in the preparation of this chapter: *Dawn* [Karachi]; *Economist* [London]; Foreign Broadcast Information Service, *Daily Report: South Asia*; *New York Times*; and *Washington Post.*)

Chapter 5

Akhtar, Hamid Saeed. *A Study of Pakistan Military Law.* Sialkot, Pakistan: Modern Book Depot, 1977.

Amnesty International. *Annual Report, 1992.* New York: 1992.

Amnesty International. *Pakistan: Human Rights Safeguards.* New York: 1990.

Askari, M.H. "Keeping Afloat?" *Herald* [Karạchi], September 1991, 79–81.

Ayub Khan, Mohammad. *The Evolution of Judicial Systems and Law in the Sub Continent.* Peshawar, Pakistan: n.p., n.d.

Babar, Sabihuddin. "Law and Martial Law," *Newsline* [Karachi], July 1990, 24–25.

Banuazizi, Ali, and Myron Weiner, eds. *The State, Religion, and Ethnic Politics: Afghanistan, Iran, and Pakistan.* Syracuse, New York: Syracuse University Press, 1986.

Barnds, William J. *India, Pakistan, and the Great Powers.* New York: Praeger, 1972.

Bhatti, Manzoor Hussain. *Crime, Punishment, Prison, and Juvenile Delinquency.* Lahore: Siraj-ud-din, 1976.

Burke, S.M., and Lawrence Ziring. *Pakistan's Foreign Policy.* (2d ed., rev.) Karachi: Oxford University Press, 1990.

Burki, Shahid Javed, and Craig Baxter. *Pakistan under the Military: Eleven Years of Zia ul-Haq.* Boulder, Colorado: Westview Press, 1991.

Buzan, Barry, and Gowher Rizvi. *South Asian Insecurity and the Great Powers.* New York: St. Martin's Press, 1986.

Cheema, Pervaiz Iqbal. *Pakistan's Defence Policy, 1947–58.* Basingstoke, United Kingdom: Macmillan, 1990.

Cohen, Stephen P. *The Indian Army: Its Contribution to the Development of a Nation.* Berkeley: University of California Press, 1971.

Cohen, Stephen P. *The Pakistan Army.* Berkeley: University of California Press, 1984.

Cohen, Stephen P. *The Security of South Asia.* Urbana: University of Illinois Press, 1987.

"Country Survey: Pakistan," *Jane's Defence Weekly* [Coulsdon, United Kingdom], 18, No. 19, November 7, 1992, 29–42.

Cronin, Richard P., and Barbara Leitch LePoer. *South Asia: U.S. Interests and Policy Issues.* (No. 93–243F.) Washington: Library of Congress, Congressional Research Service, February 12, 1993.

Eliot, Theodore, and Robert Pfaltzgraff. *The Red Army on Pakistan's Borders: Implications for the United States.* Washington: Pergamon-Brassey's, 1986.

Farani, M. *Police Laws Manual.* Lahore: Lahore Times, 1981.

Ganguly, Sumit. *The Origins of War in South Asia: Indo-Pakistan Conflicts since 1947.* Boulder, Colorado: Westview Press, 1990.

Haqqani, Hussain. "Politics of Defence," *Far Eastern Economic Review* [Hong Kong], January 9, 1986, 24–28.

Harrison, Selig S., and Geoffrey Kemp. *India and America after the Cold War.* Washington: Carnegie Endowment for International Peace, 1993.

Hersh, Seymour M. "On the Nuclear Edge," *New Yorker,* 69, No. 6, March 29, 1993, 56–73.

Husain, Noor A., and Leo Rose. *Pakistan-U.S. Relations: Social, Political, and Economic Factors.* Berkeley: Institute of East Asian Studies, 1988.

Hussain, Mushahid. "Pakistan Army: A Profile," *Friday Times,* November 25, 1992, 21. Joint Publications Research Service, *Daily Report: Near East and South Asia.* (JPRS-NEA-93–010.) January 21, 1993, 21.

Ispahani, Mahnaz. *Pakistan: The Dimensions of Insecurity.* London: Brassey's for International Institute for Strategic Studies, 1990.

Jalal, Ayesha. *The State of Martial Rule: The Origins of Pakistan's Political Economy of Defense.* New York: Cambridge University Press, 1990.

Jane's All the World's Aircraft, 1991–92. Alexandria, Virginia: Jane's Information Group, 1991.

Jane's Fighting Ships, 1992–93. Ed., Richard Sharpe. Alexandria, Virginia: Jane's Information Group, 1992.

Kennedy, Charles H. "Islamization and Legal Reform in Pakistan, 1979–1989," *Pacific Affairs,* 63, No. 1, Spring 1990, 62–77.

Kennedy, Charles H. "Islamization in Pakistan: Implementation of the Hudood Ordinances," *Asian Survey,* 28, No. 3, March 1988, 307–16.

Kennedy, Charles H. "Managing Ethnic Conflict: The Case of Pakistan." Pages 123–1433 in John Coakley, ed., *The Territorial Management of Ethnic Conflict.* (Regions and Regionalism Series, No. 2.) Portland, Oregon: Frank Cass, 1993.

LePoer, Barbara Leitch. *Pakistan-U.S. Relations.* (No. IB9404.) Washington: Library of Congress, Congressional Research Service, June 16, 1994.

Longer, V. *Red Coats to Olive Green: A History of the Indian Army 1600–1974.* New Delhi: Allied, 1974.

Martindale-Hubbell International Law Digest. New Providence, New Jersey: Reed, 1993.

Masood, Sabri. *The Pakistan Police Act with Rules.* Lahore: Pakistan Law, 1977.

Menezes, S.L. *Fidelity and Honour: The Indian Army from the Seventeenth to the Twenty-First Century.* New Delhi: Viking, 1993.

The Military Balance, 1994–1995. London: International Institute of Strategic Studies, 1994.

Muqeem Khan, Fazl. *The Story of the Pakistan Army.* Karachi: Oxford University Press, 1963.

Nadeem, Azhar Hasan. *The Punjab Police in a Comparative Perspective.* Lahore: Progressive, 1989.

Nelson, Reginald. *The Pakistan Penal Code with Commentary.* Lahore: n.p., 1985.

Pakistan. Federal Bureau of Statistics. Statistics Division. *Pakistan Statistical Yearbook, 1985.* Islamabad: 1985.

Pakistan. Federal Bureau of Statistics. Statistics Division. *Pakistan Statistical Yearbook, 1991.* Karachi: 1991.

Pakistan. Ministry of Finance. *Pakistan Basic Facts, 1984–85.* Islamabad: 1985.

Pakistan Bar Council. *Report on the Proposed Establishment of Courts of Qazis Ordinance.* Lahore: 1982.

Riza, Shaukat. *The Pakistan Army, 1: War 1965.* Lahore: Army Education Press, 1984.

Riza, Shaukat. *The Pakistan Army, 2: 1966–71.* Lahore: Services Book Club, 1990.

Rizvi, Hasan-Askari. "The Legacy of Military Rule in Pakistan," *Survival,* 31, No. 3, May–June, 1989, 255–68.

Rizvi, Hasan-Askari. *The Military and Politics in Pakistan.* Delhi: Konark, 1988.

Rizvi, Hasan-Askari. *Pakistan and the Geostrategic Environment: A Study of Foreign Policy.* New York: St. Martin's Press, 1993.

Rose, Leo, and Noor A. Husain. *U.S.-Pakistan Relations.* Berkeley: Institute of East Asian Studies, 1985.

Rose, Leo, and Kamal Matinuddin. *Beyond Afghanistan: The Emerging U.S.-Pakistan Relations.* Berkeley: Institute of East Asian Studies, 1989.

Sisson, Richard, and Leo Rose. *War and Secession: Pakistan, India, and the Creation of Bangladesh.* Berkeley: University of California Press, 1990.

Spector, Leonard. *Nuclear Weapons and South Asian Security.* Washington: Carnegie Endowment for International Peace, 1988.

Stockholm International Peace Research Institute. *SIPRI Yearbook: World Armaments and Disarmament.* New York: Humanities Press, 1992.

The Strategic Balance, 1992–93. London: International Institute for Strategic Studies, 1992.

Tetley, Brian. *Defenders of Pakistan.* Lahore: Ferozsons, 1988.

Thornton, Thomas P. "Between the Stools: U.S. Policy Towards Pakistan in the Carter Administration," *Asian Survey,* 20, No. 10, October, 1982, 955–77.

Thornton, Thomas P. *Pakistan: Internal Developments and the U.S. Interest.* Washington: Foreign Policy Institute, 1987.

Thornton, Thomas P. "U.S.-Pakistan Relations," *Foreign Affairs*, 68, No. 3, Summer, 1989, 142–59.

Tiwari, Chitra K. *Security in South Asia: Internal and External Dimensions.* Lanham, Maryland: University Press of America, 1989.

United States. Department of State. *Country Reports on Human Rights Practices for 1992.* (Report submitted to United States Congress, 103d, 1st Session, Senate, Committee on Foreign Relations, and House of Representatives, Committee on Foreign Affairs.) Washington: GPO, 1993.

United States. Department of State. *Country Reports on Human Rights Practices for 1993.* (Report submitted to United States Congress, 103d, 2d Session, House, Committee on Foreign Affairs, and Senate, Committee on Foreign Relations.) Washington: GPO, 1994.

United States. Department of State. *International Narcotics Control Strategy Report.* Washington: GPO, 1992.

Vertzberger, Yaacov. *The Enduring Entente: Sino-Pakistan Relations, 1960–80.* New York: Praeger, 1983.

Waseem, Mohammad. "Pakistan's Lingering Crisis of Dyarchy," *Asian Survey*, 32, No. 7, July 1992, 617–34.

Wirsing, Robert G. *Pakistan's Security under Zia, 1977–1988: The Policy Imperatives of a Peripheral Asian State.* New York: St. Martin's Press, 1991.

Ziring, Lawrence. *Pakistan: The Enigma of Political Development.* Boulder, Colorado: Westview Press, 1980.

Glossary

fiscal year (FY)—July 1 to June 30; FY 1994, for example, ran from July 1993 through June 1994.

gross domestic product (GDP)—A value measure of the flow of domestic goods and services produced by an economy over a period of time, usually one year. Only output values of goods for final consumption and investment are included because the values of primary and intermediate production are assumed to be included in final prices. GDP is sometimes aggregated and shown at market prices, meaning that indirect taxes and subsidies are included; when these have been eliminated, the result is GDP at factor cost. The word *gross* indicates that deductions for depreciation of physical assets have not been made. *See also* gross national product.

gross national product (GNP)—Gross domestic product (*q.v.*) plus the net income or loss stemming from transactions with foreign countries. GNP is the broadest measure of the output of goods and services of an economy. It can be calculated at market prices, which include indirect taxes and subsidies. Because indirect taxes and subsidies are only transfer payments, GNP is often calculated at factor cost by removing indirect taxes and subsidies.

haq mehr—Promissory gift from the bride's in-laws at the time of marriage. A kind of bridewealth based on Islamic traditions stipulated in the marriage contract, to be paid to the wife in the event of divorce or her husband's early death.

hudood (sing., *hadd*)—The most serious kinds of crime in Islamic law, such as those pertaining to theft and adultery.

imam—Generally, the leader of congregational prayers, implying no ordination or special spiritual powers beyond sufficient education to carry out this function. The word is also used figuratively by many Sunni (*q.v.*) Muslims to mean the leader of the Islamic community. Among Shia (*q.v.*) Muslims, it indicates the particular descendant of the House of Ali who is believed to have been God's designated repository of the spiritual authority inherent in that line. The identity of this individual and the means of ascertaining his identity have been the major issues causing divisions among the Shia.

International Monetary Fund (IMF)—Established along with the World Bank (*q.v.*) in 1945, the IMF is a specialized agency affiliated with the United Nations and is responsible for stabilizing international exchange loans to its members (including industrialized and developing countries) when they experience balance of payments difficulties. These loans frequently carry conditions that require substantial international economic adjustments by the recipients, most of which are developing countries.

jizya—A tax imposed on non-Muslims in a Muslim state meant to compensate the state for the protection given to non-Muslims who are not permitted to serve in the military.

muhajir—Immigrant or descendant of immigrants from India who fled to Pakistan after partition in 1947.

mujahidin (sing., *mujahid*)—Fighters of a jihad, a Muslim holy war; Afghan freedom fighters.

mullahs—Generic term for members of the Islamic clergy; usually refers to preachers or other low-ranking clerics who have not earned the right to interpret religious laws.

mustahaqeen—Muslims deserving of receiving *zakat* (*q.v.*) as stipulated in the Quran, such as the poor, the needy, recent converts to Islam, those who do the good works of God, and those who collect and disburse *zakat.*

Nizam-i-Mustafa—Rule of the Prophet, i.e., rule by sharia (*q.v.*) law according to Zia ul-Haq's use of the term.

Pakhtuns—Term used for speakers of Pakhtu̦ or Pashto, who are frequently called Pathans or Pashtuns. The tribes north of Peshawar are mostly Pahktu speaking, those south of Peshawar mostly Pashto speaking.

pakhtunwali—Tenets of the Pakhtun code of honor.

Pathans—Pakhtuns (*q.v.*).

pir—Successor to the founder of a Sufi (*q.v.*) order or of a local subdivision of an order; in the Sufi tradition, a religious man considered to have mystic powers.

rupee (R or Re; pl., Rs)—The national currency, consisting of 100 paisa. From 1947 to 1972, Pakistan was a member of the sterling area, but in 1971, when the United States dollar was devalued, the rupee was unpegged from sterling and pegged to the dollar at the rate of Rs4.76 per US$1. On May 12, 1972, the rupee was devalued from Rs4.76 to Rs11 per US$1. In February 1973, when the dollar was again devalued, the rupee maintained its value in terms of gold, and its value in relation to the dollar rose to Rs9.90 per US$1, where it remained until January 1982. After January 1982, the rupee was pegged to a market basket of currencies important to Pakistan's trade. The rupee subsequently depreciated steadily against the dollar, reaching Rs30.30 to US$1 at the end of February 1994. Notes are printed in denominations of Rs 1,000, 500, 100, 50, 10, 5, 2, and 1. Coins are minted in denominations of Rs1, as well as 50, 10, 5, 2, and 1 paisa.

sharia—Islamic law. Based on the Quran and the sunna (*q.v.*) with interpretations of Muslim jurisprudence. There are four major Sunni (*q.v.*) schools (of which the Hanafi is dominant in Pakistan) and one Shia (*q.v.*) school (Jafariya).

Shia—The smaller of the two major subdivisions of Islam. In Pakistan, the two principal subgroups of Shiism are the "Twelvers" (Ithna Ashari), who follow the same system as the majority group in Iran, and the "Seveners" (Ismailis or Agha Khanis).

South Asian Association for Regional Cooperation (SAARC)—Comprises the seven nations of South Asia: Bangladesh, Bhutan, India, Maldives, Nepal, Pakistan, and Sri Lanka; headquartered in Kathmandu. Founded as South Asia Regional Cooperation (SARC) at a meeting for foreign ministers in New Delhi on August 1–2, 1983; the group was renamed when the 1983 agreement was ratified at the inaugural summit meeting at Dhaka, Bangladesh, on December 7–8, 1985. SAARC's goal is to effect economic, technical, and cultural cooperation and to provide a forum for discussions of South Asia's political problems.

Sufi—A follower of Sufism, or Islamic mysticism.

sunna—In common usage, refers to the deeds and utterances of Muhammad that form the basis for the practice of the Muslim community.

Sunni—The larger of the two major subdivisions of Islam, followed by a majority of Pakistanis.

ulama (sing., *alim*)—Islamic scholars.

World Bank—Informal name used to designate a group of four affiliated international institutions: the International Bank for Reconstruction and Development (IBRD), the International Development Association (IDA), the International Finance Corporation (IFC), and the Multilateral Investment Guarantee Agency (MIGA). The IBRD, established in 1945, has as its primary purpose the provision of loans to developing countries for productive projects. The IDA, a legally separate loan fund but administered by the staff of the IBRD, was set up in 1960 to furnish credits to the poorest developing countries on much easier terms than those of conventional IBRD loans. The IFC, founded in 1956, supplements the activities of the IBRD through loans and assistance designed specifically to encourage the growth of productive private enterprises in the less developed countries. The MIGA, founded in 1988, insures private foreign investment in developing countries against various noncommercial risks.The president and certain senior officers of the IBRD hold the same positions in the IFC. The four institutions are owned by the governments of the countries that subscribe their capital. To participate in the World Bank group, member states must first belong to the International Monetary Fund (IMF—*q.v.*).

zakat—Islamic system of social welfare based on an alms tax on wealth held more than a year.

Index

Contributors

Craig Baxter is Professor of Politics and History at Juniata College, Huntingdon, Pennsylvania.

Mary Louise Becker is an independent scholar and consultant in South Asian political and economic development.

Peter R. Blood is Senior Research Specialist for Asia at the Federal Research Division, Library of Congress.

John D. Rogers is Lecturer on Social Studies, Harvard University, Cambridge, Massachusetts; and Visiting Research Fellow, Center of South Asian and Indian Ocean Studies, Tufts University, Medford, Massachusetts.

Thomas Perry Thornton is Adjunct Professor of Political Science and Asian Studies at the Johns Hopkins University and Georgetown University.

Anita M. Weiss is Associate Professor of International Studies at the University of Oregon.

Published Country Studies

(Area Handbook Series)

550–65 Afghanistan
550–98 Albania
550–44 Algeria
550–59 Angola
550–73 Argentina

550–111 Armenia, Azerbaijan, and Georgia
550–169 Australia
550–176 Austria
550–175 Bangladesh

550–112 Belarus and Moldova
550–170 Belgium
550–66 Bolivia
550–20 Brazil
550–168 Bulgaria

550–61 Burma
550–50 Cambodia
550–166 Cameroon
550–159 Chad
550–77 Chile

550–60 China
550–26 Colombia
550–33 Commonwealth Caribbean, Islands of the
550–91 Congo

550–90 Costa Rica
550–69 Côte d'Ivoire (Ivory Coast)
550–152 Cuba
550–22 Cyprus

550–158 Czechoslovakia

550–36 Dominican Republic and Haiti
550–52 Ecuador
550–43 Egypt
550–150 El Salvador

550–28 Ethiopia
550–167 Finland
550–173 Germany, East
550–155 Germany, Fed. Rep. of
550–153 Ghana

550–87 Greece
550–78 Guatemala
550–174 Guinea
550–82 Guyana and Belize
550–151 Honduras

550–165 Hungary
550–21 India
550–154 Indian Ocean
550–39 Indonesia
550–68 Iran

550–31 Iraq
550–25 Israel
550–182 Italy
550–30 Japan
550–34 Jordan

550–56 Kenya
550–81 Korea, North
550–41 Korea, South
550–58 Laos
550–24 Lebanon

550–38 Liberia

550–85 Libya
550–172 Malawi
550–45 Malaysia
550–161 Mauritania
550–79 Mexico

550–76 Mongolia
550–49 Morocco
550–64 Mozambique
550–35 Nepal and Bhutan
550–88 Nicaragua

550–157 Nigeria
550–94 Oceania
550–48 Pakistan
550–46 Panama
550–156 Paraguay

550–185 Persian Gulf States
550–42 Peru
550–72 Philippines
550–162 Poland
550–181 Portugal

550–160 Romania
550–37 Rwanda and Burundi
550–51 Saudi Arabia
550–70 Senegal
550–180 Sierra Leone

550–184 Singapore
550–86 Somalia
550–93 South Africa
550–95 Soviet Union
550–179 Spain

550–96 Sri Lanka
550–27 Sudan
550–47 Syria
550–62 Tanzania
550–53 Thailand

550–89 Tunisia
550–80 Turkey
550–74 Uganda
550–97 Uruguay
550–71 Venezuela

550–32 Vietnam
550–183 Yemens, The
550–99 Yugoslavia
550–67 Zaire
550–75 Zambia

550–171 Zimbabwe